THE DEVIL PREFERS MOZART

Anthony Burgess (1917–1993) was a novelist, poet, playwright, composer, linguist, translator and critic. Best known for his novel *A Clockwork Orange*, he wrote more than sixty books of fiction, non-fiction and autobiography, as well as classical music, plays, film scripts, essays and articles.

Burgess was born in Manchester, England and grew up in Harpurhey and Moss Side. He was educated at Xaverian College and Manchester University. He lived in Malaya, Malta, Monaco, Italy and the United States, and his books are still widely read all over the world.

Paul Phillips is the Gretchen B. Kimball Director of Orchestral Studies and Associate Professor of Music at Stanford University. He is the author of *A Clockwork Counterpoint: The Music and Literature of Anthony Burgess*, published in 2010, and essays on Burgess published in six other books, including the Norton Critical Edition of *A Clockwork Orange*. He has conducted many Burgess compositions including numerous first performances and the premiere recording of Burgess's orchestral music, released by Naxos in 2016.

ALSO BY ANTHONY BURGESS
AVAILABLE FROM CARCANET

Collected Poems (2020)
The Ink Trade: Selected Journalism,
1961–1993 (2018)
Revolutionary Sonnets and Other Poems (2002)

ANTHONY BURGESS

THE DEVIL PREFERS MOZART

ON MUSIC AND MUSICIANS 1962–1993

edited by
Paul Phillips

CARCANET
LIVES & LETTERS

First published in Great Britain in 2024 by
Carcanet
Alliance House, 30 Cross Street
Manchester, M2 7AQ
www.carcanet.co.uk

A CIP catalogue record for this book is
available from the British Library.

ISBN 978 1 80017 308 8

Book design by Andrew Latimer, Carcanet
Typesetting by LiteBook Prepress Services
Printed in Great Britain by SRP Ltd, Exeter, Devon

The publisher acknowledges financial
assistance from Arts Council England.

CONTENTS

PART III
BURGESS AND HIS MUSIC

PART IV
PERFORMERS AND PERFORMANCES

PART V
OPERA

Dedicated to the memory of
Richard Taruskin and Kevin Jackson,
inspiring mentors and friends

THE DEVIL PREFERS MOZART

Anthony Burgess's brilliance as an essayist and passion for music are united in this collection, the most complete compilation to date of his writings on music. *The Devil Prefers Mozart* comprises seventy-five chapters of essays, reviews and letters plus the occasional interview or transcription. Approximately a tenth of the entries are published here for the first time, with most of the previously published items drawn from the *Observer* (16), *The Listener* (9), *The Times* (2) and *The Times Literary Supplement* (11), the *New York Times* (4) and *New York Times Book Review* (1), as well as the *Independent*, the *Guardian*, the *Spectator*, the *Daily Mail*, the *Evening Standard*, the *Musical Times, Classical Guitar, High Fidelity* and a few other publications. Several essays were published in Italian translation in *Corriere della Sera* (8) and in French translation in *Harmonie-Panorama Musique* (2) or its successor, *Harmonie hi-fi conseil* (1). Except for the omission of 'Shaw as Musician' from *One Man's Chorus*, whose content overlaps with 'Tuned to the Future' (since both are reviews of the same edition of George Bernard Shaw's music criticism), all essays on music previously published in *Homage to QWERT YUIOP (But Do Blondes Prefer Gentlemen?)* and *One Man's Chorus* are included in this volume.

The book is structured in five parts, with the chapters in each (except Part II) arranged more or less chronologically according to when they were written. Part I, *Musical Musings*, is a varied assortment of writings on topics ranging from Shakespeare in Music to Punk to Beatlemania. Part II, *Composers and Their Music*, is arranged by composers' dates, from Claudio Monteverdi to Kurt Weill. Part III, *Burgess and His Music*, comprises a varied assortment of essays, articles, letters, programme and liner notes, plus an interview.

Part IV, *Performers and Performances*, and Part V, *Opera*, consist mainly of essays, articles, and reviews. The commentary at the end of the volume aims to contextualize each chapter with pertinent background information.

Conjoining entertainment with education, Burgess's prose sparkles with wit and erudition. Many texts are on his favourite subjects: Mozart, Beethoven, Wagner, opera, his own musical compositions, and the relation between words and music. There is an emphasis on British composers – especially Elgar, Holst, Walton and Britten – and authors especially connected with music, such as Shakespeare, Shaw and Joyce. We are reminded of (or first learn about) composers such as Cowen, MacCunn and Mackenzie; entertainers such as Gracie Fields, Bombardier Billy Wells and Tony Hancock; and films by Charlie Chaplin, Ken Russell and Luchino Visconti. Of particular interest are the essays, reviews and letters related to those musicians whom Burgess knew personally – John Sebastian, Larry Adler and Yehudi Menuhin – and the references to and exchanges with the music journalist Hans Keller, who got under Burgess's skin like no one else.

My acquaintance with many of these texts dates back to my research in the late 1990s and early 2000s for *A Clockwork Counterpoint: The Music and Literature of Anthony Burgess*, in which many of them are cited. Since the publication of that book in 2010, evidence has emerged that contradicts certain autobiographical myths that Burgess propagated for decades; Simon Johnson's landmark archival research, cited in the commentary on Chapter 47, *The Making of a Writer*, is of especial importance, setting the record straight about the 'Beautiful Belle Burgess'. The scores of numerous Burgess compositions that were considered lost when *A Clockwork Counterpoint* was published have been located since, including the Sonata for Violoncello and Piano in G Minor (1945); Concerto for Flute, Strings & Piano in D Minor (1951);

Rhapsody for Bass Tuba and Orchestra (ca. 1991); and two pieces for harmonica and guitar composed for John Sebastian (1972). While detailed musical description and analysis of these works would exceed the scope of this volume, most are mentioned as they relate to particular writings.

Burgess has his quirks and shortcomings. He is certain that when Lady Macbeth urges the Thane of Cawdor to 'Screw your courage to the sticking-place', she alludes to the tuning of a lute (which may not be the case) and that there's a *von* in Hans Richter's name (there isn't). Beethoven did not include so-called 'Turkish music' (extra percussion beyond timpani) for the first time in his Ninth Symphony, François Habeneck was not conducting Berlioz's *Benvenuto Cellini* when he took out his snuffbox, Leopold Stokowski was not originally named Stokes, and Cathy Berberian does not sing 'The Owl and the Pussycat' on *Stravinsky: The Recorded Legacy*. But such minor lapses (which are all identified and explained) do not greatly diminish the overall pleasure of this book, which combines interesting subject matter, strong opinions and stylistic elegance in a way meant to appeal to a wide range of readers interested in music. And then there are the words! The Burgessian vocabulary encompasses such terms as theodician, multiguous, parthenogenetical, stichomythia, quinquennium, apodemoniosis, and apothaneintheloish. These are defined in the notes, but readers who recoil at such sesquipedalian extravagance may want to head for the exit now.

A word about style. The reader is kindly asked to accept this book's stylistic inconsistency as an unavoidable consequence of the way it straddles both sides of the Atlantic. While most of the writings in this collection were written for the *Observer, The TLS, The Listener* and other British publications, a sizable number were published in the *New York Times* and various American periodicals. As a result, most of Burgess's writings accord with British usage while some follow American spelling and style.

Burgess's idiosyncratic style presents challenges to the editor. He frequently breaks up compound words like 'someday', 'forever', and 'concertmaster' into two words yet omits the hyphen or space in compound words such as 'middle-aged' and 'double bass', rendering them instead as 'middleaged' and 'doublebass'. Often there are different forms of an expression – for example, 'finger-click' (in *The Observer*) and 'finger click' (in *Homage to QWERT YUIOP)* – in different versions of the same text. In all such cases, I have exercised my best judgment in choosing which form to include.

Most titles in the typescripts are underlined (like <u>Ulysses</u>) while in newspapers like the *Observer* or the *New York Times*, they are often indicated by quotation marks (i.e., 'Ulysses' or "Ulysses"). For uniformity, titles are consistently rendered in italics (*Ulysses*) unless quoted from a letter or cited within a quotation. Aïghetta Quartet is spelled throughout this volume with two dots over the 'i' even though the diæresis is often omitted in the source texts. Misspelled proper nouns – like Infante (not Enfante) in the title of Ravel's *Pavane* in Chapter 38, and Stéphane Grappelli (not Stephane Grappelly) in Chapter 62 – are corrected without comment, and names that are repeatedly rendered inaccurately, like 'Hans von Richter' and 'Frederick Cowan', are corrected throughout. When original typescripts are unavailable, one cannot know if Burgess wrote German nouns like *zigarettenpause* (Chapter 60) in lower case intentionally or if an editor was responsible. In such cases, these terms are capitalized as they would be in ordinary German usage.

Notes are used primarily to explain obscure literary, cultural and historical references; to identify correspondences with Burgess's life and work, especially his novels and music compositions; and to point out connections between different parts of this book. On the assumption that most readers possess prior knowledge of classical music, notes are not provided for most of the well-known composers and performers mentioned except to comment on particular aspects of a work or individual.

The Devil Prefers Mozart is both a compilation of Anthony Burgess's dazzling music journalism and testimony to his lifelong devotion to music. If one dates the beginning of his sixty-three-year-long involvement with music to his revelatory hearing of Debussy's *Faun* around 1930, then the writings in this collection, dating from 1962 through 1993, neatly cover the second half of that period while recalling musical memories from decades prior. In sum, this volume is – like most of Burgess's books – part biography, part autobiography, part history and part fiction.

Paul Phillips
9 September 2023

ACKNOWLEDGMENTS

Since my research on Anthony Burgess extends back more than twenty-five years, it is virtually impossible to acknowledge everyone who has provided assistance along the way but essential to begin with the late Liana Burgess. If she had not granted me access to her late husband's papers, materials and music compositions in 1997, this research could hardly have begun. The Harry Ransom Humanities Research Center at the University of Texas at Austin furnished critical early support by awarding me an Andrew W. Mellon Foundation Research Fellowship in 1999, with Dell Hollingsworth and Lisa Jones providing exceptional assistance with the Burgess archive that the Ransom Center had just acquired at the time. The International Anthony Burgess Foundation and its first director, the late Professor Alan Roughley, were also essential, as were numerous individuals at the Université d'Angers associated with the Anthony Burgess Centre, notably Professor Ben Forkner, its first director, and archivist Valérie Neveu. The librarians at the Orwig Music Library at Brown University also provided vital assistance during those initial years of research.

The recent work that led to completion of this volume would not have been possible without the support and assistance of Andrew Biswell, Director of the International Anthony Burgess Foundation in Manchester, and former Deputy Director Will Carr, who both provided key documents from the IABF archive for this collection and assisted the project with vital information and encouragement. I wish to acknowledge Tamar Barzel, Head of the Stanford University Music Library and Archive of Recorded Sound, and her wonderful team, which includes Ray Heigemeir, Vincent Kang, Nathan Coy and Benjamin Bates, for their support, and my Stanford colleagues, including Stephen Hinton and my dear wife Kathryne Jennings, both of whom provided very helpful suggestions. Generous assistance was also provided by Sarah Sussman (Curator of French and Italian Collections and Head of the Humanities and Area Studies Resource Group of the Stanford University Libraries); John Shepard (Curator of Music Collections at the Jean Gray Hargrove Music Library, University of California-Berkeley); Sarah Horowitz (Curator of Rare Books & Manuscripts, and Head of Quaker & Special Collections) and Katherine Hong of the Haverford College Libraries; and Professor Steven Cox (Curator, Special Collections & University Archives, Pittsburg State University). For assistance with translation, I gratefully acknowledge Veronika Schubert, Enguerrand Horel, and Giancarlo Aquilanti, and for her help in bringing this book to publication, I offer my sincere thanks to Georgia Glover of David Higham Associates.

I am extremely grateful to Jeremy Menuhin for granting permission to print letters written by his father Yehudi Menuhin, and to the Cosman Keller Art & Music Trust for granting permission to print writings by Hans Keller. Additionally, I am especially grateful to Simon Johnson for granting permission to include material from his unpublished monograph 'The Beautiful Belle Burgess: A Biography of Elizabeth Burgess – The Mother Anthony Burgess Never Knew'. Thanks to his meticulous research, there is now a clear distinction between fact and fiction in Anthony Burgess's accounts of his maternal family history.

Finally, I wish to thank Michael Schmidt of Carcanet Press for publishing this book, and editors Andrew Latimer and Maren Meinhardt for their important contributions. I am extremely grateful to all of them for their advice, assistance and support. Much effort has been expended to make this book as informative and accurate as possible, and free of mistakes, but for any errors that remain, I bear sole responsibility.

ABBREVIATIONS

ACC   *A Clockwork Counterpoint: The Music and Literature of Anthony Burgess* (Phillips)
HQY   *Homage to QWERT YUIOP*
LW   *Little Wilson and Big God*
SCW   *Stravinsky: The Composer and his Works* (White)
TMM   *This Man and Music*
YH   *You've Had Your Time*

NOTE

Citations that occur in both *This Man and Music* (1982) and the Irwell Edition of *This Man and Music* (2020) are indicated by 'TMM' followed by a pair of page numbers or page ranges separated by a slash, as in 'TMM, p. 23/43' or 'TMM, pp. 18/38-39'.

PART I
MUSICAL MUSINGS

1. THE WRITER AND MUSIC

I have been thinking about the musician as hero since reading John Wain's new novel *Strike the Father Dead.*[1] Jeremy, Mr Wain's hero, is a jazz pianist – or so he tells us. I used to be a jazz pianist myself, and I was not always convinced that Jeremy was doing much more than going through the motions – as though acting the part in a film with a dubbed sound-track.

The musician as hero has attracted a number of novelists, but it used to be the great romantic composer instead of the jazzman – Lewis Dodd, for instance, in *The Constant Nymph.*[2] I have never been really happy about Dodd's *Symphony in Three Keys,* since the whole point about a tonal symphony is its key unity. But Margaret Kennedy always seemed to me like the lady in Oscar Wilde who didn't care a bit for music but was extremely fond of musicians.[3] The appeal of the great romantic composer is not his talent but his temperament, and this is true even of the biggest novel ever written about a composer – *Jean Christophe,* by Romain Rolland. The hero is all storm and stress, an amalgam of the personalities of Beethoven and Wagner, great lover and fiery revolutionary. There is not much room left for mere music.

The fact is that much of a composer's life is sheer physical drudgery, and that is no subject for the romantic novelist. The writing of an opera or symphony is extremely hard work, and only one novelist has been willing to show it – Thomas Mann. His *Doctor Faustus* is the only novel of any importance which has created a really credible composer. His name is Adrian Leverkühn, and we are not merely told of his greatness, it is demonstrated to us: his works are closely analysed; we can almost hear them. And the smell of ink, the long agony of orchestral scoring, is built into the book.

There is no important English novel about a musician, though there have been several good ones – Stanley Middleton's *Harris's Requiem*, for instance.[4] It has taken a long time to break down the tradition among English men of letters that music is an inferior art – a sort of mindless literature, sound without sense. I think Dr Johnson, who was tone-deaf, helped to create this attitude. Shakespeare would not have understood it; Shakespeare knew music from the inside. Only a man who had actually tuned a lute could make Lady Macbeth say: 'Screw your courage to the sticking-place'.[5]

Robert Browning rehabilitated music by making it a pretext for demonstrating his own brand of nineteenth-century optimism, but Samuel Butler was the first English novelist to take music seriously. As with Shakespeare, we get music from the inside. Since Butler, only two important novelists working in English have really put music into their writing – James Joyce and Aldous Huxley. Joyce, in the 'Sirens' episode of *Ulysses*, comes as near to a genuine synthesis of literary and musical techniques as seems humanly possible. Huxley, as he has just demonstrated again in *Island*, knows everything, but his musical insight and erudition are really formidable. Again, it is music from the inside – the accidentally added seventh in the piano improvisation of *Crome Yellow*; in *Antic Hay* the fingers of Gumbril, which learn Emily's body as they once learned a Mozart sonata.[6] It was Huxley who showed, in *Point Counter Point*, how fiction could be musicalized.

I still think that the novelist has much to learn from musical form: novels in sonata-form, rondo-form, fugue-form are perfectly feasible. There is much to be learnt also from mood-contrasts, tempo-contrasts in music: the novelist can have his slow movements and his scherzi. Music can also teach him how to modulate, how to recapitulate; the time for the formal presentation of his themes, the time for the free fantasia.

In a general sense, though, the practitioner in words should be interested in a cognate art: he should know where literature ends and music begins. Swinburne did not know this: he tried to make his verse do a job that music could do far better. But of Swinburne this story is told: for a joke, somebody played *Three Blind Mice* to him on the piano and told him it was an old Florentine air. 'Ah yes', said Swinburne when it was finished, 'it evokes the cruel beauty of the Borgias'.

The Listener, 1962

1 As quoted in 'Did You Hear That?'. The first sentence continues, 'said Anthony Burgess in "The World of Books" (Home Service)'

2 In *The Constant Nymph*, a 1924 novel by Margaret Kennedy, two cousins fall in love with a young composer named Lewis Dodd. After he marries one of the women, the younger one dies of a broken heart.

3 A reference to Lady Fermor in Oscar Wilde's short story 'Lord Arthur Savile's Crime: A Study of Duty', in which Monsieur de Koloff, the Russian Ambassador, tells 'poor Lady Fermor, right out before every one, that she did not care a bit for music, but was extremely fond of musicians.'

4 Renowned for his perceptive portrayal of provincial life and the lives of ordinary people, novelist Stanley Middleton was a co-winner of the Booker Prize in 1974 for *Holiday*. In *Harris's Requiem* (1960), Thomas Harris, a coal miner's son and classical composer, writes a requiem after his father's death to honour people who have been forgotten and neglected.

5 While this may refer to the tuning of a lute, another possible explanation involves animal slaughter. In the OED, 'sticking place' is defined as 'the point at the base of the neck of an animal where the knife is thrust in, either to slaughter or bleed

the animal; the lower part of the neck or throat'. The earliest citation, from *Foure bookes of husbandry* by Conrad Heresbach (transl. Barnaby Googe), predates *Macbeth* by four decades. The term may also refer to a crossbow, in which a wooden screw is turned to pull the string taut. When the screw cannot be turned further, it is at the 'sticking place' and ready to be released. The expression could refer to any or all of these.

6   In *The Pianoplayers*, dedicated 'To Liana, *che conosce tutta la scala cromatica dell'amore*' (To Liana, who knows the entire chromatic scale of love), Burgess would employ a similar theme: 'A Female Body… is not just a pleasing shape with a hole in it. It is more like a musical instrument made of flesh and blood that has music waiting inside it but only for properly trained hands to coax out.' *The Pianoplayers*, p. 93

Shakespeare in Music, edited by Phyllis Hartnoll
London: Macmillan, 1964

Dr Samuel Johnson, that Berlin Wall of taste, may be taken as the patron saint of all literary men who lack a musical ear and somehow glory in lacking it. The 'dissociation of sensibility' which began in the Age of Reason goes further than the art of literature; it cracks up the whole corpus of art, turning a former continent into a number of islands. Since Johnson's day, the right ear has gloried in not knowing what the left ear is doing. It comes as a shock to some writers to be told that the arts of literature and music are cognate, and that you cannot successfully practise one without knowing the scope and limitations of the other. Swinburne, lacking this knowledge, tried to make his poetry a kind of pure music. Richard Strauss, with a kind of neurotic perverseness, made his music a sort of impure literature. To go back to the world of Shakespeare, in which the distinct but germane functions of literature and music were instinctively but perfectly known, is to encounter the life of a lost Eden, the air healthy, the food wholesome, no walls up anywhere.

John Stevens's essay – the first of the four that make up this admirable book – concerns itself with music as an aspect of Elizabethan drama. Shakespeare is, naturally, in the foreground, but it is salutary to be reminded that his virtues, in awareness of the function of music as in everything else, are great but not unique. Marlowe's *Doctor Faustus* must strike many a musician as a ready-made libretto (strange that no British composer has set it as it stands), with its arias, duets, ensembles, antiphonal Good and Evil Angels, sung exorcism scene, Seven Deadly Sins ballet, dances of devils, chorus commentary. There is something in the very blank verse of early Elizabethan drama – the cut-and-thrust of stichomythia, the binding of one line to the next with an echoing word – that suggests a near-musical heredity (were Seneca's closet-dramas perhaps not intoned rather than spoken?). Apart from all this, the Elizabethans knew precisely when and how to make music serve a dramatic end, the place for hautboys and the place for the 'broken consort', the delicately judged need for song or chorus, and Shakespeare, first among his peers, excelled here as in everything.

But there is something else in Shakespeare, something qualitatively different from the mere expertise of his fellows, and that is an apparent intimacy with, as it were, the two outer ends of music – the physical process of its making, the metaphysical significance of its make-up. When we hear Lady Macbeth telling her recalcitrant lord to 'screw your courage to the sticking-place', the reference is evidently to the tuning of a lute, the small agony of a delicate technical act. The Pythagorean disquisition in *The Merchant of Venice* is well known, though its curse on the unmusical has been ignored by too many. Ulysses's speech on the necessity of order in *Troilus and Cressida* uses the image of the untuning of a string, and one cannot doubt that this was no mere conventional trope – Shakespeare physically *heard* the untuning and in it was aware of the unholy jangling of what had been the music of the spheres.

But Shakespeare's musicianship has been made most evident to the world in the sheer craft of his lyrics (Charles Cudworth gives us an exhaustive historical survey of the settings of these). I doubt if the eagerness of three centuries of composers to make songs out of Shakespeare's words has had very much to do with mere reverential duty. Schubert heard the lyrics, and the music came. Jazzmen like Duke Ellington and Johnny Dankworth are too busy for bardolatry.[1]

Shakespeare is a god, but he was also a man of the theatre, and he knew which words would set and which would not. Simplicity – even conventionality – of theme, variety of vowel and diphthong, concentration on voiced consonants rather than unvoiced – these are the big lyric secrets. Sometimes, as in 'Take O take those lips away', meaning goes under and is not greatly missed. Once, in Pandarus's dirty song in *Troilus and Cressida*, the sound of orgasm only comes to shocking life when we hear the setting: it looks like mere harmless nonny-nonny on the page.[2]

*

Sometimes setability spills over from the functional lyric to the blank-verse speech. Vaughan Williams's *Serenade to Music* ('How sweet the moonlight sleeps upon this bank') joins Johnny Dankworth's very interesting 'If music be the food of love' in drawing words away from context, diminishing Shakespeare by *enclosing* him, however exquisite the result. Parry's setting of John of Gaunt's dying speech does what many political orations do with that great metaphorical catalogue – sets up an unfortunate confusion in the ear of the listener who remembers how the speech ends: '... Is now leased out, I die pronouncing it, / Like to a tenement or pelting farm'. How far should composers work in Shakespeare's service and how far merely use him?

This is the area where the book is of most interest. Write incidental music for Shakespeare's plays (songs or entr'actes) and there is the possibility that it may be swallowed up in the shadow of his mountain. Only those songs with the most general of themes survive in the repertory (like Quilter's or Warlock's or Schubert's): here the composer can assert himself. How many sets of incidental music are now heard in the concert-hall? After Mendelssohn's *Midsummer Night's Dream* music one can think of little, and even with Mendelssohn, as Roger Fiske reminds us here, we have less a true theatre overture than a symphonic poem. Sonata form is scrupulously fulfilled, but with subtleties of variation in the recapitulation section which suggest a pictorial aim (Bottom's ophicleide under Titania's fairy-music). The great Shakespearean orchestral scores have nothing to do with the theatre, but they have, in a miracle of transference, a great deal to do with Shakespeare. There aren't many of them. Berlioz's *Queen Mab* Scherzo is an exact musical equivalent of Mercutio's speech, not an ideal accompaniment for it. The composer touched that area of the mind which antecedes either words or music: here he met Shakespeare. I am glad that Dr Fiske spends so much space considering the greatest Shakespearean orchestral work of them all: Elgar's *Falstaff.* This astonishing symphonic poem achieves the ultimate penetration. The form is literary in that it follows the Falstaff story (though the two brief interludes reach a dimension no purely verbal art could touch); the themes themselves derive from that pre-articulatory region where the image trembles between music and poetry. Music is an international art, but only an Englishman could have composed *Falstaff.*

Yes, you will say, but don't we have Verdi? Winton Dean's remarkable essay on Shakespeare and Opera must convince most of us that we only have Verdi because we have Boito, and his account of the transmutation of *Othello* into *Otello* (a miracle of a libretto if ever there was one) illuminates the whole problem of turning great plays into great operas. Mr Dean's survey makes us gape with horror and wonder: the ineptitudes, the misunderstandings, the butcherings – can such things really have been? I said earlier that *Faustus* will set to music almost as it stands, but Shakespeare's length and complexity renders music supererogatory as well as (if we can achieve the music at all) calling for the expansiveness of a whole *Ring* for a single play. The librettist's job is to render down existing greatness into something potentially great, to concentrate on a structure equivalent to, but different from, that of the original, to provide opportunities for the poetry which is now music but himself to eschew anything like the verbal intensities which are strongest when they are spoken. Can Shakespeare's words be used in a libretto? Only when they carry a minimal poetry, as in Holst's admirable *At the Boar's Head*. Benjamin Britten's *A Midsummer Night's Dream* is all Shakespeare (though Shakespeare shifted totally to a fairy's-eye-view), yet this is a young and unbuttoned bard whose poetry is more decorative than expressive. The comedies, though not all that easy, are easier than the tragedies, and if we want an operatic *Hamlet* or *King Lear* (though this must be a near-impossibility) we must look for a new Boito.

That this is a useful book, as well as an eye-opening and provocative one, is attested not solely by the comprehensiveness of the descriptive and historical treatment but by the catalogue and composers' check-list that fill the last 80 pages. It is a worthy contribution to the quatercentenary celebrations, and it is not only for musicians but for all who consider themselves lovers of Shakespeare, whether their starting-point be the study, the theatre, or the critic's laboratory. A great artist throws his beams on every human endeavour. The sundering waters are dried up, and the islands are revealed once more as limbs of the total continent of art.

The Musical Times, 1964

1   In 'Song and Part-Song Settings of Shakespeare's Lyrics, 1660–
    1960', Cudworth writes, 'Johnny Dankworth, too, has added to the
    repertory of Shakespearean jazz with various settings, including a
    very attractive "If music be the food of love", as well as a vocal version
    of part of Duke Ellington's "Such Sweet Thunder".' *Shakespeare in
    Music*, p. 87

2   Act III, sc. 1 (lines 120-5):

> These lovers cry 'O ho!' they die,
> Yet that which seems the wound to kill
> Doth turn 'O ho!' to 'Ha ha he!'
> So dying love lives still.
> 'O ho!' awhile, but 'Ha ha ha!'
> 'O ho!' groans out for 'ha ha ha!' – Hey ho!

3. MUSIC AT THE MILLENNIUM

That we should respond with a special kind of fearful expectation to the year 2001 more than to any other in the future – except perhaps 1984 – can be explained partly by the glamor of a certain Kubrick film. The year 1000, according to our Anglo-Saxon chroniclers, was to be a time of great prodigies, full of sin, murder, and anti-Christ, and presumably 1001 was to be no better. Yet 1000 and 1001 turned out to be very much like 975 and 976. People attach mystical significance to numbers to such an extent that terms like 'millennium' and 'chiliastic' imply a quantum leap change in the whole structure of human society.

This is all nonsense, of course. We're twenty-five years away from 2001, and, if what has happened in the past quarter-century is any guide, we'd be unwise to expect to enter a world of fable, especially in the arts. The arts don't truckle to time. The arts have their own in-built notions of pastness and futurity. I have on my desk now a copy of Wyndham Lewis' *Blast*, a magazine that lasted two violent issues. When I show it to young people and ask them when they think it was produced, they usually say 1951 or 1960 or 1969. They are surprised when they see the real date: 1915. Give to a wholly innocent ear some bars of Schoenberg's *Pierrot lunaire* (1912) and then a chunk of Stravinsky's 1959 atonal writing (say, the pieces for piano and orchestra).[1] If there is a time-response at all, it is as likely to reverse history as to confirm it. For me, in music and literature alike, the period 1912–39 is much more futuristic, more 2001-ish than anything that has come after.

Before considering the hellish question of what sorts of music will be available for the year of 2001, we ought to glance at and then push out of the way the new audio-technical wonders we can expect. Stereophonic recording and reproduction is already giving place to quadriphonic, as though man had four ears. As a sort of musician, I have always been doubtful about the value of such marvels, but this may be my age showing. I had my first formative musical experience in 1929, when I heard Debussy's *L'après-midi d'un faune* on a homemade crystal set; nothing since, for me, has been able to touch that old black magic. I clung to an HMV acoustic phonograph until I went to Malaya in 1954, there to find the tropical heat deforming my short-play records, turning them into licorice saucers. Like everybody else, I became a high fidelity man. I am not, however, all that impressed by music that bounces all around the room like a ball or – to put it another way – antiphonalizes from speaker to speaker. The *spatialization* of music, which is what today's audio experts are concerned with, has something to do with the primacy of the eye that is central to our age. Music jumps from ear to ear like a live thing: you can almost see it. *Videor, ergo sum.*[2] I need not, as Mr. Chips used to say, translate.[3]

Along with the refinement of the techniques for reproducing music, we may expect, by 2001, an increased difficulty on the part of the ear itself to cope with these refinements. The acoustic irony of the near future will be merely a grosser version of what we find surrounding us now. Muzak in restaurants, airports, even government buildings is desensitizing the general capacity to take in musical sounds as meaningful statements. When we are sufficiently, though gently, nagged, we no longer take in nagging as speech. The diminishing of musical sound to a permanent whisper is complemented, at the other end of the scale, by its augmentation to a level undreamt of even by Berlioz. The amplified guitar group can be, to my generation, an experience that touches the threshold of pain. But a younger generation takes the new sound level for granted and, conceivably, hardly hears Muzak at all. When Hans Keller interviewed some plentifully haired but not very talented pop musicians on television, he apologized for not being able to accept their loudness easily: 'I was brought up on chamber music.' The response was aggressive and derisive: 'Ugh, we bloody well wasn't,' or words to that effect. By 2001 we shall have, without doubt, a generation unable even to *hear* chamber music.

On the other hand, I have the utmost confidence in the capacity of some of the young to master traditional instrumental techniques and to bring them, by the end of the millennium, to a point that would leave a resurrected Liszt and Paganini gasping with disbelief. The musical talent currently available in America, especially in traditional ensemble work, is incredible. Whether the technical expertise is matched by musical understanding is another question. The language of music, lauded and prized for its ability to transcend mere verbal language and to act as a sort of world auxiliary of the emotions, is a frail and subtle thing, and its qualities are not easily transmitted either by great executants or great teachers. The language of the music of, say, the classical era owed a good deal to instrumental limitations that the composer accepted and tried to exploit. Trumpets and horns could do little more than hammer out a tonic and dominant, but Mozart made a glory out of this inarticulateness. In the near future, if not already, trumpets and horns as sprightly as clarinets, double basses as swift and sonorous as violas, will dissolve the physical obstacles of art that the composer used to delight in exploiting.

And what stretched strings and air-filled cylinders cannot do, synthetic sounds are already learning to do with frightening efficiency. I think, however, that disenchantment with synthetic music-makers is already on its way. It's all too easy, this Moog-musicalizing; easy because the parameters of the admissible and inadmissible are hard to define.[4] No art should ever be too easy, and the easiness of the musical art – for the lowlier talent – began when the barriers between consonance and dissonance went down and, indeed, the chromatic scale was democratized. What was artistic agony to Schoenberg, Berg, and Webern is a cinch to their followers. What I predict we will see, or hear, coming about in 2001 are the beginnings of a synthesis that has nothing to do with Moogs.

Various ways of composition are available to the composer today. He can use a style generally diatonic, with chromatic trimmings – a style, that is, that acknowledges a hierarchy of notes of the traditional European scale and pays some kind of homage to a key-center. This mode of composition has its most blatant exponents among the pop practitioners and the writers of film scores. 'Serious' composers are frightened of keys and major and minor and modal scales. However, as musicians like Darius Milhaud showed, this traditional kind of music could be sophisticated, made apt for 'seriousness,' by multiplication of key-centers in the kind of composition known as polytonal. Polytonality was so marked, however, by Milhaud's own personal method that to use it seems all too often like creating a Milhaud pastiche.

There remains what Schoenberg bequeathed and Stravinsky eventually yielded to – serialism. But is serialism enough? Even Schoenberg seems to have thought not.[5] When art develops, it should 'enclose' what goes before, as Beethoven encloses Haydn. The looked-for synthesis of the end of the millennium is a composer of personality strong enough to create an individual language out of the century's three main heritages – the diatonic, the serial, and the polytonal – *without the aid of literary texts*. One makes this last condition because the urgent formal need of the music of the future is the development of structure analogous to Beethovenian symphonic structure: musical argument at length, intellectuality manifesting itself structurally, not doctrinally. Perhaps the most considerable of contemporary composers, Luciano Berio, is still able to create *at length* only when he has the prop of the extramusical: text, noise, and quotations from others' music.[6] Music does not need language, any more than language needs music.

Generalization is never enough. Let us present a practical scenario for a composer of 2001. He is commissioned to write a piano concerto.[7] He has a free hand, all the instrumental resources in the world, a virtuoso performer capable of anything. Because a concerto imposes a particular relationship between a soloist and an ensemble, our composer is not at liberty to use the pianoforte in a 'concertante' way, making it a mere part of the orchestra. Because a concerto demands a considerable degree of exposition of technical resource, or showing off, he has to think in terms of duration greater than that, say, of a Webern vignette. Twenty minutes? Thirty? Because of the variety of pianistic modes to be exhibited, there must be a variety of styles, rhythms, and tempos. Our composer will, whether he likes it or not, end up with the 'natural' alternation of slow and fast or active and contemplative. He may end with the traditional three movements or the Brahmsian four. If he feels, so shackled, that he is truckling too much to the past, he ought to reflect that he is confusing tradition and 'nature'. We all have to submit to the basic rhythms of the body, of the seasons, of the alternations of mood that are built into the human psyche.

If he is wise, our composer will not disown the traditional 'romantic' orchestra merely because Strauss or Elgar used it before him. No composer *has* to use three flutes, two oboes, *cor anglais*, two clarinets, bass clarinet, two bassoons, double bassoon, and so forth, but he might at least consider, before disrupting or jettisoning his woodwinds, that here is God's plenty. The orchestra is the end-product of a long and painful evolutionary process, and it asks not to be disowned because it belongs to the dirty 'past', but to be used in new and individual ways. It can bear subtraction (as in Constant Lambert's *Rio Grande*, where the woodwinds go), and it can bear addition (electronic effects, the typewriter of Hindemith's *News of the Day*, the nightingale of Respighi's *Pines of Rome*), but never wantonly, out of mere puritanism or the desire to shock.[8]

The composer must now think out his themes – always with contrast in mind. There may be contrasting themes, or there may be contrasting aspects of the same theme: it seems that we are, by nature, committed to a sonata view of a theme or a variational one. There is no reason why he should apologize to the world for thinking in tonal terms, to begin with. The introduction of a polytonal element thickens the plot, introduces argument, and can lead the way naturally to the conversion of a tonal theme into an atonal one:[9]

I needn't say that the aesthetic value of the work will depend less on the techniques used than on the power of the composer's personality to express itself in highly individual statements – but always within the framework of a piece of music essentially 'extrovert', public, even blatantly designed for display. Such musical personalities are at present frequently shackled because of fear – fear of being vulgar, obvious, outdated. Perhaps 2001 A.D. will, musically, be less a time for odysseys into the new than a beginning of synthesis, upgathering what the past has had to offer and seeing how a limitless musical language can be put together out of the fragmented dialects lying around us. Joyce's *Ulysses* is an exercise in the use of 'total' verbal language. We need that kind of achievement in music. But why should we have to wait until 2001?

High Fidelity, 1976

1   *Movements* for piano and orchestra (composed 1958–9). Burgess
    would have heard this work performed live the previous year at the
    premiere of his Third Symphony. See Chapter 44 *Symphony in C.*

2   I am seen, therefore I am – a play on Descartes's *Cogito, ergo sum*: I
    think, therefore I am.

3   The phrase *'haec olim meminisse juvabit'* (literally, 'someday it will be
    a pleasure to remember these things', or, metaphorically, 'one day
    we'll look back on all this and laugh') from Virgil's *Aeneid* occurs
    in Aeneas's speech to his fellow Trojan warriors after they've been
    shipwrecked following the Trojan War. In James Hilton's 1934
    novella *Goodbye Mr. Chips* (later adapted into the 1939 film), the
    Classics teacher Mr. Chipping says *'haec olim meminisse juvabit* – of
    course, I need not translate' upon receiving a retirement gift from his
    students.

4   Bob Moog created the first commercial synthesizer, which he
    introduced in 1964. Wendy Carlos popularized it in 1968 with the
    hit album *Switched-On Bach*, which featured Carlos's arrangements
    of Bach compositions performed on a Moog synthesizer, and
    subsequently with the soundtrack for *A Clockwork Orange*, Stanley
    Kubrick's 1971 film adaptation of Burgess's 1962 novel. By the late
    1960s and early 1970s, numerous rock bands, including the Beatles,
    the Rolling Stones, the Doors, the Grateful Dead, and Emerson,
    Lake & Palmer, had used the Moog synthesizer on recordings or in
    live performances.

5   Schoenberg returned to composing tonal music toward the end of
    his life.

6   *Sinfonia,* perhaps Berio's most famous work, is a multi-movement
    orchestral piece that incorporates musical quotations from dozens
    of composers (including Bach, Beethoven, Brahms, Debussy, Ravel,
    Mahler, Stravinsky, Schoenberg, Berg, Boulez, Stockhausen and
    Berio himself) and text from writings of Claude Lévi-Strauss,
    Samuel Beckett and others, which are vocalized (spoken, whispered,
    shouted) by eight amplified voices.

7   At the time that he wrote this article, Burgess was composing a piano concerto of his own – Concerto for Pianoforte and Orchestra in E♭, a 33-minute work in three movements completed on 1 July 1976.

8   *Pines of Rome* (1924) was the first orchestral work to utilize recorded sound – a specific recording of a nightingale that is played in the third movement.

9   The 'tonal' version (top line) in the musical example is closely related to the main theme of the second movement of Burgess's piano concerto:

4. PUNK

The word has been with us quite a time. To Shakespeare, a punk was a prostitute. In America, it changed its sex and was regularly used to designate worthless and vicious young hoodlums. In present-day very much non-Shakespearian England it has become adjectival and vague, denoting rubbishy. Attached to various kinds of underart, it snarls an underdog defiance: I'm cheap, filthy, a social reject, but by Christ I'm fackin prahd of it. This pride in a verbal badge of inferiority is very British and, I think, not well understood in America. The Kaiser called the British forces in Flanders 'a contemptible little army', and the term 'The Old Contemptibles' became an honourable sobriquet. During World War Two there was even a song called 'We're the sons of the Old Contemptibles'. When a Socialist minister said the Conservatives were vermin, Conservatives went round proudly wearing lapel-badges showing three lice argent couchant.[1] The punk rock kids of England are following a well-established tradition. They're making the attributes of the social reject into positive virtues, which means in practice turning them into the language of a sort of art. The group known as the Sex Pistols creates a lifestyle out of excreting on the Queen's portrait, vomiting before the press cameras, using language of a gratuitous filthiness on all occasions. They have cut discs which were promptly banned because of their obscene content; the rejection was expected and even welcomed as a proof that the punk was true punk. The Sex Pistols became the most famous rock group in Britain before firing a single shot.

The punk movement manifests itself chiefly in music, meaning song and the manner of delivering that song. The song is about defying society, but it is also about defying earlier defiers of society. In England, society vaguely means a structure of rule, privilege and taste which has its seat in the South-East, or the Home Counties. During this jubilee year, many English people have had occasion to reflect on the usefulness of the Royal Family as a definer of the socially acceptable. We take it for granted that the Queen will eat roast beef but not Lancashire hot pot, that she will see a play by Terence Rattigan but not one by Beckett, that her tastes in general accept the bland but reject the violent.[2] She stands for a certain kind of spoken English, for field sports, for church on Sunday, for reticence and decent manners. She is what the art of the defiant has to defy.

The trouble with the art of the defiant in England is that it does not express a genuinely revolutionary urge. It does not seek to replace the existing order with something new; it merely snarls at the existing order, and that snarl really means a deep, not often conscious, desire to be accepted by it. The history of all defiant art in Britain since the 'fifties has been the same. John Osborne wrote *Look Back in Anger*, which screamed at the Establishment, but the Establishment gradually and gently took that play to its bosom: one can imagine the Queen going to see it and saying: 'How charming'. The mad screamer at established order becomes a court clown. All the angry young men of the 'fifties are now pillars of society, trying to behave like that irascible clubman Evelyn Waugh, who was hungry for a knighthood. The Beatles began as a rough provincial voice, demanding that remote Liverpool be taken seriously in patrician London. They smoothed themselves out, became not merely respectable but highbrow, were received by Her Majesty and admitted to the Order of the British Empire. The miniskirt was an act of defiance, but it too became merely charming, epicene rather than a challenge to the tepid sexuality of established order, and the most delightful miniskirts were to be seen in the Royal Enclosure at Ascot. Mary Quant, mother of the miniskirt, also joined the Order of the British Empire and is now a very orthodox arbiter of middle-class elegance. Perhaps the Rolling Stones have held out longest against the enbosoming [sic] of the Establishment, but they are now very very rich, and there are no rich rebels.

Now the Sex Pistols and the rest of the punk people naturally despise those defused defiers of the 'sixties and earlier 'seventies. The point about punk is that it is poor, it cannot afford the highbrow surrealism of the Beatles or their flirtations with Stockhausen: punk uses the old British working-class argument that you cannot have education without money.[3] More reasonably, it despises the expensive technology with which the Rolling Stones present themselves. Money can buy anything, from a phrase like 'Lucy in the sky with diamonds' to the electronic extravaganzas which frame the songs of David Bowie. The punk people pride themselves on poverty and, through a working-class solecism, on illiteracy. Their songs are crudely put together, and they are accompanied by chord sequences of excruciating naiveté, which the punk boys regard as a return to simplicity. Simplicity is beyond their skill, though it was never beyond the skill of the Beatles.

All that the punk singers can bring to the presentation of their songs is the gesture of sexual obscenity or of impotent rage. There is a lot of the caged simian gibber about the performances of the Sex Pistols. If the Rolling Stones breathe a rather frightening power (one feels that if Mike Jagger were not fundamentally a nice boy, a credit to the London School of Economics, he could lead a fairly effective revolution), the punk people seem to admit their own impotence. They are the voice of Britain's economic recession, which always hits youth hardest. Their little songs, following that solecism again, are musically and verbally poverty-stricken, which the works of that real protest man, Bob Dylan, were not. We are poor, and our songs are poor, so they seem to proclaim. Visually, they wear with snarling pride the marks of the downtrodden. Hair is cropped because long hair holds lice. Clothes are not patched, since patching denotes skill and a seedy desire for respectability; their gaping holes are held together with safety-pins.

Already we are observing how the badges of indigence are turning into a new kind of chic. The Sex Pistols are growing rich, and the stylised symbols of poverty mock real poverty. This is not new: for years now the well-heeled jeans-wearers have been having their tears and frays devised by cunning couturiers. The safety-pin has become a most elegant little engine. You can buy very expensive dresses carefully ripped and held together by safety-pins of gold or silver. The blunt razor-blade worn as an amulet is another piece of punk couture: it evokes not merely poverty but the days of wartime shortage. More, it is one of the properties of *Nineteen Eighty-Four* and carries an edge of tamed menace. In Britain everything is at length folded into humorous cosiness. The Union Jack itself, a symbol of empire, became a mere piece of calligraphy for shopping bags and kitchen aprons. Revolution in England is something that, like patriotism, amuses the people and keeps off the *tedium vitae*.[4] Punk is busy making faces and snarling dirty words, but it is already becoming mere, and very transitory, décor. It is very important indeed for foreigners (which includes, alas, Americans) to recognise how imperturbable British society is. You cannot shake that structure with its pliable steel cat's cradle of classes. Either everybody ends up wearing a collar and tie, or else the collar-and-tied confer a grace and elegance on the discarding of them. Certainly the rebel cannot win, nor does he really wish to. He may stick a safety-pin on to the nose of the Queen in effigy but never a dagger in her heart. He wants her to accept him; he is her errant son. Note that the pin is a pin of safety. The French (who are fairly busy with punk couture) call it an *épingle anglaise* but also an *épingle de sûreté*. *Sûreté* is what even the reddest British rebel is after.[5]

I note with some shock that my name is being associated with the British punk movement, and that the *New York Times* has even called me its godfather.[6] This is because of a novel I wrote some seventeen years ago, called *A Clockwork Orange*, a novel I have never particularly cared for. When this novel is mentioned in the press, it is usually the Kubrick film made from it that is meant. This presented a highly memorable kind of thug lifestyle, complete with costume and maquillage, but I do not think it has anything to do with punk. My own book suggested a kind of expensive elegance, rather Elizabethan with its built-up shoulders and codpieces. Punk is really a rejection of· all the varied types of elegance that earlier youth movements bred, from the Teddy boys (or Edwardian strutters) to the mods and rockers. It is closer to the very unattractive skinhead cult, with its shaven skulls, navvy boots and displayed galluses.[7] It is indeed the vocal fulfilment of that brutal and inarticulate phase in the not very interesting history of juvenile life-styles. Punk is dying as I write these words. If it has significance it is in its capacity to show how easily the foul-mouthed and talentless can prevail these days, how unsure our aesthetic standards are. British youth, like American and French and Upper Slobbovian youth, needs a good kick in the pants and a bit of solid education.[8] It needs also to be reminded occasionally how very very dull its mouthings, shrieks, and unmuscular spasms are.

The Daily Mail, 1977

1   In heraldry, *argent* connotes the silver of a coat of arms while *couchant* refers to an animal represented as lying with the body resting on its legs and the head lifted.

2   Sir Terence Mervyn Rattigan was a British dramatist and screenwriter whose genteel plays were typically set in upper-middle-class society and meant to appeal to affluent playgoers with conventional tastes. The plays of Samuel Beckett typically feature bleak, tragicomic situations in a modernist style.

3   Karlheinz Stockhausen was a leading avant-garde German composer whose experimental use of electronic music influenced a wide range of musicians including the Beatles, most notably in 'A Day in the Life' (1967) and 'Revolution 9' (1968). Stockhausen's face appears on the cover of the *Sgt Pepper's Lonely Hearts Club Band* album, fifth from left in the top row, between Lenny Bruce (left) and W.C. Fields (right).

4   boredom of life

5   *épingle anglaise* means 'English pin'; *épingle de sûreté* is 'safety pin'.

6   'Punk's "Horror Show"' from *The New York Times*, 30 June 1977, p. 19 © 1977 The New York Times Company. All rights reserved. Used under license. See Commentary for further information.

7   The heavy boots worn by construction or railway workers are known as 'navvy boots', the term 'navvy' deriving from 'navigator' for the eighteenth-century manual labourers who dug canals or worked on other civil engineering projects; 'galluses' are suspenders. 'Navvy Boots On' is a song by the Irish singer Liam Clancy.

8   Slobovia (or Slobbovia), derived in 1946 from Al Capp's cartoon strip 'Li'l Abner', connotes an underdeveloped and unenlightened fictional country in a remote location like Siberia.

5. WHY PUNK *HAD* TO END IN EVIL

Three events in my immediate life, seemingly disconnected at first, appear now to be disclosing a common theme. The first is the election of a new Pope.[1] The second is my reading of Lord David Cecil's life of Jane Austen. The third is the arrest of a character called Sid Vicious – bass guitarist with former Punk group The Sex Pistols – on a charge of murder.[2] The most authoritative voice of Christendom now comes from a nation which has had a Godless regime imposed on it against its will. At last, I feel, we are going to hear some plain words spoken about the oppressive state and the oppressed human soul. It seems as if we are entering into a period of open confrontation between the forces of light and the dark. The biography of Jane Austen reminded me that life could once be lived happily and productively in a country rectory, without the excitement of drugs and violence and indiscriminate sex.

What has gone wrong with us all since her day? There has been, of course, a gradual erosion of moral authority in British society abetted by the leaders of Church and State, but this has generally been regarded as a good thing. It is good, we've been taught, to be released from all those moral taboos and their corollaries – taboos of good manners and good taste. Men and women are free: the Pope would be the first to assert this basic doctrine of Christianity. But we ought to consider what the term means. To be free possibly signifies to be free to choose between the better and the worse, but we have to know what the better and the worse are. There have to be standards of conduct, taste and social behaviour, and we have to be taught them. Nobody is free not to know the nature of human freedom.

To various generations of the young, freedom has meant the overthrowing of the past – all the past, indiscriminately.

This is sometimes known as anarchism on the model of the Russian Bakunin, who taught that as soon as you'd jettisoned the past you had nothing to face but a rosy future.[3] But, unfortunately, values and standards of behaviour are things we can only learn from the past. If we decide to build our anarchism on natural impulses, uncorrected by the lessons of the past, then we will build it on the satisfying of immediate pleasures. I don't think this is enough. Pope John Paul II and Jane Austen agree with me.

When pleasures are freely available – without taboos, without moral standards – they are freely enjoyed, but the enjoyer discovers, to his surprise, that the enjoyment quickly diminishes. We are not free to enjoy the eightieth cigarette of the day as much as we enjoyed the first one. When simple pleasures diminish, they have to be made more complex, more dangerous. Simple sex can lead to rape or bestiality. Eventually it may lead to murder. This is one of the consequences, or fruits, of total freedom. Or, put it another way, total freedom leads to total enslavement.

The hippie communities of Southern California started out as groups of innocent boys and girls who believed that all Governments were evil, and good could only be recovered in free primitive communes. They didn't seem to realise, until people like Charles Manson came along, that evil can exist anywhere, and, that if you get rid of the rules that restrain evil, you'll quickly find prayer meetings turning into orgies of mutilation and death. There is evil in all of us. We keep it down with self-knowledge and loyalty to traditional rules. Eliminate traditional rules and, unless you're a saint, you'll not only be in trouble – you'll be in the ultimate trouble.

Like the person who calls himself Sid Vicious. The phenomenon of Punk started out innocently enough – as a childish repudiation of traditional values: no more faith, patriotism, decency, or even good manners. So long as this new cult of anarchy was controlled by a little common sense, meaning a little self-ridicule, it could do no harm – not even when it expressed itself in public obscenity, blasphemy and vomiting. But it became chic, it was a new thrill and it generated new, and profitable, gimmicks of behaviour and dress. The new thrill of spitting, or worse, in the public's face, was soon not enough. There were no standards, moral or aesthetic, to tell the devotees of Punk what exactly might be enough. It had to end up in the taking of heavy drugs. It had to end up in the devaluation of human life. There is no limit to new pleasures when old pleasures wear out so quickly – no limit except dissolution, which means death for somebody.

The pseudonym of the character at present awaiting trial is highly significant. Vicious means addicted to vice. Vice means sensual excess, self-destroying self-indulgence. Vicious, to the young man who adopted the name, was a mere silly toy, a joke. Vice was another name for rejection of the values of the past. These young men were playing with fire from the start, and they probably didn't know it – or, if they did, perhaps they thought it didn't matter. Unfortunately it does matter. We can't throw over standards inherited from the past without considering, very, very carefully, the consequences of what we're doing. And if we're too stupid to want to think about these things, our moral betters ought to get in there and explain, kindly but insistently, what precisely is involved in living the so-called free life. In other words, we can listen to the Pope, and read Jane Austen.

The Daily Mail, 1978

1   Karol Józef Wojtyła was installed as Pope John Paul II on 16 October 1978 and served as pope for over twenty-six years until his death on 2 April 2005. He supported the reforms of the Second Vatican Council, attempted to improve relations with Judaism, Islam, and the Eastern Orthodox Church, and is credited with helping to end Communist rule in Eastern Europe.

2   John Simon Ritchie, known as Sid Vicious, was arrested in New York on 12 October 1978 for the murder of his American girlfriend Nancy Spungen. After serving time in prison for violating a bail agreement, he died of a drug overdose in Greenwich Village on 2 February 1979 the day following his release from Rikers Island.

3   The Russian anarchist Mikhail Alexandrovich Bakunin espoused the creation of self-governing workplaces and communes.

6. MUSICAL AUTODIDACT

George Grove by Percy M. Young
London: Macmillan, 1980

I gained what general musical education I have from the *Radio Times* of the 1930s (a magnificently highbrow publication) and from *Grove's Dictionary of Music and Musicians*. The latter I would read as a boy in the Moss Side (Manchester) Public Library, while my father played the piano in the pub opposite. I realise now that it must have been the original edition (started in the 1870s), since Wagner was presented as the leader of the 'modern school' and the French horn still had crooks. The article on Beethoven was by Sir George Grove himself. There will be almost nothing of 'G' left in the new Grove, due out next year, but the name will not die. The *Dictionary* was one of the big Victorian creations, like the Crystal Palace and the Britannia Tubular Bridge.

Grove, who was brought up to be an engineer, had a lot to do with that bridge, as also with the construction of the Morant Point Lighthouse in Jamaica, the Gibb's Hill Lighthouse in Bermuda, the London and Birmingham Railway, and the Joint Railway Station in Chester. He had no hand in the erecting of the Crystal Palace but, when it was moved to Sydenham, he was put in charge of its musical programmes as Secretary of the Crystal Palace Company. The connection between engineering and music, strong in the Victorian era, is more than a matter of structural affinity, though Elgar, for instance, was given to bringing up bridge-building images when discussing music. He saw Beethoven's Fifth Symphony as a kind of Forth Bridge and himself, in comparison with the great pontifex, as a mere tinker. (In his Concert Overture *In the South* he gives us a remarkable representation of a Roman viaduct.) It may be said that the character of public Victorian music-making was determined by public works. You get a lot of workers together and turn them into a choir. You keep miners out of mischief by teaching them to play brass instruments (themselves triumphs of engineering). As far as you can, you insist on sacred music. Handel's *Messiah* was made for the Crystal Palace, with its vast space and reverberant organ. When Frederick Delius jeered that Sir Hubert Parry would have set the whole Bible to music if given the chance, he was raising the voice of secular, indeed atheistical, reaction to a musical tradition more pious than aesthetic.

The Germans, who nevertheless played a large part in British musical activities, called England *das Land ohne Musik*. They were both right and wrong. Wrong because the British musical impulse was never more powerfully expressed than in the eighty years of Grove's life, when there were beefy choirs bawling everywhere and drowning ill-tuned strings, when royal dukes proclaimed, on the strength of 'Sumer is icumen in' and unheard Purcell, England's musical greatness – always in strong Teutonic accents. Right because, though there had indeed been creative greatness in the past, there was little in the present. There were no important Victorians until Elgar, of whose work Grove, dying in 1900, knew only *King Olaf* and the Bavarian Highlands songs.[1] Taste was mediocre; Mendelssohn was a god because he had set God to music; all the conductors had to come from Germany.

But if, despite Europe's unwillingness to be impressed, there has been greatness since, Grove may be said to have prepared the way for it. He became Director of the Royal College of Music and, in 1894, was able to hear its orchestra – with Gustav Holst playing the trombone and Vaughan Williams the triangle – perform a symphony by the black Coleridge-Taylor.[2] In the audience was August Jaeger, to be immortalised as 'Nimrod' in the *Enigma Variations*. The British musical future was stirring. And Grove's book on Beethoven's symphonies was establishing a tradition of elegant musicology to which Donald Tovey, Cecil Gray, Ernest Newman and Percy M. Young, Grove's biographer, were to belong.

Grove did not call himself a musician. Professionally qualified as an engineer, he had taught himself music from scratch, like your present reviewer. Bernard Shaw however said: 'He is always the true musician: that is, the man the professionals call 'no musician' – just what they called Beethoven himself.' Shaw saw that Grove grasped musical truths by instinct, the way of the inspired amateur. Wagner himself was that sort of man, according to Shaw. Give the first three bars of the 'Meistersinger' Overture to a professional – Stanford or Prout or Higgs – and he would not harmonise them like Wagner: he would follow the rules too much. We are aware of inspired amateurism in so many of the great Victorian enterprises – philology with its amateur monument the OED, political theory, colonial administration.

It was not only music that Grove served. He worked at Biblical scholarship, assisting Stanley with 'Sinai and Palestine' and joining the panel of experts who produced a 'Dictionary of the Bible'. He published 'The Story of David's Early Life' and a geography primer. He was literary adviser to Macmillan.[3] His amateur polymathy and the variety of his interests caused him disquiet; the age of the specialists was beginning, and he belonged to the Renaissance. He had an honorary doctorate but no university education. The 'Oxford swells' whom the great Murray of the OED feared represented, as they still do to the autodidact, a closed world of genuine scholarship. But they were incapable of producing a 'Dictionary of Music and Musicians'.

Brought up in the 'holy village' of Clapham, Grove developed a quiet religious scepticism in his old age, but the iron ethos of British Protestantism always lay heavy on him. He ceased to love his wife, who was little help to him, and he adored from a distance his young Irish pupil at the RCM, Edith Oldham, to whom he wrote plaintive letters full of passion that was doomed to be unfulfilled. Dreaming of an impossible infidelity, he had to keep an eye on threats of sexual irregularity in his own College: one of his instructors was given to seducing female students in the service of art.

Sexual repression was perhaps one of the conditions of Victorian achievement. Perhaps also music – which Freud distrusted because it was too close to the id – was something of a surrogate for physical passion. None of us will ever understand music. The coming New Grove, with its 18,000 pages, will try to teach us everything about it except what it is really about.

Dr Young's biography is a masterpiece of lucidity. A borough councillor, the official historian of Wolverhampton Wanderers (for whom he had interpreted in Germany), a writer on football, a member of a number of statutory health bodies, Dr Young has already published some sixteen books on music and musicians, particularly Elgar. He is a living witness to my belief that musicians write better than literary men. It is all a matter of ear.

The Observer, 1980

1 The cantata *Scenes from the Saga of King Olaf*, Op. 30, is a setting of Longfellow's *The Saga of King Olaf*, a poem about Olaf Tryggvason, the historical figure who brought Christianity to Norway. *From the Bavarian Highlands*, Op. 27, is a set of six choral songs that Elgar composed after a holiday in Upper Bavaria with his wife Alice in autumn 1894. The orchestral versions of both works premiered in 1896, the Bavarian Highlands songs having first been arranged for chorus and piano in 1895.

2 See Chapter 37 *In Tune with the Popular Soul*.

3 Alexander Macmillan, who co-founded Macmillan Publishers in 1843 with his brother Daniel (grandfather of Harold Macmillan, the British Prime Minister from 1957 to 1963).

The New Grove Dictionary of Music and Musicians, 20 vols.,
edited by Stanley Sadie.
Washington, D.C.: Grove's Dictionaries of Music, 1980

Tennyson said something about the repetition of a common
word turning that word into a wonder. Literary men and
women who know something about music occasionally shake
themselves awake from the torpid acceptance of all that sound
that nowadays surrounds us – never has there been so much
music, and so much of it imposed upon us – to marvel that it
should all have its provenance in a piano handspan of twelve
notes and an assortment of noises. Next year is James Joyce's
centenary (*The New Grove Dictionary of Music and Musicians*
will remind you of this: there are literary men there as well as
musicians) and I have devised a musical version of *Ulysses* in
celebration.[1] I have spent the last two months in orchestrating
the music, and, on my resumption of literary work, I am struck
by one great difference between the two activities: for writing
words I need a dictionary; for writing notes I have to assume
a total knowledge and control of the medium. This is because
I am not dealing with meanings. And yet, writing music, I am
presumably trying to communicate. What is the nature of that
communication?

This is a question asked more by *littérateurs* than by
musicians. If a musician were to worry about the semantics of
his art he might well be struck dumb: as with riding a bicycle
(Johnson could see no bicycle would go: you bear yourself and
the machine as well), you must not let consciousness intrude
too much.[2] When, as a boy of fourteen who thought his
future lay in musical composition, I pored over the old *Grove*
(a second or third edition of the original) in my local library

reading room, I had enough of the musician's instinct to take it for granted that Beethoven expressed recognizable human emotions: how this was done was not for me to inquire. Sir George Grove himself wrote the Beethoven article, as he had written a few years previously a whole book on the Beethoven symphonies, and he was full of the assumption that music dealt in love, anguish, triumph and visions of heaven. Bernard Shaw, in a memorable article on the Beethoven book in the *Saturday Review,* praised Grove for avoiding technical twaddle about the subdominant ('which I could teach to a poodle in two hours'), and rhapsodizing in the manner of 'The lovely melody then passes, by a transition of remarkable beauty, into the key of C major, in which it seems to go straight up to heaven'.

Beauty? Heaven? In what way beautiful? How to heaven? The nineteenth century did not ask these questions much. If they did not wish to ask them, preferring instead to concentrate on the poodle twaddle of modulation via the Neapolitan sixth, nevertheless Victorian musicians accepted that a symphony discoursed personal emotion and could attain a vision of sublimity. In Victorian Britain music was heard in terms of morality and promoted among the children of Utilitarianism as a device of temperance and uplift. The original *Grove* is a typical expression of the educative urge of the day, the work of a musical amateur (as Murray of the *OED* was a philological amateur), as well able to supply a dictionary of engineering or of biblical geography as to oversee a compendium 'from which an intelligent enquirer can learn, in small compass, and in language which he can understand, what is meant by a Symphony or Sonata, a Fugue, a Stretto, a Coda' and so on. Music was enlightenment and a kind of religion.

Our views of the morality of music have changed, as our views of so much else have changed since 1945 and the beginnings of the revelations of the true depths of Nazi infamy. The Germans were for long regarded as the most musical people in the world, and they did not cease to be musical – though their repertory was reduced on racist grounds – when they became Nazi. George Steiner has an essay in his *Language and Silence* in which he wonders at the mentality of the death-camp commandant who could, after a day supervising the liquidation of Jews, go home to weep tears of pure joy at a broadcast of a Schubert trio or a recorded Schumann *Lied*. His wonder is misplaced if we consider that the nineteenth-century musical aesthetic was wrong, and that the feelings engendered by music have nothing to do with Kant or Goethe or the New Testament. We can thrill to the *Meistersinger* Prelude as Hitler did, but the imagined referent of the emotion had better not be too closely considered. The Nazis could hear in the last movement of Beethoven's Ninth Symphony an expression of Nazi aspirations. Those aspirations are no more present in the music or, indeed, the words than are visions of Christian democracy or of white supremacy in Smith's Rhodesia, which used the *Ode to Joy* as a national anthem.[3] Freud feared music because it was too close to the id. St Augustine was 'torn between three attitudes to music: exaltation of musical principles as embodying principles of cosmic order; ascetic aversion from music-making as carnal; and a recognition of jubilation and congregational song as respectively expressing the inexpressible ecstasy and promoting congregational brotherhood'.

I quote here from F. E. Sparshott's essay on the Aesthetics of Music, noting the happy accident of taxonomy which places acoustics and aesthetics, or sound and the meaning of sound, close together in the very first volume. Sparshott's approach is diachronic, as is everybody's approach to everything (look up Trombone to find which pedal notes are practicable and you plunge into history rather than immediate need), but he ends with his own questions:

A final problem arises not within music but on its borders: the edges of the arts are becoming blurred. Can and should we continue to think of music as an art distinct from all others, or should we once more face the prospect that, as Roger Bacon and Wagner suggested in their different ways, the future of music lies within some comprehensive form of aesthetic activity? It is a problem on the frontiers of philosophy and sociology, for it may be that music as we have known it is proper to a phase of civilization that is passing away.

We have, in fact, despite the pondering of individual aestheticians, come no nearer to a common understanding of what music tries to do and, moreover, the notion of what we call music is becoming confused. The phase of civilization represented by *Grove I* was both too sure of itself and too limited in its definitions. We are in the Cage age, in which the hieratic pretensions of music to be superior to mere natural noise are being questioned, and the presentation of a fixed measure of silence can be an acceptable auditory experience. We have things in the new *Grove* which its superseded great-grandfather had, despite the claims of democracy and the expansion of the Empire, to regard as too far away from Beethoven to take seriously – the music of the dance hall and the popular theatre and the gongs and noseflutes of people in loincloths.

We have great stretches of ethnomusicology and articles on jazz and pop and popular musicians. In that vastest expanse of any musical compendium – B to Petros Byzantios – Irving Berlin tinkles in the key of F sharp, the only key he could manage, near to Berlioz, and the Beatles (the late John Lennon, by the way, did *not* produce *In His Own Write* in the 1970s) precede the troubadour Beatriz de Dia.[4] There is, in the whole twenty volumes containing over 22 million words, a brilliantly informed comprehensiveness mostly touched by the tentativeness of an age not so sure of itself as the expansive time of *Grove I*.

It is as well, when first probing the utility of a new and massive compendium, to test it in an area vaguely eccentric. Last August my friend John Sebastian died. He was an American harmonica player of repute, and for him I composed two works with guitar accompaniment – a bagatelle and a sonatina.[5] More recently I have composed for two harmonica players still happily with us – Tommy Reilly (he and I played an unnamed rhapsody on my sixtieth birthday and television) and Larry Adler.[6] Both Adler and Reilly have brief but flavoursome entries, but John Sebastian is not there.

The article on the Harmonica tells us how the instrument works, its range, who manufactures it. It does not tell the prospective composer for the instrument what chords can be played on it. Under the biography of Villa-Lobos there is mention of a harmonica concerto – it was in fact commissioned by John Sebastian – but there seems to be no means, under either his entry or that of Harmonica, of mentioning that his cadenza for the instrument was unplayable and had to be rewritten by the performer. Now this is obviously an instance of my asking too much, but only the comprehensiveness of the new *Grove* would tempt me to ask at all. Another performer, for whom I wrote a song in the *Bahasa Negara* of Malaysia, is the soprano Cathy Berberian, who gets a mention in the article on Luciano Berio (they were married; he wrote much for her) but no entry of her own.[7] One of the finest of the younger American composers is Stanley Silverman (whose latest opera was favourably reviewed in the *TLS*).[8] He and I produced an Oedipus cantata performed in New York.[9] He is not in the new *Grove*, though Bob Dylan and Elvis Presley are. Is it I who put the kiss of documentary neglect on musicians with whom I have associated? You cannot have everybody, but it seems you have to have every minor Nordic teacher and folksong-collector whose name ever began with K.

But musicians happy to see Krengel, Krenn and Krenz may well grumble at space wasted on Eric Fogg, who worked for the BBC North Region and committed suicide. He was a Manchester composer who wrote a bassoon concerto in D for Archie Camden. I am interested in minor British composers, having aspired to be one myself, and am generally satisfied with the way the new *Grove,* if not the musical world without, deals with them. If Sacheverell Coke is not here, Josef Holbrooke is (much quoted for his use of banks of saxophones in Forsyth's *Orchestration),* and also Cyril Scott and Dame Ethel Smyth. On Havergal Brian a judgment is made which is applicable to most of the figures of the British musical renascence – that the fresh and idiosyncratic are juxtaposed with the banal and conventional. The major British composers are well covered, but we do not find in their entries the same concentration on tangibles as we find in the articles on Mahler and Bartók and especially Hindemith – music-type illustrations of compositional procedures, the physical nature of their styles. I realize that Imogen Holst has a sort of monopoly of her father, but I should have liked, for a change, a non-filial view, with examples of his superposed fourths (which, not being much of a Mahlerian, I had not till now realized were to be found in Mahler) and the triadic daring of the *Hymn of Jesus* and the *Choral Symphony.*

The articles on Mozart (a specialization of the editor, Stanley Sadie, who had better be congratulated now, though in parenthesis, and recommended for the next honours list), Beethoven, Wagner and the rest can hardly be overpraised. They are not merely informative, they are sometimes thrilling in the manner of literature. If musicians write so well, and incidentally show so much knowledge of literature, it seems in order to plead once again for literary people to know something about music. I can imagine modern Stendhalians who will read Philip Gossett's essay on Rossini with great delight and then become worried when they meet his analysis of the 'slightly tipsy Offenbach cancan' which, in an F major context, 'first deploys a curious melodic D flat and finally rings out a truly bizarre F sharp'. There are, as I well know, many men most learned in opera who cannot even read a score. T.S. Eliot, who, as a man whose work was set to music and who wrote about the relationship between the two auditory arts, has an entry here, loved the later Beethoven quartets and yet probably did not know much about the Neapolitan sixth.

If we want to know what a Neapolitan sixth is, what does *Grove* tell us? It tells us that it is the first inversion of the major triad built on the flattened second degree of the scale. It usually precedes a V-I cadence and it functions like a subdominant. If I were trying to explain it to a non-musician I would, after telling him that it is called Neapolitan because it was popular with the eighteenth-century Neapolitan school – Scarlatti, Pergolesi, Cimarosa, others – bang out an F major triad on the piano, root position, meaning F in the bass, and then slide the A, C and F which occupy the right hand up to the black keys immediately north of those three white notes (there's your Neapolitan sixth) and then slide back again. The function of the chord? In Beethoven certainly to effect fairly remote modulations. The earlier works change from key to key by the fairly mild process of adding a sharp or a flat; the last quartets modulate by sliding by semitones: that is where the Neapolitan sixth comes in. I cannot put it any more simply in words, but I can show it on a keyboard. The 'intelligent enquirer' of Grove's 1879 foreword could not, in fact, get much from a compendium. Music cannot be explicated in words. *Grove* does not provide a musical education from scratch. You have to be pretty far gone in music before you can use *Grove* at all.

It is no good looking up *Tristan und Isolde*. In Percy Scholes's *Companion to Music* you will find a summary of the plot, act by act; in *Grove* you will have to read the whole article on Wagner. But *Grove* will tell you all about the *Tristan* chord, which may puzzle literary men who consider they have a claim on the opera. And yet without knowing something about this chord – the opening chord of the Prelude: f - b - d sharp - g sharp – you cannot hope to know much about the genesis of modern music. E. Kurth wrote a whole book about the 'crisis' in romantic harmony which the *Tristan* chord engendered, and so did M. Vogel *(Der Tristan-Akkord und die Krise der modernen Harmonielehre)*. The article *Armonia* in the Enaudi *Encyclopedia* starts off with the chord. Its mystery lies in the fact that it has a place in traditional functional harmony and yet the first sounding of the chord seems to imply the breakdown of tradition.

This brings us to atonality and twelve-note composition. The article by George Perle and Paul Lansky may be regarded as typifying the clarity of exposition and depth of scholarship (confirmed, as in every entry, by a most comprehensive bibliography) which characterize the new *Grove*.[10] The article is, as it has to be, wholly technical. It begins: 'The dissolution of traditional tonal functions in the early years of the twentieth century gave rise to several systematic attempts to derive a total musical structure from a complex of pitch classes that are not functionally differentiated.' If we want this to be translated into 'human' terms we must go to O.W. Neighbour's article on Schoenberg, where we will see a photograph of Schoenberg, in Tyrolean costume, scraping a cello with the rest of the Fröhliches Quintet (*c*1895), the first fiddler being Fritz Kreisler. We may read about physical hardship as well as eventual racial persecution, the reluctant necessity to create a new musical language against all the odds, the sympathy Schoenberg felt for those who could not go along with him.

You will also meet the personal elements in the music: 'The trio of the scherzo incorporates the popular melody *O du lieber Augustin,* the words of which end with the tag, 'Alles ist hin', as a private reference to his wife's liaison with Gerstl.' The biographies of most composers – perhaps with the sole exception of Rossini – are pretty wretched reading. Penury, sickness and lack of understanding are perennial elements; our own age introduces the particular villainy of the Nazis (who drove out the Aryan Christian Hindemith as well as the Jews) and the dubious refuge of Hollywood.

But the film music which Schoenberg could not compose ('Are you trying to save my life by killing me?') was written by others, some of them also distinguished exiles, and it has earned at last the tribute of a most absorbing survey by Christopher Palmer and John Gillett. Here we learn that, for *The Devil and Daniel Webster,* 'Herrmann used the sound of telegraph wires singing at 4 am to characterise Mephisto and had the overtones of C printed on the negative in the form of electronic impulses so that when the film was projected a phantom fundamental was produced', and that underscoring the action of animated films is known as 'Mickey-Mousing'. While we are in this area of music brought to the people, we may note that Pop and Popular music are carefully distinguished, though the long article with the latter title sees acid and punk rock and the rest as part of a continuum beginning with Pinsuti, Denza and Balfe and perhaps even earlier. It is refreshing to find such objective and literate treatment of phenomena like Elvis Presley, who started with the kind of material Bill Haley had used but 'was a much better musician and a more dynamic personality, and in his singing style, gestures and stage deportment... often emphasized the sexual implications of rock and roll more than other white musicians had dared'. And so, after the Jaye Consort of Viols, to Jazz, surveyed by Max Harrison, whose seriousness of approach is confirmed in his final quotation from Schoenberg: 'The higher an artistic ideal stands, the greater the range of questions, complexes, associations, problems and feelings it will have to cover; and the better it succeeds in compressing this universality into a minimum space, the higher it will stand'.

This is fine history and excellent discography, but it might have been better for a few music-type illustrations and a closer consideration of jazz harmony, which is a kind of instinctual impressionism, and of the 'blues scale', whose flattened thirds and sevenths Harrison finds to be 'in no way specifically African, nor negroid, still less exclusively American.' I find no entry for Symphonic Jazz, so I must learn about *The Rio Grande* under Lambert (another neglected British composer) and the *Rhapsody in Blue* under Gershwin. Charles Schwartz, in his two columns and a bit, finds the Jewish *frailach* in Gershwin's rhythms and disillusions us by telling us that the opening clarinet glissando of the *Rhapsody* was not the composer's own work but a joke of Paul Whiteman's clarinettist, Ross Gorman. Proportions are always just. Gesualdo follows shortly after Gershwin and is given twenty-one pages, more than three of them devoted to lavish extracts from his madrigals. Stravinsky, according to Lorenzo Bianconi, misunderstood Gesualdo, as did Lowinsky, who assigned the eccentric Prince of Venosa to 'an imaginary, heroic history of visionary prophets'. Bianconi finds in him 'an exhibitionist and at the same time secretive individualism... socially and historically conditioned by his melancholy evasion of history and society'. Gesualdo, as is perhaps too well known, murdered his wife and her lover in the act and then retired to cultivate a style too advanced for Wagner, let alone the seventeenth century as we think we know the seventeenth century.

Indeed, browsing in *Grove* shakes one's complacent view of Western musical history as a straight progressive line, exhibiting, with the adoption of once-forbidden tonalities or brass instruments with keys, ever more efficient modes of expressing states of feeling or building allegories of divine order (if music is really concerned with these things: we don't know and we shall never know). A small Scandinavian composer whose name begins with K is using Stravinskian discords while Grieg is selling bonbons filled with snow (Debussy's metaphor). Even Dvorak, in the Ninth or 'New World' Symphony, is using consecutive secondary sevenths before history properly allows (that second movement, incidentally, was intended to be in C, but Dvorak had found chords suitable for getting from E minor to D flat), and Puccini, whom history tells not to administer musical shocks, shocks with the bare fifths of the third act of *La Bohème*. And Gesualdo uses processions of unrelated triads in what looks like the manner of Vaughan Williams but, of course, is not. Even when the chromaticisms of Purcell's early anthems and string fantasias sound 'curiously modern', Jack Westrup, in his admirable essay on the composer, tells us that 'they are a logical extension of the practice of his immediate predecessors, particularly Locke.'

Over a hundred pages are given to Opera – a substantial book in itself, with a team of expert authors too numerous to list here, though the editor is among them. The literary lover of the form need fear no technicalities. The strength of the survey is indicated by the firmness of its definitions and by its willingness to plunge at once into exemplification. 'Music can strengthen, subtilize or inflect any words that are uttered on the stage. It can also carry hints about words or feelings that are left unexpressed.' Examples? The accompaniment to the aria *'Le calme rentre dans mon coeur'* in Gluck's *Iphigénie en Tauride*, where the uneasy throb of the violas 'contradicts the singer's words and instructs the listener that his calm is illusory'. The new theme in the closing scene of *Das Rheingold*, which tells the auditor that an idea has just struck Wotan – great and noble but as yet unspecified. Duets of lovers or conspirators in thirds, sixths or octaves to show unity of sentiment or purpose. And one of the major problems of the form is adumbrated in the general preamble: should primacy be given to the word or the music? Two operas have taken this question as their theme – Salieri's *Prima la musica e poi le parole* (1786) and Strauss's *Capriccio* (1942).

We know where the true primacy lies – in dramatic success. In the theatre the claims of both literature and music are subdued to what will work and earn money. The greatness of Verdi and Puccini was never wholly musical. Both knew as much as their librettists, if not more, about the dramatically feasible. Mozart, too, knew more than Metastasio but was not big enough to prevail over the Laureate of the Empire. And, in pursuing dramatic success, composers are not to be subjected to the analyses of textbook musicians shockable by irregularities. Jean-Jacques Rousseau is not thought much of as a musician, but he deserves his long entry in *Grove* because *Le devin du village* and *Pygmalion* inaugurated respectively the age of the *opéra comique* and the tradition of the melodrama. Daniel Heartz tells us of weak part-writing, parallel fifths in *Le devin*, but rightly adds: 'It is needless to ask whether a work of genius such as this opera is 'good' – it held the attention of several generations and continued to form musical tastes to the time of Berlioz.'

One is glad to see that another literary man is considered in his role of musical amateur – Ezra Pound, reviewer of music as 'William Atheling' for the London *New Age*, one of the founders, through his Rapallo concerts in the 1930s, of the modern cult of Vivaldi and, above all, innovative composer of the opera *Villon*. Among the music critics honoured by inclusion, Bernard Shaw leads all the rest in a lively two columns from Robert Anderson which not only summarizes the achievement of 'Corno di Bassetto' but also indicates the musical provenances of some of the dramatic effects in the plays – the mixture of Wagner and *Die Zauberflöte*, for instance, in the fourth play of *Back to Methuselah*. Shaw's master, Samuel Butler, who believed music had stopped with Handel, produced, we are told in a brief dismissive essay, very frigid and worthless pastiches of his idol. Shakespeare, who was not Shaw's master, and on whose connection with music whole large volumes have been written, is granted only four pages. Of Shakespeare's own presumed musicality little is said. The two themes which appear solmized in respectively *Love's Labour's Lost* (C-D-G-A-E-F) and *King Lear* (the first four notes of Addinsell's big tune in the *Warsaw Concerto*) are not mentioned, neither is his imperfect understanding of the term 'jack' in the sonnet on his lady playing the virginals nor his vivid use of a lute-tuning metaphor in *Macbeth*.[11] But 'his shrewd assessment of music's power to contribute to drama' is not neglected. It influenced Goethe in *Egmont* and *Faust* and, more interestingly, Verdi's and Boito's *Falstaff.*

Of the immense and lightly carried scholarship in the articles on old music I will say nothing. Indeed, there is nothing more to say about the whole great achievement, a masterpiece of Britannico-American collaboration with notable contributions from Europe. The quality of production is very high, with fine and always relevant illustrations and no typographical error that I have been able to spot. The computer's presence is indicated only by its ignorance of morphemes. Longish monosyllables like *schemes* look like polysyllables to the electronic eye and undergo line-end hyphenization. This is an innovation we have to get used to.

Sir George Grove has, as he has to have, his own brief entry. To call the new *Grove* '*Grove*' at all may seem merely an act of national piety. A man once boasted that he had possessed the same axe for forty years, except for three new hefts and five new blades. Still, we may accept a kind of mystical continuity and find in this astonishing compendium the fulfilment of an aim essentially Victorian. I understand that the new *Grove*, which represents on the part of Macmillan – the original publisher and the true blazon of continuity – an investment of more than three million pounds, will have to last us for fifty years. It is doubtful whether in 2031, Western or universal man will have come any closer to an understanding of what music is or what it does. The new and presumably still vaster *Grove* that will come out then will be another monument to a sustentive mystery.

Times Literary Supplement, 1981

1   See Chapters 48 *Musicalising* Ulysses and 49 *Blooms of Dublin*.
2   The parenthical quote comprises lines 5 and 6 from William Empson's poem 'Invitation to Juno'.
3   As leader of the Rhodesian Front government in Salisbury, Ian Douglas Smith led the minority White government in Rhodesia as Prime Minister from 1964 to 1979, during the period that extended from Zambian independence in October 1964 until the declaration of independence from Britain in 1979, when the name of the country changed from Rhodesia to Zimbabwe.
4   *In His Own Write* was published in 1964 by Jonathan Cape.
5   *Panique* and *Sonatina in C for Harmonica & Guitar*. See Chapter 68 *John Sebastian – A Personal Reminiscence*.
6   For Tommy Reilly, Burgess composed *Romanza* for harmonica and piano. For Larry Adler, Burgess wrote *Pieces for Harmonica* in 1980 and *Sonatina for Harmonica and Guitar* in 1986. See Chapter 67 *Hand to Mouth*.
7   This sentence, which does not appear in the *TLS* review, was added to 'Wandering Through the Grove' (WTG) in HQY. Cathy Berberian was an American mezzo-soprano who

specialized in performing contemporary music in the US and Europe. In YH (p. 235), Burgess mentions that he 'had written a setting of a Malay *pantun* for her, with alto flute and xylophone accompaniment.'

8   *Madame Adare*, produced at New York City Opera in 1980.

9   *King Oedipus,* for Speaker, Chorus, and Orchestra, was performed on 16 May 1973 in New York at the Whitney Museum, with Burgess narrating. See ACC, pp. 130-2.

10 George Perle was an American composer, music theorist, and professor at Queens College in New York City. Paul Lansky, who studied with Perle at Queens College, is an American composer who taught at Princeton University from 1969 until his retirement in 2014. In WTG, these two names are conflated as 'George Perle Lansky'.

11 'Screw your courage to the sticking-place.'

8. TURNING THE HANDLE

The Hurdy-Gurdy by Susann Palmer with Samuel Palmer
Newton Abbot: David & Charles, 1980

Samuel Palmer is the son and Susann the mother. Samuel is an instrument maker. He made a hurdy-gurdy with which the mother fell in love. This book, exhaustive as to both text and (very beautiful) illustrations, is a pledge of love. In a brief foreword Professor Francis Baines (composer, leader of a consort of viols, hurdy-gurdy player) reports that 'the Victoria and Albert Museum, London, say that scarcely a day goes by without inquiries concerning hurdy-gurdies. That can mean only one thing – that it is high time there was a book about them. And here it is.' He might have said more – that the book is a labour of love and so on. For my part I do not think we shall need another book on the hurdy-gurdy for a long, long time. What we may need is a brief demonstration on radio or television of hurdy-gurdy-playing – the sound, that is, as opposed to the mere technique. Mrs Palmer is as exhaustive on the technique as on the history.

The very name of the instrument lends itself to a pejorative view of both its sound and its social status. Etymology? 'C.18', says the new Collins: 'Rhyming compound, probably of imitative origin.' The name seems first to occur in print in Bonnel Thornton's 'Ode on St Cecilia's Day' in 1749:

> With dead, dull, doleful, heavy hums,
> And dismal moans,
> And mournful groans,
> The sober hurdy-gurdy thrums.

Before that it had more dignified names – symphonie, sanfoigne, chamfogne, cymphan, syphonie, chyfonie, cyfonia,

70

phonphogne, fonfonia. There seems to be a Joycean conflation of *symphony* and *chiffon* in some of those terms, the cloth or rags connoting the beggars who played the instrument, though perhaps primarily the cloth-covering of the strings which ensured a sweet hushed tone. This brings me, perhaps belatedly, to what the thing is and how it works.

It is a stringed instrument with a handle. The handle turns a hidden wheel against which the strings vibrate. There is a manual keybox whose keys operate tangents that shorten the strings and thus discourse melody. The keybox has black keys which produce a diatonic scale and white keys for chromatic inflections. The better class of hurdy-gurdy – like that used once by the French aristocracy – had or has two octaves; the lowlier or rural version had to be satisfied with one and a half. There is a tonic drone, as on bagpipes; a tonic-dominant drone is possible too. The effect, so far as I can judge, is of a one-stringed fiddle accompanied by a viola or cello playing on two open strings. I am assured that the sound is endearingly simple and altogether charming.

Its appearance is well recorded in pictorial art. A twelfth-century carving on the cathedral of Santiago de Compostela shows two kings or angels operating one hurdy-gurdy – sensible division of labour: one for grinding, the other for playing. In the eleventh-century York Psalter, King David's harp is accompanied by a recognizable cymphan or phonphogne. And so, in almost unbroken succession, up to 1979, with a picture of Samuel Palmer himself churning and fingering a very lovely hurdy-gurdy with a smile of quite religious rapture. Perhaps the most famous reproduction of the instrument is to be found in Hieronymus Bosch's *Hell*, where a miniature demon turns the handle but nobody attacks the keyboard. We may term this an apodemoniosis of a humble and harmless discourse of melody which gave much innocent pleasure during several centuries.[1]

I can have nothing but praise for a book which fills in, so eruditely and charmingly, a gap in most people's musical and social knowledge. Admiration, too, for the publishers, who assuredly have produced no bestseller. What is now called for, I think, is a visit to Samuel Palmer's workshop in Whitechapel and a demonstration of fonfonia-playing. His mother has done him proud.

Times Literary Supplement, 1981

1 This neologism connotes the condition of extreme or excessive demonization of a blameless thing. The word *apodemoniosis* combines the Greek prefix ἀπο- (apo-) [off, from, away; quite] with *daemōn* (Latin) or *demon* (French or English) [an evil spirit or malevolent supernatural being] and -ωσις (-osis) [a condition of disease, disorder, excess, or infection].

9. THE WELL-TEMPERED REVOLUTION

A Consideration of the Piano's Social and Intellectual History

I, who earn my living by writing fiction and literary criticism, must, before opening the piano lid, present credentials for daring to summarize the social history of a musical instrument. I am called to the task, I suppose, by the voices of my ancestors, who were Lancashire Catholic with a fierce admixture of Irish. Living in a Protestant country which, until the Catholic Emancipation Act of 1829, forbade adherents of the unreformed faith to qualify for the learned professions, my family, which never lacked either spirit or talent, worked mostly in a field for which degrees and diplomas were unnecessary – that of popular entertainment.[1] When my ancestors did not keep taverns, they performed in them or in that extension of them, the British music hall. My mother was a soubrette and my father a piano player.[2] He would not use the term *pianist* of himself, considering that it ought to be reserved to artists who performed on the concert platform, to which he was never good enough to be elevated. His place was the orchestra pit. He worked in variety theaters but mostly in cinemas in the silent days before 1929, either alone or with a random bunch of other musicians. He had, without being a virtuoso, as full a grasp of the capabilities of the piano as any professional performer I have ever known. He could switch from ragtime to Chopin; he was a brilliant improviser.

When, in about 1933, I wished to take up the piano myself, he gave me little encouragement. He had become embittered by the growth of mechanical music and the death of the cinema orchestra. Now, like his father before him, working as a pub landlord, he rarely touched the instrument that had been his livelihood. I taught myself the piano by discovering the position of middle C on the keyboard and in the printed music, and I travelled on from there. I never became more than a middling amateur, better at big chords than at nimble passage-work, but I did grow into a competent composer. A few years ago I composed a concerto (in a kind of E-flat) for piano and orchestra.[3] It is dedicated to the memory of my father, whose craft brought him little money and a measure of hard work and suffering. It is too difficult for me to play, and it would have been difficult for him, who was always impatient with written notes. It was written for a pianist; both he and I have been merely piano players.

*

An upright piano was part of the furniture of my father's house. It was part of the furniture of most lower-middle-class homes in the early years of this century. It was not always played; the minor profiteers of the First World War would install one as an emblem of mild prosperity and garnish its top with framed photographs and gewgaws. Sometimes, when there were daughters in the family, these would be given inexpert lessons on the instrument to justify the existence of the stool. This reversed the natural process of musical education. Oboists and bassoonists do not take to the oboe or bassoon because there happens to be one in the house. They hear the sound of the instrument at a concert or on a record or the radio and fall in love with it. If they are lucky, the instrument is imported into the home and the love affair is promoted under more or less expert instruction. Woodwind teachers, unlike the lady who has a card in her window that reads PIANO LESSONS $X PER HOUR, are usually professional performers. Myra Hess, a great pianist, used to complain about the prevalence of ill-taught and unenthusiastic young piano players. If, she said, the kitchen sink had had an arrangement of copper wires beneath it, whining daughters would have been led by the ear and made to play that.

The piano is the instrument that everyone knows. I have composed music for bassoon and bass tuba, yet I have never handled either instrument.[4] There is no person alive in the Western world who has not handled a piano. It is familiar, but it is still fascinating. Young children hammer it, instinctively recognizing that it is a percussion instrument. When they discover that there is a sustaining pedal, they face the anomaly that fires the composer for it – the fact that a kind of complicated tuned drum can also, like the human voice, prolong its notes. The long keyboard, with its uncountable ivory teeth and regular pattern of duo-trio-duo-trio black keys, is soon recognized as presenting visibly the entire range of pitches, from below the lowest note of the double bassoon to above the top note of the piccolo. It is not quite an orchestra, but orchestral music does not sound absurd on it.

More than any other instrument, it seems to make sound visible. The range of a flute or clarinet is not manifested in its appearance, since the mysteries of overblowing are involved in the making of its higher notes. The stringed instruments are mere stretched wire. The piano shows what triads and sevenths really are. The infant Grieg found out the dominant ninth by simply playing alternate white notes. The black notes make up the ancient pentatonic scale, on which any fool can play Chinese or Scottish music. Any fool can play two kinds of glissando. Anyone not quite a fool can be shown, in half an hour or so, how to play the three principal chords of C major. Of course, the piano is also the most difficult instrument in the world to master. The trombone is nothing to it.

Let us see what this instrument is made of. There is an iron frame, somewhat in the shape of a harp, laid against a wooden plank. There are tightly stretched steel strings screwed to the extremities of the frame. There are eighty-eight hammers to hit the strings. This is the simple basic structure, but in fact it is overlaid with subtleties that are triumphs of sophisticated technology. The hammers are not crude and brutal strikers; they are delicately fitted with felt-covered heads. The strings are, for the greater part of the range of the instrument, grouped in closely set threes, producing the same tone in triplicate. This makes for fullness of sound, a kind of orchestrality. A modern piano sounds fuller than one of the pioneer models chiefly because of this triple tuning to the same pitch – except in the lower regions, where two strings are enough, and, lowest of all, where there is but one long, thick, chiming cord of copper. The pioneer pianos were fitted with bichords, not trichords.

When attenuated softness is required, there is a mechanism for cutting off one string of the trichord. The printed designation for this effect is inaccurate: *una corda*, '[play on] one string'. One is actually playing on two. This fossilizes the situation of the old bichordal piano. The restoration of trichordal fullness is shown, justly, as *tre corde* – '[play on] three strings'. In the shifting between two and three there is that characteristic alternating of soft and full which gives the instrument its full name – *pianoforte*, or 'quiet-loud'.

Hammers strike the strings, then, but not with the uncontrolled vibrancy of nature. There has to be a mechanism for killing the sound at will. To stop sound suddenly there is a damper, a small piece of felt with a wooden reinforcement, which can lie against the strings and quell their vibrations. When we play a note, the hammer flies toward the strings and the damper automatically lifts off; the note vibrates as long as nature permits or art requires. The finger, having struck, stays on the key, and the damper stays away from the trichord. Remove the finger, and the damper goes back to the strings and stops their vibrations at once. There are no dampers for the topmost strings because these make sounds with very little duration.

The craft of using the feet, it is said, is almost as important as the art of the hands. When the right foot depresses the right pedal, the sustaining pedal, all the dampers are removed from their places of rest against the strings. Sound rings out even when the fingers are removed or shifted elsewhere on the keyboard. A chord of two hands can be played in the upper, middle, and lower regions successively, and if the sustaining pedal is depressed, the effect is of an orchestral *tutti*. When the left foot holds down the left, or soft, pedal, a shifting mechanism prevents the hammers from hitting the entirety of the trichord or, lower down, bichord or unichord. It produces a thinning or muffling effect. On grand pianos it is usually the keyboard itself that responds to the touch of the left foot on the left pedal. The keyboard shifts slightly, taking the whole action with it. The hammers are gently moved off center, and we have the *due corde* effect which we call *una corda*. The foot is lifted from the pedal, and we are back to *tre corde*. It is possible to be a kind of virtuoso of the feet. Nothing betrays the bad amateur more than abuse of the sustaining pedal.

Once seen, examined, explained, the piano seems as rational as the wheel. But unlike the wheel, it came fairly late into human history. When it came, musicians were not long in wondering how they had ever managed without it. In a sense, it had always been there *in potentia:* its existence is implied even in the Old Testament, where there is talk of psaltery and dulcimer. The psaltery was a kind of primitive harp attached to a sounding board; the player woke the strings to life with a plectrum. This produced in time those keyboard instruments which seem to be, but are not, ancestors of the piano. Both the virginals of Shakespeare's time and the later, highly sophisticated harpsichord of Bach and Mozart are derived from the psaltery; there is a mechanism for plucking the strings. True, the perfecting of this mechanism – by which the depressing of a key leads instantaneously to the twanging of a wire – was slow to be achieved, and the piano owes much to it; but the quantum leap to felted striking and singing prolongation needed inventive genius. If the psaltery was plucked, the dulcimer was hit with hammers; in this action there slept for millennia the concept of the piano.

The term *piano e forte* was applied to a musical instrument as early as 1598, but the instrument, invented by Paliarino of Modena, seems to have combined a virginals (the plural is awkward with a singular article; the Elizabethans called it a pair of virginals) with a small organ. This seems to have been a cumbersome way of attaining two opposite functions out of the same keyboard: attack and duration. The instrument has not survived, and we have learned about it late, from some letters discovered in 1879. The point is that the term – like *television* – was contrived before the thing itself. Musical inventors knew what they wanted, but they were slow in devising the peculiar machinery of strike and release which we take so much for granted today.

Between the harpsichord and the pianoforte stands the clavichord. This does not pluck the strings with a quill; it pushes them with a kind of brass coin called a tangent. The pushing has to be gentle to prevent the strings' going out of tune. I have a clavichord, modern, Italian-made, and find it a very exasperating instrument. It is desperately quiet, a mere producer of whispers; but it has nuance, variety of tone, even vibrato. The harpsichord which I have in another room is, by comparison, a brash clatterer. Bach loved the clavichord. It is a very domestic instrument, suitable for playing to one's wife when the children are in bed. The neighbors will never complain about a midnight session; they will be quite unable to hear it. The player can hardly hear it himself.

*

In 1709 Scipione Maffei visited Prince Ferdinand de' Medici in Florence. The Keeper of the Prince's Musical Instruments was Bartolommeo Cristofori (1655–1730), and he appears to have made a kind of harpsichord with hammers instead of quills. Maffei wrote home about its possibilities, describing with some enthusiasm its capacity for alternating piano and forte, 'the gradual diminution of tone little by little... a diversity and alteration of tone [of which] the harpsichord is entirely deprived'. This seems to have been the genuine prototype of our modern piano. It had a double lever to make the hammer fly fast and a check to prevent the hammer from bouncing. There were two strings to a note and a sliding device to achieve the subdued *una corda* effect. It was the apotheosis of the dulcimer. Cristofori called it a *gravicembalo col piano e forte*. His fellow Italians did not much care for the instrument, and Cristofori had to sustain himself by making harpsichords, reserving his invention for occasional private demonstrations. The interesting question is: What music was played upon it? I like to imagine that Cristofori was a composer himself and wrote pieces – post-baroque, pre-romantic – to exhibit the scope and range of a machine unhappy with harpsichord clatter or clavichord whispers.

Gottfried Silbermann (1683–1753) worked at piano manufacture in a country more amenable to musical revolutions than Italy. It is known that Frederick the Great of Prussia acquired several Silbermann pianofortes (Bach's biographer Forkel puts the number at fifteen). It is known too that Bach was unenthusiastic about Silbermann's instruments – weak in the higher register, action too stiff – and that it was Bach's strictures that made Silbermann labor at improvements. It is also known that Frederick summoned Bach to Potsdam and made him improvise a fugue, on a royally composed subject, on one or another or several successively of the Silbermann creatures. Out of this triple encounter – Bach, king, piano

– came the *Musical Offering* but, so far as we know, no conversion of the aging composer to the new keyboard sound. With his *Well-Tempered Clavier* he exhibited the essential condition of the music that must be written for the piano – the availability of twelve major and minor keys, made possible by tempering or falsifying the natural scale – but it was left to his three sons, Wilhelm Friedemann, Carl Philipp Emanuel, and Johann Christian, to develop the new music, based on free access from one key to another, which the new instrument craved.

The problem of musical composition may be expressed like this: How is it possible to achieve a piece of music which, without help from words liturgical or secular, can be of a length and weight commensurate with those of a piece of literature? One answer lies in the fugue or the passacaglia, which, as Bach *père* spectacularly demonstrated, could be of long duration and of an intellectual complexity and emotional profundity matching, say, Milton's *Lycidas* or Shakespeare's *Hamlet*. But a passacaglia, being a set of variations on an unvarying ground bass, is limited in key, and a fugue rarely travels beyond three or four closely related keys (say, A minor, E minor, C, G, D minor, F). There is not enough drama in either form. Drama was to come with the sonata, which the Bach sons pioneered and developed. The piano, with its capacity for alternating forte and piano, its ability to sustain long crescendos and diminuendos, its ability to *surprise,* was an instrument admirably suited for drama. With equal temperament and new devices for getting from one key to another, the sonata was, within less than a century, able to convey the range and variety of the novel or the narrative poem.

It is necessary to say something about equal temperament in relation to the piano. Tuning the instrument in such a way as to make it subtly out of tune with nature is a skilled art; the professional piano tuner was not long in coming after the instrument itself. The nature of his skill, and the cussedness of nature, can be demonstrated easily enough. Assume for the sake of explanation that the tuner starts with the lowest A of the instrument and that he moves up octave by octave and makes each successive A conform to the one before. With each jump of an octave the number of vibrations of the string per second doubles. If the lowest A has x vibrations per second, the ones after will increase their vibrations in the proportions $2x, 4x, 8x, 16x, 32x, 64x, 128x$. The tuner tunes the octaves first, then the fifths, in the manner of a string player. The tuning route goes from A to E to B to F-sharp to C-sharp. C-sharp may (contrary to nature) be read as D-flat, and we can then proceed to A-flat, E-flat, B-flat, F, C, G, D, A. With each jump northward the vibrations do not, as in the case of octaves, double; they are multiplied by 1.5. If we multiply 1.5 by 1.5 again and again, we do not arrive at 128; the top A would be too sharp. To make the top A consonant with the bottom A, the tuner must cheat. He must make the fifths slightly flat. He must so organize his tuning for the rest of the keyboard that all semitones are equal (hence equal temperament). Nature does not acknowledge this democracy. Her C-sharp is sharper than D-flat, but in the tempered scale they are the same note. By means of this cunning adjustment the pianist has all the major and minor keys to journey through, whereas the old natural temperament – which many harpsichordists of Bach's day adhered to – did not permit travel to more than a few, the rest sounding out of tune.

What the new music suitable for the equal-tuned piano had to learn was how to get from any one key to any other, and as rapidly as was consonant with post-baroque drama. There were certain chordal devices such as the diminished seventh, which Bach had used, but only, often in quick chromatic sequences, for an effect of baroque brilliance. The same chord, which is made up of minor thirds, can be used for instantaneous moves from one key to another, sometimes very remote:

The first chord in each pair is always the same chord as far as its sound is concerned, though it can be seen that for the purposes of 'grammar,' the notations vary. Another chord, unknown to Bach and Handel, that was to be immensely useful to composers of sonatas was the augmented sixth, which in sound if not notation is identical with the dominant seventh. It is this identity of sound that enabled Beethoven to indulge in dramatic 'puns':

No baroque composer was able to move, by one step only, from the key of D-flat to the key of C – the nearest key in physical location but the farthest away in the key cycle. The equal-tuned piano became, with the development of the sonata and its wide-ranging capacity for sudden shifts of emotion, the instrument *par excellence* of the romantic movement. But first it had to serve the intermediate phase of the rococo.

*

What is the rococo? In music as in architecture, it is a mode of creation that rejected the complications of the baroque – complications that often appeared to twist the raw material (stone or sound) into patterns that strained the possibilities of the material to the limit. Rococo meant a fundamental simplicity – harmony instead of counterpoint – but a tendency toward surface decoration which, as with a wedding cake, went beyond the needs of sheer nutrition. Rococo can be vulgar. With Haydn and Mozart it maintained a tastefulness and a charm rarely betrayed into ostentation for its own sake. If the baroque in music served, at its most typical, the emotions of established religion, rococo presented an image of aristocratic stability, garnished with ornaments, prepared to employ set formulas and tags without apology – though with Mozart, such properties were miraculously transformed into the personal and idiosyncratic. It is not my purpose to evaluate the achievements of the great composers of the pianistic era but to consider the impact of the instrument itself on society. It was in the rococo period that the piano began to trundle its way through the Western world. We may associate the growth of its popularity, and the development of technique suitable for playing it, with Muzio Clementi.

William Beckford, the author of *Vathek* and the builder of the architectural folly called Fonthill – which fell down and was meant to – had a cousin, Peter Beckford, who was in Rome in 1767.[5] There he heard a fifteen-year-old keyboard prodigy, son of the silversmith Clementi, and he bought the services of the boy for a term of seven years. Beckford had made his money out of Jamaican sugar and hence slavery, so this purchasing of a young white musician seemed to him a natural enough transaction. In London, helped by Beckford's wealth and influence, Clementi rose to the heights as a composer for pianoforte, as executant, and as cembalist (conductor at the keyboard) in the Italian Opera. It was as a piano virtuoso that he met Mozart in a kind of competition under the aegis of the Emperor Joseph II and earned the contempt of the greater musician as a mere mechanic, a show-off charlatan, skilled at playing thirds and sixths and octaves with great rapidity, but lacking taste, feeling, and expression. Yet, while Mozart wrote great music in many forms, Clementi specialized in pianistics; he showed the future directions of piano technique. Thirteen volumes of his works were published by Breitkopf in Leipzig.

Clementi's financial success as a virtuoso enabled him to buy his way into the British publishing firm of Longman and Broderip, which put out sheet music of great mediocrity but immense popularity among the now growing piano-playing public. In the firm was a young man named Frederick William Collard, soon to become a skilled manufacturer of pianos. Clementi may be said to have become the mediator between the piano as a structure and the piano as a producer of sound. The works of Mozart and Haydn and, later, Beethoven were for the most part beyond the capacities of the new piano-buying public. This public preferred the showy mediocre, the descriptive novelty (like 'Pigmy Revels' and 'The Enraged Musician'), the easy variations on Scottish melodies, to the profound and exacting sonatas of the masters. Érard in France (to which country the import of English pianos was not at the time permitted) promoted his own instruments with the same commercial fervor as Clementi and his colleagues in London. Some of the instruments made on both sides of the Channel exploited the extramusical with shameless commercial greed – 'Turkish' effects such as pedals for cymbals and drums, even (with one of Clementi's models) a revolving cylinder that converted the piano into a music box.

The situation as regards the proliferation of the piano, its mass introduction into bourgeois homes with more money than taste, is similar to that of the guitar in our own age. The instrument is played as a glorified ukulele (popular in the twenties), not as a one-handed harpsichord. Its great exponents like Segovia are not followed; amateurs are content with minimal effects made spectacular through electronic amplification. There was, in the days of skiffle, a wholly mechanical guitar which, upon the pressing of buttons, gave a tonic, a dominant, and a subdominant chord. The popularization of an instrument has little to do with the popularization of great music composed expressly for it. The history of the pianoforte has nothing essentially to do with the history of great music.

Tireless in promotion of the piano and in a wholly healthy desire to make money, Clementi must not be totally written off as a serious musician. He produced a *Gradus ad Parnassum*, or series of technical studies, which Beethoven himself admired. There was a public for this, as there was for his charming but superficial sonatinas. Music publication became a big business. Breitkopf in Leipzig had invented a technique for printing music with movable type. Gottfried Christoph Härtel took it over but abandoned it for engraving on pewter plates. Clementi went to Leipzig to negotiate with Breitkopf and Härtel for British Empire rights to their publications. Publication and piano making went together, as though manufacturers of electric stoves should also be dealers in foodstuffs. Wherever Clementi traveled he set up agencies for the importation of pianos and piano music – Moscow, St. Petersburg, Berlin. He was the most energetic of promoters.

He was not the only one. By 1800 the piano had become an indispensable piece of furniture in the homes of the genteel. In that year Matthias Müller created the first upright. John Isaac Hawkins of Philadelphia made an even better upright, the ancestor of the one we use today. Charles Jarvis, an immigrant Scotsman, set up his own factory in the same town. It is interesting to note that the division of function, or development of component specialization – usually thought of as Henry Ford's major contribution to mass production – began with the manufacture of pianos. By 1802 Broadwood in London was turning out 400 pianos a year, and the Érard factories in Paris were exporting madly to all the countries that were locked in Napoleon's Continental System. The instruments, though mass-produced, did not as yet settle to standardization of form. There were uprights that were made to look like upended grands and were called giraffe pianos.

Some had the appearance of dressing tables, complete with mirrors. The Victorians, to whom ornamental excrescence was a necessity of life, produced gothic monstrosities. But by the middle of the nineteenth century the two major shapes had evolved to something like their final forms. All that had to be done was to extend the range from the limits inherited from the harpsichord. The piano now goes up to the high C just outside the range of the piccolo. It also, on some models, goes down to a low C unattainable by any instrument of the orchestra. I played on such an instrument recently on BBC television; it was the piano favored by Oscar Peterson, who was on the program with me. Fortunately there was a masking device to make my bottom note the familiar A. Progress can go too far.

*

To the general public there are only three kinds of heroic musical executants – the singer, the violinist, and the pianist. The greatest of these is the pianist. He is on his own. He may be backed by an orchestra, but he can do well enough without. It may be significant that the rise of the pianistic hero belongs to the Napoleonic era. Napoleon himself had an Érard piano, though it is doubtful he ever played it (despite his early boasting of a perfect knowledge of compositorial technique). Beethoven is the first of the Napoleonic pianists, but to the uncultured public outside Vienna, he meant less than the now forgotten Daniel Steibelt. Steibelt was the first in the long line of traveling virtuosos whose technique and taste were less than perfect but who had a gift of showmanship and could play very fast and very loud. With him begins the cult of personality. He was a German with an English wife, who accompanied him on the tambourine. Johann Tomaschek, describing a Steibelt recital in Prague in 1800, writes: 'The new combination of such diverse instruments so electrified the gentlefolk that they could hardly see their fill of the Englishwoman's pretty arm, and so it came about that Steibelt's female friend [Tomaschek apparently was doubtful of their marital status] was easily persuaded to give lessons on it.... Steibelt remained in Prague for several months and in due course sold a large wagonload of tambourines.'

Steibelt, like many a pianistic showman after him – Liberace, for instance – knew his limitations and wisely kept quiet about them. When he played in Vienna, he made sure first that Beethoven was unlikely to be in the audience. He was well aware of Beethoven's supremacy in the pianistic field, and he did not aspire to rival him. He was content to travel widely, arrive late for concerts (unpunctuality has always gone down well with frivolous music fanciers), and make money. Beethoven had music to write and did not move far out of Vienna. Had he chosen to cover the great concert circuits of the world, he would have shown up the charlatans. For it is he more than anyone who has provided the romantic prototype of the Napoleonic pianist – wide-eyed and wild-haired, a great smasher of pianos, a purveyor of storm and stress and fireworks as well as heartrending lyricism.

With the Napoleonic era came the birth of the romantic movement, in literature, painting, and decor as well as in music. Romanticism is best thought of as art that exalts the individual above the collective, emotion above reason, impulse above form. With Napoleon we have the first great instance in history of the victory of human personality over mere brash circumstance: the strong man, immensely gifted, more intuitive than intellectual, a believer in free will but also in destiny, imposes the images of his creative genius on inert traditional social forms and breaks them. The Napoleonic personality becomes, in the field of artistic endeavor, the Byronic. But the greatness of Beethoven cannot well be encompassed by a mere movement. To call Beethoven either classical or romantic is to limit his achievement. True, his work is the expression of the motions of an individual mind, but form is not crushed under their tempestuous impact. The Third Symphony, the *Eroica*, the supreme expression of the Napoleonic age, expands inherited classical sonata form. In the final works, especially the quartets, new forms are generated, but the principle of form is not denied. There is nothing of the rhapsodic about Beethoven. Beethoven is not Liszt.

It is in his impatience with the strictures of the rococo that Beethoven seems to show himself as a romantic. With him the piano seems to crack and strain under the weight of emotions too tempestuous for mere wood and wire to bear. Pianissimi alternate with fortissimi; fortissimi threaten the instrument with dissolution. Human emotion that seems to have its basis in moral struggle is almost too great for physical expression. The iconographs of Beethoven that young people wear on their T-shirts provide the popular image of the musician as he should be – torn, tormented, arrogant, aggressive, emotionally unpredictable, heroically muscular. Mozart will not do, nor will Haydn. Even Handel, who would hurl kettledrums in his rages, fails to fit the archetype. The ignorant public wants its musicians to be fierce and scowling and to have long, unruly hair. Or used to want them like that. Now it is prepared to listen to ordinary-looking young men and women as long as they have prodigious technique. But the Beethovenian image holds; it was transmitted to Pachman, and Paderewski, though not to Rachmaninoff, who always looked like a higher mathematician glooming over an equation.[6]

In 1809 Mendelssohn was born, in 1810 Schumann and Chopin, in 1811 Franz Liszt. The age of the romantic piano was beginning. These composers remain, to the general public, more amenable than the gigantic Beethoven. They do not make his emotional, moral, and intellectual demands. They are capable of sentimentality. Mendelssohn wrote salon pieces that delighted Queen Victoria and Prince Albert and were not outside their pianistic competence. Schumann produced albums of easy sketches for the beginner. Chopin can be difficult, but he sings to the heart. Liszt's pyrotechnics are beyond the amateur, but in the *Consolations* and *Liebesträume* he yields riches to the moderate technique. Chopin and Liszt, more than Mendelssohn and Schumann, sum up romantic pianism. They also provide something dear to the public heart: an aura of gamy eroticism. Chopin's affair with George Sand, Liszt's uncountable affairs with princesses, as also with Lola Montez, seem to rub off onto the piano itself.[7] The piano, with them, seems to become a monstrous aphrodisiac. With Chopin and Liszt there was also a property nearly as thrilling as the erotic – a colorful nationalism, productive of, with the one, polonaises and mazurkas and, with the other, Hungarian rhapsodies. Here were two composers ready-made for Hollywood, though Hollywood has never done them justice.

The essence of romantic pianism has, to the general public, been best manifested in the piano concerto, wherein one brave and brilliant musician tussles with a gigantic force of strings, wind, and percussion. It is Cyrano de Bergerac fighting a hundred paid bravos. Alternatively, it is the piano taming the orchestra and teaching it the pleasing postures of subservience. As we may expect, it is not the finest concertos that have been the most popular. Beethoven's fifth, the *Emperor*, is insufficiently erotic; Chopin's two are indifferently orchestrated; the Schumann is slight, with insufficient hammering; in Brahms's first the piano seems an intruder (indeed, the work was first conceived as a symphony, and it sounds like it). The second Brahms is considered tuneful, though there is a regrettable lack of fireworks. It is only with the Russians Tchaikovsky and Rachmaninoff that the absence of show-off pianistics is excused by heartlifting, if somewhat banal, melody and the pounding of chords under the soaring of unison strings. As always happens, the epigone is preferred to the original, and the most popular concerto of the last forty years has been Richard Addinsell's Warsaw Concerto – not properly a concerto at all, since it has only one movement which, through the suspension of disbelief engendered by the film in which it was first heard, *Dangerous Moonlight*, nevertheless presupposes the existence of two others.[8] Addinsell seems to have borrowed his main theme from four notes sung by Edgar in *King Lear*, which Shakespeare presents in sol-fa notation – fa-sol-lah-mi. Here we have secondhand Rachmaninoff, spurious emotion, banality difficult neither to hum nor, in a best-selling simplified version, to play on the joanna of a military canteen.

The public will always be given what it wants. It did not want the whole of Rachmaninoff's *Rhapsody on a Theme by Paganini*, but it did want the sentimental movement from it which inverts, in D-flat, the original violin motif. It wants the introduction to Tchaikovsky's first concerto but not the rest of the work. It wants a particular sound rather than a particular structure, and it likes that sound to be associated with cinema. A British film called *Love Story* introduced a pseudo-concerto called *Cornish Rhapsody*, and yet another, *The Dream of Olwen*, had an eponymous gallimaufry of arpeggios, runs, and simple aspirant melody. The piano became debased, a machine for conveying shopgirl emotions. It has always had this capacity for debasement, inseparable from its popularity. 'The Maiden's Prayer' and 'The Robin's Return' were written for it. The oboe and flute rarely sink so low. Some see its ultimate debasement in its exploitation as an instrument for jazz and its derivatives, but this is an attitude both snobbish and unrealistic.

*

Before saying anything about the piano as a New Orleans whorehouse excitant or postcoital comforter, I must discuss the deromanticization of the instrument. Whatever jazz is or is not, it is not romantic. It tends toward dryness and understatement. There is no room for the languors of *Tristan* in it, except in the satirical form of the trio of Debussy's 'Golliwogg's cake walk.' The time of Debussy was also the time of rag. What happened with piano impressionism was a removal of the human element, a refusal to use the keyboard for imitating sobbing and orgasm or expressing Beethovenian aspiration and struggle. Jazz is also inhuman in that it exploits the animal rhythms of the blood and leaves out the cerebral cortex.

Debussy's two volumes of *Préludes* show what impressionism is about. He presents – in titles that appear at the end of the pieces, like afterthoughts – images of the natural world. Where people appear – like Mr. Pickwick or General Lavine or the girl with flaxen hair – they are reduced to paintings or puppets. The depiction of nature – fog or wind or a sea with sails on it – appropriately employs what seems far more natural to the piano-playing fingers than the structures of traditional music. Take, for instance, the whole-tone scale, which Debussy first heard in Javanese music at the Paris Exposition. It is pure color, and it is also pure pianistics. Play three notes on three black keys, then three notes on three white keys, and you have one of the two forms of it. It comes naturally. It is a scale but also a chord, and the sustaining pedal may be held down while it gurgles up the keyboard. It is natural to wish to employ all five fingers when playing a chord, and Debussy gives us not simple Mozartean triads but triads with added seconds and sixths. He often, as in 'La cathédrale engloutie,' has whole sequences of these chords. They do not follow the traditional logical pattern (tonic followed by subdominant followed by dominant and so on) but subsist as patches of pure color. Consecutive fifths and sevenths used to be banned, but in Debussy they are part of the basic language.

What we are encouraged to hear in impressionistic music is the entire spectrum, though often obscured by pedalic mist, of the harmonic series. It is into these component notes that the struck string naturally flowers. Increase of lip pressure on the metallic tube of the trumpet or trombone carries the player up the ladder of the series. The resonance of a note is a blur of its upper partials. Mozart as an infant is said to have fainted on hearing a trumpet for the first time; his ear was catching the whole range of the harmonic series in the note sounded and reacting in awe and fear. In the music of the past the upper partials were allowed to follow nature and merely be faintly implied. In impressionistic music there is explicit sounding of the partials, which contributes to the pointillist richness of the music of Debussy and his followers.

Some composers of music which, though not itself jazz, acknowledges the influence of jazz actually use the whole harmonic series as a cadential chord. The chordal sound of jazz and its derivatives is manifestly different from that of Beethoven or even Wagner, but it is close to that of Debussy. A common chord of C may have an A added to it and sometimes a D as well. A minor chord may have an added major sixth (E added to G, B-flat, and D, for example), thus implying agreement with Schoenberg's assertion that the minor scale and its chords do not exist in nature. Jazz pianism is essentially impressionistic. When Bix Beiderbecke put down his trumpet and wrote *In a Mist* for piano, he was paying one of the first jazz tributes to Debussy.

Early jazz kept to hymn-tune harmonies, but it was not long before impressionistic chords came in. Melodically its rhythms were closer to those of speech than to the formalized patterns of traditional song. Certainly jazz piano insists on a new way of using the instrument. Its music defies traditional notation. It is far from easy to learn. And if it is harmonically impressionistic, it can also favor the dry, pecking sound of the baroque. Some jazz keyboard players have even gone back to the harpsichord. The sustaining pedal is not loved. The soft pedal might as well not have been invented. The pianoforte is, in jazz, a forte.

It must be admitted that jazz is not so popular as its tame derivatives. Jazz is gamy, earthy, and still has a quality of black deprivation as well as of African wildness. It began with brothel pianos but also with spirituals, street parades, and funerals, and no matter how refined by great sophisticates like Duke Ellington, it remains removed from music's mainstream just as its mastery lies beyond the technique of the traditionally trained pianist. It is the derivatives – show songs, commercial swing, and so on – that showered sheet music on the parlor piano from the end of World War I to the time of the rise of the guitar and the falling out of favor of the once indispensable domestic keyboard. This music itself was domesticated into the insipid and easy. Meanwhile lessons were taken, and there were newspaper advertisements beginning, 'At first they laughed when I sat down at the piano. But when I began to play a hush fell on the room. I played the first movement of Beethoven's immortal *Moonlight* Sonata. When the last notes died away I was surrounded. I was nearly deafened by admiring voices. "Who was your teacher? How did you get that beautiful singing tone?" I told them...'

For piano lovers like H.G. Wells, who did not have the time to learn the boring techniques of pianism, there was the pianola, about which the Prince of Wales, at a public dinner, made a joke. 'A sick man had his body covered with paper, on which his doctors pricked the locations of his various ailments. When they had gone, he threaded the paper into his pianola, and it played "Nearer My God to Thee".' This mechanical marvel was, however, more than a kind of decorative treadled phonograph. The living masters recorded their interpretations of the classics for it. A genuine pianist as opposed to pianolist could play duets with his betters. Stravinsky even composed for it.[9] But the techniques of a less limited mode of recording and reproduction were improving, and the radio was joining the phonograph, often under the same lid, in rendering the piano (which now was considered as taking up too much space) more or less obsolete.

From the days of the virginals on, a keyboard instrument sat in the homes of the bourgeoisie and the aristocracy to sweeten life with an art never well understood (who can say what music is trying to tell us?) but curiously necessary. No home has ever been able to subsist, even at the most brutish level, without music. Now there is too much music, and none of it is homemade. There is no thrill in playing Beethoven's symphonies as piano duets when the works in their original form are ready to blast out of the quadrophonic engine. If, rarely, it is felt that the house is bare without a keyboard, this is more often powered by electronic impulses, with ready-made chords and bongo drums activable at the touch of a switch. The piano is no longer a preserve of the amateur; it has returned to the professionals.

*

Professional pianism has attained a technical excellence beyond the dreams of Liszt. Concert and recital programs exhibit an eclecticism that ranges from William Byrd to John Cage, with the late rococo and the romantic still, as in the nineteenth century, providing the bulk of the nourishment. To the average uninstructed listener who knows what he likes, the piano is an instrument for big chords, wide-ranging melodies, Chopinesque decorations. The contemporary composer brutally disregards these prescriptions, having decided that the piano is what children have always known it is – a percussion instrument. It is, of course, also an instrument for two hands capable of independent action, a multiple picture of a chromatic scale that does not exist in nature, and a gymnasium for prodigious leaping. The pushing of these four aspects of the piano to the limit accounts for much of the music written for it since, say, 1912 – the year of Schoenberg's *Pierrot Lunaire*.

A kind of manifesto for the new way of using the piano appeared ten years after *Pierrot Lunaire*, when Paul Hindemith attached to his *Suite für Klavier* a series of 'directions for use', which included 'Take no notice of what you learned in your piano lessons'; 'Play this piece very wildly yet strictly in rhythm, like a machine'; and 'Regard the piano as an interesting kind of percussion instrument and treat it accordingly'. This injunction was not meant too literally. It was not, for instance, intended to encourage the emergence of the 'prepared piano' under John Cage. I once examined a Steinway in which steel bolts had been screwed among the strings and pieces of rubber inserted above and beneath them. I have heard, as items in Cage's percussive experiments, the strings hand-plucked, the keys banged with the elbows, and the iron frame struck with a kettledrum stick. I have seen Cathy Berberian seeming to vomit into the body of the open instrument, though actually merely using it as a resonating chamber for her voice.[10] Cage has even exploited the silence of the piano, making the visual appearance of the player at the keyboard a focus for the attention of the audience while they listen to the fringes of silence – coughs, sneezes, passing traffic.[11] All this may be interpreted as mockery of a great instrument, but the piano, a beast of burden as well as a king, can take it.

The fact that the two hands can achieve a measure of rhythmic independence led to experiments with tonal independence, as in Béla Bartók's bitonal works. Indeed, as

Debussy demonstrated, the co-existence of a bank of black keys above an endless bed of white ones invites the simplest kind of bitonality, which Stravinsky exploited in *Petrouchka*, in which the key of G-flat major opposes but also conjoins with that of C major. Debussy's 'Brumes' in the second book of the *Préludes* is essentially an exercise in this kind of bitonality. And the fact that the semitones on a piano keyboard are, contrary to nature, exactly equal makes the instrument ideal for dodecaphonic composition. The violin and cello do not hold with semitonal democracy, any more than does the open trumpet or horn, but the piano can do anything the composer asks with a tone row. It can leap in a single melodic line from the highest A-flat down to the lowest B-natural and then to the middle D-flat with grotesque agility:

The piano has always permitted clowning, from Haydn's middle C to be played with the nose up to Chico Marx's stiff finger chopping seasoned with glissandi. It has submitted to systematic detuning for Berg's *Wozzeck*. It will, with dignity, consent to be an unplayable monument, a piece of industrial archaeology, like the Gaveau upright that is one yard away from my typewriter – unplayable and beyond repair, but once the property of the great Parisian cabaret star Josephine Baker.

The firm Gaveau has disappeared, along with Pleyel and Érard, though the three names are kept alive by Schimmel of West Germany. Bechstein now belongs to Baldwin of America. The Jasper Corporation of Indiana owns Bösendorfer of Vienna and makes the Kimball, besides running Herrburger Brooks in England. Steinway is part of the Columbia

Broadcasting System. Blüthner keeps itself to itself in East Germany. In Japan, at the biggest piano factory in the world, that of Yamaha, which also makes motorcycles, there is an annual output of 160,000 instruments for the home market and 41,000 for the rest of the world. From the Soviet Union the Estonia piano has been visiting the West – a solid artifact with an action made by Herrburger Brooks. The Chinese are working on piano manufacture. Despite those occasional sadistic competitions, sometimes televised in Great Britain, in which teams compete to see which can smash a piano to wood and wire most speedily, the creature that Cristofori invented (if it really was Cristofori) seems in no danger of dying.

*

My final meditation is on the metaphysical significance of the piano or pianoforte or fortepiano or *Hammerklavier.* Was it mere accident that it arose in an era of European *Sturm und Drang*? Is it possible to think of Napoleon's wars with an accompaniment of harpsichord twangings or clavichord whispers? Music is different from literature in that it can extend its vocabulary only through technological innovation. The epics of Homer are fully winged literary art, but the music of that epic period is no more than harps and flutes. Shakespeare's *King Lear* could not be matched by Dowland or John Bull. It was only in the middle years of the nineteenth century that the resources of music – harmonic, structural, instrumental – had arrived at a pitch where literature could not merely be rivaled but actually overtaken. Think of a young Jesuit priest, Gerard Manley Hopkins, stirred by the news in *The Times* on a winter day in 1876, brooding on its story of the wreck of the *Deutschland* in the Thames estuary, wondering how the tragic tale of five drowned nuns, exiled from Germany under Bismarck's anticlerical laws, could be commemorated in

English verse.[12] The resources of the poetry of Wordsworth and Tennyson were inadequate for the expression of horror and hard-won reconciliation to God's will; Hopkins had, using sprung rhythm and head rhyme, to make poetry imitate Wagnerian music. Music had become the most expressive of the arts.

Wagner had much to do with the extension of music's capacity for expression. His art depended not only on the pushing of chromaticism to the tonal limit but on the invention of new instruments. The trumpet now moved with the ease of the flute; it was no longer restricted to the bugle calls of the harmonic series. Contrabass trombones, Wagner tubas, Parsifal bells, anvils, squadrons of horns and harps combined with complete woodwind families and an army of strings to convey the images of cosmic passion which his personal genius, and the inscrutable urgings of the *Zeitgeist,* forcefully dictated. It is possible, perhaps necessary, to view the piano as the keyboard counterpart of the new orchestra.

Because the function of this orchestra was, in the great music dramas, to depict the psychological turbulence that lay under the sung words, so the pianoforte served, in those contradictory lyrical musical monodramas called *Lieder,* to deliver the subtext of the melodized poems of Goethe and Grillparzer. The piano became essentially a medium for German *Innigkeit.* And yet the Germans did not invent it.

The irony is that Cristofori's fellow countrymen have never done much with the pianoforte. There are no great Italian sonatas or concertos, unless we except the achievement of Busoni, who, being of Alto Adige stock, was drawn naturally to Teutonic art. The French, exploiting the piano impressionistically and neoclassically, have deliberately avoided invoking the dangerous human depths which, in courage or folly, the Germans have courted ever since Napoleon shook them into a sense of nationhood. The piano, we may say, was invented for the benefit of the emerging German soul. It is the essential post-Napoleonic instrument, the reflection in miniature of the Wagnerian orchestra.

Under the Weimar Republic the piano was reduced and mocked. It was not raucous enough for the Nazis, and yet, with artist's insight, Charlie Chaplin in his *The Great Dictator* saw that it was a true voice for the brooding, inchoate dreams of an egomaniac like Hitler. Hitler used the piano only for its bass wires; with these the rebellious generals were strangled. In Visconti's *La Caduta degli dei (The Damned)*, it plays the *Liebestod* while Röhm's SA is massacred.[13] In the postwar world its function is mainly historical: it feeds a romantic nostalgia with the concertos of the Russians or calls up the tortured and triumphant soul of Beethoven.

In Leonard Bernstein's musicalization of Auden's *Age of Anxiety*, the piano symbolizes alienation. 'Confronted by the mass of the orchestra', says Peter Conrad in his *Imagining America*, 'the soloist... testifies to an existential division, the self's separation from reality. The piano plays beside the orchestra, and doesn't belong within it. The orchestra twice rebuffs it... The piano is also excluded from the solemn optimism of the epilogue, which is the revelation of faith.' That applies, however, only to the original version of the work, first performed in 1949. When he revised it in 1965, Bernstein allowed the piano soloist 'a final confirmatory cadenza... The way is open, but, at the conclusion, is still stretching long before him.' The piano has become a lonely instrument playing febrile jazz, brooding, introspective, neurotic. It has outlived its romantic past.

It is necessary for us to shake ourselves out of this identification of an artifact with a historical period, with a national soul or a half-articulated metaphysic. Ultimately the piano is a most ingenious structure in which, under the hands of Rubinstein, or the single hand of a Wittgenstein, opposites are reconciled and acts of magic performed.[14] The note begins to decay at the very moment of striking, but the illusion of durability holds. The instrument is a tuned drum, but it is also a human voice. Other stretched strings or vibrating air columns are competent to express a single aspect of the universe and the human life that tries to feel at home in it, but only the piano can attempt, in however miniaturized a form, the total picture. That is why it continues to deserve our homage and our wonder.

The Lives of the Piano, 1981

1   The Catholic Relief Act of 1829, also known as the Emancipation Act, removed restrictions on British Roman Catholics that had been imposed during the late eighteenth and early nineteenth centuries. Prior to passage of this act, Catholics also had been unable to purchase land, inherit property, practice their religion freely without civil penalties, hold civil or military offices, or serve as members of Parliament.

2   As Simon Johnson has demonstrated, Burgess's mother was neither a soubrette nor a music hall performer. See commentary on Chapter 47 *The Making of a Writer*.

3   See ACC, pp. 199-201.

4   Burgess composed 'Nocturne and Chorale for Four Bassoons' on 17 October 1980 at Kenyon College. An undated, incomplete score of 'Allegro moderato' for four bass tubas is probably the work identified in *This Man and Music* as '*Homage to Hans Keller* for four tubas', the title that concludes the catalog of compositions (composed 1934-82) listed in the 'Biographia Musicalis'; TMM, p. 40/61. In response to an inquiry dated 15 October 1991 from the American tubist Jay Rozen regarding 'Nocturne and Chorale for Four Bassoons' and *Homage to Hans Keller*, Burgess sent

Rozen a postcard from London, postmarked 23 Dec 1991: 'At the moment I'm composing a work for you – Rhapsody for Bass Tuba & Orchestra. I hope to have finished it in the New Year. Then I will send it.' Around 2010, the score was discovered in the archive of the International Anthony Burgess Foundation.

5   William Thomas Beckford was an English novelist, art collector, travel writer, and plantation owner who was briefly instructed in music by Wolfgang Amadeus Mozart. Heir to a great fortune from his father, a former Lord Mayor of London, Beckford was described in contemporary newspapers as 'the richest commoner in England'. In 1782, he began writing the Gothic novel *Vathek, an Arabian Tale* (alternatively titled *The History of the Caliph Vathek*). Written in French, it was translated into English by Reverend Samuel Henley and published in 1786 as *An Arabian Tale, From an Unpublished Manuscript* with the false claim that it had been translated directly from Arabic. After several years in exile following a sexual scandal, Beckford returned to England with a plan to build a Gothic cathedral in southern Wiltshire as his new home. The erection of Fonthill Abbey lasted from 1796 until 1813, but Beckford's Folly, as it came to be known, was plagued by unsound construction methods that left the structure unsafe. In 1822, after a severe financial setback, Beckford sold Fonthill Abbey and its contents, and three years later, the abbey's tower, which had collapsed several times during construction, fell down for good. In 1845, a year after Beckford's death, all but a small remnant of the building was demolished. His cousin Peter Beckford, author of *Thoughts upon Hunting*, the authoritative guide to the art of the foxhunt, is chiefly remembered for his patronage of Clementi.

6   Vladimir de Pachman was a pianist of Russian-German ancestry, born in Odessa, who specialized in Chopin's music. Also known as Vladimir von Pachmann, he cultivated an eccentric performing style characterized by odd gestures and speaking to the audience during his recitals.

7   Under her pseudonym George Sand, the French novelist and journalist Amantine Lucile Aurore Dupin became one of the leading European writers of the Romantic era. Rebellious in both her writing and personal behavior, she wore men's clothing, smoked tobacco in public, and engaged in romantic affairs with men and women. Eliza Rosanna Gilbert, an Irish dancer and actress born in County Sligo, gained fame as a Spanish dancer under her stage name Lola Montez. In 1844, she met and had an affair with Franz Liszt, and later became the mistress of King Ludwig I of Bavaria, who granted her the title Gräfin von Landsfeld.

8   The film *Dangerous Moonlight* came out in 1941, forty years before Burgess wrote this essay.

9   In 1917, Stravinsky composed 'Study for pianola', which was issued by the Aeolian Company Ltd., London, as a pianola roll. (His subsequent orchestral arrangement of it, called 'Madrid', is the last movement of his *Four Studies for Orchestra*.) He also created pianola arrangements of *Petrushka* and *The Rite of Spring*. In 1919, Stravinsky composed the first two scenes of *Les Noces* for pianola, harmonium, percussion, and two cimbaloms before ultimately scoring the complete work for four pianos and percussion.

10 'Her singing techniques were avant-garde, and they made much of gulps, hockets and seeming to vomit into the body of a grand piano.' This description of her performance of Berio's Joyce songs at the Third International Joyce Symposium, which took place 14-18 June 1971 in Trieste, appears in *You've Had Your Time*, p. 235.

11 *4'33"*. Dating from 1952, it is in three movements and written for any instrument or combination of instruments, with the instruction that the performer(s) not play during the entire duration of the piece. *4'33"* consists of the environmental sounds that the listeners hear while it is performed and epitomizes Cage's belief that any auditory experience may be considered music.

12 Burgess composed *The Wreck of the Deutschland*, a one-movement oratorio, around the time of this essay, completing it on 8 March

1982. It is a complete setting of Hopkins's text for baritone solo, SATB chorus, and large orchestra, about 32 minutes in duration.

13 Literally *The Fall of the Gods*. The members of the SA (*Sturmabteilung*, lit. Storm Detachment), the original paramilitary wing of the Nazi Party, were known as the Brownshirts. Their aims were to intimidate Jews and other victims of Nazi oppression while providing protection for Nazi rallies and gatherings. Ernst Röhm, an early ally of Hitler, co-founded the SA and was later its commander. When Hitler perceived Röhm as a potential rival for power, he ordered his execution, which took place on 1 July 1934 in Munich.

14 Arthur Rubinstein, a peerless interpreter of Chopin who played in public for eight decades, is considered one of the greatest pianists in history. After losing his right arm in World War I as a soldier in the Austro-Hungarian army, pianist Paul Wittgenstein, the son of the wealthy industrialist Karl Wittgenstein and an older brother of the philosopher Ludwig, commissioned Ravel's Piano Concerto for the Left Hand plus works by Britten, Hindemith, Korngold, Prokofiev, Schmidt, Tansman, and Richard Strauss, thereby creating a repertoire of music for the left hand.

Shaw's Music, edited by Dan H. Laurence
London: Bodley Head, 1981

There are nearly 3,000 pages of Shaw the musicologist, and I have finished reading them with no notable sense of fatigue. This is remarkable, since there is nothing more tiring than the company of a man whom vegetarianism and teetotalism have rendered horribly energetic, who would never bring any essay to an end if it were not for the pressure of space, and is never in the wrong – or, if he is, takes care to put himself in the right in a later footnote.

Shaw on music is endlessly readable because he is endlessly knowledgeable. He is also remarkably prophetic. Some of the things he was saying about music and musicians a century ago, eccentric in their time, are commonplaces today. As a Wagnerian, and a partisan of the 'music of the future', he was ready for Schoenberg before Schoenberg was born. When (in Volume III) he at last heard the Five Orchestral Pieces, he had evidently been awaiting them since *Tristan,* and he could even forehear the final note of the last of the pieces.[1] He foretold a British musical renaissance while British academics were churning out pale imitations of *Elijah.* He was not surprised by Debussy's whole-tone scale, and he speculated as to whether Debussy had been brought up next to an organ factory, since organ pipes are tuned on a whole-tone system.[2] His blind spot was Brahms, but after all he was a Wagnerian.

Non-musical Shavians have generally assumed that their idol was able to sustain so unstaunchable a flow of musical journalism through verbal trickery, egotistical bluff, and a background of domestic vocalism and scrambling through operatic scores at the piano. He had, in fact, a very thorough musical training, though he despised the academies. Like all of us musical autodidacts, he taught himself the elements with the Novello primers. He knew the entire terminology of the craft but took no pride in it. He liked to pretend that Elgar, of whose greatness he never had any doubt, did not know what the supertonic was, and it was to Wagner's credit that he ignored the rules about consecutives and could not write a fugue (though in fact Wagner did write one, and a very good one, in the *Meistersinger* Overture).

Time was quick to prove Shaw right about the futility of an academic training. A great number of the British oratorios (with dismal libretti by provincial journalists), pseudo-symphonies, tone-poems and rhapsodies which he noticed in the *Star* and the *World*, were dry and professorial, and they used fugue as a substitute for inspiration. A good two-thirds of the works he dutifully heard have sunk like the lead they were. He is unerring in his spotting of structural weaknesses, and his scorn for the level of literary taste of Victorian composers, as well, naturally, of Victorian literary men, is eloquent but at the same time good-tempered. There is never any bile in his writing, this all having been absorbed by fruit and nuts, and if he is called ass he smilingly responds with idiot. And, indeed, only the idiots called him ass.

A lot of music critics have no practical knowledge of the making of music, and one very famous critic, who has an amusing battle with Shaw in the indulgent correspondence columns of that age of cheap paper, was even to extol the conversion of music into a purely subjective experience. This was Ernest Newman, himself to replace Shaw as the leading British Wagnerian, who once sympathized with a composer for forgetting the limits of the violin strings and giving them notes below the low G.[3] Shaw has no use for this interiorizing of music. He is to the fore in the controversy about the changing over to French pitch, and full of advice to clarinettists about how to adjust their instruments. He worries, along with Elgar, about how to strengthen the orchestral bass, and is learned about obsolete boomers like the ophicleide (which Shaw's suicidal uncle had played). He knows all about the voice, having been taught it by the great Lee of Dublin, and is ready to tell Jean de Reszke, the famous cigarette-smoker, all about headnotes.

His main task, though, is to chasten taste, and his taste is faultless. Too many of his readers believe that even the feeblest sacred cantata is superior to the strongest secular piece by virtue of its being about God and his prophets. Shaw wades in, fearless of charges of blasphemy, to assert that Elijah and Jeremiah and St Paul are bores and Sigmund and Sieglinde, though incestuous lovers, are not. His eye is always on art which, in the Oscar Wilde manner, he appraises with the rigour of the moralist.

I once briefly as a boy met Shaw at Malvern (he was not gracious; I wanted his autograph and he said I could never afford it), and I can't help considering him as a great man of my time. It is something of a shock to find him so firmly placed among great historical musicians. He was a mature man when Wagner died (he remembers his erratic beat as a conductor, his sour neuralgic look, and the relief with which the Philharmonic hailed his replacement by Richter); he saw Dvořák and Clara Schumann and wrote for an Oslo paper on Grieg's first London recitals.

He saw through Cowen and Mackenzie but found merit in MacCunn's *Land of the Mountain and the Flood*, which, ninety years after its first performance, has at last become popular.[4] He deplored, predictably, the 'working out' section, 'which Mr MacCunn would never have written if his tutors had not put it into his head. I know a lady who keeps a typewriting establishment. Under my advice she is completing arrangements for supplying middle sections and recapitulations for overtures and symphonies at twopence a bar, on being supplied with the first section and coda.'[5]

Shaw was no composer himself. Dr Laurence, who has done the expected fine job of editing, reproduces a setting of Shelley, done by the young Shaw, which Samuel Butler would have sneered at. Shaw reserved musical structure, along with an operatic spectrum of voices, for his plays. *Back to Methuselah* is his *Ring* and *Man and Superman* his *Don Giovanni*. How important a musician Shaw was this collection at last testifies.

The Observer, 1981

1   'I was quite proud of myself for guessing which was to be the final chord of the fifth Orchestral Piece, which was more than I'd been able to do in the four previous ones.' From a letter to Cedric Glover sent in 1914, and quoted by Dan H. Laurence in his 'Introduction' (Vol. I, pp. 21-2). Volume III covers the years 1893–1950, which explains Burgess's reference to that volume regarding a performance that would have taken place in 1914; however, no review of Schoenberg's Five Orchestral Pieces, Op. 16, nor any reference to that work, appears in that volume.

2   It wasn't Shaw who speculated about Debussy, but rather a Parisian acquaintance of his who wondered whether Debussy had worked in an organ factory (not been raised next to one): 'I once met a Parisian who had heard of Debussy, and even had a theory that he must have been employed in an organ factory, because of his love of the scale of whole tones.' Vol. III, p. 642.

3   *Grove's Dictionary of Music and Musicians* describes Ernest Newman as 'the most celebrated British music critic in the first half of the twentieth century.' After serving as music critic of *The Manchester Guardian* (1905–6), *The Birmingham Post* (1906–19), and *The Observer* (1919), he was music critic of *The Sunday Times* from 1920 until his death in 1959. He was also the author of books on Richard Wagner, Hugo Wolf, Richard Strauss, and others.

4   Frederic Hymen Cowen was an English composer, conductor, and pianist; his surname is consistently misspelled as 'Cowan' in the source texts and is corrected throughout this volume. Alexander Campbell Mackenzie and Hamish MacCunn were both Scottish composers, conductors, and teachers. Shaw's review of MacCunn's *The Land of the Mountain and the Flood*, composed in 1887, appeared in *The Star* on 11 March 1890. Sometimes called 'the archetypal Scottish overture', its title comes from *The Lay of the Last Minstrel* (Canto vi, stanza 2, line 4) by Sir Walter Scott. After its inclusion in the 1968 EMI recording *Music of the Four Countries* performed by the Scottish National Orchestra conducted by Alexander Gibson, *The Land of the Mountain and the Flood* became the theme of the BBC television series *Sutherland's Law* (1973–76), whence derived its popularity. In a stanza about British composers in *Byrne*, the music of MacCunn (misspelled as McCunn) is considered especially Scottish in nature: 'McCunn, true, rather overdid the sporran.' See *Byrne*, p. 19.

5   Vol. I, p. 950.

11. THE RUINATION OF MUSIC

I wish to make a plain statement about the condition of music in our time. As a moronic sub-art, an anodyne for adolescents, it subsists and even flourishes. As an art dedicated to the plumbing of the depths of the human soul, or (and this amounts to the same thing) the disclosing of heavenly visions, it ceased to exist at about the time of the death of Mozart.[1]

This, of course, does not mean that music died with the last notes of the 'Jupiter' Symphony, but rather that music ceased to be an art capable of (a) purveying an image of that social stability which mirrors the final stability of heaven and (b) functioning without the aid of non-musical references. With the Austro-Hungarian Empire – that ancient dead tyranny which we are now beginning to see as a lost utopia – music had a social function. Through the dance, and that exaltation of the dance which is the classical symphony, the glory of a tranquil state was affirmed. With the arrival of Beethoven we began to hear the voice of the frantic ego denying the importance of the community and asserting the pre-eminence of the self. This is sometimes called romanticism, and it is often interpreted in terms of the French revolution and the Napoleonic fury which followed. However we view the greatness of Beethoven and Wagner, we cannot listen to them as pure music: we have to take into account those extra-musical elements called variously literary or mythic or programmatic. We hear the beginnings of musical dissolution in the very opening bars of Beethoven's First Symphony, which deliberately shock with a dissonance and state that the idiosyncrasies of the composer's personality are of greater interest than symbols of social stability.

We may know Mozart well, but few of us have a clear image of the man: his personality is subordinate to his artistic function. Most of us can draw the stormy countenance of

109

Beethoven from memory. Even when we don't have the face imprinted on record sleeves or T-shirts. With Beethoven personality dominates music. That personality has little to say except: 'I am here – I, I, I.' Take the Fifth Symphony. The basic rhythm of the first movement was, from the very first performance on, permitted to mean something other than pure music. Beethoven said it was the basic song of the yellowhammer, but he also said: 'Thus Fate knocks at the door.'[2] During the Second World War the two opening measures spelt V for Victory. A purely musical content was never enough. Towards the end of that movement Beethoven inexplicably stops the pounding rhythm to insert, in *adagio* tempo, the plaintive tones of an oboe soliloquy. What does it mean? We do not know, but we do know that the voice of the ego is intruding. Music as a communal experience has ceased to be enough: the cry of the lone and dissident ego has to be heard.

What I am saying in effect is that music, after the great stable age of Haydn and Mozart, began to be a kind of inarticulate literature. The inarticulacy was recognized by Hector Berlioz as an untenable contradiction, and he decided that music had to be converted into either autobiography or fiction. The classical composers were content to write concertos for violin or piano, oboe or viola; Berlioz has to call his viola concerto *Harold in Italy* and make of it a musical interpretation of Byron's *Childe Harold*. More, in his *Symphonie Fantastique* he gives us a Gothic novel, in which a drugged artist has visions of dissolution and death and the musical technique is permitted the colourful crudity of the professional novelist, temporarily tired of words, taking on the tasks of the amateur composer. From Berlioz on, apart from the recidivism of Schumann and Brahms, music could no longer function without a literary programme. Musical form was no longer dictated by the conventions of a stable society, themselves deriving from the binary rhythms of nature; it became literary form applied to the spinning of notes.

Perhaps the most spectacular decadence was to be observed in the symphonies of Mahler and the symphonic poems of Richard Strauss. Mahler's symphonies are pure autobiography, not easily understood without reference to his own tortured life. When Mahler's music is at its most tortured, it is at the same time at its most banal. Thus, personal agony is often expressed in the rhythms of a street organ playing some such nugacity as '*Ach du lieber Augustin*'. Sigmund Freud explained this to the composer in an hour or so at a railway station. The child Mahler had witnessed a bitter quarrel between his father and mother while a street organ was discoursing that tune: popular banality had become a symbol of personal agony. Mahler's audiences had to attend to the tearing-apart of Mahler's soul on a huge orchestra. This was exhibitionism, bad taste, and Beethoven had decreed that it was good art. Mozart would have been embarrassed.

Richard Strauss said that music could take over the province of literature. If you heard his symphonic poem *Don Quixote* you had no need to read the book, except perhaps to clarify the meaning of the music. In his opera *Salome*, the words of Oscar Wilde became supererogatory: the huge orchestra could say all that had to be said about the obscenity of kissing the severed head of Saint John the Baptist. When, in 1907, the score of the opera was published, Arnold Schoenberg studied it with care. He recognized what had begun in the first measures of Wagner's *Tristan und Isolde* had at least begun to be fulfilled in the music of Strauss: the stability of tonality had at last collapsed, and the way was open for the anarchy of the twelve-tone scale. In the music of Schoenberg and his successors we have the intellectual notion of formal coherence but the auditory actuality of personal neurosis. Music as a symbol of social stability was no longer acceptable.

It depended in its very language on meanings only apparent to the composer himself or the circle around him.

This is pretty well the situation as we find it today. These words are prompted by the first performance of the latest work by Pierre Boulez who, after years of struggling to find a new musical language, has at last come through with a composition dependent on words, electronic noises, spatial disposition of vocal and instrumental forces, and a use of intervals which denies the universal validity of the scale which was good enough for a tradition stretching from the middle ages to the final quartets of Beethoven, to say nothing of the glorious stable age of Haydn and Mozart.[3]

I am not denying the composer's right to produce whatever music he wishes, and, as a composer myself, I claim the right to fabricate idiosyncratic and even eccentric sonorities. But we have lost something since the Beethovenian revolution. We have lost the right to understand what we hear, to regard the language of music as a social construct analogous to the language of words. When M. Boulez speaks on French television, he does so with a clarity quite Mozartian. Why should music claim for itself the privilege of unintelligibility? It is a pity that it should be only on the discs of the rock-groups that the language of tradition – though wilfully distorted and sometimes mocked – should sound loud and clear. The greater realm of music has been hit by a great sickness, and none of us knows where to look for a cure.[4]

The Times, 1981

LETTERS TO THE EDITOR
The Times
11 January 1982

Music's death
From Mr Hans Keller

Sir, Delusion need not be invalidated, merely diagnosed. 'The day the music died' by Anthony Burgess (December 29) removes, amongst other geniuses, what is perhaps humanity's greatest mind altogether from the music lover's understanding: Beethoven.

Musical incompetence and incomprehension as well as sheer ignorance are the cornerstones of an essay whose publication in *The Times* we musicians fail to understand: replacing fact with fantasy, it can only make sense to those similarly afflicted.

Yours sincerely,
HANS KELLER,
3 Frognal Gardens, NW3
December 30

1   The Italian translation of this essay, published in *Corriere della Sera*, takes its title, *'Forse con Mozart finisce la musica'* (Perhaps music ended with Mozart), from this idea. Called 'The Ruination of Music' in the typescript, the essay was published as 'The day the music died'; for remarks about the title used by *TLS*, see Commentary.

2   The yellowhammer is a European bird (*Emberiza citrinella*) whose call was cited by Czerny as the inspiration for the opening theme of the Fifth Symphony: 'the song of a woodland bird: the yellowhammer gave him (Beethoven) the theme for the C minor Symphony.' [Carl Czerny, ed. Paul Badura-Skoda: *Über den richtigen Vortrag der sämtlichen Beethoven'schen Klavierwerke: Anekdoten und Notizen über Beethoven* (1852) (Vienna, 1963), p. 18.] See also 'The Theming Magpie: The influence of Birdsong on Beethoven Motifs' by Sylvia Bowden in *The Musical Times,* Summer 2008.

3   Evidently a reference to *Notations I-IV* or *Répons. Notations I-IV,* premiered in Paris in June 1980, received its first performance in the UK in September 1981, performed by the Orchestre de Paris conducted by Daniel Barenboim at the Royal Albert Hall to conclude the 1981 Proms. *Répons* premiered in October 1981 at the Donaueschingen Festival. *Pli selon pli*, an older work by Boulez (composed 1957-62) that he revised in the 1980s, includes vocal soloists; *Notations I-IV* and *Répons* do not.

4   The typescript ends with this closing paragraph, which was included in the Italian version published in *Corriere della Sera* but omitted from the essay published in *The Times* as 'The day the music died'.

Strange that in the twenty thick volumes of the new *Grove's Dictionary of Music and Musicians* the subject does not once arise. And yet the making of sweet sounds to accompany savoury mouthfuls goes back to the very egg of civilisation. One of our primal images is of warriors sucking marrow bones while the bard plucks strings. Throughout the history of music, no reasonable instrumentalist or composer has seen it as a demeaning of his craft to have it compete with the rattle of knives and forks. Handel's music was for *use* – to be drowned by the royal fireworks or in the royal cups – and the same could be said of all music until Beethoven. But as Beethoven would not hammer the keys unless there was perfect quiet (one word, belch, or tinkling of a coffee spoon and he would yell: 'I play no longer for such pigs'), so you may say that food and music separated with the coming of the romantic era.

Let me explain that. When composers lived by princely patronage they had no rights. Haydn was paid by Prince Esterhazy to provide such music as His Highness needed – and that meant music for banquets as well as settings of the *Te Deum*. When composers no longer had noble patrons – they began to disappear when Napoleon stormed over Europe – they inflated their egos and denied that music was for use any more: music was to be listened to, very closely; music was the expression of the composer's personality; the composer was important, he was even God. You couldn't eat ice cream while listening to a Chopin nocturne or carve a joint to the sound of Beethoven's Ninth Symphony. Music split itself up into the serious and the light – a division that would have made no sense to Handel, Haydn and Mozart. Serious music was for the concert hall; light music was for everywhere else.

It was above all for the dining room. Or the tea room. In my boyhood not even the meanest restaurant was without its resident trio – piano, fiddle, cello. I have played the piano in such an ensemble myself. There were no formulated rules as to what one played to accompany eating, but it was tacitly assumed that Bach fugues and Brahms sonatas were not wanted. The sounds had to be sedative rather than exciting. No military marches, no jazz. Waltzes, yes. Selections from musical comedy (Victor Herbert, not Cole Porter), fine. Saint-Saëns's dying swan. The Intermezzo from *Cavalleria rusticana*. Nothing to make the adrenalin flow, for adrenalin impedes the secretion of the digestive juices. Nothing sexy, angry, patriotic. Keep it safe, keep it light.

The choosing of music for eating has, as I imply, always been a pragmatic business. No expert will tell you what music goes best with soup or joint or soufflé. Only one composer ever took the job of making *Essensmusik* or eatmusic with Germanic seriousness, and that was Richard Strauss. In the incidental music he wrote for the banquet scene in Hofmannsthal's version of *Le Bourgeois gentilhomme*, the food itself is described. The trout comes from the river Rhine, so we have to have the river music from Wagner's *Rheingold*. For the roast mutton, Strauss's own description of a massacred flock of sheep in his symphonic poem *Don Quixote* makes a dissonant appearance. The ice cream is accompanied by Strauss's version of *Funiculì Funiculà* to show that it comes from Naples. Coffee is poured to the trickle of a strain from Bach's *Coffee Cantata*. All this is serious only in the sense that you have to have a pretty serious knowledge of music to be able to catch the references; for the rest it is vaguely witty but, from the digestive angle, not very helpful.

But at least Strauss's dinner music is *structured*, which is more than can be said of the damnable muzak that papers the walls of most public eating places these days. Structuring is important in dinner music, because a dinner is itself structured. Indeed, a banquet presents a recapitulation of the world's history. We begin with the world as a hot soup in which primitive life-forms swim, go on to the fish, the fowl, the mammal, and end with subtle human artifacts like cheeses and puddings. A good well-balanced meal is a kind of poem of the development of life. It deserves appropriate music.

Such music should begin with flow – for both soup and fish. Watery origins for both may be suggested by light works with a lot of piano arpeggio: you may even get away with a John Field or Chopin nocturne. I would personally prefer one of the *Arabesques* of Debussy – the one in E major which is all flow. A peppery soup – mulligatawny, for instance – needs flow-music with a certain piquancy in it, and you may try Rachmaninov or early Prokofiev or perhaps John Ireland. If you wish to be specific about the fish course, there is a fine aquarium piece in Saint-Saëns's *Carnival of the Animals*, as also in the ballet music of Holst's *The Perfect Fool*. That aria in Haydn's *The Creation* which deals with great whales is not appropriate: a whale is a mammal, and we in Britain gave up eating whalemeat in about 1950.

Let us, when we get on to the poultry, not deign to give any music to a battery chicken, unless it be Mossolov's violently Soviet *Factory: the Music of Machines*.[1] Good game requires music with a northern tang – a suggestion of the bagpipe drone, the Scots snap. Debussy's piano piece *Bruyères* would do nicely, or the Scherzo from Mendelssohn's Scots Symphony. And now to real meat. Bach's Choral Prelude 'Sheep May Safely Graze', with its suggestion of ram's bells and its pastoral placidity, will help down a rack of lamb. For beef avoid toreador music (specifically bullfight marches) and have something of quiet but solid nobility: Beethoven may rage in heaven, but a Beethoven slow movement is very much in order. The best beef music I know, however, is the central tune in the Jupiter movement of Holst's *Planets*, especially when played on strings and six horns, but an organ version will do very well.

Cheeses demand music from the place of origin: it would be stupid to accompany a good Brie with the 'Song of the Volga Boatmen'. But should a Canadian Cheddar have *'Chantez Alouette'* or a tune from the Cheddar Gorge? I think Ravel's fine suite *Le Tombeau de Couperin* would do very well for any French cheese, some Henry Purcell for Stilton or double Gloucester, and very distant yodelling for a Swiss *fondue*. This means, I think, that Swiss cheese must usually be avoided.

The dessert? This depends on whether it is a complex artifact or some ready-made confection dragged from the icebox. Debussy called Grieg's music 'bonbons stuffed with snow' and I have always found this piquant Norvegian admirable with cold light sweet things – practically anything of his will do, except the scene from *Peer Gynt* where Åse tediously dies. I think with the coffee (which, despite the American custom, should be served apart from the dessert and fortified with a liqueur) one can risk something fierily Brazilian, though at a distance. If you are illegally handing round Cuban cigars, play some music from Tampa – if there is any.

Readers will, I fear, think that I am being facetious. I am not. I have always taken both food and music seriously, and I have composed both, though not at the same time. My son goes even further than I: he is a professional *cuisinier*, French-trained, and also a player on the oboe and the baroque bassoon.[2] We have had long discussions about the junction of the two great arts and have even produced menus on which the musical items (transferred from records to a continuous magnetic tape) have been listed along with the wines. We recognise, however, that there is no substitute for live performers, and that a versatile and intelligent trio ought to be enough. Even a piano will, at a pinch, do. But make sure your dinner-players are not too intelligent. I knew one pianist who played Swedish music when caviar was served (he knew it was lumpenfish, not the genuine Beluga) and cattily started on 'How much is that doggie in the window?' when the venison appeared. That dinner ended without music.

Cuisine, 1984

1 The Soviet composer Alexander Vasilyevich Mossolov is best known for his 1926 composition *Iron Foundry*, Op. 19, which uses a full orchestra to evoke the sound of a factory in operation. This example of Soviet futurist music was originally a movement of *Stal (Steel)*, a ballet created to glorify industrialization and 'the worker'.
2 Andrew Burgess Wilson also played the English horn and recorder.

Anybody can write a sort of melody. Give, as the Chinese do, each note of the musical scale a number. Do re mi fa so la ti do: 1 2 3 4 5 6 7 8. You can turn your telephone number or car registration number into a sequence of notes.[1] This is perhaps not long enough for a true melody, but it will yield a theme. A theme may be defined as a scrap of melody crying out to be developed – not just into a true melody but into a whole symphonic movement, into a whole opera. All music begins with a germ like that, and it may lie sleeping in a passport number.

But we all know that the great melodies of the world are not made in that manner. The great melodies of the world arrive without warning. They spring out of nowhere, and they are only given to the great musical geniuses. Perhaps there is an analogy between the language of speech and the language of music. In every spoken phrase, even in a single word, a melody may be lurking. Take the phrase that comes in a poem by Edgar Allan Poe – 'the tintinnabulation of the bells'.[2] Recite that often enough, and the sheer rhythm – regardless of meaning – will generate a musical phrase.

'La ci darem la mano'. Da Ponte gave that phrase to Mozart in the opera *Don Giovanni,* and Mozart heard in it the melody which begins an exquisite duet. In one of Beethoven's last string quartets we hear the question *'Muss es sein?'* (Must it be?) and the answer *'Es muss sein'* (It *must* be!).[3] Beethoven goes to the trouble of placing the words under the notes. They are not intended to be sung, since the musicians are string-players, not vocalists; the composer is merely being honest enough to disclose the inspiration of his theme.

But great melodies are not often bound to words. Bach's Air on the G String or the marvellous theme of the Choral

Prelude *Wachet Auf* are clearly pure sound which owes nothing to verbal inspiration. Where did they come from? Anyone who, like myself, has composed music may give some sort of an answer. A melody arrives in the mind. It seems to be something remembered, something that has always existed but been long forgotten. Then it suddenly appears. Occasionally this melody is genuinely something remembered – something written by somebody else. This can cause trouble – lawsuits for plagiarism. There was a popular song in the 1920s called 'Yes, We Have No Bananas'. This is made up out of Handel's 'Hallelujah' chorus, the folksong 'My Bonny Lies Over the Ocean', and the aria 'I dreamt that I dwelt in marble halls' from Balfe's opera *The Bohemian Girl.* Plagiarism? Possibly. Popular song-writers used to plagiarize all the time. Sheer memory? Possibly again. Who knows? These things are difficult to prove in a court of law.

The truly great tune resembles no other. It has certainly come from heaven, or from nowhere, and it usually comes when unexpected. But it sometimes comes when it is needed. Imagine that you are commissioned to compose a symphony. This is to be performed in two months' time by a great symphony orchestra. The least difficult work will be the orchestration, which will come last. The most difficult will be finding themes for the first movement. Here you will require two main groups of themes, one aggressively masculine, the other delicately feminine. These themes must be capable of development – that is, turning into other themes, combining in counterpoint with other themes, turning into great soaring melodies. The urgency of the commission will sometimes force your unconscious mind into producing melodic germs full of potential. Or some little melody composed in childhood will suddenly present symphonic possibilities. For another great mystery about melody is that it is more likely to come to you when you are seven than when you are seventy.

The mystery remains. But in an age like ours, which doesn't approve of mysteries, the production of great melodies is no longer regarded as one of the jobs of the composer. Be honest, and consider which pop or rock song of the last twenty years contains a genuine melody. You will hear fine melodies in, say, George Gershwin or the Beatles, but few in the music of the Rolling Stones. The sexual impulse in the rhythm, or the content of social protest in the words, will seem to the new generation more important than sheer melody.

What applies to popular music applies even more to the music termed serious. The dodecaphonic composers, led by Arnold Schoenberg, showed the way to a mechanical mode of composition very popular with the young products of the music academies. You make a theme out of the twelve notes of the chromatic scale – a theme of just twelve notes, for one of the rules is that no note may come more than once – and then you play this theme backwards or upside down or upside down and backwards. Your musical skill will lie in the management of tone colour, of dynamics and climax, but not in the creation of melody as we used to know it. You will find such music damnably hard to sing.

There are people around who say that there can be no more great melodies. They say that, with so few notes in the musical scale, all the original themes must already have been written and there is no point in looking for new ones. This is nonsense. There is still an infinitude of books to be written out of the twenty-six letters of the alphabet, and there is still an infinitude of melodies to be generated out of twelve notes and the innumerable rhythmical combinations of these which wait to be exploited. We have just got out of the habit of thinking melodically. This is very bad for us, since there is nothing in the world more heartening than a great tune.

Where would the French Revolution have been without the *Marseillaise,* a tune written by a soldier named Rouget de Lisle, who was suddenly touched by inspiration? Where would the communist revolution have been without the *Internationale* (a far inferior tune to the *Marseillaise*)? But greater than tunes are those fifty-minute streams of melodic invention we call symphonies and concertos. These are always the products of conscious skill and ingenuity, like works of engineering, but they could not exist without those spurts of melodic inspiration from the unconscious mind. We do not know what strange inner force is at work spinning away at themes and tunes, but we bow down to the results. The great mystery of music remains.

The Courier, 1986

1 While living in Rome in 1973, Burgess turned part of his phone number into a fugue subject by converting 5-8-2-1 into the notes G-C-D-C. From this subject, he composed a fugal exposition that he gave to pianist-conductor John Covelli, with whom he was working on *Cyrano* at the time. See ACC, pp. 208-9.

2 'The Bells', written by Poe in early 1848 and published posthumously 1849.

To the tintinabulation that so musically wells
    From the bells, bells, bells, bells,
        Bells, bells, bells—
    From the jingling and the tinkling of the bells.

3 fourth movement of Beethoven's String Quartet No. 16 in F major, Op. 135

14. INTRODUCTION TO *PIANOFORTE: A SOCIAL HISTORY OF THE PIANO*

Carl Dahlhaus, reviewing this book in *Die Zeit*, said *'Ein Thema hat seinen Autor gefunden'* – 'a subject has found its author'. The pianoforte has certainly found an author of the right race (and, whatever his race, certainly a very good author), for, despite its name and its origins, the piano, or *Hammerklavier* as Beethoven memorably called it, was one of the great implements of German romanticism. It had been preceded by various keyboard instruments whose charm we still recognise, but when strings began to be hammered, instead of delicately plucked, the soul of a turbulent era found the voice it needed.

A virginals, an instrument that our Virgin Queen played and played well, has a keyboard identical with that of the piano, though much shorter, and its successor the harpsichord also looks like an attenuated and very elegant piano, though sometimes it has, like an organ, two manuals. But both are thin-stringed, and the plectrum that plucks the strings cannot sustain the sounds that are produced. The clavichord, which strikes instead of plucking, gives out an even fainter note than its elder sisters: it is a suitable instrument for a very small apartment with very thin walls and unmusical neighbours. All these instruments are played today, our era having been taught by Stravinsky, as well as by jazz, to reject romanticism and return to the dry pecking tone of the Age of Reason. Edward Heath showed the jazz pianist Oscar Peterson how to make use of the clavichord in a small combo (it would never do in a big band or an electronically amplified rock group), and the style of jazz piano – dry, sardonic, and with little use of the assertive sustaining pedal – owes more to Bach than to Liszt.[1]

The piano begins its true career as the instrument of men and women who lived in the age of Napoleonic imperialism.

If the harpsichord is the Alexander Pope of music, the piano is its Lord Byron. True, it was used by Haydn and Mozart, and the young Beethoven who followed Mozart, but much in the restrained spirit of the harpsichord. Its romantic possibilities only began to be exploited when a new philosophy came to Europe. The French Revolution looked forward to the collapse of all the old despotisms. It preached freedom, but this turned out to be freedom for a new despot. Napoleon Bonaparte may have pretended to liberate nations in the name of that revolution, but his liberations were really conquests in the name of himself and his hard-eyed Corsican family. The concept of the hero had come back into the world, and as Carlyle's *Hero and Hero Worship* reminds us, heroism did not necessarily have to take the form of the military conqueror. In Byron the hero is a man who detests war but glorifies his own ego. He loves largely, suffers from perturbations of the soul, is essentially solitary and tries to commune with Alps and rivers. He is an animated grand piano.

Technically, the pianoforte – so called because its tone could range from loud to soft, whereas the harpsichord always plucked the same number of decibels – owed its novelty to a capacity for sustaining notes and for damping them. Piano-engineering has not changed much since the time when Beethoven was given a Broadwood piano (which he called a *Hammerklavier*[2]) and thanked the makers in horrible French.[3] A harpsichord has, in its middle and upper ranges, a pair of stretched wires for every note, but a piano has three strings for each note, of great strength and tension, except in the lower stretches, where a single string as powerful as a cable tolls like a bell, and in the highest of all, where resonance does not matter. A padded hammer strikes. If the note is to be sustained, as a note in the orchestra is sustained, the right foot depresses a pedal. If an effect of muffled softness is required then, the left foot pushes down another pedal, and only one string of each trio of strings is struck. This explains the directions one sees in piano music – *una corda* (one string) for the soft pedal, *tre corde* (the whole three) when the pedal is released.[4] At the same time, many dynamic gradations are permitted by the varied striking force of the hands on the keyboard.

This is clearly an instrument for the expression of a romantic personality, perhaps psychically unstable in the terms of the Age of Reason, quick to move from a whisper to a shout, capable equally of melting softness and frenzied noise. Its pitch range is greater than that of even the orchestra of Richard Wagner or Richard Strauss – it can go higher than the piccolo and lower than the double bassoon. Its effect is that of a one-man orchestra, and Franz Liszt demonstrated, by making piano versions of the Overture to *Tannhäuser* and the Prelude to *Tristan and Isolde*, that, though palpably inferior to the orchestra in tone-colour, it could easily attain its expressive range. Try playing the Venusberg music on a harpsichord.

Dieter Hildebrandt has a lot to say about the great nineteenth-century composers and performers, who were not, of course, all German. But we have to think of the romantic movement as a Teutonic phenomenon. It arose out of rejection of the imperial ambitions of the Corsican upstart, and, in defying Napoleon, Germany may be said to have found its soul. Germany certainly found that it was possible to be a nation instead of a parcel of principalities and duchies. And if Germany was not the Austro-Hungarian Empire, which produced Liszt, the same language was spoken in Vienna and Prague as in Berlin and Weimar. The Germanophone unity was finally decreed by Adolf Hitler, and this was, though perverted, a natural conclusion to the cult of the pan-Teutonic romantic ideal.

Certainly, the great monuments of the pianoforte repertoire, which have not been diminished in the age of Stockhausen and Boulez, have come out of Germanophonia.

Chopin, leaving Poland to earn fame in the West, composed the lyrical poetry of the instrument, but the epics came from Beethoven, with the sonatas that demonstrate the whole gamut of pianistic possibilities and the five great concertos. It is the piano concerto which best expresses the romantic spirit, and, though Poland produced two, Norway one, and France (before Ravel) none worth talking about, the German-speaking territories, with Beethoven, Schumann, Liszt and Brahms, exhibited magisterially the heroic implications of a single man fighting, and being reconciled with, an orchestra of a hundred. Berlioz represented Childe Harold, who is really his author Byron, in a solo viola poeticising against an orchestra, but he should properly have chosen a piano. He did not, however, play the piano, and he is one of the two romantic composers who failed to exploit its power. (Wagner, of course, is the other, though even he has had, in certain productions of *Parsifal,* four grand pianos in the wings to simulate the chiming of bells.) Berlioz made up for his lack of pianism by employing bigger and bigger orchestras.

It is Franz Liszt who stands out as the great romantic hero of the instrument. Some say that his technique would easily be overshadowed by some of the soloists of our day, but there is no living virtuoso who finds the most difficult of his piano pieces easy. In Liszt, as in Chopin, the superb composer for the instrument is conjoined with the superb practitioner. If Chopin took pianism far, Liszt took it much farther. His hands were exceptional, and his management of them such that he could hold glasses of water on both – even in passages of great speed – without spilling a drop. But it was not just a matter of developing technique; it was a matter also (and this applies to Chopin as well) of finding in the sonorities of the piano new possibilities for romantic music in general. Chopin breaks the harmonic rules nearly a century before the academies give their permission: he has consecutive fifths and sevenths, like any jazz pianist. There is something in pianistic procedure which demands this kind of unorthodoxy. In Liszt we find every possible harmonic innovation – from the Scriabinesque dissonance to the Debussyan whole-tone chord. The piano, being a romantic instrument, foreshadowed the breakdown of classical order in music. The hint of what was to come in the twentieth century can even be heard in later Beethoven.

With Claude Debussy, who liquidated, on behalf of France, the long musical hegemony of Germany and the Austro-Hungarian Empire, the experiments of Liszt reach their consummation. Romanticism became impressionism. The piano ceased to be heroic, and the poet of the keyboard expressed not himself but the essence of external nature – water, mist, flowers, storm, heat, frost – as well as unemotional artefacts like a picture postcard of a Spanish scene or figures on a Greek vase. But the capacity of the piano to peck like one of its tinny ancestors, to blur through use of the sustaining pedal, to arpeggiate, to complement the great speed of scale work with the solemnity of huge sustained chords, to wage war between the black keys and the white (out of this came the polytonality of Stravinsky's *Petrushka*) served modernism as well as it served the romantic heyday. Nowadays, no composer is quite sure what to do with the instrument, and the 'prepared piano' of John Cage is a sign of dissatisfaction with what it always wishes to invoke, even when the cat walks over it or a child bashes it with his tiny fists – namely, the spirit of Liszt. When Cage makes his performer sit at the instrument and do nothing we have reached the limit of dissatisfaction. To appreciate what the piano was always meant to be about, we must go back to the heroic days which Dieter Hildebrandt so ably chronicles.

He calls his book *Der Roman des Klaviers. Roman* means either 'novel' or 'romance' (which once meant the same thing: nowadays a romance can only mean a debased form of the novel, the speciality of Bills and Moon, to use David Lodge's inspired spoonerism).[5] In that his survey is about a romantic instrument, *The Romance of the Pianoforte* is in order as a translation of his title. But I like to feel that the whole story of the instrument has the qualities of a novel – thrilling, with mercurial characters, an evocation of the erotic and the perilous. Whether there is a happy ending I do not know. But, though we lack a modern Liszt or Chopin, to say nothing of Beethoven, we do not lack brilliant interpreters to bring their wild-eyed century back again. The romance of the piano is probably not yet over.

Pianoforte: A Social History of the Piano, 1988

1 Sir Edward Heath, British prime minister from 1970–74, was an accomplished pianist and author of *Music: A Joy for Life* (1997), his musical autobiography.

2 The repetition of the word 'Broadwood' in the phrase 'Beethoven was given a Broadwood piano (which he called a Broadwood)' is evidently an editorial error. In Chapter 23 *Notes from the deep*, Burgess writes, 'he did want a pianoforte – once called by him, in a gust of patriotism, a *Hammerklavier*', which suggests that *Hammerklavier* belongs here as well.

3 '*Mon très cher Ami Broadwood! Jamais je n'eprouvais pas un grand Plaisir de ce que me causa votre Annonce de l'arrivée de cette Piano...*' and so on (p. 27). Thomas Broadwood shipped the fortepiano to Beethoven from London in December 1817. It required a seven-month journey for the piano to reach Trieste by sea, whence it was hauled by cart to Vienna. Having arrived slightly damaged, it was repaired at Beethoven's behest by his friend, the Viennese piano builder Nanette Streicher.

4   The fuller description of *una corda* in Chapter 9 *The Well-Tempered Revolution* explains that when the soft pedal is depressed, two strings (*due corde*) are struck, not one.

5   Mills & Boon is a romance imprint of the British publisher Harlequin UK Ltd. Founded by Gerald Rusgrove Mills and Charles Boon in 1908 as a general fiction publisher, Mills & Boon has long specialized in romances generally considered low-brow and formulaic. Over a hundred Mills & Boon novels are published each month. In David Lodge's 1984 novel *Small World: An Academic Romance*, Cheryl Summerbee is a British Airways check-in clerk at Heathrow Airport who loves reading romance novels, especially ones published by 'Bills and Moon'.

15. BLEST PAIR OF SIRENS?

I take my title – less the query – from John Milton, who apostrophised voice and verse as holy seducers and 'pledges of heaven's joy, sphere-born harmonious sisters'.[1] In Milton's time, and in all the time before it, music and liturgy, or music and lyric poetry, went together in the sense that the meaningful art gave meaning to the meaningless one. Music, however we like to associate it with nameable moods and emotions, means only itself, which is as good as saying that it means nothing. If, in the old pre-symphonic days, you wanted to compose music unassisted by the crutch of words, you were limited to fairly short forms – the dance, the air, the fugue. The mass, the oratorio and the opera could be lengthy because the words ensured that they were, but it was only with symphonic form that music could stand on its own – wordless, telling no story, concerned only with a pure sonic argument – and do so for a length of time impossible to Purcell or Bach.

The symphonies of Mahler and Bruckner take length to the limit. Sonata form perhaps spent itself with those masters, and music seems to have found it hard to breed a self-referring form that should supersede it. Probably if Hector Berlioz had not been overwhelmed by Harriet Smithson's Paris performance as Ophelia on 11 September 1827 (the year of Beethoven's death) the hybrid known as the symphonic poem would not have so speedily arrived. For the *Symphonie Fantastique* pays a perfunctory service to the form that Beethoven seemed to have exhausted: it has sonata elements – first and second subject, development, recapitulation and so on – but it is really a symphonic poem in five cantos. Romanticism in music, finding symphonic form too 'classical', had to go back to literature.

This year's Proms seem to be acknowledging rather lavishly the debt that music owes to the sister art. Haydn, true father of the symphony, appears with only his No. 44 and No. 101, and both of these have subtitles – 'Trauer', or funeral, and 'Clock' – which, for those who cannot take their music neat, anchor at least some of the notes to the world outside. Richard Strauss does far better with seven items, of which only the *Metamorphosen* can be termed unliterary. Schoenberg's three pieces all have literary referents; Walton has two Shakespeare suites; Britten brims with poetry. This is to say little of what is actually sung, not just played. Debussy's only orchestral contribution – the music for D'Annunzio's *Martyrdom of St Sebastian* – bows down to words, and the Prom planners are so keen to accommodate the vocal Debussy that they give us the early *Blessed Damozel*. Delius is present with only the highly secular *A Mass of Life*, balancing Verdi's *Requiem*, which at least sounds secular, mourning for Manzoni in greasepaint.

The wealth, if not preponderance, of music with literary associations raises the old question of what precisely music can do with literature. Richard Strauss thought music could take literature over: there is no need to read Cervantes when you have the key items of *Don Quixote* presented in the orchestra far more succinctly than in the original words. But if those 'Variations on a Theme of Knightly Character' were played titleless, would the newcomer to the music even have an inkling as to what it was really about? Like the banal barrel-organ theme of Mahler – which Freud explained to the composer between trains – would the clichés on the viola suggest an external programme or merely sound like motiveless parody? The listener needs the title taken from the book, but he needs the book as well.

Symphonic poems always have to assume that the listener is at least as cultivated in literature as the composer. It is useless to take in Tchaikovsky's *Francesca da Rimini* without knowing that the music is meant to be two large helpings of hell with a couple of sinning lovers between them. If nobody really wants to hear the same composer's *Manfred*, it is because nobody knows Byron's poem. I have never heard *Hamlet*, nor do I greatly wish to, but I can guess what Tchaikovsky's music is like – generalised action and atmosphere but no soliloquies, something that would serve equally well for the *Ur-Hamlet* or *The Spanish Tragedy*. There is, I think, only one symphonic poem that transcends its literary – or in this instance sub-literary – origins, and that is *Till Eulenspiegel*.

Music can convey atmosphere but not narrative facts – except in the widest, most cinematic, way (here the hero hurries on horseback; here he savours dawn on a mountain-top). There is an attempt in this year's Proms to see how three very different composers convey the atmosphere of a dramatic work that has been saved for the stage only by being musicalised. Maeterlinck's *Pelléas and Mélisande* has become Debussy's. It is to be done, semi-dramatically, at the Proms, as is Sibelius's music to the play, a humble servitrix to the verbal content. Schoenberg's symphonic poem, lushly late-Romantic and sometimes very loud (I remember the composer at a pre-war rehearsal asking: 'Is the bassoon to hear?' It was not to hear: the trombones drowned it) is there to remind us that we can learn little of the flavour of a piece of literature from its musical translation. Only the words can, clinging sometimes like fingers to the ledge of audibility, convey the primary intention. There is no lack of verbal audibility in Debussy.

We shall hear what Strauss thought of Nietzsche in *Also sprach Zarathustra* (whose opening has virtually been taken over by Kubrick's *2001*), and how Nietzsche confirmed Delius's atheistic vitalism in *A Mass of Life*, but the two Nietzsches are hardly compatible. The framers of the Prom conspectus are making a good deal of the literary inspiration behind many of the works to be performed, but the inspiration is really not much more than pretext. Shakespeare or Byron or Goethe may start a composer off on his exploration of themes and sonorities, but there will not be much of the poet left at the final double bar.

There are, I think, only two items, both Shakespearean, which provide a literary stimulus as well as profound musical satisfaction. They are both entitled *Falstaff*. Elgar's symphonic study makes too much of Sir John the knight, as opposed to the Manningtree ox with the pudding in his belly, but it is astonishing that we should be aware of the knight at all, the slim page too, and know that we are in a Worcestershire orchard with him and Justice Shallow. This work is a very curious miracle. Of the Verdi-Boito *Falstaff* one has to say first that it transcends its origins in *The Merry Wives of Windsor*. Boito could not, of course, have written the libretto at all without the cumbersome bardic farce (which we can, if we wish, believe that Queen Elizabeth ordered Shakespeare to write, much against Will's will), but a joint genius produced a Sir John who can be related to the rounded round figure of *Henry IV*. What is happening in the orchestra qualifies the buffoonery of the stage. This is another miracle. Why that greybearded Vice should be behind two of these is a question for Maurice Morgann, and he is long dead.[2]

This year's Proms, in their yoking of two arts, will help to disabuse some of us of the notion that the sphere-born harmonious pair are, when brought together, equal in their sirenian seductiveness. But the music will always swallow the literature, grateful for it as a note-weaving pretext. Setting words, it will reduce them to sound without much semantic content. Music needs literature, but the reverse is not true. Not even Falstaff needs any music except the Cheapside waits, though he will hear in it proof that he is the cause of wit in others. Post-Beethovenian music cries out for a scaffold. Literature graciously accords it, then gets on with its own job.

The Listener, 1988

1   'At a Solemn Music', written in 1633–34 by John Milton, begins:
        Blest pair of Sirens, pledges of Heaven's joy,
        Sphere-born harmonious Sisters, Voice and Verse,
        Wed your divine sounds, and mixed power employ,
        Dead things with inbreathed sense able to pierce;
2   Maurice Morgann, an eighteenth-century colonial administrator
    and Shakespearean literary scholar, wrote *An Essay on the Dramatic
    Character of Sir John Falstaff.*

The Archbishop of New York, Cardinal John O'Connor, has solemnly damned the cult of the rock music known as heavy metal. He alleges the Devil rampages in it and leaps into the souls of its devotees. Two cases of apparent demonic possession have been exorcised in New York in the past few months, and heavy metal music, according to His Eminence, has had something to do with both. He has made his condemnation pretty general, but he has picked out one song by one singer – 'Suicide Solution' by Ozzy Osbourne – as responsible for a Californian adolescent self-slaying. Osbourne is British, and other British rock musicians have come in for more secular attacks – notably Motörhead, Iron Maiden and Saxon. Satanism and suicide – these are highly reprehensible British exports. We must try to take Cardinal O'Connor seriously.

First though we have to divide all music – not just rock – into two components – the inner and the outer. If music is played at a volume of up to 100 decibels it can make the adrenalin gush, quicken the heartbeat and, especially in combination with alcohol, arouse very violent instincts. This is the outer aspect. Play the scherzo of Beethoven's Ninth at an excessive volume and you will equally promote mindless aggression. The twenty minutes of Ravel's *Boléro*, if loud enough, can kindle a murderous frenzy. Play a typical rock effusion pianissimo and you will do little harm. It is not the inner component that arouses rage, except perhaps in the genuinely musical. The trouble with heavy metal is that without the insistent beat, greatly amplified, there is not much left. And indeed very little rock music goes on very long. Its composers, if we may call them that, have not acquired the skill to develop their material for more than a minute or so. The jungle drums which Cardinal O'Connor seems to be evoking, and which are pummelled for the sole purpose of arousing a kind of religious frenzy, go on for hours. Rock only seems to do that.

As for the suicidal influence of music, we have to listen to the genuine stuff to find the harmonies and rhythms capable of awakening the death urge. The music of Frederick Delius, I have always maintained, is dangerous to the unstable adolescent. Three years ago I took a young man to a performance of Wagner's *Tristan and Isolde*. The following day he slit his wrists – fortunately not lethally, though that was his intention. No music ever composed stimulates the urge to die more powerfully than the third act of that opera.

But there are probably worse things music can do than invite suicide or awaken small demons. Music can drive nations to war. To Adolf Hitler, Wagner's opera *The Mastersingers* summed up German aspirations. The music itself is probably harmless – indeed, most of it is ravishing – but the image which it encloses and which it raises to the level of ecstasy is one of a nation that will do anything to glorify its culture. It reverberated in Hitler's head while he devoured Europe. If Europe was to be Teutonised, the music of Wagner was to be the spiritual agent. The only piece of Nazi music that is still played – and is, in fact, excessively popular – is the *Carmina Burana* of Carl Orff. Though it is a setting of tavern songs sung when Germany was called the Holy Roman Empire, its rhythms are suitable for beer-bloated stormtroopers ready to hit out at Jews. And, if we want an example of hyper-chauvinistic music from our own shores, this must be the trio of Elgar's first *Pomp and Circumstance* march, given patriotic words and roared out by a youthful audience on the last night of the Proms. Fortunately, there is something ironic in the lusty tune. Also, if you listen carefully, something neurotic and self-doubting. Give your audience free beer and a large number of encores, however, and its effects could be devastating. The Albert Hall might be burned down.

In other words, we have to accept that music can be dangerous. Sigmund Freud was scared of it because it was too close to the id, that irrational volcano of sheer animal energy which has to be controlled by the ego and submitted to the approval of the super-ego. St Augustine, a millennium and a half before Freud, was frightened of the animal element in music but accepted that a good rousing hymn could promote Christian solidarity. Music, in a well-organised state on the lines of Plato's *Republic*, needs watchdogs, or rather listenhounds. The Archbishop of New York is asking for a rating system, on the analogy of films, so that parents may stop their children's ears to the grosser and more seductive noises. This is very platonic. Plato said that you could have this kind of music but you couldn't have that.

I accept there is a limit to that outer component we call volume. Serious music uses volume with artistic effect – it swells from a pianissimo to a fortissimo and back again, with a forte or a mezzo-piano in between. This makes volume an inner component. Music that has to have volume imposed from the outside is less than music: it is the raw material of a deliberate acoustic battering. Some years ago, a learned classical musician interviewed on BBC TV a pop group that had recently come to the fore but, like many pop groups, was to fade into drugs, death and oblivion.[1] The learned musician was kind about the tunes of the pop group but unhappy about the noise. 'I was brought up on chamber music', he explained. Almost as one boy, the group responded: 'Well, we bloody well wasn't'. And the trouble is that there is a whole generation that cannot take music in at all unless at a volume that a true musician would regard as brutally excessive.

For the sake of their own acoustic well-being, something will have to be done about this. It is a matter of auditory health. Children in the Trastevere district of Rome listen, at the time of their local festivals, to musical noise far in excess of anything the New York young could take. Their hearing powers have been ruined. Even close to, they cannot hear the murmuring of a Roman fountain. A law ought to be passed to cut down on public decibels – meaning the tuneless din blasted forth from public house loudspeakers. It is auditory pollution. But so is the insidious piped music of airports, hotels and restaurants. None of us should be given music unless we ask for it.

As for the inner component of pop, whether it clangs heavy metal or not, it is so puerile as to be totally harmless. We have come a long way from the time when, with the music of Richard Rodgers, Cole Porter and George Gershwin, the world, young or old, could have tunes in common. There is in pop or rock a watery neutrality that can only be given a semblance of meaning by being equipped with a heavy monotonous beat. It is suitable for the unformed young and it is to be despised more than feared. Noise is a different matter. His Eminence is right there, but the Devil has better things to do than respond to its inanity. The Prince of Darkness is an intellectual and he likes Mozart.

Evening Standard, 1990

1   The same anecdote is related in Chapter 3 *Music at the Millennium*, where the 'learned classical musician' is identified as Hans Keller.

17. BEATLEMANIA

Beetles are *scarabei*.[1] The Beatles were four young men from Liverpool, on the north-western coast of England, who gained world fame as a group of popular musicians. In their collective name they combined certain puns. 'Beatle' referred to the strong beat of their songs, a rhythmic ictus that became less important than the melodic content; it also carried an echo of the place-name Bootle, a district of Liverpool with which they were associated. As 'Beatles' is pronounced like 'beetles,' there was a certain wilful self-disparagement in their name: here we are, mere insects, ready to be crushed under foot. Such masochistic humour is highly British. When they were first heard, there were plenty of critics prepared to use the name as a ready-made device of condemnation. But popular adulation, especially among the young, soon made the critics see wit, originality and melodiousness where previously they had heard nothing but banality.

The musical talent was considerable though untrained. The four young men – John Lennon, Paul McCartney, Ringo Starr and George Harrison – shared an academic background, if it can be so called, that had nothing to do with music. They were alumni of the Liverpool College of Art, which was notable chiefly for the sartorial tastes of its students.[2] The Beatles wore their hair long but not wild; it was carefully sculpted. Their clothes were neat, restrained, the jackets without lapels. The Beatles never looked like gentlemen of the British Establishment, but they proclaimed no anarchy. Respectability was tempered by a certain irony.

It is just thirty years since the Beatles began to crawl into prominence. It is just twenty-five years since the release of their most popular album, *Sergeant Pepper's Lonely Hearts Club Band*. That title is either absurd or devious, according to our preference. A Lonely Hearts Club is, presumably, a group of solitary people looking for love and companionship. They are unlikely to form themselves into an aggressive musical group under an irascible army sergeant (pepper is *pepe*).[3] The cover design betrays the Beatles's origins as students of commercial art, and also a certain pretentiousness, a bid for intellectual acceptance, since it contains portraits of great painters, writers and musicians of the past. The songs of the album are also touched by pretentiousness. Ringo Starr, the drummer, had a vocal compass of some five notes, which he employed in 'Yellow Submarine'. The song is childish, and it was much sung by children, but the application of 'yellow' to a submarine was considered by some to have a surrealist, even a psychedelic, significance. Another song in the album is 'Lucy in the Sky with Diamonds', which has references to a girl with kaleidoscope eyes and taxis made out of newspapers. This is genuine and gentle surrealism. But the best of the Beatles was to be found in songs about suffering and bewildered members of the Liverpool working class, as in 'Eleanor Rigby' and 'She's Leaving Home'. The sincerity, a rare property in popular song, was controlled and never sank to the sentimental.

This album was a product of immense electronic subtlety. The Beatles had first been known as three young men singing and strumming guitars (not very well) to the percussive accompaniment of Ringo Starr, whose charm was great but whose talent inconsiderable. With the help of genuine musical and technical experts, the Beatles became a recording phenomenon. The montages of their recorded songs could not be reproduced on the stage or in the television studio, though such films as *Yellow Submarine*, an animated cartoon in which caricatures of the Beatles wandered through strange landscapes, were able to exploit the surrealistic and the psychedelic to the limit. They brought a slight musical acquaintance with the possibilities of the symphony orchestra, the experiments of

Stockhausen, the subtleties of electronic synthesis, to men who knew all about these things. They appealed on many levels. There was a tendency to take them too seriously.

America took them to its great heart and exaggerated their significance. I remember being commissioned by an American magazine of large reputation to present them as the four new evangelists. Charles Manson, the serial killer, saw himself as the cleanser of the world and found justification in the Book of Revelations. There, he said, the coming of four archangels was prophesied. They would wear steel breastplates. They were clearly the Beatles, and the breastplates were metallic guitars. At the time of the Beatles the bloodstained Messiah would come, and this was to be Charles Manson.

Perhaps the true significance of the Beatles, and the Beatlemania that flourished for some years, was more sociological than artistic. They came at a time when the British provinces were beginning to assert themselves against the intolerable dominance of the metropolis. For far too long, London had decreed intellectual, aesthetic, social, and even moral modes, and the provinces were expected to follow. The entertainments industry, with its centre in London, had been willing to draw on the immense fund of talent in the provinces while at the same time despising it. In the 1950s, the provincial underclass bit back. John Osborne's play *Look Back in Anger* initiated the cult of the 'angry young man', and this was associated with the appearance of rebels from the North in various plays, films and novels, who disputed London's claim to be the arbiter of thought, manners and morals. The Beatles were a comparatively late addition to the trend.

They came from a part of England – the great port of Liverpool – which was cut off from the Protestant mainstream of the south-east. The Reformation had never really reached the county of Lancashire, of which Manchester and Liverpool are the major cities, and native Catholicism, with an interfusion of immigrant Irish, was, where tolerated, not encouraged.[4] Until the Catholic Emancipation Act of 1829, British Catholics had been denied higher education, and such talent as they had was not permitted to express itself in the learned professions. There was only one profession available – a distinctly unlearned one – and that was the popular theatre. The Beatles came at the end of a long tradition of Lancashire singers, actors and, above all, comedians. I say 'end' advisedly. They did not initiate a new trend in entertainment. After them came the genuinely anarchic rock groups, like the Sex Pistols, disaffected, obscene and, above all, illiterate. They were a late manifestation of provincial assertiveness, though ironic, self-disparaging. Their songs were singable as the songs of the old provincial music halls had been. The songs that have come after are not singable at all, and their words make little sense.

They stood not only for the proclamation of provincial talent but also for the new status of the youth of Britain. The Second World War had made it very clear to the ordinary citizens of the country that there was a profound fissure between the rulers and the ruled, the metropolitan and the provincial, the young and the old. In the 1960s, an era when, as the Prime Minister Harold Macmillan was always pointing out, the British people 'had never had it so good', young people had jobs and money. The money could be spent on modes of fantastic dress and diversion decreed by such of their cunning elders as knew all about the exploitation of youth. The age of the miniskirt, the disco, the record-player, was the age of the Beatles. They were young, decent, nonconformist but not anarchic, and they provided the words and the music for the generation of which they were already senior members. The Beatles proclaimed that youth could have a voice if it wished, and here was that voice.

The adulation, as I say, was excessive, and John Lennon, Americanised and living in New York, was the paradoxical victim of that excess. He was assassinated by a young man who claimed that the motive for the murder was pure adoration. This seemed to exemplify Oscar Wilde's statement that 'each man kills the thing he loves'.[5] The violent death of one of its members, and perhaps the most talented, signalled the end of the Beatles. Its surviving members have produced songs of no great merit, and Paul McCartney has dared to produce a *Liverpool Oratorio* in which most of the technical expertise was provided by Carl Davis.[6] The Beatles were not enough of musicians to sustain a genuine career in the art. They belong to a brief epoch, and a rehearing of the work provokes nostalgia. But their voice was unique. Since it was stilled, the metropolitan centres of culture have not dared to ridicule the art of the provinces. And Liverpool, a great decaying city, a moribund port, has achieved a cultural dignity it is not likely ever to lose.

Corriere della Sera, 1992

1   The Italian word for 'beetles' is *scarabei*.
2   Only John Lennon attended Liverpool College of Art. He entered in October 1957 but was an indifferent student and did not graduate. Paul McCartney and George Harrison attended The Liverpool Institute, a grammar school located next door to the college. Ringo Starr, whose education was interrupted repeatedly by poor health and prolonged hospitalizations, did not attend school beyond the age of fifteen.
3   Since this was written for an Italian newspaper, Burgess translates 'pepper' (*pepe* in Italian) for its readers.
4   See Commentary to Chapter 34 *Gentlemen v. Players*.
5   From 'The Ballad of Reading Gaol', line 37
6   Composed in collaboration with Carl Davis to commemorate the Royal Liverpool Philharmonic Orchestra's 150th anniversary, it premiered at Liverpool Cathedral in June 1991 and was released that October as an album that rose to #1 on classical charts worldwide.

PART II
COMPOSERS AND THEIR MUSIC

18. PEARLS BEFORE SWINE

The Letters of Claudio Monteverdi, translated and introduced
by Denis Stevens
London: Faber, 1980

When Monteverdi started writing the letters in this volume,
Shakespeare had just produced *Hamlet;* when the letters ended,
with his life, the London playhouses had been closed and the
Civil War was already raging. The music of England during
that period was remarkable, so remarkable that Europe did
not despise it. But the music that Monteverdi was composing
– in Mantua, Venice and Parma – was revolutionary. Its place
in the history of Western music is comparable with that of
Wagner and Schoenberg. Monteverdi invented opera –
specifically *opera seria*, though he had *opera buffa* also in mind.
In instrumental usage he was moving towards the concept
of the modern orchestra. He was using, to the annoyance of
some of his contemporaries, unprepared discords in his vocal
writing. He was founding the baroque tradition, replacing a
rigid mode of counterpoint with one more melodic and freer-
flowing. On even the shortest list of supreme composers his
name has to appear. And yet this superb artist was a slave to
giddy patrons, a man trying to present images of order in an
age notably disordered, subject to indigence and fear (at least
on his son's behalf) of the Holy Inquisition, always forced to
fulfil the postures of humility before men unworthy to rule his
bar-lines.

It is something of a shock to find that Monteverdi and
Mozart – separated as they are by an epoch of vast historical
changes – yet share, almost without even the smallest variation,
the same situation of grovelling for patronage, turned into
disregarded journeymen summoned at a finger-click for the

composing of carnival dances or masses or operas or *Te Deums*. The great change in the situation of European composers occurs with the advent of Beethoven, the first free musician, who had indeed patrons but was prepared to treat them abominably, who wrote pretty well what he wished, who never had to endite elaborate self-scourging epistles ending with 'Forgive me, I beseech you, for so much inconvenience, while with all my heart I make a most humble reverence and kiss your hand…Your Most Illustrious Lordship's most humble and most grateful servant' (Monteverdi to the Marquis Alessandro Striggio, at Mantua, 8 July 1628).[1]

In a letter to the same nobleman (18 December 1627) Monteverdi writes that his son Massimiliano has been in the prisons of the Holy Office for three months, 'the reason being that he read a book which he did not know was prohibited'. What is notable about the attitude of the distraught father is the lack of anger. Later he writes to the Marquis: 'I understand from your most considerate letter that you happened to speak personally to the Most Reverend Father Inquisitor (a favour so great that it makes me blush)…' No blasting of the cruel cleric to hell: that would be a later, post-Beethovenian, luxury. We cannot blame anybody or anything, but we have to confess that, after 400-odd pages of most eloquent self-abasement, we grow angry ourselves at the expenditure of so much epistolary skill on the making of elaborate reverences.

What, on the recommendation of this very fine translator, we have to do is consider these letters as pieces of music. The architectonic instinct of Monteverdi is expressed here, as much as in his madrigals, in the organization of periods which have the effect of counterpoint. In perhaps the only letter which expresses subdued rage at wounded dignity (a just rage, since Monteverdi was now at the peak of honour and not far from death) the shaping skill is at its peak – 'much more rhetorical in style,' says Stevens, 'than the majority of them, and so planned that the subject of the exordium is separated from the main verb by nearly half the length of the letter.' Monteverdi was by now Director of Music at St Mark's and servant of the Most Serene Republic of Venice. A bass singer in the cathedral choir, Domenico Aldegati, spoke insulting words in public, saying:

> The Director of Music belongs to a race of big cut-throats, a thieving, cheating he-goat, with many other wicked insults, and then he added: 'And I call him and whoever protects him an ass, and so that each one of you can hear me, I say that Claudio Monteverdi is a thieving, cheating he-goat, and I am telling you, Bonivento, so that you can go and report it as coming from me.'

(Bonivento was at the time paying out money to the singers given to him by the nuns of St Daniele for a vespers service.)

One thing may be said of the various nobility to which Monteverdi so humbly (and yet with a kind of structural dignity) writes, and that is that they were all musical enough to be worthy of detailed technical accounts of what Monteverdi was trying to do in his commissioned music. Some of the revelations of artistic problems are absorbing. What should be done, in a kind of masque of the months, to represent the goddess Discordia? As a discord was, of its nature in those distant pre-Schoenbergian days, only justifiable in terms of resolution on to a concord, it was not possible to write her music as consistent dissonance. Therefore it was not strictly possible for her to have a harmonic accompaniment for her song. Perhaps the song should be speech? Nay, perhaps even a kind of *Sprechgesang*? If Monteverdi thus foreshadowed *Pierrot Lunaire*, at least in intention, he was also willing to anticipate Strauss's *Don Quixote* by suggesting that the sounds of zephyrs and tempests be handed over to the brass and woodwind. His imagination was incredible, but it was always held in check by the commission on hand, the exigencies of singers' and instrumentalists' talents, and the subtle acoustic problems of the various places of performance. Today's composers are totally free. There is nothing they dream up that cannot be done. But freedom, though a fine political concept, is not really of much use to the artist. Monteverdi exemplifies the paradox of the muse in chains and yet soaring.

The frontispiece to this book is the reproduction of an oil painting of the composer done by Domenico Feti and to be seen in the Galleria dell'Accademia in Venice.[2] It is a very remarkable portrait. The upper half of the face is that of Samuel Beckett, brooding on but writing nothing of the *merde universelle*. The ears reach out for sound like radar dishes (at least, the ear we can see does that). But the total effect, long hidalgo nose and grey beard and mustachios, will do for Don Quixote (did Strauss have this picture in mind when he wrote his 'theme of knightly character'?). It is a portrait of the archetypal artist set upon by the stupidities of the world. All Monteverdians will buy this admirable volume, a work of astonishing care and scholarship, but all concerned with the place of the great musician in a setting not quite worthy of him (apart from the irrelevancies of wars and disease and highway robbers) should at least dip into it.

The Observer, 1982

1   Alessandro Striggio the Younger served at the court of Mantua, the city of his birth, and died of the plague in Venice. He is chiefly remembered for writing the libretto of Monteverdi's opera *Orfeo* in 1607.

2   The painting in Venice is a copy, by an unidentified artist, of 'Portrait of an Actor' by Feti (or Fetti), which hangs in the Hermitage Museum in Saint Petersburg. The personage in the painting, depicted holding a harlequin mask, is thought to be Tristano Martinelli or Francesco Andreini, both of whom were actors, and is no longer regarded as a portrait of Monteverdi although it does bear resemblance to the painting of him by Bernardo Strozzi and the etching from the title page of *Fiori poetici* (Poetic Flowers), a 1644 book of commemorative poems written for Monteverdi's funeral.

19. HANDEL, NOT HÄNDEL — A TRICENTENNIAL TRIBUTE

He was a big man, given to corpulence, of immense strength and uncertain temper. He would hurl a kettledrum at a stupid leader of the orchestra, kick a hole in an out-of-tune double bass, throw a temperamental soprano out of the window. His appetite was enormous and notorious. His face, often sour and forbidding, could flash into a smile that was like the sun breaking through clouds. He was absolutely without malice and of scrupulous honesty: he said what he thought and he always paid his debts. He never married, but we know nothing of his mistresses: his discretion was remarkable. He was witty. When a violinist concluded a long and rambling cadenza, he cried out, so that the whole concert hall could hear him, 'You are welcome home, Mr Dubourg'.[1] A friend remarked on the atrociously bad music that was being played at Vauxhall Gardens in London, and he said: 'You are right, sir, it is very poor stuff. I thought so myself when I wrote it.' He was an astonishing practical musician, graceful at the harpsichord, thunder and lightning at the organ, a brilliant violinist when he deigned to pick up the instrument, a sonorous singer when he took the trouble to sing. And, of course, he was conceivably the greatest composer that Germany ever produced. Beethoven thought so. England claims him as one of her own glories.

He began life on 23 February 1685, in Halle, and he was baptised into the Lutheran Church as Georg Friederich Händel. In Italy he called himself Hendel, as also on his first visits to England, but later he designated himself George Frideric Handel, without the umlaut.[2] This is the name you will see carved below his statue in Westminster Abbey, and it was under this name that he became a British citizen. This change of citizenship looks to some Germans like a defection.

But the same thing may be said of the Elector of Hanover's becoming King George I of Great Britain. The British people have had German monarchs on the throne ever since the death of Queen Anne, the last of the Stuarts (who were, of course, Scottish), and these monarchs, once they learned English, became very British. George I never learned English, and he had to have a German-speaking first minister. That is how the office of prime minister came into being. As for Handel, who forgot much of his German but never learned to speak English like an Englishman, he was too cosmopolitan to be considered anything except a citizen of Europe who happened to be living in London.

Handel shares a tercentenary with Domenico Scarlatti, an admirable composer with whom Handel once engaged in a harpsichord-playing competition and, naturally, won, but also with another German composer on much his own level of genius – Johann Sebastian Bach, who was born on 21 March 1685. In this celebratory year it is tempting to look for affinities between them and even to enquire whether they ever met. They did not; on their travels they kept missing each other. In August 1703 Handel visited the great Buxtehude at Lübeck to see what chance there was of succeeding him as organist of the Marienkirche. One of the conditions of obtaining the post from the ailing and ageing master of the fugue was to marry his daughter, who was ugly and past her first youth. Handel withdrew. Two years later Bach went to Lübeck on the same mission, found the marital conditions still in force and likewise withdrew. This is the only instance we can find in the lives of Bach and Handel of a shared ambition and a common prudence. For the rest, each went his own way.

As a young organist and composer in Hamburg, Handel seemed likely to become no more than a competent musician of the known and admired northern German stamp – strong on counterpoint, weak on melody, an earnest engineer of complex fugues. Fortunately he was invited by Prince Ferdinand de' Medici, son and heir of the Grand Duke of Tuscany, to visit Italy (though at his own expense). This brought him into the southern sunlight and the florid world of Italian opera. He had already composed Italianate operas in Hamburg, but the scores that survive show a certain stiffness and a lack of melodic freedom. He needed contact with the Italian voice, and in Florence and Rome he got it. Italy turned him into the composer we know – master of instrumental writing, skilful in motets, but, more than anything, the supreme man of the theatre. Italy softened his German angularities, infused southern sensuousness into his melodic lines, taught him the art of pleasing rather than elevating.

He left Italy for Hanover, where he was appointed *Kapellmeister* to the Elector. One of the conditions of appointment on which he insisted was an immediate year of absence in London. The Elector made no objection: he knew that Queen Anne was dying and that he himself would soon be in London too: Hanover and London were to become twin centres of the one dynasty. In London Handel rehearsed his future. For the new opera house built by Vanbrugh, dramatist and architect, situated in the Haymarket and called the Queen's Theatre, he composed an Italian opera, *Rinaldo*, which took the town by storm.[3] It anticipated much of his later London theatre work, with its florid castrati, its special orchestral effects (vulgar, some said), its highly memorable tunes, and its elaborate staging, with live sparrows twittering in the grove of the heroine Almirena. Handel had entered show business.

When George I was crowned, Handel's career as an adoptive Englishman began. Unlike Bach, he was engaged in the purveying of music on the open market. He joined the London middle class, but he had profound aristocratic connections from the monarchy down. Like Beethoven, he was undeferential and even abusive to his noble patrons, being ready to rail at his pupil the Princess of Wales for not taking her music with the right seriousness. Like Beethoven, he was too honest and too dedicated an artist to earn lordly rebuke, which, anyway, he would not have taken lying down. The aristocracy sometimes accepted him with the good-humoured tolerance appropriate to a large and unruly dog. It is said that he earned the displeasure of the king and ingratiated himself by composing the Water Music. This may be apocryphal. Handel was ready enough to subdue himself into a kind of easy servitude to the Duke of Chandos as his resident composer.[4] But he was happier in the situation of a free musician selling performances of his operas and oratorios on the open market, though he did not disdain the king's purely artistic patronage.

Handel composed innumerable operas on a multitude of classical themes, usually in Italian, for it was Italian opera that London best liked. *Ottone, Floridante, Flavio, Admeto, Giulio Cesare, Acis and Galatea* poured from his pen. He was a rapid worker who did not disdain to work out his themes at the keyboard. His melodies smell of improvisation more than midnight oil. They often derive directly from the rhythms and tonalities of the words he set. The need to fulfil many commissions and to meet deadlines (in the manner of a good musical journalist) led him not merely to cannibalise his own earlier works but to steal from other composers. This was very much in order in an age that had not yet thought of copyright: Bach stole from Vivaldi, Handel stole from composers now forgotten. T.S. Eliot once said: 'Minor artists borrow. Major artists steal'. Stealing, they make what they steal into something greater than it was.[5]

We must imagine Handel as being thrown into a lifelong fever of theatre business, trying to give the public what he thought it wanted, quarrelling with singers and instrumentalists, wooing prima donnas from abroad with fabulous fees, attending to matters not only of music but of stage scenery and lighting, introducing ballet and, if need be, performing dogs, astonishing the ears of the public with bells, masses of brass, contrabass kettledrums, worrying over box office receipts. He filled in the acts of his operas with organ concertos which he played himself, mostly improvising. Besides the theatre, he had to occupy himself with ceremonial odes, an occasional Te Deum, music for a firework display in Green Park to celebrate the Treaty of Aix-la-Chapelle in 1749, a chorus – 'See the Conquering Hero Comes' – for the Duke of Cumberland, returning to London after slaughtering the rebellious Scots at Culloden.[6] He could be contrapuntally complex, like Bach; he could be almost naive with his four-square melodies and simple block chords. He never wrote anything too difficult to play or to listen to. When the first performer of Schoenberg's violin concerto told the composer he needed a violinist with six fingers, Schoenberg said: 'I can wait.' Handel was not like that.

Like any man of the theatre, Handel had to be stoical about flops. And none of his successes ever equalled that of *The Beggar's Opera* (still very much alive, even when travestied in Brecht's *Dreigroschenoper*). This brilliant work, in a mixture of criminal slang and elegant lyricism, was written by John Gay, with traditional and popular tunes arranged by Dr Pepusch. Handel never thought highly of Pepusch's musicality; he compounded contempt with jealousy when *The Beggar's Opera* seemed likely to run forever.[7] Its success indicated that the British public was ready to prefer *opera buffa* in English to *opera seria* in Italian. Handel was ready to take the English language seriously.

It was in that curious hybrid form known as the oratorio that Handel showed his command of the tones and colours and rhythms of English verse. We can date the beginning of this phase in his career exactly. On his birthday, 23 February 1732, a performance of *Esther* was given in the Crown and

Anchor tavern in the Strand. The subject was drawn from the Old Testament but there was none of the wooden reverence appropriate to a sacred subject. The work was given with stage action, mostly by boys of the Chapel Royal, and the chorus, in the ancient Greek manner, commented on the action – not, however, from the stage but from the orchestra. Princess Anne, Handel's pupil, wanted the production transferred to the King's Theatre, and this was done after a massive revision of the score occasioned by a couple of bad pirated performances in York Buildings. But there was no stage action. The Bishop of London forbade it. Nevertheless, this static presentation, with books in the singers' hands, was an immense popular success. Italian singers took the leads, but, said a contemporary report, they 'made rare work with the English tongue, you would have sworn it had been Welsh.'

It is interesting to contrast the devotionalism of Bach's settings of religious subjects with the secularism of Handel's. Of course, Bach kept to the New Testament, while Handel felt free to regard the chronicles of the Children of Israel as material closer to myth or fairy tale than to the word of God. *Solomon* is even erotic: the arrival of the Queen of Sheba has the excitement of glandular arousal, the nuptial chorus is sung while the fabulous pair are already in bed. But, with *Messiah*, Handel produced a work wholly devotional and yet totally lacking in pietistic postures. This, composed at red-hot speed, remains his best-loved work in the British Isles (it was first performed in Dublin to immense Celtic enthusiasm), and, from the purely technical viewpoint, a model of compromise between the more severe baroque forms and a melodic drive wholly popular. And it demonstrates superlatively Handel's mastery of the prosody of English.

Here we have a problem. It is virtually impossible to appreciate Handel's greatest choral works without recognising that they are wedded to the English language. They will not easily translate, not even into German. French and Italian versions are a virtual impossibility. I am thinking particularly of the great secular odes, settings of John Dryden – *Alexander's Feast* and *A Song for St Cecilia's Day* – where the exactness of the matching of music to words is almost miraculous. And in the settings of John Milton's *L'Allegro* and *Il Penseroso* we find a totally English lyricism combined with orchestral scene-painting that seems to express a love of the English countryside only a native Englishman might be expected to feel. In his novel *The Way of All Flesh*, Samuel Butler describes English peasants attending church and says: 'For some reason, the tune of Handel's 'Here the ploughman near at hand/Whistles o'er the furrow'd land' got into my head. How marvellously old Handel understood these people!' So he did. His music is the music of a great humanist.

But how can music be anything but the pleasing combination of mere sounds? There is a mystery here, never to be explained. Playing a fugue from Bach's *Well Tempered Clavier*, I feel myself to be in a wholly intellectual world. Playing the 'Pastoral Symphony' from *Messiah* I smell the night frost and see the smoking breath of the shepherds watching their flocks outside Bethlehem. I do not know how Handel does it, but his music conveys the totality of the human makeup – flesh, emotions, intellect, but more flesh and emotions than intellect. Much of the effect of the Hallelujah Chorus in *Messiah* derives from a total simplicity – block chords, unaccompanied vocal lines, a tone of affirmation which is wholly physical.

We call Handel a baroque composer, but the term does not wholly fit. 'Baroque' works for Bach: with him it implies great complexity of texture, as it does in the sculptures of Bernini. A baroque sculptor takes stone and makes it behave like paper. Bach makes the voice behave like a trumpet and the trumpet behave like a voice. Possibilities are pushed to the limit. Not so in Handel. He had no technical limitations, but he recognised the limitations of his audiences. If he had given them a double fugue in the manner of Bach, they would have walked out. He knew that his paying customers were of the British middle class – not over-cultivated, a little hypocritical in their approach to religion, lovers of broad effects and a good tune. When Gluck came to England, he told him: 'Do not give them complicated stuff. The English like to beat time and stamp their feet.' (Later he said: 'Gluck knows as much about contrapunto as my cook.')

There is another sense in which he may be deemed a composer wholly suited to the English. He knew English music, and particularly the music of Henry Purcell. At a performance of Handel's *Jephtha*, a certain Mr Savage said to the composer: 'This movement, sir, reminds me of old Purcell's music.'[8] Handel replied: 'Oh, go to Teufel. If Purcell had lived, he would have composed better music than this.' It was through writing in the tradition of Purcell – broad tunes of the kind to which King Charles II had loved to beat time, bold harmonic effects which occasionally broke the rules – that Handel joined himself to the British artistic *ethos*. But, being a foreigner, he was assumed to know more about music than any native musician. That has been the British way: in music the foreigners (and, since Handel, particularly the Germans) always know best. This enabled the Germans to call England *Das Land ohne Musik* and the English to concur in the libel.

But it is true that Handel, for all his acquired Englishness, began a tradition that persisted all through the reign of Queen Victoria and her consort – the tradition that England was musically barren ground which it was the duty of the Germans to fertilise. The Handel-type oratorio, discoursed by musical amateurs, became the basic fodder of musical Britain. Handel, without knowing it, served the Industrial Revolution. The underpaid workers were encouraged to forget their social wrongs by forming choirs and brass bands and singing *Messiah*.

Mendelssohn obligingly produced sacred oratorios in the manner of Handel, and so did every visiting foreign composer – Dvorak, Gounod, Liszt. British composers, almost until the outbreak of the First World War, could only make their name by setting mediocre sacred librettos with fugal tricks and massive choral effects. Handel, without intending to, did a lot of harm.

He had a long career, made money, lost money, knew his share of mental and physical suffering. Eventually, like Bach, he went blind. He had already composed *Samson*, an oratorio based on Milton's *Samson Agonistes*, and the aria 'Total Eclipse' brought tears to its auditors, who heard Handel's anguish in the blinded giant at the mill with slaves in Gaza. Handel shed no tears for his condition, and his native Lutheranism reconciled him to the abiding truth of human misery. He could be seen on his knees in St George's church in Hanover Square (the God of the Anglicans was probably also Luther's), making his peace, asking heaven for nothing. Heaven had already given him much, and hard work had given him more. When he died he was buried in Westminster Abbey, joining British artists who had helped to bring glory to a race not generally thought of as caring much for its artists. He is celebrated this year as a great cosmopolitan musician, but the British may be forgiven if they consider George Frideric Handel as their own property.

Corriere della Sera, 1985

1   Matthew Dubourg was an English violinist, conductor, and composer who began working with Handel in London in 1719. For many years, Dubourg was one of the leading musicians in Dublin, where, on 13 April 1742, he led the orchestra in the premiere of Handel's *Messiah*.

2   See *Byrne*, p. 19, and ACC, p. 383.

3   The dramas and architecture of Sir John Vanbrugh were considered radical for their time. His plays defended women's rights in marriage and were notable for their sexual explicitness.

4   From 1717-19, Handel was resident composer for James Brydges, the first Duke of Chandos, at Cannons, his grand country house in Little Stanmore, Middlesex.

5   In his 1920 essay 'Philip Massinger', published in *The Sacred Wood*, T.S. Eliot wrote: 'Immature poets imitate; mature poets steal; bad poets deface what they take, and good poets make it into something better, or at least something different.' A similar quote has been attributed to Igor Stravinsky: 'A good composer does not imitate; he steals.'

6   The music for the Green Park firework display is commonly known as *Music for the Royal Fireworks*, HWV 351.

7   Its run of 62 consecutive performances, which began on 29 January 1728, was the longest in British theatrical history to that time.

8   William Savage was an English composer, organist, and singer chiefly known for his association with Handel, whose oratorios he sang.

Handel and His World by H.C. Robbins Landon
London: Weidenfeld and Nicolson, 1984

Handel by Christopher Hogwood
London: Thames and Hudson, 1984

Handel: The Man and His Music by Jonathan Keates
London: Victor Gollancz, 1985

These three books, published to coincide with his tercentenary, concur in finding Handel the composer great and Handel the man formidable. The stories of his physical ebullience in the service of bad temper are well-known – the hurled kettledrums, holes kicked in double basses, castrati thrown out of windows. His capacity for food and drink was gargantuan, but we know little about his sexual appetites. He did not marry, yet no scandal – even in these detailed biographies – attaches to his amorous life. He had the integrity, candour, piety and corporeal bulk of Dr Johnson.

If Beethoven is generally accepted as first of the German composers, we ought to remember he granted the palm to Handel. And yet we regard Handel as very much our own, a pragmatic artist working in a medium that has never been much regarded by either the State or the Church, in a country that, though it became a province of Hanover, was without *Kapellmeisters* or paid court composers. Handel developed his genius in the hurly-burly of London theatre business, where one had to exert a powerful personality if one wished to prevail. I still find it hard to persuade Germans and Frenchmen that his name was Handel, not Haendel or Händel; concert posters in Europe insist on the heresy of the umlaut. But it was with an unmodified 'a' that he became a British citizen. His Germanicity is being stressed this year in Halle, where he was born – 23 February 1685 – and both sides of the wall are inevitably relating him to Bach, with whom he shares his tercentenary.

They never met: they kept missing each other. They both applied for the same job – successor to Buxtehude as organist of the Marienkirche at Lübeck – but both had the good taste to withdraw when marriage to the old sick fugalist's ugly middle-aged daughter was made one of the conditions of employment. For the rest they went their own ways. Bach worked in a closed world which did not have to admit artistic compromise; Handel accepted the need to yield to the conditions of a popular art. Handel's audience would, if he had stayed in Germany, have been a cultivated aristocratic one. In London he served chiefly the middle-class, whose limitations he was quick to learn. His audiences did not want mirror fugues or canons at the ninth; they wanted good tunes and solid four-square rhythms, with the complications of the Baroque reserved to vocal ornamentation and not the musical textures. They wanted showmanship and they got it. They also got melodic lines of immense beauty and subtlety, and orchestration of great illustrative power.

They also got, when Handel turned from Italian to English, unexampled skill in matching verbal and musical rhythm. Though it is said that Handel forgot most of his German without gaining a corresponding mastery of spoken English, no British-born composer has been more sensitive to English verse. In the setting of Milton's *L'Allegro*, he may be thought to go too far in having 'Laughter ho-ho-ho-ho-ho-ho-ho-holding both his sides', but he could never resist the broad effect. It was the show business element in him.

Samuel Butler, who wrote music in imitation of Handel, found in him a humane quality difficult to define: he understood people; even in that same *L'Allegro* he somehow expressed his affection for the ploughman and the shepherd and the English landscape that bred them. The humanity of his art, which is only organised sound, is a doubtful quality, but it may come out in a charitable understanding of what people can *accept* in music. *Messiah* is wholly acceptable in that a sacred theme is approached not with the postures of conventional piety or an assumption that God can best be praised in a state of discomfort. This divine music entertains. We go to the Bach *Passions* as to church, to *Messiah* as to the theatre. Some of the sacred oratorios home unerringly to the entertaining elements in their texts – the plague of frogs that oppresses the Egyptians, the arrival of the Queen of Sheba and the nightingales that put her to bed with Solomon.

H.C. Robbins Landon's book has admirable illustrations which show the turbulent world that Handel set out to conquer. The public was fickle, fashions changed. The passion for Italian opera gave way to the adoration of what John Gay did in his Newgate Pastoral.[1] *The Beggar's Opera* made more money for Dr Pepusch, with his not very brilliant harmonisations of popular tunes, than the wholly original Handel had ever earned. But Handel did not repine; he got into the act and worked with Gay giving the public what it wanted – though, like Shakespeare, he always gave it rather more than it wanted. With the form which he made very much his own, the sacred oratorio, he created a new taste which the following century so thoroughly assimilated that it became the sound of the Crystal Palace and the whole expansive industrial epoch. *Messiah* is the most British thing that we have, and it is still very much alive.

Christopher Hogwood's book is the work of a man who has conducted Handel and been especially acclaimed for his interpretations of *Messiah*. H.C. Robbins Landon is a Bostonian who professes music at Cardiff, strictly a rococo man (Haydn, Mozart). Jonathan Keates is a novelist who teaches English at the City of London School. It's good to see three different temperaments and specialisations coming together in homage to Handel. All the books are sharply particular, avoiding general laudations and looking at the scores as well as the fireworks. All of them teach us new things. I had not previously realised how the echo of the pipe-playing Abruzzesi Shepherds in the Piazza Navona at Christmas had got into the pastoral symphony of *Messiah*. All Handel's works were for occasions – not for the gratuitous giving out of his soul. We get the occasions. The books also join in being suffused with a deep affection for their subject. It would have been difficult for them to be otherwise.

The Observer, 1985

1   In a 1716 letter to Alexander Pope, Jonathan Swift proposed the idea of a stage work set in Newgate Prison, asking, 'What think you, of a Newgate pastoral among the thieves and whores there?' Their friend John Gay converted Swift's concept of a pastoral musical play into a satirical one called *The Beggar's Opera*.

Christoph Willibald Gluck died in 1787, but it's unlikely that this bicentennial will arouse the same enthusiasm as George Frederic Handel's three hundredth birthday did in 1985. Gluck was not the sort of composer whose life would make a thrilling film. He lacked the Falstaffian ebullience of Handel, the romantic disorder of Beethoven, and the enigmatic mixture of refinement and vulgarity that made up the character of Mozart. Nor is he known for much more than a couple of operas that do not draw the crowds as *Otello* and *Tosca* do. This year there will probably be a dutiful trotting out of *Iphigénie en Aulide* or *Orfeo* in the opera houses of the world, but there will be a sense of disappointment in audiences accustomed to the rhodomontade of Verdi or the lachrymosity of Puccini, to say nothing of the apocalyptical thunder of Wagner. Gluck always seems a little too bland. He lacks salt and pepper.

The truth is that without Gluck some of the developments of romantic opera would not have been possible. Opera, after all, should not be gymnastic vocal display from tenors and sopranos who have lost their figures and have never cared much about acting. Opera should be the apotheosis of drama, like *Wozzeck* or *Lulu*. We should feel that we are watching comedy or tragedy tuned to the highest possible pitch, in which music is the servant of human conflict and reconciliation. Before Gluck's time it had not been like that. Opera-lovers were lovers of the human voice, especially if the range was phenomenal and castrati could purvey a perverse thrill with incredible *roulades* and stratospheric tremolos.

The fact that Gluck, by the standards of Mozart and Wagner, was not much of a musician was something of an advantage to his concept of opera. He felt no compunction to show off musically. He had a fine melodic gift, but his orchestration was thin, his bottom lines were unadventurous, and he had no great gift for counterpoint. When he came to London the great Handel said: 'Gluck know as much contrapunto as my coke.' That last word may mean 'cook' or something more vulgar. Gluck could not, like Bach or Handel, dash off a convincing fugue. There was a certain meagreness about his music. He entertained Londoners by playing on the musical glasses (glasses filled with variable amounts of water and struck with a little hammer), and that was rather different from Handel thundering away on the full organ.

We cannot explain the thin musical endowment by referring to the thinness of his musical education. His father Alexander, who became head forester to the Duchess of Tuscany in Reichstadt (now Liperec) in northern Bohemia, tried, like many fathers of musical geniuses, to suppress his son's talent, probably revealed after a few local lessons in violin and perhaps cello. The boy ran away from home at the age of thirteen and tried to earn his living by playing on one instrument or the other. In Prague, where he had the chance of a formal musical education, he preferred to teach himself the elements of composition and to learn about opera by going to it. He escaped the domination of German style by listening to Vivaldi, Albinoni, Lolli and Porta, whose works filled the Prague Opera House. He went, inevitably, to Vienna, only apparently to come under the influence of another Italian, Sammartini. It was not till he was twenty-seven that, in Milan, he composed his first opera, *Artaserse*, with a libretto by Metastasio.

Metastasio was the poet of the imperial court, and he wrote innumerable libretti, not many of which have survived. But he part-fathered over eight hundred operas in the sense that his libretti were used again and again by a variety of composers. This situation implies a kind of homogeneity in the opera world, a lack of powerful individuality on the musical side. We cannot imagine Verdi being satisfied with a second-hand libretto or, for that matter, one not tailored exactly to his musical style. Metastasio, who considered himself a great man, regarded the musical settings of his stiff and heroic dramas as a mere tribute to the action or inaction. He was closer to Gluck in this than Gluck himself perhaps realised. But if, in the mature Gluck, the drama came first, it was through a fusion of music and words and not the predominance of the latter.

The eighteenth century was a great period of travel for musicians who had not secured sinecures in princely or archiepiscopal courts. Gluck went to London, where Handel, despite the gibe about his lack of contrapunto, gave him professional support. Gluck even put on an opera before the Duke of Cumberland. *La caduta de' giganti* was a political opera in that it was a vocal compliment to the Duke's massacre of the Jacobite Scots at Culloden in 1745. Then Gluck travelled the German princedoms until, nearly forty, having caught gonorrhea but still made a prosperous marriage, he settled in Vienna. It was there that he wrote *Orfeo ed Euridice*, to a text not by Metastasio but by Calzabigi. Paris and Vienna became the twin foci of his mature experiments in opera. He wanted to outlaw the baroque, though the baroque was partly in his nature and had been exemplified in most of his operas, few of which we now hear. The baroque was display and decoration. The new, reformed, opera was action, drama, psychology, character.

If we listen carefully to *Orfeo* we will hear how Gluck made a virtue out of the simplicity imposed on his music by his comparative lack of skill. He exploited his weaknesses. Music did not get in the way of the direct impact of the drama. With Gluck we begin to see that librettos will in future have to be written for one composer only and that the wholesaling of a poet like Metastasio belongs to the utilitarian past, the age of purely decorative music. Gluck's musical slenderness is really an athletic property: it goes along with a forceful energy; at the same time, as we know from the Dance of the Blessed Spirits in *Orfeo*, it is not incompatible with an almost heavenly serenity. Compare the vision of Hades and the vision of Elysium, put side by side in Act Two of *Orfeo*, and the breadth of Gluck's genius cannot be in doubt.

In the melodic field, perhaps only Mozart and Handel share with Gluck the ability to convey an almost unbearable emotional poignancy in a major key with the simplest of harmonies. This can be heard in Orfeo's aria 'Che faro senza Euridice', which is one of the universally known and loved melodies, and in 'O malheureuse Iphigénie', sung by the heroine of the opera named for her. He is not afraid of invoking the antique – as in the instrumentation of *Orfeo* – and this produces a mythical remoteness which does not war with the emotional immediacy. The opening storm scene of *Iphigénie* shows how he could attack the audience with a pictorial directness which, without doubt, Wagner was to recall in the opening of *Die Walküre*. Wagner learned a good deal from Gluck.

So did Mozart, who attended all the rehearsals of the Vienna production of *Iphigénie*. The ballet music in Gluck's *Don Juan* left its mark on *Don Giovanni*, and so perhaps did Gluck's trombones. The March of the Priests in *The Magic Flute* is surprisingly similar to the chorus 'Chaste fille de Latone' in *Iphigénie*. As opera-goers know Mozart better than Gluck, these debts tend to be missed.

But it was the two great figures of early romantic opera, Berlioz and Wagner, who acknowledged the greatest debt to the forester's son from Reichstadt. *Les Troyens*, long neglected, especially by the Paris for which it was written, is at last being accepted as Berlioz's masterpiece. Gluck taught Berlioz how to deal with myth, how to reconcile the sense of classical remoteness with the immediacy of human passion. He even influenced the orchestration of that prince of orchestrators – the menace of a horn call, choral unisons against seething textures of instrumental sound. Wagner owed to Gluck the concept of continuous musical action, driving out the convention of opera as a set of separate arias and ensembles divided by dry recitative.

The question is always arising, even now: which is the important part of opera – the words or the music? Should the composer bow to the drama or accept a formal scheme of musical numbers? Richard Strauss's opera *Capriccio*, set in the time of Gluck, is one of the magisterial examinations of the problem. It may be said that the problem was solved for the first time by Gluck, in whom the claims of drama and music are exactly balanced, and there is an artistic compromise wholly satisfying to the aesthetic sense. It is the beauty and skill of the Gluckian solution which makes him an important figure in the world's music and, in this bicentennial year of Gluck's death, compels our homage.

written, 1987; published in *One Man's Chorus*, 1998

Mozart in Vienna 1781–1791 by Volkmar Braunbehrens
London: André Deutsch, 1990

Dr Braunbehrens gives us only one scrap of Mozart in music type – the main theme of the slow movement of the *Coronation* Concerto (K. 537). He puts this in his preface, an attempt at hiding it from the general reader. The extract has an empty bass stave. Mozart improvised his accompaniment to the melody but never wrote it down. Some hack filled in the left-hand line for the publication of the score in 1794, and this ever since has been taken as authentic Mozart. Depart from it, and the critics will curse you. This illustrates Dr Braunbehrens's general contention that we do not know as much as we think about the later Mozart, and that we are too often rebuked for replacing a legend with a documented truth or, just as frequently, with a total blank.

He calls the unauthentic or legendary Mozart by his supposed middle name, Amadeus, which Mozart never used. He translated the baptismal Theophilus as Amadé or Amadeo, and the Latinisation, like the left hand of K. 537, has been left to others. Shaffer's play and Forman's film *Amadeus* proclaim falsehood in the very title. Salieri did not poison Mozart (Braunbehrens has written the biography of that amiable not quite second-rater); Mozart was not given a pauper's funeral; nor, in his brief life, did he giggle and play silly games. Billiards, yes, but studying the roll of the ball was part of the creative process that went on and on, making Mozart polite but always a little *distrait*. The young man presented here is civilised enough to be welcome at court, highly intelligent, not good at money matters (he spent what he earned, which was considerable). His professionalism is never in doubt, nor is his integrity as a husband and a father.

Mozart fathered so much music that we tend to ignore his more palpable children. He had six of these. Raimund, Johann Thomas Leopold, Theresa Costanza and Anna Maria hardly survived birth, but Karl Thomas died at seventy-four after a career as a tax official, and Franz Xaver Wolfgang, who considered himself a failed musician, passed away at fifty-three. A two in six survival rate was average for the time. Constanze, Mozart's wife, ill for a good deal of her life, nevertheless lived until she was eighty. She and her two sons were crucial agents in the transmission of the truth about the great man, as well as the preservation of his works. Biographers have been catty about Constanze, even dragging her into the poisoning legend, but she seems to have been a loyal wife and widow, musical enough to understand her innovative and sometimes difficult husband. Mozart was uxorious. All this makes sad reading for those who like their geniuses to live scandalous lives.

Mozart, as the ten-year output shows, had little time for iniquity or even honourable liaisons of the Beethovenian kind. He was a hard-working freelance. Leaving the employ of Count Hieronymus Colloredo, the archbishop of Salzburg, he set up shop as composer, performer, teacher. There are romantic elements in his music, but his approach to the art was closer to Hindemith than to the lover of the Constant Nymph.[1] Music was for use; nothing was produced except on commission or for his own needs as a professional. To suggest that he lived in a state of chronic inspiration would be to go too far. The work was done, and if inspiration added gratuitous grace, so much the better.

He did right to leave dull Salzburg for ebullient Vienna. Dr Braunbehrens does right to avoid the excessive close-ups of the hagiographer and to let his camera roam over the elegant dirty city. Thus, we may glimpse Mozart on horseback or, on an evening when there was no paid music to be made, walking to his masonic lodge. Freemasonry stood for intellectual enlightenment. When we hear clarinets in E flat, Mozart is uttering masonic music. A foolish theory once had it that he was murdered by a member of his lodge for divulging masonic secrets in *The Magic Flute*. This may be taken as a masonic allegory, but the mysteries of that work are surely generic, not sectarian.

Another allegation holds that Mozart's operas were not popular, and that *Le Nozze di Figaro* was condemned by the Emperor as a work of wanton subversion. Not so. And if some affirmed that Salieri was the greater composer of operas, this was because Salieri wrote hardly anything else and Mozart's skill in other genres, as well as in keyboard virtuosity, was considered distinction enough for one young musician without bringing *Don Giovanni* in as well. Nor will the view that Mozart's music was excessively difficult to understand hold water. The story of a steady decline in popularity ending in poverty is another myth to be exploded. *The Magic Flute* was playing to full houses while he lay on his deathbed. He was never in Elgar's position. Indeed, Mozart has never experienced a decline in reputation. With the arrival of Beethoven, music began to admit extraneous elements, such as the composer's ego. Mozart is of the Age of Enlightenment, when the symphony confirmed the social stability of a great empire.

The last days of Mozart will, to many readers, be more compelling reading than the relentless chronicle of work done. There is no mystery about the commission of the Requiem: this was not a dark emissary from the underworld but a certain Count Waisegg who sent a certain Puchberg to ask Mozart's price for defunctive music for the prematurely dead Countess.[2] The work was unfinished by the master, who went down with a kind of rheumatism ('It began with swelling in his hands and feet, which he was soon unable to move', reports Georg Nikolaus von Nissen, who got the details from Constanze). In fifteen days he was dead. The poison theory was sheer gossip which poor Salieri solidified into false history by denying it when near death himself. Mozart was, as Keats was to be, over-bled by his physician. His loss of two litres of blood exacerbated his debility. The death certificate nowadays would say something about cardiac arrest consequent on rheumatic fever.

The strange-seeming facts about Mozart's burial have to be referred to the funerary ordinances brought in by the Emperor Joseph II. Funerals were costing too much. Constanze would have had to spend half a year's imperial salary on a mass, candles, knells, an escutcheon, an oration, and three lay brothers (though these cost only a florin each). There was a cult of common graves and reusable coffins – all in the service of hygiene and economy. Mozart's body was probably thrust into a pit holding from four to six corpses – no degradation, mere custom. The gothic myth of the sudden bad weather which sent the mourners scurrying is not borne out by the meteorological records. If they did not accompany the hearse as far as the grave, this too followed custom. That grave has been sedulously sought, but it will never be found. Braunbehrens is not sorry, since there was too much ghoulish interest at the time in the recovery of outstanding skulls. Goethe retrieved Schiller's skull from the charnel house in Weimar and kept it at home. Haydn's skull was wrenched from his grave in the very year he died (1809). Mozart was spared this indignity.

Next year we celebrate the bicentennial. This useful book gets in early. I was, incidentally, asked to write a brief opera in rococo style with Mozart as the leading character. This cannot be done. He did nothing but write music.

The Independent, 1990

1 the character Lewis Dodd in Margaret Kennedy's novel *The Constant Nymph*. Cf. Chapter 1 *The Writer and Music*, note 2.

2 an allusion to Ravel's *Pavane pour une infante défunte* (Pavane for a dead princess).

Beethoven by Maynard Solomon
London: Cassell, 1978

Musical composition, more than any other creative activity, shows how far the imagination can function independently of the rest of the human complex. A writer's arthritis or homosexuality or sweet tooth will often come through in a spring sonnet. An armless sculptor cannot sculpt well, no matter how prehensile his toes. A blind painter cannot paint at all. Frederick Delius, blind and paralysed, produced fine music. Beethoven, deaf, cirrhotic, diarrhetic, dyspnoeal, manic, produced the finest, and healthiest, music of all time. This is not, of course, to say that the composer's art operates totally in its own autonomous world. Delius found it necessary to tell his amanuensis, Eric Fenby, that those long-held D-major string chords had something to do with the sea and sky and the wind arabesques could be seagulls. Gustav Mahler put trivial hurdy-gurdy tunes in his symphonies until Freud, between trains, told him why. Although Beethoven's music is about sounds and structures, it is also, in ways not easily demonstrable, about Kant and the tyrant at Schönbrunn[1] and Beethoven himself, body soul and blood and ouns.[2] To read Beethoven's biography is to learn something about what his music is trying to do. Not much, but something.

Maynard Solomon's book is the latest in a long line dedicated to telling the truth about Beethoven as Schindler would not see it and as Thayer, who had to rely heavily on Schindler, was not able to see it. It was only in 1977, at the Berlin Beethovenkongress, that Herre and Beck proved that Schindler had fabricated more than 150 of his own entries in the Conversation Books. Moreover, the hagiographical tendency of many biographies got in the way of presenting the squalor, the clownishness, the downright malice, the drinking and drabbing. It was not right for the composer of the Ninth Symphony and the last quartets to vomit crapulously and frequent brothels. Solomon has no desire to 'fashion an uncontradictory and consistent portrait of Beethoven – to construct a safe, clear, well-ordered design; for such a portrait can be purchased only at the price of truth, by avoiding the obscurities that riddle the documentary material.' At the same time he is prepared to call on Freud and, more, Otto Rank to elucidate the obscurities.

Beethoven was named for his grandfather, a Kapellmeister at the electoral court of Cologne, and identified with him, going so far as to wish to deny the paternity of Johann Beethoven and to acquiesce in the legend that he was the illegitimate son of a king of Prussia – either Friedrich Wilhelm II or Frederick the Great himself. He denied his birth year of 1770, despite all the documentary evidence, alleging and eventually believing that he had been born in 1772. His contempt for the drunken, feebly tyrannical, not too talented court tenor who was his father seems not to have been matched by a compensatory devotion to his mother: after all, he was prepared to put it about that she had been a court whore. Beethoven wanted a kind of parthenogenetical birth proper for the messianic role he envisaged for himself.[3] He would willingly turn a woman into a mother if she was too young for the part. That he regarded mothers as supererogatory is proved by his turning himself into the father of his nephew Karl, execrating his sister-in-law as the 'Queen of the Night', pretending that the Dutch *van* of his name was really *von* so that he could use aristocratic clout in the courts to dispossess the poor woman of her maternal rights.

He broke free of Viennese musical conventions to assert a new masculine force, appropriate to the Napoleonic age, which should be characterized by rigour of tonal argument and a kind of genial brutality. The legend about his dedicating his Third Symphony to Bonaparte and then tearing up the dedication page after the assassination of the Duc d'Enghien is still to be accepted as true, but Solomon makes it clear that Beethoven was strongly drawn to the tyrant. Vienna's musical talent assembled at Schönbrunn to welcome the conqueror, but Beethoven alone was not invited. He resented this. He arranged a performance of the *Eroica*, expecting Napoleon to turn up. Napoleon did not turn up. Beethoven was not altogether the fierce republican, the romantic artist shaking his fist at despots. He owed much to his aristocratic patrons; he dreamed of receiving honours at the Tuileries. He had his eye to the main chance. He liked money. He was ready to sell the same piece of music to three different publishers at the same time and pocket three different advances.

He also had his ear, even when it was a deaf one, to the exterior world of sonic innovations. When Schoenberg was told that six fingers were required to play his Violin Concerto, he replied: 'I can wait.' Beethoven did not want six fingers, but he did want a pianoforte – once called by him, in a gust of patriotism, a *Hammerklavier* – that could, there and then, crash out his post-rococo imaginings. The fourth horn part of the Ninth Symphony was specially written for one of the new valve instruments: Beethoven knew a man near Vienna who possessed one. He was a great pianist and a very practical musician. His orchestral parts were hard to play but not impossible. Impossibility hovers, like a fermata, above the soprano parts in the Ninth, but sopranos were women, mothers, sisters-in-law.

It is only through the vague operation of analogy that we can find in a symphony like the *Eroica* – a key work, the work that the composer believed to be his highest orchestral achievement – the properties of the Kantian philosophy and the novels of Stendhal. This music was necessary to the age, but not because of its literary programme. One attaches literary programmes at one's peril to Beethoven's work, even when he says of the yellowhammer call of the Fifth: 'Thus Fate knocks at the door.' Give Beethoven a text and he does more than merely set it. *Fidelio* is a free-from-chains manifesto typical of its time (though more in Paris than in Vienna), but it is also vegetation myth, with Florestan as a flower god, woman most loved when the female lion becomes the faithful boy, mother into son, the composer himself incarcerated in his deafness. It is, as well, much more, and the much more is not easily explicated. The music works at a very deep psychic level, subliterary, submythical, multiguous.[4] When Donald Tovey said that the *Leonora* No. 3 rendered the first act superfluous, he spoke no more than the truth. With the American Solomon's excellent book (though not as excellent as our own Martin Cooper's) we know a little more about the man but nothing more about the mystery of his art. That was to be expected.

The Observer, 1978

1   Napoleon Bonaparte. On 13 October 1809, a seventeen-year-old German named Friedrich Staps sought an audience with Napoleon at Schönbrunn in order to assassinate him. Apprehended by an aide to the self-declared emperor, Staps was given the opportunity to speak with Napoleon, who questioned him personally about his intentions and offered him clemency for the intended crime. Staps refused the pardon and was executed by a firing squad on 17 October 1809. His last words were, 'Liberty forever! Germany forever! Death to the tyrant!'

2   a reference to *Ulysses*, where, on the first page of the novel, Buck Mulligan says 'For this, O dearly beloved, is the genuine Christine: body and soul and blood and ouns' during his blasphemous parody of the Roman Catholic mass. The phrase 'blood and ouns' was a rude medieval epithet for Christ's blood and wounds.

3   parthenogenesis: reproduction from an ovum without fertilization. The usual adjectival form is parthenogenetic.

4   multiguous: having two or more meanings

The Nine Symphonies of Beethoven by Antony Hopkins
London: Heinemann / Seattle: University of Washington
Press, 1981

Having dealt with No. 8 in F major, before engaging the
heavy work of analysing No. 9 in D minor, Antony Hopkins,
perhaps needlessly but certainly with a decent sense of
proprieties, justifies or excuses what he feels may be regarded
as 'a somewhat frivolous approach to what is unquestionably
a masterpiece'.[1] He means this sort of thing: '…the strings
buzzing anxiously as the woodwind search for a triad that
refuses to materialise. (How can it when they are coupled in
pairs? Triads need – "lesh think… *three* notes").'[2] The slanginess
perhaps encourages the slackness of 'coupled in pairs', as if
things could be coupled any other way. I have to regret these
occasions on which Mr Hopkins lets himself down. They do
not come often but they are shocking when they do come.
Discussing the opening bars of the last movement of the
Eroica, he says that they are an impressive-sounding hoax,
'roughly comparable to the late and lovable Tony Hancock
giving us a few lines of *King Lear* by way of a warm-up.
"This should impress the natives," Beethoven seems to say as
he lets loose a torrent of semiquavers in the strings.'[3] That is
unworthy because it drags a great universal artistic experience
into a region of insular cosiness. Who in Seattle knows who
Tony Hancock was?[4]

And yet I cannot but approve of the anthropomorphic
approach, which was Sir George Grove's and also Sir Donald
Tovey's. But Tovey would quote a few bars of Bruckner and say
'Here is Sir Charles Grandison's drawing room'.[5] This is a cut
above Hopkins's 'Did you say "KNOCK-KNOCK-KNOCK?"

ask the strings incredulously. "YES WE DID!" reply the other instruments. *Strings:* "Oh..." *(quietly). Wind and brass:* "Hum..." *(pensive).*[6] In fact this imagined colloquy does suggest what is happening in the orchestra, but only on a surface which robs the exegesis of dignity. But Hopkins's search for comedy is incessant, except when 'The tempo changes to *Poco Andante* and a divinely beautiful variation ensues'.[7] The finale of the *Eroica* may be both comic and divinely beautiful, but it is much more besides. If it is about anything it is about Prometheus, a fact which Beethoven spells out by blatantly borrowing from his own *Prometheus* ballet music. The humour is heroic, suitable for a relaxed conqueror, but not one who is playing postman's knock.[8]

The problem of how to write about music is still with us, and, as Hopkins says:

> It seems to me that there are two approaches to analysis; one is to apply the chilling hand of the anatomist, applying the correct labels according to musical terminology – 'here the subject is inverted in augmentation over a pedal-point on the mediant' etc.; the other is to describe what happens in less abstruse terms – 'the string chords increase in intensity as horns and trumpets pound out the all-pervasive rhythm'. I detest the first method and avoid it insofar as I can; inevitably I am often guilty of the second. However, both are merely descriptions of events and as such do not necessarily interpret what is happening.[9]

Yet, saying that, he does not at all allude to a method genuinely opposed to the technical one. An orchestral score might well carry indications like *intensificandosi* and *martellando* (hammer or pound out). It seems as if for the moment he is ashamed of stating what the true alternative is. It is, of course: 'The bassoons hiccup drunkenly and the first violins utter a prim protest, while the muted violas, less exhibitionistically, croon what sounds suspiciously like a version of "Show Me the Way to Go Home".'

Hopkins is a composer himself, and he knows that long work on a full score generates an anthropomorphic approach to the various instrumental groups. I do not mean that the composer visualizes violinists and oboists; I mean that, in Disney fashion, he endows the instruments themselves as tonal entities with a kind of thwarted free will. The trombones cut into a flute solo, and it seems rude and angry though (since they are totally under the composer's control) only factitiously. The trumpets have been quiet for a long time: time they said something. Before long the score becomes a kind of cartoon zoomorphic drama. But this drama is parallel to the true drama of the music. It is this surface cartoon which too often takes over in detailed musical analysis – and not only in Mr Hopkins's painstaking, generally enjoyable and often enlightening commentaries. There is in many professional musicians, however, an unfortunate tendency to the schoolmasterish or choirmasterly. I remember the *Musical Times* of the 1930s and its references to the 'bonny stroke' of Handel's 'Laughter ho-ho-ho-ho-ho-holding both his sides' and 'spunky tunes' in Haydn's finales. Worst of all, I remember the late Dr Herbert Howells rebuking me for not at once spotting that a particular chord was the Neapolitan Sixth.[10] 'Come, come, don't you eat ice cream?' I was at the time mature and even bearded. I swore something and knew I had failed.[11]

Mr Hopkins is at his most valuable when he is, forgetting for the moment to be colloquial and breezy, absorbed in technicalities. The First Symphony in C major begins, as all the world knows, with a dominant seventh on C. Traditionally the opening bars of an opening allegro should state the key of the whole work vigorously and unequivocally, and here is

Beethoven suggesting that his symphony is really in F, not C. This has been taken as an example of Ludwig van's spunky quirkiness or perverseness. Hopkins shows that the whole first movement is based on chains of dominant seventh-tonic assertions of keys that are not C, and that the opening surprise is an announcement of intention. Similarly he takes the C sharp in the first movement of the *Eroica* – a surprising shift on the part of an E flat bugle call – and relates it to the D flat section of the coda, asking us, without facetiousness, to marvel at an enharmonic mystery. It is precisely when he is dealing in augmentations on mediant pedals that he is at his most brilliant and instructive.

He cites Beethoven's notebooks and shows how initial banalities are transformed, by hard work as much as magic, into pregnant themes. He has a very sharp eye and ear for odd three-note wisps of accompaniment (as in the finale of the Fifth) which are turned into bursts of lyricism or energy. The other side of him, the desire to communicate in human terms, blends admirably with the technical anatomist when he comes to the Pastoral. Here he has Beethoven's own imprimatur to find the rustic *cornamusa* or *ciaramella* in the first bars and to suggest that themes burgeon like leaves in what follows; to invoke Beethoven's own interest in the tonalities of streams and rivers and justify the muddiness of the bass chords at the opening of the second movement; to impose chronological time on musical duration and suggest that the storm takes place at night and the shepherd's song is heard on Sunday morning.[12]

As a composer and conductor Hopkins is aware both of Beethoven's occasional miscalculations (second violins unsupported and inaudible) and the difference in numbers and balance between his orchestra and ours. Beethoven's apparent ineptness – or misogynistic cruelty – in giving his sopranos long high-held As is excused by reference to the semitone difference between his A and ours. Sing the killing A in the Ninth Symphony as A flat (though only experimentally, not, God help us, in the concert hall) and it becomes easy enough. Hopkins is full of practical knowledge. The three horns still approach the trio of the Scherzo of the *Eroica* with some trepidation: at least the first horn, who has to play an uncovered high E flat, is not happy about it. Hopkins's triumph is, like Beethoven's, the long and intricate Ninth. His references to the Choral Fantasia, in which the piano tries out instrumental recitative in preparation for the speaking basses of the last movement of the Ninth, are relevant and helpful. His last words combine tellingly the coolness of the analyst and the elation of the mere listener:

> Immense descending scales in the strings seem to draw curtains over the biggest stage in the world, the sopranos climb to a top A for the last time, the orchestra scampers to a finish, proclaiming the glory of D major to the last. It is the tonal goal of the entire symphony from the first groping elusive dominant to the ultimate triumphant affirmation of the joyous tonic.[13]

All that we need after this is an extract from Grillparzer's funeral oration: 'The last Master of resounding song, the sweet lips that gave expression to the art of tones', etc etc.[14] Hopkins celebrates the living artist in a way that that artist, once he had had Tony Hancock and football choral singing explained to him, would probably have approved. This is a book of very considerable value. If it does not obviate our need to read Tovey, it renders Grove's treatise unnecessary. It contains Grove's spirit but much much more.

Times Literary Supplement, 1981

1   Hopkins, p. 241

2   Ibid., p. 240

3   Ibid., p. 92

4   Seattle is the location of the University of Washington Press, Hopkins's publisher. The English comedian and actor Tony Hancock was best known for his BBC series *Hancock's Half Hour* (1954-61).

5   In Samuel Richardson's 1753 epistolary novel *The History of Sir Charles Grandison*, the protagonist is a staid character who consistently behaves in a moral and socially acceptable manner.

6   Hopkins, p. 92

7   Ibid., p. 98

8   Also known as 'post office', postman's knock is a kissing party game usually played by teenagers.

9   Hopkins, p. 241

10 In a Letter to the Editor published in the *TLS* on 15 May 1981 (p. 545), David Willcocks of the Royal College of Music points out that 'In the course of his review, Mr Burgess refers to the 'late Dr Herbert Howells'. Dr Howells is still very much alive, though as he is in his eighty-ninth year he is very much less in the public eye than he was.' Herbert Howells, who was born in 1892, died in 1983 at the age of ninety.

11 See LW, p. 350.

12 The Italian word *cornamusa* means bagpipes, while *ciaramella* is a double-reed instrument, descended from the Medieval shawm and related to the piffero, belonging to the oboe family.

13 Hopkins, p. 285

14 Loc. cit.

Beethoven and the Voice of God by Wilfred Mellers
London: Faber, 1983

Ten years ago Professor Mellers published *Twilight of the Gods: The Beatles in Retrospect*. Two years ago came his *Bach and the Dance of God*. Now Beethoven is in on the theodicean act.[1] But, of course, he always was. It has never been enough for Beethoven to have spun notes for money and diversion: he has always purveyed the struggle of the soul in the direction of the divine vision. The latter term has to be used in a Pickwickian sense, since the Nazis, who had a better claim on Beethoven than the Christian democracies, presumably found in him a spiritual uplift appropriate to the Final Solution. We know what God does *not* mean to Professor Mellers. He says: 'I am not and never have been a Christian, and... I subscribe to no creed religious or political.'[2] The God he finds in Beethoven is an eclectic entity – illuminist, Blakean, masonic – but, since music cannot propose anything except self-referring structures, he has to be concerned with exalted motions of the mind induced by music. The Mover has to be outside his scope, but, through the free use of metaphor and a wide range of literary and theological citations, he persuades himself that a kind of ultimate reality shines through.

Anybody who loves music has to be worried about the romantic assumption that it contains meanings expressible in words. When Professor Mellers deals, as he does brilliantly, with the *Missa Solemnis,* he is on safe verbal ground. Beethoven is setting the words of the Latin mass and is clearly searching for musical patterns which are metaphors of those words. He is also a good freemason like Mozart, making use of symbols associated with the rituals of the craft – like the three opening 'knocks' – and sonorities (clarinets, bassoons, strings of major thirds) associated with freemasonry. There is even a masonic key – E flat. It requires, of course, an extreme eclecticism to reconcile Catholicism with freemasonry, since the Church has traditionally condemned secret societies, but music can effect the reconciliation because its meanings are not explicit.

Where there *are* meanings in the music itself, as opposed to the words set, these, surely, are imposed rather than immanent. 'The "goal" of the Mass, tonally, is G major, which for Beethoven as for Bach is the key of blessedness,' says Mellers. Again, 'B minor, for Beethoven as for Bach, is a key of suffering, whereby a synthesis between God's D major and Man's B flat major occurs and, "for the time being," finds haven in G major's benediction.'[3] I find this very hard to take.

The musical journalist Hans Keller said on the occasion of the 150th anniversary of Beethoven's death that Ludwig van was conceivably the greatest thinker of the nineteenth century.[4] He did not mean by this that Beethoven, in his spare time, worked out a coherent philosophy that makes Kant and Hegel look like schoolboys: he meant, I think, that Beethoven's musical structures exhibit an intellectual strength analogous to that of the inspired metaphysician. If I say that this sounds to me very much like nonsense, I shall have to submit to a Kellerian knock-down argument of coarse abuse.[5] It seems to me that the task of musicologists is to exhibit and explain musical patterns and not to confuse the analogy with the identification. Mellers does not try to turn Beethoven into a metaphysician, but he does try to exhibit him as a mystic. Let us see what he does with the great piano sonata in C minor and major, Op. 111.

After an admirable technical description of what happens in the opening bars of the Arietta, we get this:

'Garlic and sapphires in the mud/Clot the bedded axletree': but only momentarily, since parallel thirds and sixths, thrusting up in this fastest version of the boogie rhythm, end the variation at the apex of the Arietta's ecstasis. A corporeal music has transcended time and the body.[6]

Later, true to the spirit of 'Little Gidding', we have: 'After a baptism in the waters, a scorching in the pentecostal fire, and a *conjunctio oppositorum* of earth and air.'[7] The sustaining pedal is down, and we hear the blur of bells. If we have at all been seduced by Mellers's combination of exact technical analysis and mystical exegesis, we can break free from him when he quotes Herbert Whone's *The Hidden Face of Music* with approval: "'If [a man] is able to resonate himself he becomes a thing of beauty, as we find indicated in the French *belle*... There is worldly strife (which we see reflected in the dialectic of the Latin words *bella* and *bellum*, beautiful and war)... The bell begins to ring for joy when a man finds his own way back to pure being!'"[8] Add to this a fancied derivation of *bell* (cognate with *bellow*) from Hebrew B and el, signifying the Being of God, and you will understand why so much musicology has a bad name.

I would never go so far as to assert that music has no relevance to human experience and that it is no more than a string of tensions and releases, some stronger than others, but I would suggest that it is ultimately undescribable except in terms of its physical content. The oboes and bassoons play a semibreve F major chord and the strings, *ppp*, rush up and down in staccato semiquavers. There's nothing wrong with that. When the chord becomes an expression of ecstasy and the semiquavers are the impotent assault of minor devils on Mansoul, then I get worried.[9] I should imagine that the tensions and releases of Beethoven have as much to do with visceral problems as with the fight towards the ecstatic vision.

We do not know what music 'means', but there is no harm in looking for tentative literary analogues if these assist appreciation of the sheer sounds. To approach Beethoven with the aid of Martin Buber, Descartes, Meister Eckhart and Nietzsche seems to me to be a presumptuous stepping outside of the musicologist's province. On the other hand, Professor Mellers's purely musical analyses of some of the Beethoven sonatas are perfection, and I recommend his book for those alone. His title, however, is clearly blasphemous.

The Observer, 1983

1   theodicy: the perception of divine attributes in the acts of humans in a way meant to 'justify the ways of God to men'. Having previously viewed the Beatles and Bach through this lens, Mellers focuses here on Beethoven.
2   Mellers, p. viii.
3   Ibid., p. 361.
4   In HQY (p. 544), the line is changed to, '...Hans Keller, one of whose modes of musicological argument is dyspeptic bad temper, said,...'
5   Their mutual animosity arose in the 1960s, when Keller's advocacy of pop music's artistic worth incurred Burgess's wrath, and escalated in 1982 with the publication of Burgess's essay 'The day the music died' in *The Times*, the premiere of *Blooms of Dublin*, and Keller's reaction to both. See Chapters 11 *The Ruination of Music* and 49 *Blooms of Dublin*.
6   Mellers, p. 261. The quotation begins with the first two lines of Part II of 'Burnt Norton', the first of Eliot's *Four Quartets*. During the course of Mellers's 34-page discussion of Op. 111 (Ch. 4, 'The Water and the Fire', pp. 240-73), he refers, in addition to Eliot, to Blake, Shakespeare, Thomas Taylor, Donald Francis

Tovey, Fritz Rothschild, the Book of Common Prayer, Herbert Whone, Lao-Tse, St John Chrysostom, Tertullian, Thomas Mann, Plutarch, Dante, Schindler, and Meister Eckhart.

7   Ibid., p. 264. 'Little Gidding', the last of the *Four Quartets*, addresses the theme of spiritual renewal through the combined image of fire and Pentecostal fire for the purpose of purification and purgation.

8   Ibid., p. 265.

9   A reference to John Bunyan's 1682 novel *The Holy War Made by King Shaddai Upon Diabolus, to Regain the Metropolis of the World, Or, The Losing and Taking Again of the Town of Mansoul.*

26. THE NINTH

Symphonic composers after Beethoven have been, for the most part, scared of writing a tenth symphony or anything numerically beyond that. Shostakovich in the Soviet Union and Havergal Brian in England have, it is true, taken their symphonies into the teens, but there's a sense that what Shostakovich calls symphonies are often – especially with the later, choral, ones – only that in a Pickwickian sense. They might as well be called symphonies since they're neither symphonic poems nor concertos. Havergal Brian, our prize neglected symphonist, went on composing beyond the Beethovenian limit with little hope of ever being performed. He was not, as it were, challenging the master in the concert hall. Gustav Mahler wrote a Number Nine in D – major, not Beethoven's minor – and his Number Ten was finished by Mazzetti, so that Mahler could not be posthumously accused of outnumbering Beethoven.[1] Ralph Vaughan Williams's Number Nine is a kind of divertimento, a game with strange instruments, a sort of self-mockery at numerical effrontery.[2] Of course, we've all heard a mock-up of what might have been Beethoven's Tenth, but we accept the Ninth as representing the consummation of symphonic form. There's a holy number there. Indeed it may be said that there's only one Ninth.

We tend to bow deep down before the work as the final testimony of what can be done with sonata form on a large scale. Brahms, Beethoven's true successor, didn't advance the form much, except in his Fourth, where the scherzo is a full-length symphonic movement and not a mere glorification of the dance, and the finale is a passacaglia, taking us back to Bach. Sibelius was to develop the symphony by way of compression rather than expansion, and his Seventh amounts to a symphonic poem without a programme. Elgar expanded enormously, expressed the spirit of an age which did not understand where it was going, and the formal element is less important than the implied programme. Ernest Newman had no doubt that Elgar's two symphonies were symphonic poems. In a word, Beethoven sowed no seeds, any more than James Joyce did in the novel. His innovations were there for his own use. He could learn from Haydn but nobody could properly learn from him.

We bow down to the work, I say, but we do not have to consider it the best of Beethoven's symphonies. Beethoven himself had no doubt that the *Eroica* was his finest orchestral exercise in sonata form. It is not, like the Ninth, a hybrid. To finish a symphony with a choral setting of an ode by Schiller is, despite the ingenuity with which the passage is made from the orchestral to the vocal, a kind of irrelevance. We don't feel that the sung finale follows naturally on from what has gone before. We may even have our doubts about the literary element that creeps into the *Eroica* in the scherzo and the finale. The finale is a set of variations, just like the finale of the Ninth, but it spells out its literary content very obliquely. The theme for the variations is taken from Beethoven's *Prometheus* ballet music, and it's natural to think of the preceding scherzo as representing the mythical hero, the fire-filcher, being chased by the gods. The Napoleonic element in the first two movements we know about – the conqueror's life of action followed by his funeral march; then comes the apotheosis into a Greek myth. This is all very non-musical, and the symphony is supposed to be entirely a musical argument. But Beethoven lived on the verge of the Romantic explosion and music was ceasing to be pure.

Mozart's symphonies are pure in the sense that nothing extraneous intrudes – no associations, no ego in conflict with an essentially public or social form. But the impurity of intrusion is in the *Eroica* and, very blatantly indeed, in the first movement of the Fifth. In the recapitulation of that movement the allegro quaver urgency is halted for a barless passage marked adagio, in which a solo oboe gives out what sounds to me like a signal of the composer's presence. A private significance is made manifest: I am here, Beethoven, not the anonymous purveyor of public entertainment but a suffering individual. *Sturm und Drang*. Struggle and eventual triumph. Music is becoming autobiographical, even getting ready for Berlioz. And in the Ninth music is becoming political. That Ode to Joy was once an Ode to Freedom.

Beethoven's previous symphonies had all been turned out with the healthy speed we associate with the productions of a popular novelist. Number 1 in 1800, 2 in 1803, 3 in 1804, 4 in 1806, 5 in 1808, 6 in the same year, 7 and 8 in 1812, the year of Napoleon's retreat from Moscow. But then comes a gap of eleven years before the appearance of the Ninth. A lot of thought had gone into it, and a lot of history had flowed by. Buonaparte was dead, and the Romantic movement in England and Germany had spent a great deal of its force. Beethoven had four years of life ahead of him, to be dedicated to the inner voices of the last quartets. But of course all he had was inner voices. Only the non-musician will wonder that it was possible to hammer together so vast a sonic structure as the Ninth without the possibility of its making an auditory impact on the brain that created it.

To all composers, whether they are deaf or not, music is an inner experience related to the pencilling or inking of signs on music paper. The reality is in the skull and it is encoded in crotchets and quavers. The physical sound is a bonus, rich in harmonics: there is no inner substitute for the braying of a horn or trumpet. But music is a mental argument. The cinematic image of the composer working at the piano is nonsense and always was. The composer does not need sound. But eventually his signs must be realised as sound, and then there may be difficulties. Beethoven was not always able to judge adequately – that is, in terms of brute acoustics – what would or would not be audible. This explains the tendency of contemporary conductors to double the woodwind so that it will be heard over the strings. Beethoven's imagination never failed him, but his grasp of acoustic realities had become inadequate. I sometimes think also that he did not quite realise what the effect would be of a particular harmonic sequence in the trio of the scherzo. It works, it is very effective, but it surprises, and I don't think that Beethoven meant, at that point, to surprise. I say no more.

There is one marvellous instance of the deaf composer's extreme practicality that has to be mentioned. In those days the trumpets and horns had a very limited use in the orchestra. They were mostly confined to sets of bugle calls whose pitch could be altered by a change of crooks – attachments which raised or lowered the tone. When you read a score of the period and see 'Horn in C', you know that the cornist has put a crook on which gives him the harmonic series based on that note. Soon he may have to change it for one in E or A. Nowadays our trumpets and horns have valves and they can play chromatic scales as if they were flutes or clarinets. Valves were just coming in at the time of the Ninth. At least Beethoven knew of a horn-player who had one of the new valved instruments just outside Vienna, He roped him in for the Ninth and wrote for him a fourth horn part of considerable range and agility. We are, orchestrally, moving towards modernity here. Four horns and, in the last movement, trombones as well as a range of percussion known at the time as 'Turkish music'.

It is dangerous to try to attach a programme to the three purely orchestral movements – to talk of struggle in the first and second and something like peace in the third. A lot of pseudo-poetic nonsense has been uttered about the D minor opening, with the first main theme striving upwards through the mists and eventually asserting itself. The misty symphonic opening, which became as acceptable a cliché as the old loud statement which bade listeners attend, stems from here. It is in nearly all Bruckner's openings, as well as in Vaughan Williams's 'London' Symphony and Sibelius's Fifth. The real wonder of the movement is the closeness of the argument and the utter unseductiveness of the material. There is nothing here to whistle, nothing to please. This is as close as music can conceivably get to something like a philosophical disquisition. When it bangs out its final D minor chord, unprolonged, dismissive, brusque, it is the end of the argument. It is a movement to admire. Not many listeners like it. You are not meant to like Kant's *Critique of Pure Reason* either.

We do not move out of D minor for the second movement. The mood is the same but the theme is less intellectual. If we wish to speak of the terror of nightmarish pursuit we may. W.H. Auden has some lines which convey the quality of the music:

> 'O where are you going?' said reader to rider,
> 'That valley is fatal where furnaces burn,
> Yonder's the midden whose odours will madden,
> That gap is the grave where the tall return.'[3]

The rhythm of that is also Beethoven's. But, being a scherzo, the movement is also a joke. What the musician finds interesting in it is the change from duple to triple, units of two bars to units of three. The introduction is something that every composer wishes he had thought of first – so simple, so effective, so frighteningly humorous: the arpeggio of D minor descending, with the timpani giving the mediant of the chord. And the simplicity of the trio, for which we anticipate the sunny key of D major in the choral finale, is almost insolent. The escape from the comic nightmare of pursuit is in a return to childhood, whereby you hope that you will be too small and insignificant to be of interest to the pursuing giants. But it is an anticipation in more than tonality of the last movement. There's plenty of childishness there too – or innocence, if you like, the necessary condition for being joyful. I can't help being reminded of the last page of Aldous Huxley's *Point Counter Point*, in which the horrible Burlap and the recently seduced Beatrice take a bath together. 'What fun they had. The floor was quite wet with their splashings. Of such is the kingdom of heaven.' But it may be out of order to suspect much irony in Beethoven. Irony is a very British commodity. At the end of the scherzo the steady eye of childhood exorcises the demons, who collapse ignominiously. This seems as authentic as the end of a fairy tale. There was a good deal of the *kindisch* in Beethoven.

There has been a displacement of scherzo and slow movement. In effect the energy of the scherzo has been an aspect of the power-drive quality of the first movement, not, as normally, an anticipation of the speedy finale. Beethoven has, then, given us a very large lump of D minor, has, as it were, got the minor element out of the way before settling to the confidence and stability of the major. The slow movement is in B flat major, with pendants in D major – two flats alternating with two sharps. It is not an exercise in thought or contemplation. It seems to be a demonstration of pure sonic beauty, than which – if it goes on too long – nothing can be a greater bore. I mean the sensation of going round and round in a circle in which the revisitations are marked chiefly by more and more florid decoration. It is a beautiful movement, no doubt, and Wagner was aware of it when he lifted the first three notes of the main melody, complete with their harmonies, for the opening of the 'Preislied' in *Die Meistersinger*. Its beauty is exhaustive. I am always glad when it is over.

Beethoven clearly had great difficulty in effecting the changeover, in the finale, from the purely orchestral to the orchestral and vocal. He begins with a ghastly discordant fanfare which the cellos and basses do not like. For the first time in the history of music we have to accord to mere instruments the capacity to behave like human beings. This is an anthropomorphic approach which makes me uneasy. The story of the introduction to the movement can be spelt out in words, and that makes me uneasy too. Music is music and words are words, and one should not try to do the job of the other. The orchestra is obviously searching for a theme, and that *schreckliche* fanfare expresses frustration at not finding one. The themes of the preceding three movements are paraded, and the cellos and basses are petulant – they don't want any of these, though they concede that the slow movement is passable. Then a new theme appears, a genuine melody, and the cellos and basses consent to try this out themselves, without accompaniment. Then there is a return to the discord of the opening, a fresh expression of frustration. Clearly, with so vocal a melody, what is needed is a human voice. They get a human voice, who addresses the instruments of the orchestra as if they were a Walt Disney zoo. 'O friends, not these sounds. Let's have something more cheerful.' And then the highly vocal new melody in D major is justified by having words put to it. The words are by Friedrich von Schiller, who died in 1805, between the third and fourth symphonies. They belong to his 'Ode to Joy' – *an die Freude*. Originally this had been *An die Freiheit* – to freedom. But joy is a less controversial and subversive subject than freedom. Strength through joy. *Arbeit macht frei*. Neither term meant very much in the Nazi vocabulary. Here are the opening words:

> *Freude, schöner Götterfunken,*
> *Tochter aus Elysium,*
> *Wir betreten Feuertrunken,*

Himmlische, dein Heiligtum.
Deine Zauber binden wieder,
Was die Mode streng geteilt,
Alle Menschen werden Brüder
Wo dein sanfter Flügel weilt.

Sometimes translated as

Joy, thou glorious spark of heaven,
Daughter of Elysium,
Hearts on fire, aroused, enraptured,
To thy sacred shrine we come.
Custom's bond no more can sever
Those by thy sure magic tied.
All mankind are loving brothers
Where thy sacred wings abide.

One is, or should be, doubtful about addressing joy in this manner. Joy can come from anything – even, to the Nazis, from liquidating Jews. The joy of a punch-up. The joy of gang-rape. Give me *Freiheit* or give me death. We can all do without Joy, unless we have a wife or sweetheart of that name.

What, apart from the words, are we to think of the melody? Many of us have been brainwashed into regarding it as the greatest ever penned. It has been the national anthem of repressive Rhodesia, and it is the continental anthem of the new Europe. In the 1960s it was turned into a pop-song (naturally not with Schiller's words) but it never reached the top ten.[4] It is not, in my view, a great melody – Beethoven was not naturally a great melodist, not as Schubert was – but it is suitably simple with a touch of rhythmic subtlety. Beethoven harmonises it exquisitely before he lets the voices take over. What is more interesting than the melody are the strategies which Beethoven employs to represent the main phases of the poem.

For instance, the solo tenor sings about the stars in the courses, propelled by joy, and Beethoven has to find an orchestral accompaniment which expresses the stellar sublime. His solution is to fabricate a comic little march on the woodwind. There is something grotesque about it, and the grotesquerie is perhaps right, for the sublime and the ridiculous are, as Napoleon was always saying, but a hairsbreadth away from each other. The late Sir Donald Tovey, for whom Beethoven could do no wrong, was convinced of the stroke of genius in this comic little display of military strutting matching the march of the firmament. All I can say is – well, at least interesting.

When – in the English words (I cannot at this moment remember the German ones) the chorus cries 'I embrace ye, O ye millions, here's a joyous kiss for all', Beethoven makes marvellous use of the trombones.[5] He doesn't need harmonies here. He is preparing us for the next stage of simplicity after pure monody. The simplicity of the chorus's main final statements is the simplicity of the round – as basic and infantile as 'Three Blind Mice'. Joy can be loud, but it cannot be complex. It is elemental, and it needs elemental noise. This Beethoven gives us in full measure.

During the last war, in 1943 I think it was, performances of Beethoven's Ninth were given simultaneously in London and Berlin. Neither performance was better than the other, though the German chorus naturally sang in German, more authentic than the British version in English. The applause was the same for both. Beethoven and Schiller were saying something that made equal sense to the Nazis and the democracies. If *Freude* had been changed to *Freiheit*, there would have been a subtle change of *nuance*. But the Ninth was protected from the start from being political because of the very vagueness of *Freude*. Listeners in Vienna probably felt no unease at hearing a word reminiscent of the great Jewish father of psychoanalysis whom they'd expelled. Music is curious in that it has no real human content. Opera, of course, is different, and Beethoven composed one opera – *Fidelio* – of which no Nazi performance has, to my knowledge, been remembered. That was certainly about letting decent men out of an unjust prison and extolling freedom as a political essence. But the Ninth Symphony remains what it always was – a gorgeous tapestry of sound whose sense lies in its tonal patterns, not in what the words are saying. Is it the greatest music ever composed? I doubt it. I will not say what, in my view, surpasses it, apart from Purcell's *The Fairy Queen* and Elgar's *The Dream of Gerontius*. We're all entitled to our own aesthetic judgements. But to hear it always has the quality of an occasion. It is astonishing what that deaf man, living in unredeemable squalor and pain, could do with twelve notes. It makes us start believing in the indomitability, and perhaps even the immortality, of the human spirit. Whatever that is.

Broadcast on BBC Radio 3, 14 December 1990

1   The typescript reads, '…his Number Ten was finished by Mikory, so that Mahler could not be posthumously be [sic] accused of outnumbering Beethoven.' The most widely performed and recorded completion of Mahler 10th is by Dereck Cooke; there are none by anyone named Mikory. The American composer Remo Mazzetti, Jr., produced several completions of Mahler 10th beginning with one written from 1983–5 and another completed in 1989 not long before this essay was written. One of Mazzetti's completions was recorded in 1994 by the St. Louis Symphony Orchestra conducted by Leonard Slatkin; another was recorded in 2000 by the Cincinnati Symphony Orchestra led by Jesús López Cobos.

2   By 'strange instruments', Burgess presumably means the flügelhorn in B♭, tenor saxophone in B♭, and two alto saxophones in E♭ that Vaughan Williams includes in the otherwise traditional instrumentation.

3   first stanza of Auden's 'O Where Are You Going?', which echoes the traditional folk song 'The Cutty Wren' on which it is based ('O, where are you going?' said Milder to Molder).

4   'A Song of Joy' (*'Himno de la alegría'*), a rock song set to the tune of the Ode to Joy. Arranged by Waldo de los Ríos, who specialized in pop settings based on classical music, and recorded by the Spanish singer and actor Miguel Ríos, it sold over four million copies worldwide. In 1970, it rose to #16 on the British pop chart and peaked at #14 on the US pop chart, while reaching #1 on the US Easy Listening chart and #1 in Australia, Canada, Germany, and Switzerland.

5   *'Seid umschlungen, Millionen, diesen Kuss der ganzen Welt!'*

Fair Ophelia: Harriet Smithson Berlioz by Peter Raby
Cambridge University Press, 1982

The Anglo-Saxon musical world seems at present to be
inundated with new recordings of the *Symphonie Fantastique* of
Hector Berlioz. The renewal of interest in the work may have
something to do with the work of the musician-antiquarian
Roger Norrington, who insists on using the original
instruments and instrumental techniques for composers even
so recent as Brahms and Wagner. Richard Strauss will be next.
With his version of the *Symphonie Fantastique*, Norrington
has reverted to very rustic-sounding oboes and clarinets, and
his strings have little vibrato. He has an ophicleide rasping
away in the bass. The work sounds romantic but naive; all
modernity had been expunged. But the idée fixe still sounds
clear and chilling, high above the orchestra. The witch who
once haunted Berlioz has not been exorcised. Her name
was Harriet Smithson. It was she who convinced Paris that
Shakespeare was conceivably a great poet.

The actor-manager Samson Penley put Shakespeare on
the stage in Paris in 1822, though little could be heard over the
crash of hurled sabots and little seen through the rain of eggs,
coins and cabbages. The sight of Desdemona being smothered
appalled Parisians brought up on the classicism of Voltaire, and
they cried: *'A bas Shakespeare! C'est un lieutenant de Wellington!'*
Honest anglophobia got mixed up, in a thoroughly French
non-Cartesian way, with an aesthetic which, as Stendhal very
clearly saw, was fast disappearing. Romanticism was awaiting
its cue, but Penley gave that cue a little too soon.

In 1827 Paris, which had now become unreasonably
anglomaniacal, what with volumes of Scott and Byron on salon

tables and Windsor soap and lavender water by the washbowls, was ready for a company whose actors were drawn from the theatres at Covent Garden, Drury Lane, and the Haymarket. *Hamlet,* with Kemble in the lead, was billed for 11 September at the Odéon, and – despite the mockery of the *Courrier des Théâtres:* 'Parnassus drowned in the Thames'... 'Molière traduced by the English' – the occasion was anticipated with interest and even eagerness.

It was Harriet Smithson as Ophelia who set Paris on fire. The daughter of an acting family of no great note, English by blood but Irish by birth, she was already established in Britain as a useful all-round actress, graceful and beautiful but no Mrs Siddons.[1] To the French, unaccustomed to an uninhibited style of acting that the English had long taken for granted, she was a revelation. By the time Harriet spoke her final lines 'And peace be with all Christian souls, I pray heaven. God be with you', there was hardly a dry eye in the theatre. Men reportedly stumbled weeping out of the auditorium unable to watch further.

Practically the entire French romantic movement was in the audience: Hugo, de Vigny, Delacroix, de Musset, Deschamps, Sainte-Beuve, Barye, Huet, Boulanger, Gautier.[2] There was a young musician there too, Hector Berlioz, who was later to say:

> Shakespeare, coming upon me unawares, struck me like a thunderbolt. The lightning flash of that discovery revealed to me at a stroke the whole heaven of art, illuminating it to its remotest corners. I recognised the meaning of grandeur, beauty, dramatic truth.

He was only twenty-three, not merely dangerously young but also dangerously susceptible, and he had difficulty in separating the impact of Shakespeare from that of Miss

Smithson. She was, of course, unattainable, a goddess, the Muse, while he was merely a struggling composer spurned by his philistine family. But it is no exaggeration to state that the thunderflash of the vision of Harriet-Ophelia turned him, almost overnight, into the greatest romantic composer of the age. He tried to purge his obsession into music and produced the *Symphonie Fantastique* – a brilliant, wild, botched confection in which Harriet, rarefied into the Beloved and desecrated as the Evil One, floats transfigured as the first ever leitmotif over orchestral noises intended to match the verbal impact of Shakespeare. This was in 1830, merely three years after the death of Beethoven. Music was forced into changing into something desperately new.

With the catharsis of art, the obsession with Harriet might have ended. Berlioz fell for the pianist Marie Moke, more poetically known as Camille, and proposed marriage. But Camille deserted him for the Monsieur Pleyel of the pianofortes, and Berlioz Shakespearianly cried out on high heaven, purchased a gun, proposed a *Hamlet*-like massacre.[3] He calmed down, seduced a girl on the *plage* at Nice, and wrote the *King Lear* overture. There the whole story of tempestuous passion might have ended had not Harriet reappeared in his life. She was back in Paris, unsuccessful in repeating her former triumphs, and, by chance, attended that remarkable concert of 9 December 1832, in which the *Symphonie Fantastique* and *Le Retour à la Vie* (a weird romantic hotch-potch of music and monologue) were presented.[4] The risen composer wooed the fading star with a symphony orchestra of great size. At length they married. It was a great pity.

It is always a great pity when myth has to melt into the Monday of quarrels over ill-made coffee and unpaid bills. Berlioz was first an enchanted husband, then a contented one, then a disillusioned one. Harriet was a bad housekeeper and an imperfect mother. She never spoke French adequately.

She grew fat and drank too much. Berlioz was unfaithful and she whined with jealousy. At length, having lost the power of speech, she fell into a decline and died. Though Berlioz mourned – 'I loved Ophelia. Forty thousand brothers / Could not, with all their quantity of love, / Make up my sum' – he had the honesty to admit that his true residual emotion was pity: pity for a decayed body and a failed vocation. Disillusioned with the too too solid Harriet, he never became disillusioned with Ophelia or Juliet. The fire of that first vision remained with him and produced the best Shakespeare music in the repertory.

It is a sad but illuminating story. There remains a residuum. Harriet was the posthumous embodiment of the romantic spirit, at least to the French. Did she inspire Hugo and Musset and Fantin-Latour?[5] When Rimbaud wrote *'O belle Ophelia! belle comme la neige!'*, he was helping in the process of turning a drowned girl driven mad by grief into one of the central icons of romanticism. She is in the paintings of Delacroix, bare-breasted, wide-eyed, recognisably Harriet. The French had to discover Shakespeare sometime, and they discovered him that evening of 11 September 1827, his spirit, passionate but not really erotic, incarnated in a dark-haired Irish girl. Turn on the compact disc player and, in a few bars in C major, she is back with us.

The Observer, 1982

1   Sarah Siddons, née Kemble, was the most famous tragedienne of the eighteenth century. Best known for her portrayal of Lady Macbeth, she was a member of the Kemble family of actors, which dominated the English stage for decades. Sarah's younger brother Charles Kemble starred as Hamlet in the 1827 production in Paris that featured Harriet Smithson as Ophelia.

2   novelist Victor Hugo; poet and playwright Alfred de Vigny; painter Eugène Delacroix; writer Alfred de Musset; poet Émile Deschamps; literary critic Charles Sainte-Beuve; sculptor Antoine-Louis Barye; painter and printmaker Paul Huet; painter Louis Boulanger; and writer Théophile Gautier

3   In 1830, while Berlioz was in Italy, the Belgian concert pianist Marie-Félicité-Denise Moke, who had been betrothed to Berlioz for three months, broke off the engagement to marry Camille Pleyel, the son and business partner of the composer Ignace Pleyel, who in 1807 founded Pleyel et Cie., the prestigious French piano manufacturing company. The comment that Marie Moke was 'more poetically known as Camille' indicates confusion over her and her husband's names.

4   Heartbroken over losing Marie Moke, Berlioz composed *Le Retour à la vie, mélologue en six parties,* in 1831 in Italy. The work is a portrait of the composer's 'return to life' after recovering from deep despair. Berlioz later retitled it *Lélio* and revised it to make it seem that his misery was over Harriet Smithson rather than Mademoiselle Moke.

5   Harriet Smithson's beauty inspired portraits by numerous British and French artists, including Fantin-Latour, Boulanger, Devéria, Maile, Dubufe, and Drummond. Henri Fantin-Latour was a French painter and lithographer whose many portraits of French artists and writers included a series titled *Hector Berlioz, sa vie et ses oeuvres.* An 1888 lithograph from this group, titled 'Symphonie Fantastique: A Ball', shows Berlioz drawing Harriet Smithson's attention, with a gathering of ball guests in the background.

The Diary of Richard Wagner 1865–1882: The Brown Book,
presented and annotated by Joachim Bergfeld, translated by
George Bird
London: Victor Gollancz, 1980

This is the famous Brown Book given by Cosima von Bülow
to Richard Wagner for the notation of his feelings about her in
absence, or rather its contents, the original being calf-bound,
jewel-studded, metal-locked. Those contents are for the first
time published in their entirety. Wagner being Wagner, there
is as much cosmos as Cosima, as well as poems for King
Ludwig, attacks on anti-Wagnerians, scraps of music and, as
a bonus, those Annals out of which *Mein Leben* was written.
There is also the first outline of *Parsifal.*

Cosima was the second of the three illegitimate daughters
given to Franz Liszt by the Comtesse Marie d'Agoult. She
married Hans von Bülow, pianist, conductor, Wagnerian,
Liszt's favourite pupil, but Wagner cuckolded the patient von
Bülow and had two children by Cosima before she could get a
divorce. One of these children was Eva, named for the heroine
of *Die Meistersinger,* and it was Eva, who became wife of the
notorious Houston Stewart Chamberlain, who bequeathed
the book, her mother's own bequest to her, to the Richard
Wagner Gedenkstätte in Bayreuth.

Like many another pious relict of a great man, Eva
was not happy about granting even 'trustworthy persons'
the right to gloat over his weaknesses or indiscretions,
so she destroyed fourteen pages of the book, pasted over
another five to ensure illegibility, but, in recompense,
carefully inked over some pencil entries for their better
preservation. Cosima herself destroyed nothing written by

Wagner, except some of the letters he wrote to Mathilde Wesendonck. There have been very few female relicts of great men who were or are not in some measure enemies of the whole truth.

In 1865, when Wagner pens his first entry on the lines of 'I love you with an ultimate love', the lovers were separated for the first time: Cosima had to go with Hans to Hungary, calling in Austria on the way. Wagner writes: 'Ah, what madness! What madness! And that fool Hans who wouldn't let you go to Penzing and showed you the shops of Vienna instead!' (Wagner had lived in Penzing, a suburb of Vienna, from 1863 to 1864: Cosima had wished to see his lodgings, already sacred.) 'Can one believe it? Can one believe it? And this, if you please, is my one friend! Ah, foolish hearts! Blind eyes!' and so on.

It will be seen that Wagner has a rather one-sided notion of friendship. As for love, it finds what one has to term very Teutonic expression (meaning full of references to eternity and destiny and the soul), and not only to Cosima. In 1864, when Wagner had already vowed deathless devotion to her, he was writing to young Mathilde Maier in most affectionate terms – 'My dearest love... go on loving me.... With heartfelt kisses from your R.W.'. On 18 August 1865 he has an entry in the Brown Book about Cosima's jealousy. Eva carefully pasted this over, but Dr Bergfeld has kindly unpasted it. 'Good morning, naughty child!' writes roguish Richard. 'What a nasty letter you wrote me yesterday! And now poor M.M. has to come in for it again!' *Und so weiter.*

In 1869 Wagner and Cosima, with tiny Isolde and Eva and Siegfried on the way, were happily bedded down in the house in Tribschen. Now, at fifty-five, Wagner purrs like a great cat, madly joyous, and composes something quite unWagnerian: a cradlesong with the words

Schlaf, Kindchen, schlafe;
im Garten geh'n zwei Schafe:
ein schwarzes und ein weisses...

If baby will not sleep the black sheep will bite him, her, it. The music is in simple four-part harmony (leading note moving the wrong way) and it is penned in his characteristic clear strong script. This became part of the *Siegfried Idyll* which was played on Christmas morning, also Cosima's birthday, 1870, heard by Nietzsche and beautifully staged by Visconti in his Ludwig film.[1] From now until 1882, the year before Wagner's death, the Brown Book can be used not for plaints to the distant beloved but for verses, schemata, aphorisms. The verses include

Heil! Heil dem Kaiser!
König, Wilhelm!
Aller Deutschen Hort und Freiheitswehr!

and the aphorisms such banalities as 'The oddity of the genius in this world can be very well judged of from the stupid questions he is asked.'

I have just been reading Ronald Hayman's excellent *Nietzsche: A Critical Life*, where we see the Tribschen *ménage* from the outside and are compelled to compare the two men as thinkers, if not as composers. (Nietzsche's musical *oeuvre* has recently been played through in Milan: he is always competent, very unoriginal but quite unWagnerian). In the glow of Nietzsche's first adoration, Wagner seems an intellectual giant. The Brown Book shows a glib and fluent poet, always ready with a birthday ode for Ludwig, and a mediocre thinker. He reads widely but unsystematically; he has half-baked progressive ideas; he is a sort of Colin Wilson with musical genius.[2]

But get Wagner away from *Seele* and *Schicksal* and on to the interpretation of his own art and he becomes authoritative and absorbing. Perhaps the person who meant most to him was the Heldentenor Ludwig Schnorr von Carolsfeld, the first Tristan, who died young and is the subject of a fine eulogy which Wagner put into the Brown Book and later into the *Neue Zeitschrift für Musik*. 'The orchestra disappeared vis-à-vis the singer, or, more correctly, seemed to be included in his performance.' Wagner is shrewd and lucid and practical when he talks of the new *Übermensch* kind of singer who, 'under the inevitably acknowledged leadership of German musical art' (viz. Wagner), will require intellect as well as voice. But we always seem to be on our guard when reading Wagner, fearful that, even when discussing the range of the Wagner tuba, he may suddenly turn abstract or chauvinist or, eye on the main chance, exalt the 'high-minded Sovereign' who was really a hysterical boy.

Perhaps Hitler, another high-minded adorer of Wagner, has made us oversensitive to the proto-Nazi elements in the prose and poetry, if not in the music. The music is harmless, I think, even when Hans Sachs is telling the guilds to honour German art: there is more dangerous imperialism in Elgar's Pomp and Circumstance marches than in the Entry of the Masters. The fantastic anti-Semitism which Wagner was, in 1882, to impose on the plot of *Parsifal* but which is not yet present in the outline of the Brown Book, leaves that gorgeous score untouched.

If we excuse Wagner's anti-Semitism on the grounds of Meyerbeer's success in Paris and his own failure there (which turned all the French into Jews), we have to excuse Nazi genocide on the same grounds – the artistic failures of Hitler and Goebbels and their envy of brilliant Jewish painters and playwrights. Wagner ought at least to have been suspicious, as a universal artist, of his own racist theories. But our trepidation in turning these pages derives from an unfair hindsight. If I saw that biting black sheep as an SS officer that is not Wagner's fault.

The translation seems adequate, but I don't think Schopenhauer's *Vorstellung* should be rendered as 'conception'.[3] The book itself is necessary to Wagnerians, but it is not, meaning the man himself, all that attractive. Wagner is too arrogant and high-souled for British tastes, insufficiently Pooterish.[4] But that's true even of Goethe.

The Observer, 1980

1   The Italian filmmaker Luchino Visconti directed and co-wrote his 1973 film *Ludwig,* a biographical drama about 'Mad King' Ludwig II, who ruled Bavaria from 1864–86.

2   Colin Henry Wilson was a prolific English writer, philosopher, and novelist who wrote more than one hundred books, many of them on mysticism, the paranormal, and true crime. He viewed himself primarily as a philosopher whose purpose was 'to create a new and optimistic existentialism'.

3   Burgess had strong and particular feelings about this word, which appears in his poem 'Garrison Town, Evening' (lines 5–8):

> Each projector downs its snout,
> Truffling the blackened scene,
> Till the Wille's lights gush out
> *Vorstellungen* on the screen.

In his book *They Wrote in English* (Vol. 2, p. 553), Burgess provides a detailed explication of the poem, which he wrote in early 1942 in Eye, the town in Suffolk where he trained to become an instructor in the AEC (Army Educational Corps). Lusty sexual overtones combine with philosophical imagery drawn from Schopenhauer and Spengler to evoke an evening during the war when British soldiers 'emerge from their barracks and look for girls, who are willing to be looked for.' Burgess explains that '*Vorstellungen*', in the Schopenhauerian sense, are 'illusions or phenomena or representations...which we take for reality' while pointing out that '*Vorstellungen*' is also 'German for cinema shows'. In *Inside Mr Enderby* (Part 1, Chapter 4, section 3), Burgess attributes the poem to his fictional poet F.X. Enderby, and in his 1977 song cycle *The Brides of Enderby*, it provides the text of the fourth movement. See *Revolutionary Sonnets and other poems*, p. 19; *Collected Poems*, pp. 12-13, 369; and ACC, pp. 218-22.

4   Charles Pooter is the fictional author of *Diary of a Nobody* (1892), a comic novel by the brothers George and Weedon Grossmith. Much of the book's humour stems from Pooter's unjustified sense of self-importance and how this leads to frequent minor humiliations, with his delusions repeatedly squelched by everyday social interactions.

29. RICHARD WAGNER

Richard Wagner died in Venice just one hundred years ago, having devoted the greater part of his life of seventy years to an artistic revolution whose reverberations are still with us. He has been called, as Verdi or Puccini is more rightfully called, an operatic composer, but his vast music-dramas transcend the limitations of the traditional operatic stage. Wagner wished to create a new art-form in which music, poetry, architecture, myth, politics, religion blended in a new image of man. He had a long life of struggle to achieve his aim, and was resentful of the easier successes of operatic composers like the Parisian Meyerbeer, whose work he reluctantly admired but also detested. Meyerbeer was a Jew, and Wagner's reputed antisemitism springs from a particular enmity.

It is true, however, that many of the doctrines of Nazism seem to find their source in Wagner's writings. For Wagner was not content to compose poetry and music; he was a great muddled theorist who, in turgid German prose, issued books and pamphlets on aesthetics, morals, politics and religion and also dabbled in the murky pools of racism. It is true to say, however, that had he survived into the Nazi régime he would have abhorred everything that Adolf Hitler stood for, even though Hitler considered himself a great Wagnerian. After all, Wagner was a free artist and a vast egoist and also something of an anarchist. He was prepared to use the political power of others to encompass his own artistic ends (as he used King Ludwig of Bavaria's patronage to erect a theatre and pay his ever-present debts) but he was not a man capable of yielding to authority.

He was a sensualist, a lover of wines, perfumes, silks and the embraces of women. But, once he had stolen the wife of Hans van Bülow, a fine musician and, despite everything, a devoted Wagnerian, he remained a faithful husband and devoted father. He quarrelled with everybody – from Friedrich Nietzsche (once his disciple) to his father-in-law Franz Liszt. He was an amiable bully, angry if he was not always the centre of attention, prepared to scream if need be, but so thoroughly devoted to his concept of art that everybody forgave him and still does. And what precisely is his achievement?

His achievement in the earlier operatic works – *Rienzi, Tannhäuser, The Flying Dutchman, Lohengrin* – seems orthodox enough, but we are aware of a concentration on the inner life of his characters, expressed in music of an intensity learned from Beethoven, that is to be found nowhere in his contemporaries – except the later Verdi. When we come to *Tristan, The Ring* and *Parsifal,* we are into a world of profound symbolism, in which realism melts into myth, and great psychological depths are plumbed. Music which dares the limits of chromaticism and calls on a new kind of orchestra is in the service of human complexity. This new kind of art is not easy, it is not pure entertainment, but it is the necessary consummation of nineteenth-century thought and feeling, and it looks into the future. Out of the opening chords of *Tristan* the atonal music of our own century was forged. The 'Wagner sound' is with us in the cinema and the Frank Sinatra 'backing'.

Wagner was a German who, though often in exile because of revolutionary political beliefs which matched his revolutionary artistic doctrines, never spoke any language well except German and considered himself to be, above all, a German artist. But there is no narrow nationalism in his work, and the Nazis were mistaken when they thought they found in him a foreshadowing of their own diabolic doctrines. He remains an international voice, triumphant in torture, complex and exquisite, digging deeper than any artist of his time into the obscure depths of the human soul.

Corriere della Sera, 1983

30. RING

Bernard Shaw translated *Das Ring des Nibelungen*, quite correctly, as *The Niblung's Ring*, while others, very inaccurately, have called the work *The Ring of the Nibelungs*. True, the Nibelungs are a whole race of dwarfs, but Wagner's massive foursome of music dramas is concerned with a ring belonging to one dwarf only. The titles of the two middle dramas – *The Valkyrie* and *Siegfried* – are pretty well in English what they are in German, but the first, *Das Rheingold*, goes better in English as *The Gold of the Rhine* rather than as *The Rhinegold*, which is too Germanic, and the last, *Die Götterdämmerung*, is more dramatic as *Night Falls on the Gods* (again, Shaw's title) than as *The Dusk of the Gods* (James Joyce's version) or the commonest translation of all – *Twilight of the Gods*, which suggests a cosy tea with muffins round the fire while the lights are low. When we talk of Wagner's *Ring*, nearly everybody knows what we refer to, but not everybody knows why such an enormous expenditure of time and music paper – twenty-five years and thousands of pages, all covered with exquisite penmanship – should have been devoted to the telling of a Teutonic fairy tale which is better fitted to the nursery than to the inadequate machinery of the nineteenth-century theatre.

First, let us consider what the fairy tale is about. It is not, of course, really a fairy tale, since there are no fairies in it, but there are giants and dwarfs and deities, as well as a dragon, a magic sword, and a helmet of invisibility. It looks, on the surface, like children's stuff, but, if we look more deeply, we shall discover a very powerful political allegory. *The Ring* is about the corruption of money and power and the need for revolutionary action in a world dominated by cynical tyranny. It is closer to Karl Marx and Bakunin than to a children's tale at twilight.

What happens? Three mermaids or naiads are swimming in the river Rhine. They have a huge piece of gold there, which they love as a thing of beauty and never dream of putting on the market. An ugly little monster called Alberich comes slithering along the riverbed and he begs for the love of the three girls. They merely laugh at him, being elementals who have not learnt the social art of discretion, and, in his anger and humiliation, Alberich decides to abjure love and live for wealth. He steals the gold and sets up as a capitalist, making hundreds of other dwarfs, or Nibelungen, toil for him in a subterranean factory. Out of the gold they fashion two objects very useful to a capitalist – a ring which bestows supreme power, and a helmet which confers the gift of metamorphosis. Wearing this *Tarnhelm*, as it is called, Alberich can assume any shape he wishes, or even no shape at all.

High above the world of the dwarfs is the world of the gods, whose head is Wotan. He has a wife named Fricka and a cunning intellectual henchman called Loge. He has commissioned certain giants, decent hardworking hardhatted creatures of little intelligence but much muscle, to build a palace called Valhalla, agreeing to give in payment the goddess of love and beauty and eternal youth – Freia, after whom the sixth day of the Northern week is named. Now that the time has come for fulfilling the bargain, Wotan is unhappy about it: without Freia the gods will wither and grow old: they need to feed on her golden apples. But Loge, who can suggest no tricky or cheating way out of the contract, has heard the complaint of the maidens of the Rhine – their gold has been stolen by the dwarf Alberich. The giants say they will take the gold instead of Freia, so Wotan and Loge trick Alberich into tarnhelming himself into a toad, and off they go with the wealth. The giants now grow greedy, and Fafnir, the greediest, commits murder for it. He turns himself into a dragon and spends his life guarding the hoard, the ultimate miser, not even a capitalist.

Loge's magic makes a rainbow bridge, and over this the gods process into their new magnificent home.

So much, briefly, for the plot of the first of the four music dramas. Clearly, the gods are immoral, the giants stupid, the dwarfs ugly and avaricious (there is another named dwarf – Mime, kinsman of Alberich, whose villainy is reserved for the story of Siegfried). We need another kind of being, revolutionary, brave, of shining moral integrity. We need man and woman. Better, perhaps, we need what Nietzsche called the *Übermensch* and Shaw the superman and Wagner was content to think of as the Hero. We need Siegfried, but we shall not meet him until the third music drama of the cycle.

In *Die Walküre* or *The Valkyrie* we meet Brünnhilde, whom it is best to think of as Brynhild (it saves the trouble of looking for an umlaut). Brynhild is Wotan's daughter, but she is begotten of the Earth Mother, not his wife Fricka, and is outside the realm of dynasty and alliance and trickery: she is as pure as a god's offspring ought to be. She is one of a group of warrior maidens who carry the bodies of slain men from the battlefield to Valhalla, and they have a fearsome cry which, in *Apocalypse Now*, Mr Coppola unleashed over the napalm-stricken forests of Vietnam. From Brynhild and a chosen mortal man a new breed of heroes may come forth, but Wotan has to ensure that the divine seed dwells in these heroes, and he goes forth among the mortal women of the world impregnating them that they may produce potential heroic fathers. The father and mother of the hero who is to mate with Brynhild are named Sieglinde and Siegmund, and both are children of Wotan (who has been going round in a cloak and hat as the Stranger or the Wanderer, and in a wolfskin as a wolf). When they fall in love with each other they are ready to commit not only incest but adultery, since Sieglinde is married to a warrior called Hunding. Siegmund is a brave man but very unlucky, and he expects to be slain by the man he proposes to cuckold. In fact, he is, despite Brynhild's magical help, for Wotan, whose wife has told him she is on the side of the marital law as well as the dynasty to which Hunding belongs, steps in to enforce the law and see that Siegmund duly dies. Brynhild has not cared a damn about the law, and she is put to sleep like a fairy princess, surrounded by a wall of fire which only the coming bridegroom-hero can safely pierce. Sieglinde is pregnant with this hero, so that is all right.

In *Siegfried*, the young hero, eponymous hero I should say, is being reared by the dwarf Mime. Sieglinde died in giving birth to her son, bequeathing him a kind of broken birthright – the fragments of the sword called *Nothung* or Needful, which Wotan had thrust into a treetrunk for Siegmund, like King Arthur with Excalibur, to pluck forth. Mime does not like his adoptive son, and Siegfried detests Mime; otherwise, they get on well enough together in the forest where they live. Mime wants one thing only from Siegfried – that he should slay the dragon Fafnir and take his gold; Siegfried will then be conveniently slain himself with a bowl of soup seasoned with poison. The trouble is the forging of the sword: every sword that Mime forges Siegfried breaks with ease, jeering nastily at the poor swordsmith. There is only one unbreakable sword in the world, and that is *Nothung*, but *Nothung* is broken – why and how? Because it met the invincible spear of Wotan in that fight between Siegmund and Hunding. But Siegfried takes the fragments, melts them down, then lets the molten metal run into a sword-mould. *Nothung* is refashioned, and Siegfried goes off to meet the dragon – not out of love for Mime, but in the sheer love of dangerous adventure. He kills Fafnir and takes his ring and *Tarnhelm*: the rest of the gold he leaves as worthless. While his hand is in, he kills Mime, to the joy of Alberich, who is lurking in the background. Then, licking off some dragon's blood that has got on to his finger, he discovers that he can understand the song of a bird that is evidently trying to tell him something. There is a beautiful maiden waiting behind a wall of fire for a hero's releasing kiss. Siegfried goes off joyously. At the foot of Brynhild's mountain, Siegfried meets Wotan, in his earthly disguise as an old man. He invokes the generation gap and insults him. Wotan raises his spear, but this time it is powerless: *Nothung* snaps it in two. We are ready for night to fall on the gods and for the race of heroes to take over the governance of the world.

All Wagnerians agree that *Die Götterdämmerung* does not gear well with the other music dramas of the tetralogy. There is something very operatic about it – duets, choruses, recitatives and arias – and the Siegfried and Brynhild we have already met change their characters and become less than heroic. The music, however, is glorious – the tone poem which describes Siegfried's journey to the Rhine, the death march of Siegfried, the fire and water finale. This is the sumptuous Wagner of his orchestral maturity, but the libretto itself belongs to a much earlier period – the time when he planned a genuine opera (not a music drama) called *The Death of Siegfried*. What happens on the plot level follows logically enough from what we have already heard and seen; it is the psychological treatment that upsets us.

Most of the action of *Götterdämmerung* takes place in the hall of the Gibichungs, who sound villainous and are. Gunther, the head of this Rhineland clan, is cowardly and foolish but thinks highly of himself. He and his crafty henchman Hagen know all about Siegfried and Brynhild and the ring and the *Tarnhelm*. Hagen, though not a dwarf, is the son of the dwarf who started all the trouble, Alberich, and he has inherited from his father a powerful, and very operatic, avarice. So he wants the ring while Gunther wants Brynhild. By the use of a magic potion they make Siegfried (who, still being in search of adventures, inevitably finds his way to the hall of the Gibichungs) forget his love for Brynhild and fall for Gunther's sister Gutruna. He will, in his changed and implausible state, do anything for his prospective brother-in-law, so he captures Brynhild, who is wearing the ring he gave her, and brings her in a flash, by virtue of the *Tarnhelm*, to the Gibichung court. Hating Siegfried now, she joins in a plot to kill him but eventually finds out the truth about his strange disaffection. So she lights a funeral pyre for the dead hero, rides into the flames herself, and presides, before being consumed, over the end of everything. The hall, having a pyre in it, goes up in flames and so does Valhalla, around which the self-destructive Wotan has arranged the dry wood of the World Tree. The Rhine obligingly overflows its banks and puts out the fire, though belatedly. The ring returns to the river and thus can do no further harm. The age of capitalism is dead, but so are the gods and the planned race of heroes. It has all been rather a waste of time.

That is a very bald summary, and it says nothing about the subtlety with which the music helps to delineate character, motivation and place. But it may serve to show, for those who have picked up their knowledge of the great work from Nazi propaganda, how pessimistic Wagner was about human, or German, destiny. The Superman does not triumph: he dies. Hitler ought to have seen in his beloved *Ring* how accurately Wagner had foretold the end of the *Reich*. If Siegfried became the prototype of Nazi manhood – muscular, blond and innocently cruel – he remained even more the type of the failed hero. He had no hope of redeeming the world. Such a task had to be left to Wagner's next and last hero, Parsifal, a holy fool in search of the Holy Grail. Wagner liked to think that *The Ring* was an illustration of Schopenhauer's philosophy, which found no virtue in striving and tried to seek in passive resignation relief from the machinations of the universal Will. Very Germanic.

But Wagner was himself no man for passivity. He was energy incarnate and in many fields – not only music but also the love of women, aesthetics, sociology, ethnology, politics. It is his participation in the revolutionary politics of Europe which began with the Parisian turmoils of 1848 – the year of revolutions – that makes us see *The Ring* as a political allegory. In 1843 he became opera conductor at Dresden and might have remained there, producing other men's operas as well his own, settling into the bourgeois life of a provincial capital, if he had not become excited by the anarchic ideas of Proudhon and Bakunin.[1] He wanted a break with the past – not only socially but musically – and the works he began to sketch in 1848 and 1849 combined the desire for a reformed society with the ideal of a new, freer, kind of dramatic music. Thus, he proposed a work called *Jesus von Nazareth*, in which Christ should be a political revolutionary, and began to write the libretto for *Siegfrieds Tod* (Siegfried's Death – the original *Götterdämmerung*) – an opera, or music drama, fit for the new age which seemed to be dawning.

In 1849 there was an uprising in Dresden, and Wagner joined in it. He did not fight at the barricades, but he expended inflammatory words which made the authorities issue a warrant for his arrest. Liszt helped him to escape to Switzerland. King Johann of Saxony – whom Wagner had unrealistically begged to drop the postures of traditional power and help inaugurate the new era – later said that, had he not escaped, he would certainly have been tried and sentenced to death. In Zurich he had operatic visions which, he knew well, could never be realised in the opera houses of the old régime – a régime, alas, which did not yield to the forces of revolution. Though *Siegfried's Death* was to have most of the features of the old opera, with recitatives, arias, duets, quartets, and choruses, it was to demand orchestral forces and stage machinery (consider, for instance, that final conflagration) which could not be found in the resources of the time. Wagner began to dream of his own opera house.

In 1850 he drafted the music for *Siegfried's Death*, but, hopeless about the possibility of production, dropped it and began to work on the dramatic poems which, logically, led up to the incineration of his hero. He wrote *Der junge Siegfried – The Young Siegfried*, eventually just *Siegfried* – and *Die Walküre*, which should describe the begetting of the hero, then finally the first poem of the cycle – *Das Rheingold*. By the end of 1852 he had completed the entire *Ring* poem. He was drawing on the old German epic called *The Song of the Nibelung*, but he was imposing his own ideas. The most startling of these ideas is the highly democratic one that man is potentially greater than the gods, and that the gods, or monarchs of the kingdoms of Europe, unconsciously harbour a death-wish: they *want* to be overthrown. When he started writing the music of *Das Rheingold* in 1854, it was the need for gold – or any kind of financial security – that was uppermost in his mind. It was not until ten years later that King Ludwig II of Bavaria, who was a fanatical adorer of his work, paid all his debts, offered him a fee of 30,000 florins for completing *The Ring*, and granted him an annual allowance of 8,000 florins. Wagner wanted more than that. He wanted a Wagner theatre in Munich, but Ludwig's cabinet used this extravagant proposal to raise public feeling against him. They had other things against him too: his adulterous relationship with Cosima, the wife of Hans von Bülow and daughter of Liszt; his debts; his damnable love of luxury. Of course, what they really resented was his influence with the king. They made him flee Munich, but he came back again.

Das Rheingold was first produced in that city in 1869 – twenty years after the initial conception of the final drama of the cycle. *Die Walküre* was first heard in the following year. But the Munich opera house and its musical resources were not good enough, and the dream of a theatre of his own began its realisation, with Ludwig's help. By 1874 Wagner had set himself up in Bayreuth, living in the villa called *Wahnfried*, watching the theatre take shape. It must not be supposed that Ludwig paid for it all. Wagner gave concerts, started subscription lists, floated loans. If Hitler was to make the Bayreuth theatre a charge of the Third Reich (first having purged the enterprise of Jews, which angered Toscanini and drove him away, thus depriving Germany of the finest Wagnerian conductor of all time), neither the State of Bavaria nor the Reich of Wagner's own day cared a twopenny damn about the enormous musical vision and the home which was to enshrine it. The annual Wagner festival was a long time paying its way.

The entire *Ring* cycle was given, three times, in the summer of 1876. This parturition was the culmination of a gestation period that had lasted from 1849, though Wagner wrote other music dramas – *The Mastersingers, Tristan and Isolde* – as well as a large number of books and pamphlets and such exquisite trifles as the Wesendonck songs and the *Siegfried Idyll* during a time which, like all his times, was turbulent. In the Bayreuth theatre Wagner had all his own way, as, until 1930, his widow was to have her own way also, a way that threatened to turn Bayreuth into a museum until her son Siegfried, and his son Wieland, found new ways of solving the staging problems which have bedevilled all Wagner producers. For the trouble with *The Ring* is that it is based on an epic and remains an epic. Epic takes kindly to dragons and magic swords, as well as universal conflagrations, but the stage is unhappy about them. What *The Ring* has always needed is cinematic adaptation, but the cinema, even in Nazi Germany, was always too popular a form to accommodate Wagnerian grandeur. Television, in the hundredth year after Wagner's death in Venice, has to be forced into accepting *The Ring*. This cycle of drama, music, myth and social allegory is one of the great human achievements, and we ought to commit suicide rather than deny it to the small screen.

Let us consider briefly the nature of Wagner's artistic achievement. *The Ring* is (with the inevitable qualification concerning its final segment) not opera but a new form called music drama. Opera thrives on set numbers and, except for its recitatives and dialogue, comes closer to the four-square structure of song than to the flow of an Aeschylus or a Shakespeare. Wagner has created a kind of musical prose which flows for ever and resists being chopped up into set arias or ensembles. Moreover, the orchestra, instead of tamely supplying a rum-tum-tum accompaniment to the singers in the Italian manner, lives its own complex life and illuminates the narrative at a level which anticipates the Freudian and Jungian unconscious. Wagner generated over a hundred germinal themes, or *Leitmotive*, which symbolise objects, concepts, motivations, personalities, and these melt and merge and are transformed as the orchestral flow surges and subsides and recovers and overwhelms in what Wagner called perpetual melody.

The orchestra that he needed defeated conventional opera houses. He called for eight harps in *Das Rheingold*, as well as a phalanx of anvils. New instruments were invented so that each section of the orchestra could form its own self-contained family – heckelphones as well as English horns to drive the oboe tone down to the depths; high trumpets and bass trumpets; a contrabass trombone. Sax in Paris (father of the saxophone) fashioned the Wagner tuba, which helped to blend trombones and horns. Massed strings were divided into shimmering rainbows of sound. Orchestral players all over the world had to learn to become virtuosi. My father used to tell me of his being present at a rehearsal of the Hallé Orchestra in Manchester under Hans Richter, who had worked with Wagner.[2] The first horn player said that Siegfried's horncall in *Götterdämmerung* was unplayable. This plaint was translated for Richter, who knew no English, and he put out his hand for the horn, fitted to it a mouthpiece he took from his pocket, played the passage flawlessly, then handed the instrument back.[3] From then on there were no more complaints about unplayability. This re-education of musicians was going on everywhere, and it was all in the service of the great musical message of *The Ring*.

Music had, up to Wagner's time, been more decorative than expressive. True, Beethoven dragged the art of sound into regions of morality and philosophy in that Ninth Symphony which Wagner always regarded as his own starting-point. But with *The Ring* the urgency of the philosophical message turned music into a language more subtle and various than that of even the epic poets. The time would come when Richard Strauss, who cut his teeth on Wagner, could create symphonic poems which made verbal language supererogatory. In the late twentieth century composers are still trying to free themselves from the Wagnerian heritage. Wagner died a century ago, but we have only to listen to the opening of *Das Rheingold*, where the very groundbass of nature is heard, hardly distinguishable from the voice of the eternal river, to be seduced into feeling that *this* is what music is about, and Mozart and Haydn and even Beethoven were merely playing parlor games. It is an illusion, but a very powerful one. Wagner was the most dangerous of magicians.[4]

The Nazis have done a lot of harm to Wagner, exaggerating an antisemitism which was nothing more than resentment at the success of the operas of Meyerbeer, who just happened to be a Jew, and seeing in his transformation of the Nibelung myth the glorification of the Aryan. But Wagner is bigger than all the political ideologies, and his realistic pessimism, curiously contradicted by the sheer glory of his orchestral sound, is more in tune with our own age – which has seen *The Ring* enacted on the stage of world politics – than with the facile triumphalism of both the fascists and the communists.

He is a very modern poet and composer, as much present in Eliot's *The Waste Land* as in Joyce's *Ulysses*, and his centennial is not an antiquarian celebration: it is an acknowledgment that Wagner is a living force and probably an eternal one.

Corriere della Sera, 1983

1 Pierre-Joseph Proudhon was a socialist, philosopher, and economist who became a member of the French Parliament after the 1848 revolution. He originated the term *anarchist* and is considered one of anarchism's major theorists.

2 The name of the Austro-Hungarian conductor Hans Richter does not include 'von', yet erroneously appears as 'Hans von Richter' in the typescripts and prior published versions of Chapters 30, 33, 51, and 65. It is corrected in each. Evidently Burgess conflated the name Hans Richter with Hans von Bülow.

3 See ACC, p. 365.

4 Burgess typed 'musicians', which he altered to 'magicians' by hand.

Arthur Sullivan: A Victorian Musician by Arthur Jacobs
Oxford University Press, 1984

A French *philosophe* recently pointed out that, while the French love triplets (*Liberté, Égalité, Fraternité*, for instance), the British prefer pairs – eggs and bacon, Fortnum and Mason, Crosse and Blackwell, *Dieu et Mon Droit*, Burgess and Maclean, Gilbert and Sullivan.[1] It is rarely that a writer dares devote a book to the latter half of this last doublet or couplet, and Arthur Jacobs, having done precisely that and at length too, in doing it demonstrates why. For what of Sir Arthur Sullivan's still stands without the prop of William Schwenck Gilbert's inspired dementia? Very little, alas. There is the hymn 'Onward, Christian Soldiers.' The sacred song 'The Lost Chord' can only be performed parodically or recalled in Jimmy Durante's record about the guy who found it.[2] The big choral works – *The Golden Legend, The Martyr of Antioch* – provoked ecstasy when presented at the triennial Leeds Festivals, but nobody hears them now. The macaronically named *Overture di Ballo* and the incidental music to Shakespeare get an occasional hearing, but, even in the Savoy operas, Sullivan is being so transformed as to be robbed of his essence. The recently acclaimed Joseph Papp version of *The Pirates of Penzance* retains little more than his melodic line, and the various travesties of *The Mikado* have syncopated even that out of easy recognition.

Yet Sullivan in his day was considered to be England's answer to Mozart, Mendelssohn, Spohr and Weber, all impeccably packaged into one moral, tasteful, essentially Victorian whole. England, having done well enough in literature and having conquered a large part of the earth with Birmingham guns in order to make it accept Manchester goods, needed a great composer. Sullivan, it seems, was the only man available.

The mention of Louis Spohr in that list above points to the fallibility of esthetic judgment. Gilbert makes his Mikado propose punishing music-hall singers by making them hear 'masses and fugues and ops by Bach interwoven with Spohr and Beethoven.'[3] Few had any doubt of Spohr's greatness. Occasional performances of his works on the radio have recently surprised listeners with their revelation of a masterly, almost Mendelssohnian talent, but no revolution of standards could place him with Beethoven or Bach. Yet, knowing the shakiness of some contemporary judgments (the Beatles, Andy Warhol, Christopher Fry) we must not deride the Victorians for thinking too highly of Sullivan.[4] British music had been occluded by the great Germans who followed the Hanoverians to London, and what listeners heard in Sullivan was the revival of a native quality lost since Purcell, allied to a technique learned in Leipzig and hence not to be despised by Europe.

The trouble was that the musical establishment was not content with accepting that great musical skill could sometimes find its best expression in the lighter forms. The British proletariat was being kept out of mischief by being formed into brass bands and choral societies, and the huge choirs of the provinces had to be further uplifted by being made to sing oratorios. The duty of British composers was to provide these; if they could, as a sideline, produce the odd symphony, so much the better: the moral power of Beethoven was well known, and the English, being a more moral people than the Germans, ought to produce symphonies morally if not musically better than his. Poor Sullivan was dragged by an imposed sense of duty, which soon became an inner conviction of responsibility to his own talent, into fields where his deficiencies were nakedly exposed. This did not happen in his prime, but it began to happen when the real British musical renaissance began – with the advent of the brilliant, self-taught, neurotic, ambiguous Elgar. Sullivan, though he died young (at only 58), lived to see it.

Dr. Jacobs's very detailed biography – which draws lavishly on Sullivan's letters and diaries – records successes and failures in areas where superficial readings of his career have taught us to believe otherwise. None of the Savoy operas did as well as Cellier's *Dorothy*, which is now forgotten.[5] Sullivan's solitary excursion into grand opera – *Ivanhoe* – flopped only because D'Oyly Carte overexposed it. Comic operas that Sullivan composed with librettists other than Gilbert – *Haddon Hall*, for instance, with Sydney Grundy – did not do noticeably worse than the mythic collaborations.[6] Sullivan made a lot of money and gambled much of it away. His career must be accounted an overall success, however posterity is forced to judge it. He gave the Victorians what they wanted and, apart from musical fulfillment, he got a lot out of life – close friendship with royalty, acclaim in Germany (where the future Kaiser would quote from the First Lord's song in *Pinafore)*, the willingness of France to pamper him for money if not for music (France still cannot understand what all the G.&S. fuss is about) and a satisfactory if adulterous sexual life, previously undisclosed, with the American beauty Mary Frances Ronalds.[7]

Inevitably, with his attempt to concentrate wholeheartedly on the life and career of Sullivan, Jacobs cannot permit Gilbert to upstage him. There is no room for Gilbert's wit, scabrous and otherwise, though there has to be plenty of room for letters between the two men, if only to show what a fine letter-writer Sullivan was, as well as an outstanding diarist. His writings confirm what others said about him – that he was good, kind, urbane, courteous, and a terribly hard worker. Anyone who has ever produced an orchestral score will appreciate what Sullivan's labor was like – the long nights with twenty-odd-stave paper, dotting in his notes with exquisite neatness and the speed of shorthand, his fingers stained with incessant cigarette smoking, always – like Mozart – fighting to meet a deadline.

Unfortunately there is no space in this book to do more than indicate generally the greatness of Sullivan's talent, as opposed to his genius. The genius is in the melodies, which we all know by heart; the talent lay in what the orchestra was doing while the melodies looked after themselves – the odd sly touches like the citation of a Bach fugue when the Mikado mentions the 'ops', the contrapuntal brilliance, the capacity to make even the accompaniment to a patter song live its own organic life. Offenbach's scores are dull. With the coming of the Broadway musical, orchestration became an affair of hacks (except for Kurt Weill). No composer of light music has ever, except for Sullivan, brought to it the loving attention to detail that could only be learned in the tough, serious school of the symphony and oratorio. *The Mikado* is not just superb entertainment; it is exquisite craftsmanship of an almost Mozartean order. When America pirated his works, Sullivan was pained because he knew what New York and Boston audiences were missing, hearing as they were nothing more than a vamped pit-band transcription of the vocal score. If Sullivan was not a great composer, at least he was technically equipped to become one.

Unfortunately he was a Victorian. This meant that he had to be respectable, and musical respectability meant abiding by harmonic rules and formal restrictions sanctified by Higgs, Prout, Goss and other pundits the world has forgotten.[8] He realized what Wagner had done in the opening bars of *Tristan*, but he did not dare to follow that path. Gilbert's librettos – more subversive and sexually perverse than the audiences guessed – were his substitute for musical daring. When he dared, he could always go back to the Leeds Festival or dash off a religious motet, but the daring was, anyway, only vicarious. Bernard Shaw, the most brilliant music critic of that age, saw what was going on:

He furtively set Cox and Box to music in 1869 and then, overcome with remorse, produced Onward, Christian Soldiers and over three dozen hymns besides. As the remorse mellowed, he composed a group of songs – Let Me Dream Again, Thou'rt Passing Hence, Sweethearts, and My Dearest Heart – all of the very best in their *genre*, such as it is. And yet in the very thick of them he perpetrated Trial by Jury, in which he outdid Offenbach in wickedness, and that too without any prompting from the celebrated cynic, Mr W. S. Gilbert... They trained him to make Europe yawn; and he took advantage of their teaching to make London and New York laugh and whistle.[9]

Whatever he achieved, he did his best work with the celebrated cynic. Chiefly, probably, because Gilbert was the most accomplished lyricist who ever lived. The moral pundits would have preferred him to work with Tennyson, as he did in *The Foresters*, where the Poet Laureate's comic fairies were to sing this sort of thing:[10]

TITANIA:	Nip her not, but let her snore.
	We must flit for evermore.
1ST FAIRY:	Tit, my Queen, must it be so?
	Wherefore, wherefore should we go?
TITANIA:	I, Titania, bid thee flit.
	And thou dar'st to call me Tit?
	Pertest of our flickering mob,
	Wouldst thou call my Oberon Ob?[11]

The gust remains dual, as in Crosse & Blackwell. Dr. Jacobs must write a companion book on Gilbert and, later, bind it with this.[12]

The New York Times Book Review, 1984

1   Fortnum & Mason is an upmarket department store in Piccadilly founded in 1707. Crosse & Blackwell is a British food brand established in London in 1706. Meaning 'God and my right', *Dieu et mon droit* is England's royal motto, which appears on a scroll at the base of the coat of arms of the UK. Guy Burgess and Donald Maclean were members of the Cambridge Five spy ring who defected to the Soviet Union in 1951.

2   'I'm the guy who found the lost chord', performed by Jimmy Durante, was featured in the 1947 MGM film *This Time for Keeps*, which starred Esther Williams with a supporting cast that included Durante, Lauritz Melchior and Johnnie Johnston. Co-written by Durante and Earl K. Brent, the song was released as a 78rpm in 1947 in the US and the following year in the UK, with 'Little Bit This, Little Bit That' on the B side.

3   The quote is from this verse of 'A more humane Mikado' ('My object all sublime', etc.):

    The music-hall singer attends a series
    Of masses and fugues and 'ops'
    By Bach, interwoven
    With Spohr and Beethoven,
    At classical Monday Pops.

4   Christopher Fry was an English poet, playwright, and screenwriter, widely known for his 1948 play *The Lady's Not for Burning*. The clause '(the Beatles, Andy Warhol, Christopher Fry)' was added in HQY.

5   *Dorothy*, a three-act comic opera with music by Alfred Cellier and libretto by B. C. Stephenson, premiered at the Gaiety Theatre in London in 1886 and ran for 931 performances over the next three years, setting a record for longest-running musical theatre production that lasted until the early twentieth century.

6   Once Gilbert and Sullivan dissolved their partnership in 1889 after the production of *The Gondoliers*, the impresario Richard D'Oyly Carte sought new writing partners for Sullivan in order

to continue producing new comic operas at the Savoy Theatre. One of these was the English dramatist Sydney Grundy, who, in his only collaboration with Sullivan, wrote the libretto for *Haddon Hall*, which had a modestly successful run of 204 performances at the Savoy Theatre from 1892-93.

7   Mary Frances 'Fanny' Ronalds was an American socialite and amateur singer best known for her musical salons and her affair with Sullivan.

8   The names of Higgs, Prout, and Goss are added in HQY. See LW, p. 11, and TMM, p. 20/40.

9   *Cox in Box* premiered in 1866, was performed at charity benefits in 1867, and became popular in 1869 upon receiving a professional production. Its year of origin is given by Shaw as 1869 and was changed to 1867 by Burgess. The entire quote has been restored here to Shaw's original text, unitalicized titles and all; *Shaw's Music*, Vol. II, pp. 173-4.

10 Alfred, Lord Tennyson, generally regarded as the chief exemplar of Victorian poetry, was England's Poet Laureate from 1850 to 1892.

11 Lines from Act III, Scene ii of *The Foresters, or, Robin Hood and Maid Marian*, written by Tennyson at 82 years of age and considered among the weakest he ever wrote. According to Jacobs, Tennyson wrote this verse play around 1891 at the request of the American theatre manager Augustin Daly, who had met Sullivan in California in 1885 during the latter's visit to the US and commissioned him to provide music for the play. Titania's quatrain is altered (incorrectly) and reduced to three lines in HQY.

12 In HQY, this sentence is preceded by: 'The author of *The Bugger's Opera*, whose obscene cast list finds a place in Joyce's *Ulysses*, would never have ordered his musician to set such innocent dirt.'

32. NATIVE WOOD-NOTES

An Elgar Companion, edited by Christopher Redwood
Ashbourne, Derbyshire: Sequoia-Moorland, 1982

Elgar: The Man by Michael De-la-Noy
London: Allen Lane, 1983

I prepared for the writing of this review, apart from reading the books, by listening to a recording of Elgar's Second in E flat played by the USSR Symphony Orchestra under Yevgeny Svetlanov.[1] The question I was asking was: is Elgar exportable? Or, more pertinently, could the music of a neurotic conservative Edwardian make sense to the children of a failed socialist revolution? Judging from the scant applause at the end, the work had not made much sense. The interpretation itself strikes me as being insufficiently tentative and nervous: the first movement sounds like rejoicing in Red Square, with the odd quiet interval of brooding on the beauty of the personality of Lenin. This may be overfanciful. Perhaps if I had come innocently to the disc and been told the performance was British I might have accepted it (although knowing it was not Boult in charge), but I would have known that the brass instruments were not made in the West. The socialist economy has achieved some damnably tinny trumpets.

The truth is that Elgar used to export – to France and Germany as well as to Czarist Russia. The Germans saw the greatness of *Gerontius* before the British did.[2] Elgar had a number of Continental decorations as well as the O.M. and (the donors knew he had no son) a barren baronetcy.[3] His alleged insularity seems to be a myth of late manufacture. If he is all-English, one wants to know how exactly. Can racial elements reside in pure sound that does not set out to evoke

Ancient and Modern or clodhopping on the village green?[4] Neville Cardus, in this excellent *Elgar Companion,* compares Mahler and Elgar, finding in the former personal emotion that might be embarrassing if we are British, in the latter emotions appropriate to public celebration – a king's death, a victory in the Transvaal. Plenty of musicians hear the dropping of Worcestershire pippins in *Falstaff.*[5] I know that Elgar is not manic enough to be Russian, not witty or *pointilliste* enough to be French, not harmonically simple enough to be Italian and not stodgy enough to be German. We arrive at his Englishry by pure elimination.[6]

The *Companion* is an anthology of reminiscences and assessments we have read before, but it is good to have them together. The Enigma of the *Variations* gets thirty-two pages, complete with 'Auld Lang Syne' in the minor trying woefully to be a counterpoint to the great noble theme.[7] The man who devised ciphers in World War One liked his mysteries. The Violin Concerto has an epigraph from Le Sage's preface to *Gil Blas: 'Aqui esta encerrada el alma de...'*[8] Mr De-la-Noy thinks that soul belonged to Alice Stuart-Wortley, whom Elgar called 'Windflower', and that the guilt of the widower Elgar had much to do with his capacity for loving everybody except his own wife.[9]

Mr De-la-Noy's biography is notable for being the first to be written since the death of Elgar's daughter Carice Blake in 1970. Rosa Burley's sometimes bitchy memoir, already written then, could not be published: 'it quite simply contains comments and judgments upon Elgar and his relations with his wife that no daughter would have wanted to read.'[10] This new biography, which draws on that memoir as on others, is very candid about the relationship. Alice Elgar, older than her husband, idolised his music in a manner both encouraging and embarrassing, especially to strangers, sent the chilled Elgar to bed with seven hot water bottles and woolly bedsocks, but does not seem to have accorded him more substantial comforts in bed. Elgar could be passionate enough in his music, but Lady Elgar never fired his passion. There was a curious *ménage à trois* that lasted many years, in which Dora Penny – the 'Dorabella' of the Variations – stayed up with the composer till all hours while his wife retired early, but the piano seems to have been banging away all the time and there is no record of Dorabella's being thrown to the floor.[11]

Elgar's sexual life remains dimmer than that of Shaw – the close friend who emerges, in both books, as the only man not of the family who never doubted Elgar's greatness.[12] He wrote to Jaeger (Nimrod) in affectionate terms which did not preclude the odd 'darling', but there was no homosexuality there: Elgar went along with the judgment of his second royal master, who thought that 'men like that shot themselves'.[13] There was no bohemianism in Elgar's life, though there was much manic depression. Although he became a public figure who pretended that music was bosh and only dogs and horses worthwhile, he could behave like a failed poet nail-biting in the York Minster. Some of his public pronouncements, especially those attacking British philistinism, gave grave offence, and his professorial tenure at Birmingham – in a chair specially endowed for him – was a disaster.[14]

As a man Elgar was a typical victim of the British class system. His father was a tradesman and he himself began his career as a poor teacher and orchestral player.[15] His craving for state honours was pathetic: he wanted the barony that only Britten among composers got, and got when he was dying. He wanted intimacy with the royal family, though he knew that neither Edward nor George cared a damn about music. His sense of victimisation, which could come out even when he wore his state kneebreeches and flashed his medals, found the inevitable economic expression: he was a poor man considering the necessity of taking up violin teaching again even in honoured middle age. It seems true that he did not have much money, but, like Mozart in Auden's poem, he never had to make his own bed and there was always a team of servants, including a cook and a valet-chauffeur.[16] It was no paranoia that made him brood on neglect in his old age. The seventieth birthday concert had a wretched attendance. Mr De-la-Noy is too young to remember his death in 1934 (that was a bad spring for music: Gustav Holst and Frederick Delius also died), but I remember that the popular papers remembered him only as the composer of 'Land of Hope and Glory'. But his work is secure now, except, bafflingly, on the Continent.[17]

The Observer, 1983

1   Melodiya/His Master's Voice – SXLP 30539, vinyl LP released 1981 in the UK

2   added in HQY: (that execrable first performance – fully recounted in both books – was a huge setback).

3   OM: the Order of Merit. Established in 1902 by King Edward VII, it recognizes distinguished service in the armed forces, science, art, or literature, or for the promotion of culture.

4   *Hymns Ancient and Modern*: the Church of England hymnal

5   'Worcestershire pippins' are apples from the Worcester region; cf. *The Merry Wives of Windsor*, Act I, ii, where Sir Hugh Evans says, 'I will make an end of my dinner; there's pippins and cheese to come.' Burgess considered Elgar's symphonic poem *Falstaff* the finest musical evocation of Shakespeare.

6   added in HQY: 'That he was a great composer (hence of international significance) we ought to have no doubt.'

7   actually forty-one pages (50-90) comprising five separate essays

8   'Here is locked the soul of...'

9   In HQY, the line is changed to: '...the widower Elgar (though all widowers are guilty, being murderers) had much...'

10 *Elgar: The Man*, p. 12.

11 In HQY, the line is changed to: '...all the time (it comforted Lady Elgar and probably reassured her) and...'

12 In a Letter to the Editor published on 5 June 1983, Michael De-la-Noy asserts that 'Anthony Burgess's lengthy and much appreciated review...contains one rather odd remark. I feel it ought to be corrected in fairness to the memory of at least two great servants of music. Mr Burgess says that Bernard Shaw emerges 'as the only man not of the family who never doubted Elgar's greatness.' But Shaw's contribution to Elgar's career was minimal compared to those of Nimrod (August Jaeger, his publisher at Novello) and the young Adrian Boult. Among many others who never doubted Elgar's greatness one might include his wealthy patron Frank Schuster and Alfred Rodewald, to whom the First Pomp and Circumstance March was dedicated.'

13 Quote attributed to King George V, who succeeded Edward VII.

14 added in HQY: 'The nastiness of the great man, given the *una corda* treatment by previous adoring memoirs, especially that of the violinist W. H. Reed, comes out here, but the great man's greatness is not seriously diminished. The greatness, as always with artists, lies only in the art, which may be termed patrician and plebeian but hardly at all middle class.' William Henry 'Billy' Reed was an English violinist, teacher, composer, conductor, and long-time friend of Elgar. His book *Elgar As I Knew Him* (1936) provides detailed information about the writing of the Violin Concerto in B minor and numerous sketches for Elgar's unfinished Third Symphony that were used by Anthony Payne in his completion of that work sixty years later. Reed's later book *Elgar* was published in 1939. His tendency toward hagiography has been pointed out by Eric Blom and others; De-la-Noy remarks that Reed's books on Elgar 'go far beyond the call of duty in their reticence on personal matters.' p. 12

15 added in HQY: '– a ragged usher and a damned fiddler.'

16 Auden's 'Metalogue to *The Magic Flute*' (line 24): 'But *Mozart* never had to make his bed.'

17 added in HQY: 'Hans Keller, who cannot often be trusted to show much more than well-informed bad temper, said a perspicacious thing in 1957: 'Continental audiences will come to understand Elgar's innovations *via* Britten, just as a twelve-noting pupil of mine has come to understand Wagner *via* Schoenberg.' Keller is right to see Elgar's genius as innovative. Perhaps the Second Symphony was too revolutionary for the baffled Soviet audience on my record of Svetlanov and his tin trumpets.' The Keller quote is the closing line of 'Elgar: "The First of the New"', originally published in *Music and Musicians*, June 1957 and reprinted in *An Elgar Companion*, pp. 275-8.

33. ELGAR NON È VOLGARE

One of the great mysteries about music is that, though it speaks an international language, it remains obdurately insular. Israel resents having to listen to Wagner, and Beethoven seems to the French to be all too Teutonic. Some composers do not travel at all: like certain wines, they demand an insular palate. This seems to be true of some of the composers of my own country, England, who, despite the few kilometres of sea separating Dover from Calais, have never really entered Europe. Italians will perhaps listen to Henry Purcell and Benjamin Britten, but there is a whole body of composers in between these two who are either unknown or known for the wrong reasons.

Take Sir Edward Elgar. Born in 1857, dead in 1934 (along with two other composers not well known in Europe – Gustav Holst and Frederick Delius – and possessing, like them, a not very English-sounding name), he came at a time when English music was in bondage to the Germans. Handel had come over from Hanover with George I, who never spoke one word of English, and German-speaking Queen Victoria had decreed that Felix Mendelssohn was the new Handel. It was difficult for an English composer to write in an English style – a style that should declare its continuity from the time of a composer like Purcell or, earlier, Byrd or Orlando Gibbons or Lawes. Quite apart from the tradition of religious oratorio in the German manner, there was another German whose influence lay heavy on English music – Richard Wagner, whose orchestral sonorities were so seductive that no young composer could evade them. The musical academies of Britain taught young men to write in a 'European', which meant a German, manner. Elgar did not go to an academy: he was self-taught and earned his living as a violinist and the director of an orchestra in a lunatic asylum.[1]

When he came to compose his 'Enigma' Variations for orchestra in 1899 it was evident that here was not merely a new voice but a distinctively English one, despite the quotation from Tasso at the end of the score: 'Bramo assai, poco spero, nulla chieggio'.[2] The Englishry lay less in the orchestral sound and the harmonies – both of which owed much to Wagner – than in a peculiar humour and a peculiar self-doubting passion. The English are a humorous people, and they are frightened of expressing their emotions, though this does not mean that they are devoid of passion. In the 'Enigma' Variations Elgar is concerned with the gentle passion of friendship. He presents his theme and then presents it again with a single climax: he is expressing his love for his wife, and this declaration of affection had better be disposed of quickly so that he can get on to less embarrassing avowals. In each variation a close friend is depicted, quickly and economically. We hear an organist friend who played in Worcester Cathedral exercising his fingers. We hear another friend who had a bulldog named Dan, or, rather, in the manner of Hogarth's self-portrait, the dog is placed in the foreground and it is he we hear plunging into the river Severn and then shaking himself dry. When Elgar comes to a final self-portrait (under the initials E. D. U., which stand for the *Edu* or *Eduardo* his wife always called him) he alternates self-mockery with the briefly grandiose. We are hearing, probably for the first time, a quality we have to call Edwardian.

Two years after this composition was first presented, King Edward VII came to the British throne. Edward Elgar, soon to become Sir Edward Elgar, was born to express the peculiar quality of the new royal epoch. It was expansive, concerned with the glories of empire, and seemed to have an unlimited confidence in the future. Elgar composed a symphony in 1908 – No. 1 in A flat major – which summed up the era. There are massive soaring melodies in which horns and trumpets and trombones, playing, according to their preference, in flat keys, provide images of imperial grandeur. We are often, perhaps too often, in Westminster Abbey, attending a royal coronation. The quality of Elgar's melodic invention is such that the opening theme of Schumann's 'Rhenish' symphony has been described as Elgarian. But there are other qualities, including one of extreme tenderness that seems to have something to do with a response to the English spring. The music, however one describes it, is not European. It is bluff, pragmatic, often elusive, eloquent, ashamed of its eloquence, but not afraid to give the direction *nobilmente*. The symphony is hardly known in Europe, though there was a time when it was much performed in Germany under Hans Richter, to whom it is dedicated. I once saw and heard it performed on Italian television, but the pleasure was impaired for me by the yawning of the first trumpet, who was apparently bored by the work.

The second symphony – in E flat major – was composed in the last year of Edward VII's reign and, when performed in 1912, was obviously intended as a poem of regret at the passing of an epoch. 1912 was the year of the sinking of the *Titanic*; two more years would bring the First World War. The work is full of neurosis. The heavy brass tries to recall the glories of the reign that is gone, but the themes are distorted and become ghostlike. The work ends in a sunset glow of resignation. This is the work that Europe ought to hear. It is more sophisticated than anything by Mahler, it is wholly professional, it is probably the last of the great symphonies.

Unfortunately, Elgar has become known in Europe solely for the trio of a march he wrote. It is a good march, and the melody of the trio is magnificent, but it is not what Elgar is really about. He noted that Johann Strauss and Richard Strauss had glorified the Viennese waltz and he proposed doing the same for the military march – hence the group of orchestral marches entitled 'Pomp and Circumstance'. The title is ironic. It is a citation from a speech made by Othello on his discovery that Desdemona has been unfaithful to him. 'Farewell, the pomp and circumstance of glorious war'. These marches by Elgar seem powerfully extrovert, but if one listens carefully there are the harmonies of self-doubt, of a neurosis kept under control, of a potential hysteria. They are a profound psychological document, and one that says as much about the state of England as about the composer himself.

Consider the nature of this composer in his maturity. He had received great honours from the state, but he had little money. He was a Catholic purveying the doubts and glories of a Protestant kingdom. He was a man of passion frightened of that passion, a neurotic pretending to be John Bull. In his later days he pretended not to be a musician at all: with his field-glasses and top hat he spent much of his time in the royal enclosure at the horse races. He knew that his fellow-countrymen were philistines. Like the Europeans themselves, they knew him only for a particular tune – one to which the words 'Land of Hope and Glory' (ridiculously chauvinistic) had been set. By the year of his death the music of Europe had succumbed to a neurosis which could express itself only in the hysterics of atonalism. Schoenberg was purely neurotic; he had abandoned the ordered structure represented by tonality. Elgar had kept his neurosis under control. Mahler had not, nor had Berg and Schoenberg and Webern. Stravinsky had taken up the posture of the *pasticheur* and the mocker. Elgar had presented civic order, imperial élan, but he had been aware of the qualifying doubts, the tropical neurosis, the malaria, and the sand-fly fever. In this respect he was very much like his contemporary Rudyard Kipling.

Europe ought to listen to one of Elgar's later works, the symphonic study called *Falstaff*. If it is too 'English', then Verdi and Boito are too English too. T.S. Eliot pointed out that Sir John Falstaff is not merely an ox of a man, swinishly drunk and greedy, a thief and a coward. There is nobility in him, an immense wit and an unquenchable intelligence, and a great deal of self-doubt. He grows old and his nose becomes 'as sharp as a pen'. Verdi and Boito knew all this, and Elgar knew it too. Elgar's portrait avoids the Rabelaisian and perhaps over-stresses the nobility. But he sets the portrait, which Verdi and Boito could not do, against a background of the Worcestershire countryside which nurtured him and which Verdi and Boito knew not at all. How music can express the *physical* quality of landscape is a mystery, and only English music seems to have done it.

The music of Elgar is, after all, available on discs and cassettes, but I doubt if Ricordi in Milan is much interested. I think it is up to the adventurous music-lover with innocent ears to give the music of Elgar a trial. If I love this music, it is not because I am a chauvinistic Britisher. It is the only music I know that presents in all honesty the complex *Weltanschauung* of the early part of our century. It does not snivel like Mahler, and it does not scream like Schoenberg. It maintains a gentlemanly dignity, and it scorns to cry in public. But its heart is large.

Corriere della Sera, 1983

1   The ensemble, which Elgar led from 1879–84, comprised *attendants* and not inmates of the Worcester and County Lunatic Asylum in Powick.

2   from *La Gerusalemme Liberata* (Jerusalem Delivered), which Elgar translates on the following page as 'I essay much, I hope little, I ask nothing'.

The English Musical Renaissance 1860–1940: Construction and Deconstruction by Robert Stradling and Meirion Hughes. London: Routledge, 1993

Taking the *viva voce* part of the ARCM examination (Theory and Composition), I was asked by Dr Herbert Howells to name the great figures of the renascence which is the subject of this admirable book. I began with Elgar, and was close to physically struck down. Elgar was nothing, he'd merely built on the pioneering work of Mackenzie, Stanford, Cowen, Parry. Who was the best of the twentieth-century English song-writers? Peter Warlock, I said and still say. Wrong, wrong. It was Ivor Gurney.[1] I should have remembered that Gurney and Howells had been close friends, and that Gurney called Howells 'Howler'. He certainly howled at me. I failed, of course.[2]

It has not been easy for some of us to find a political dimension in music, but it's always been there, as *The English Musical Renaissance* exemplifies. When, with its Royal Academy and Royal College and the Albert Hall near by, South Kensington became England's Leipzig, the musical tradition that was fostered was nothing if not gentlemanly. Stanford was Anglo-Irish ascendency, Parry was almost aristocratic.[3]

When Elgar appeared, with his well-made oratorios for the Midlands and, later, his incredible *Enigma Variations* for London, he was something of an embarrassment. The son of a shopman, an itinerant fiddler, a totally self-taught composer, he in no wise conformed to the South Kensington image. His first symphony, conducted by Hans Richter, was first heard in Manchester. In Birmingham Elgar's brief and disastrous professorship was dedicated to railing at the South Kensington establishment.

And yet Elgar was loaded with white-elephant honours. Stanford wanted him tamed and, gentrified by his patrician wife, made fit to join the élite. Awkward, of course, was the fact that Elgar was a Catholic, and that he had, in *Gerontius*, dramatised a doctrine that the Church of England did not accept.[4] Catholics with provincial accents were not wanted. It was embarrassing that Elgar was so evidently a genius.

We hear Elgar still, though Europe has ceased to (except for the *Pomp and Circumstance* accompaniment to Twining's Tea TV commercials). Where are Mackenzie, Cowen, Stanford and Parry, to say nothing of Holbrooke, Boughton, and Cyril Scott?[5] We used to hear Stanford's sea songs on the last night of the Proms; Parry is firmly fixed there now with his setting of Blake's 'And did those feet?', though God knows what he thought the lines meant when he melodised them and melodised them well. The 'dark Satanic mills' are, in Blake's symbolism, churches; Jerusalem is the ultimate harmony of copulation and imagination. If you don't believe me, read the epic *Milton* to which the sixteen lines are attached.

What kind of music did the South Ken Renascence want? Nothing German, though it was hard for Stanford to keep Brahms out of his own tonalities. And yet the most English of them all went to Germany to study under Max Bruch (also to Paris to learn what he called French polish from Ravel). This was Ralph Vaughan Williams, moneyed, aristocratic, who found his voice through Tudor anthems and a folk-song tradition already near dead.

All English music subsided to the pastoral. Arthur Bliss could be fierce with his *Morning Heroes*, but *Lie Strewn the White Flocks* breathes the right grass and sheepdip. Walton was out, said RVW, as was Constant Lambert; both mocked pastoralism. And they were both, somehow, not British. As for Arnold Bax, a Londoner, he turned himself into a Fenian and, like Yeats, mourned the Dublin dead of 1916.[6] Nobody seemed to like anybody, and probably the sound of the music hardly came into it.

When music failed, it was because of political subversion. At the BBC's Coronation concert of 1937, the chief commissioned work was *These Things Shall Be*, words by J. Addington Symonds, music by John Ireland.[7] Frank Howes attacked the work as shallow, hollow and insincere. Ireland complained that even if 'one wrote better than the Holy Ghost and the Blessed Virgin Mary combined, they would still piss on one's works as insignificant rubbish.'

Hardly, in this instance, insignificant. After the lines 'And every life a song shall be / When all the world is paradise', a solo horn plays, as descant to the main melody, 'The Internationale'. And the same song of communist aspiration crashes out after the whispered question 'Say, heart, what will the future bring?' Few seem to have noticed. Yet Ireland's (and Britten's) support of the communist-led Workers' Musical Association did him no good.

But other composers, now forgotten, rose higher than Ireland to sink lower. What were the really popular works of the pre-war era? *The Immortal Hour* by Rutland Boughton, which – first performed at Glastonbury, England's answer to Bayreuth – chalked up 500 performances in London, an incredible figure for an opera. Where is it now? Boughton also blotted his copybook with a fine orchestration of that same 'Internationale'.

Coleridge-Taylor's *Hiawatha*, beloved of the late Malcolm Sargent, was always a sell-out, especially with costumes and wigwams and genuine Amerindian choreography, but the composer's radicalism – he was an African black – caused headshakes in South Kensington.[8] The third of the great dead popular works was John Foulds's *World Requiem*. Foulds was a

Mancunian, not a gentleman. He disappeared into India, and his music is not now anywhere to be found.

The fate of so much English music cannot be blamed solely on its intrinsic debility. Frank Bridge was a fine impressionist who cried aloud at his neglect. Cyril Scott's piano impressionism was highly original (we used to hear it on the radio in the 1930s). Holbrooke's orchestra, with its banks of saxophones, looks interesting: I have never heard it.[9] Even good light composers, like Eric Coates, have disappeared (except for the signature tune of *Desert Island Discs*).[10]

This survey ends in 1940, when the Germans started deconstructing our concert halls, but it could just as well, admit the excellent authors, end in 1934. In that year Elgar, Holst and Delius all died. It was a bitter triple blow.[11] Delius was of German parentage, Holst was a Swede, and both were very English (Delius was forced into the English pastoral fashion because he could make no name abroad). How do these three names, and others, stand up against the geniuses of Germany? Our authors think: not well. We, if we were honest, would deplore this incessant pastoralism. We would reject RVW's Fourth Symphony as searing modernism because its dissonances are all *appliqué*. Visiting conductors like Pierre Boulez conduct nothing of ours. We missed the boat somehow. We don't export well. Our music, as at the Proms, confirms an ironic chauvinism or encourages a cosy insularity. This book very eloquently sets it all down.

The Observer, 1993

1   The English poet and composer Ivor Bertie Gurney, best known for his songs, was a chorister in his youth at Gloucester Cathedral, where he studied with Dr. Herbert Brewer along with fellow students Herbert Howells and Ivor Novello (then known as Ivor Davies).

2   See LW, p. 350.

3   Born in Dublin, Sir Charles Villiers Stanford was educated at Cambridge followed by musical studies in Leipzig and Berlin; in 1882, at age twenty-nine, he was one of the founders of the Royal College of Music, where he taught composition the rest of his life. Sir Charles Hubert Hastings Parry, 1st Baronet, succeeded George Grove as head of the Royal College of Music in 1895; an enthusiastic sailor, Parry was elected in 1908 to membership in the Royal Yacht Squadron, the only composer ever to receive that honor. Gustav Holst and Ralph Vaughan Williams both studied composition with Stanford and Parry.

4   *The Dream of Gerontius*, composed by Elgar in 1900, relates the journey of a pious man's soul from death to God's judgment to Purgatory, where it ultimately settles. Largely a meditation on Roman Catholic eschatology, the libretto, drawn from the 1865 poem by Cardinal John Henry Newman, conflicts with precepts of the Anglican Church; for this reason, performances of *Gerontius* at the Three Choirs Festival used a revised text until 1910. (Newman was the City of London's first saint since the sixteenth century, beatified by Pope Benedict XVI in 2010 and canonized by Pope Francis in 2019.)

5   Joseph (or Josef) Holbrooke, an English composer, conductor, and pianist whose music is stylistically akin to Richard Strauss, composed numerous poems and fantasies, and applied a descriptive or poetic title to virtually every work, relatively few of which have been recorded. Rutland Boughton, best known for his opera *The Immortal Hour*, was a prolific English composer of opera, choral music, symphonies, concertos, chamber music, and songs who devoted twelve years to establishing a summer music festival at

Glastonbury and achieved great success in this effort until 1926, when his decision to join the Communist Party eroded public support for his music and the festival he had created. Cyril Scott was a prolific composer with wide-ranging interests in alternative medicine, health foods, naturopathy, philosophy, yoga, and the occult. Described by Eugene Goossens as 'the father of modern British music', Scott was admired by Claude Debussy, Richard Strauss, Igor Stravinsky, and his close friend Percy Grainger.

6   Sir Arnold Edward Trevor Bax was an English composer who remains best known for his symphonic poem *Tintagel* and seven symphonies. While studying at the Royal Academy of Music, he became fascinated with Celtic culture. Prior to World War I, he moved to Dublin, where he wrote fiction and verse under the pseudonym Dermot O'Byrne. The Easter Rebellion, or Easter Rising (*Éirí Amach na Cásca*), was an armed insurrection against British rule carried out by Irish republicans seeking to establish an independent Irish Republic. It began on 24 April 1916 during Easter Week, lasted six days, and left much of Dublin in ruins. The rebellion caused the deaths of nearly 500 people, including sixteen Irish republican leaders who were court-martialled and executed by the British government.

7   The English composer John Nicholson Ireland studied composition with Stanford at the Royal College of Music. Strongly influenced by Debussy and Ravel, Ireland developed a style sometimes called 'English Impressionism' and remains best known for his Piano Concerto, piano miniatures, and songs.

8   Cf. Chapter 37 *In tune with the popular soul.*

9   Holbrooke composed a Serenade for oboe d'amore, clarinet, basset horn, two saxhorns, five saxophones, viola, and harp, as well as a saxophone concerto.

10   *By the Sleepy Lagoon*, a light orchestral piece written by Coates in 1930.

11   'I sometimes feel that the growth of my musical sensibility came to a full stop in 1934, when Elgar, Holst and Delius died.' YH, p. 390.

Review of *Delius: A Life in Letters 1862–1908*, compiled and
edited by Lionel Carley
London: Scolar Press in association with the Delius Trust,
1983

In 1933 we celebrated the fiftieth anniversary of the death of
Wagner. In 1934 British music lost its three senior luminaries
– Elgar, Holst and Delius. And now the quinquennium has
come round, and they ought to seem as safely dead, beyond
reassessment, classic as Wagner did then.[1] But the reputations
of the three are far from settled. *The Planets* has got into the
international repertory, but we don't hear enough of the rest
of Holst to get him into perspective. Elgar is played enough,
except for the post-*Gerontius* oratorios, and we hear now,
which we did not in 1934, the strains of a neurosis qualifying
the Edwardian stability. Delius is played, I am sure, more
than he used to be – an impressionistic Nietzschean who
can promote the death-urge in the young – but many have
forgotten that he was one of the fathers of applied jazz. I met
Duke Ellington just before he died (on a plane flying from
New York to Toronto) and asked him which composer had
meant most to him. He said 'Delius' without hesitation.

This compilation by the honorary archivist to the Delius
Trust gets the composer to Florida by page 5. The sister-in-
law of his foreman on the orange estate said this about him:

> Time an' time I tell Mister Delius he ought to go to the
> church, I don't care which because the Lord don't know
> denomination. Just like he don't know color. But Mister
> Delius, he pay no mind... Long as he make his music he just
> don't mind what else.

Delius was soaking in black melody and realising that the harmonies of Brahms or Parry didn't fit. The *Florida* suite, composed in 1886–7, looks forward to symphonic jazz, and symphonic jazz is very nearly what *Appalachia* is. Going from Florida to Leipzig to learn Straussian harmony would have ruined him. He was lucky to be drawn to Grieg, whose chords Debussy described as bonbons filled with snow. Leipzig was the right musical town for the German that Delius was (just as Holst was a Swede), but he had nothing of Brahms or Max Reger in him. He needed technique, but his sensibilities were drawn to Scandinavia and France, as well as what the blacks were singing in America. His work is, when you come to think of it, a strange compound – death-urge, atheism, *Übermensch*, sex. There is nobody quite like him.

When Ravel, as in the *Scheherazade* songs, sounds Delian, it is assumed that Delius is really Ravelian, since no British composer could possibly influence a Frenchman. But the letters show Ravel to have been hard at work making piano arrangements of Delius's *Margot la Rouge*. Florent Schmitt was another of his arrangers and copyists.[2] Incredible though we would like it to be, Delius was played, known and admired in Europe long before England discovered him. There are some who would like him to have been a mere gifted amateur, but he went the whole Continental course and knew all about counterpoint. If in later life, like Elgar, he pretended technical ignorance, this was the right response to companies of philistines. There is a solidity in even the most evanescent of his scores; inside the son of a Bradford German wool-man there was an academic toughness.

The portrait of Delius we most cherish is the one created by Augustus John when the composer, made blind and paralytic by syphilis picked up in Paris, looked ethereal and frail. Ken Russell's admirable film of fifteen years ago animated this picture.[3] The Delius we see in the photographs here is young, vital, handsome, moustached, working and playing hard, rarely in disgusting Bradford, an early exile who heard nothing in British music (he and Elgar must be spending eternity in an incurable state of cold shoulder), writing in German, Norwegian and French as much as in English. His correspondents, besides Grieg, are Richard Strauss, Edvard Munch, Strindberg, Gabriel Fauré, Princess Alice of Monaco (he got an early hearing in Monte Carlo), Léon Moreau – all Europeans. He himself is Fritz, not yet Frederick. Towards the end of the compilation the English begin to appear – Granville Bantock, Vaughan Williams (who wanted lessons but got them eventually from Ravel), above all Sir Thomas Beecham.

Beecham's devotion, to be followed by that of Philip Heseltine, ensured the near-exclusive Anglicisation of the Delius cause. But the composer is settled in Grez-sur-Loing at the end of this volume, married to the painter Jelka Rosen, nursing the spirochaete and the intransigent postures of elected exile. He was a Yorkshireman, despite the German blood, and seems to most of us an incomparable tone-painter of English landscape (I don't think music can really paint anything, but we have Eric Fenby's testimony that the Delius musical images sprang out of inner visions of nature; we have also Delius's own titles). Nevertheless, despite *Brigg Fair* (whose Yorkshire folk melody he got from Percy Grainger), there was no yearning in him for a return to the English north. There was only one real north, and that was among the Griegian fjords. He created his own climate – which combines torrid Florida and windswept Norway – as he created his own moods, which are primaveral and autumnal at the same time. This book, however, places him firmly in that great artistic Europe which England has never learned properly to enter: it reminds us that Delius is international before he is British.

1   Burgess mistakenly uses *quinquennium* (period of five years) instead of *quinquagenary* (period of fifty years) to denote 1984 as the year marking the fiftieth anniversary of the deaths of Elgar, Holst, and Delius.

2   In the 1890s, the young Florent Schmitt prepared piano-vocal scores for four operas by Delius – *Irmelin, The Magic Fountain, Koanga,* and *A Village Romeo and Juliet* – and was one of Delius's few French friends during the years he lived in Paris. Schmitt was a composer who studied with Gabriel Fauré and Jules Massenet at the Paris Conservatoire, won the Prix de Rome in 1900, and became a member of *Les Apaches*, a group of Parisian musicians formed in 1903 that included Maurice Ravel, Ricardo Viñes, and later Igor Stravinsky. A controversial figure, Schmitt supported the Nazi party in the early 1930s and worked for the Vichy government in the 1940s, yet was admitted to the *Légion d'honneur* in 1952.

3   *Song of Summer*, a black-and-white television film co-written, produced, and directed by Ken Russell for the BBC's *Omnibus* series, is a video portrait of the last six years of Delius' life. The film's title comes from the tone poem *A Song of Summer*, one of several Delius compositions featured in the soundtrack. First broadcast on 15 September 1968, it starred Max Adrian as Delius and Christopher Gable as Eric Fenby. Russell described *Song of Summer* as the best film he ever made, stating that he would not have done a single shot differently.

On 28 April 1982, Channel One (postponed from 24 February 1982 on account of a strike), French television gave us Gustav Holst's symphonic suite *The Planets*, played by the Orchestre National under the direction of Lorin Maazel. To me, an Englishman, this was a great moment. At last the French were taking English music seriously. It is, I recognise, a pity that the name Gustav Holst should not sound very English. His family was Swedish, long-settled in Cheltenham, that most English of towns (full of retired colonial administrators and refined schools for girls), and, until the outbreak of World War One, Gustav Holst even called himself Gustav von Holst. There was, at one time in British musical history, more chance of success for a musician if he had a foreign name. Sir Henry Wood had to call himself Klenovsky, and Leopold Stokowski began his career as a London church organist with the name Stokes.[1] The names of a number of our modern British composers sound foreign, such as Edmund Rubbra, Frederick Delius, even Edward Elgar, though Britten speaks for Britain just as Jean Françaix used to speak for the Français.[2] In terms of idiom and inherited tradition, no composer would well be more English than Gustav Holst.

The Planets is his best-known work, and it represents a synthesis of many of the elements which were emerging in British music at the beginning of World War One. There had been a desperate struggle to free English music from the overwhelming German influence of the nineteenth century. Queen Victoria and Prince Albert had both been German, and their favourite composer had been Felix Mendelssohn. The idiom of such now forgotten composers as Sterndale Bennett, Mackenzie, Cowen, Stanford was, where it was not Mendelssohnian, Brahmsian or Wagnerian.[3] Holst's early music sounded like diluted Wagner, and it was only by concentration on such native traditions as those of ecclesiastical polyphony and folksong that emancipation from the power of the devil of Bayreuth could be achieved. The minor and major scales of classical usage had to be replaced by the ancient modes which could still be heard in folksong. There is a passage in the 'Uranus' movement of *The Planets* where we hear the distorted prancing of Morris-dancers (the Morris dance – really *danse mauresque* – is part of the British folk tradition):

Here Holst, having abandoned the scales that were good enough for Mozart and Beethoven, is contriving a mode of his own. It is hard to find a fixed tonic or dominant, and the harmonies, too, have to break away from classical tradition. Holst has two harmonic procedures – one based on consecutive triads, as in 'Mars':

and the other on superposed fourths, which, as in 'Jupiter', can even provide a melody:

We are into the modern era, but in a very British way. Though Holst is presenting the solar system, he is anchored firmly in the green fields of England and, celebrating Jupiter as the Bringer of Jollity, he seems even to transport the god to Trafalgar Square for the singing of a national song:

Watching the endless rolling of credits – *cadreurs, ingenieurs de son,* etc.[4] – after the televisual presentation of *The Planets*, one is ironically reminded how essentially lonely and painful a procedure the composing of the work was. Holst could never have foreseen that the French would have employed so great a battery of technical and artistic specialists to render his piece, or pieces, acceptable to the great French public. He was teaching music in St Paul's Girls' School, Hammersmith, London, and, on his only free days, Saturday and Sunday, he locked himself up in the music room to pen his huge score. It was a painful procedure, because Holst suffered from arthritis in the right arm and hand, and he was grateful for the existence of repeat signs, which obviated the need to write the same notes over and over again. Look at the 'Mars' movement in autograph score, and you will find that the notation of the pounding rhythm – five beats to a bar – occurs only at the beginning. The sign ✕ – which he called 'one of the joys of life' – saves him not only labour but pain.

'Mars', the first number of the suite, was drafted long before the beginning of World War One, yet it remains one of the most evocative musical images we possess of technological warfare. The march rhythm of the past is distorted to five beats: we hear not pounding feet but rumbling machines. The strings play *col legno* – with the wood of the bow, not the horsehair. Parodic trumpet calls are answered by the voice of the tenor tuba – one of the most crass or stupid-sounding of all brass instruments – and six horns, divided into two trios, stride with their consecutive triads across the endless advance of the mechanised armies. For a work conceived in 1913 it is an astonishing prophecy.

'Venus' is all strings, woodwind, harps, celesta, glockenspiel. We do not hear the trumpets and trombones and timpani, and the horns have become cool and pastoral. But there is no tame consonance: the harmonies are delicately astringent. After the opening horn-call, four flutes oppose three clarinets in the sounding of sevenths and ninths in contrary motion. We are in the presence of the bringer of peace, but it is a peace earned with difficulty and difficult to sustain.

'Mercury', the winged messenger, evokes, though only superficially, the aerial legerity of Berlioz's *Queen Mab* Scherzo. There are two key signatures in the score – two flats, three sharps – and the effect is less one of bitonality, in the Milhaud manner, than of keylessness. When the common chord of B-flat alternates with that of E major so rapidly, the tritonal flavour negates key. Key is for the earth, with all its solid certainties, but Mercury's world is the air. The trio of this scherzo is nothing more than the repetition, with shifting harmonies and tone colours, of a wisp of melody that has no time for development:

After the trio we hear one of the most incredible evocations of airy speed in all music. It is very simple: the strings rush about with tonal consecutive secondary sevenths in fourth inversion and, towards the end, a pedal rhythm on the timpani serves as bass to a solo celesta.[5] And then Mercury alights and asserts key. The final chord is the common chord of E major, but it might just as well have been B-flat. Any key will do, since Mercury is careless about his landing strip. Soon he will take to the air again.

For the god Jupiter Holst concentrates on his capacity to preside over a kind of bucolic harvest merrymaking, though, because his first theme seems to be in A minor, we are not allowed to forget his thundermaking capacity. Superposed fourths suggest not only the god's reserves of acerbity but also the sharpness of homebrewed beer. Holst takes us for a few bars to the British music hall, then, in the manner of the trio of 'Mercury', gives us a wisp of a tune in the mixolydian mode which achieves variety only through tone-colour, not development or modulation:

Then comes the great E flat song on unison strings and horns, finally taken up by the entire vast orchestra but closing not on the expected tonic chord but on a joke. The notes B-flat E-flat F, which sound like a suspension on the dominant, are converted into another idiom, that of superposed fourths, and we are back to the beginning again. Holst, when asked to provide a melody for a patriotic song called 'I Vow to Thee, My Country', was too weary to write a new one, so used this great Jupiter theme. It is a pity. In 'Jupiter', the song is one of harvest thanksgiving not patriotic fervour, and it is hard for British listeners to expunge the association. French listeners have no such problem.

The fifth and seventh movements of the symphonic suite are among the most original conceptions in modern music. 'Saturn' presides over old age, and we are in a thematic world of no certainty except the march of time towards death. But there comes a moment, contrived with extreme simplicity, when the gates of mystical revelation seem to open to the noise of bells. 'Neptune', the final movement, is himself the mystical god, the seer, and his music – in five-four time, like 'Mars', only much slower – is mostly an alternation of quiet dissonances with much arpeggio work on harps and celesta, ending with the singing of unseen female voices whose final harmonies fade into the distance. It belongs to the most disturbing music of our century. In between these two slowly treading movements comes the celebration of Uranus, the magician, highly effective and brilliantly scored but carrying too much of the flavour of Dukas's *L'Apprenti Sorcier* to those who do not realise that the main tune is a distortion of an old music hall song – 'Tonight, tonight, we'll have a good time tonight'.

The television presentation of this work was effective but misguided. Holst wrote for a large orchestra, and the resources of French television were able to give him more than he asked for – eight horns instead of six, eight timpani instead of six. The sound was thrilling. But the visual aspects of the presentation emphasised the space age too much. Maazel and his players seemed to be dressed in elegant astronaut outfits. Each movement was partially accompanied by visual materials which showed the planets themselves: the astrological meaning of the planets, which is what the work is about, was totally ignored. Holst was not attempting physical depiction. He was interested in astrology, and the subject-matter of his work is the influence the planets have traditionally been held to exert on men's lives. The music is startalk, but it is not astronomical.

Not only astrology but other aspects of the occult and strange affected Holst's thinking and hence his music. Perhaps his greatest choral work – *The Hymn of Jesus* – is a setting of part of the Apocrypha. The atmosphere is not conventionally Christian, but it is certainly mystical. There is an incredible moment when the word 'light' is set, on divided voices, to a discord consisting of the chords of G and F-sharp. Holst was drawn strongly to the more recondite expressions of religious experience. He learned Sanskrit in order to study the *Rig Veda*, and he wrote an opera on a theme out of it, as well as some choral hymns which are settings from the same mystical codex. Introspective as he was, he was also, as parts of *The Planets* make clear, an earthy man, fond of steak, good burgundy, rousing songs, the bustle of the Hammersmith market on a Saturday evening. He wrote simple music for the string players of the girls' school where he taught, but nothing in Holst is exactly simple. There is a moment in the *St Paul's Suite for Strings* when two English tunes are brought together:

The upper melody is an old folk song called the Dargason, and it is in six-eight time. The lower melody is, I think, well enough known in France. It is 'Greensleeves', in three-four time, attributed to King Henry VIII. The collocation seems improbable, but Holst makes it appear that the two tunes came from the same brain. In his capacity to produce astounding novelties with simple means, he belongs to the great composers. I hope that *The Planets* will not, to French audiences, be the beginning and end of Holst. He wrote better work, and the French deserve to hear it.

Typescript, 1982

1   The myth that Stokowski was originally named Stokes has long been discredited; see *Stokowski: A Counterpoint of View* by Oliver Daniel and *Stokowski and the Organ* by Dr. Rollin Smith. The rumor originated in the 1930s and was repeated in print by pianist Oscar Levant in his book *The Unimportance of Being Oscar*. Stokowski's birth certificate, proving the authenticity of his name, can be viewed at the Family Records Centre in London.

2   A stanza of *Byrne* (p. 19) addresses this topic in verse. See also ACC, p. 383.

Strange that the names of English-born composers
Should often sound (Delius, van Dieren) foreign:
Holst, Rubbra, Finzi, Elgar – names like those, as
Though the native stock skulked in a warren
Shivering at Calliope's bulldozers.
McCunn, true, rather overdid the sporran.
That Handel was staunch British to the end'll
Still be denied by Huns who call him Haendel.

3 Sir William Sterndale Bennett was an English composer, pianist, and conductor who led the Royal Academy of Music for the last decade of his life.

4 cameramen, sound engineers

5 The strings play consecutive seventh chords in third inversion, not fourth.

The Heritage of Samuel Coleridge-Taylor by Avril
Coleridge-Taylor
London: Dennis Dobson, 1979

I knew Samuel Coleridge-Taylor before I knew Samuel Taylor
Coleridge. My father strummed the 'Petite Suite de Concert'
on the piano, Pier bands would play the *Othello suite*. I was taken
to hear the choirs of mills and factories perform *Hiawatha*.
Avril Coleridge-Taylor's citation of the opening bars of the
'Ballade' for orchestra brings back vividly the experience, in
my adolescence, of hearing it live – probably conducted by Sir
God Damfrey, as Peter Warlock called him, at Bournemouth.[1]
Coleridge-Taylor was a part of popular British musical life
and *Hiawatha* still lives on, as solid an annual ceremony as
Messiah. His daughter recalls hearing a blues version of
'Demande et Réponse' belting out of a London railway
terminus public address system. That would be 'Question and
Answer', a popular waltz I well remember playing at army
dances. Coleridge-Taylor is far from forgotten, but he is not, I
think, represented any more in serious orchestral concerts. Sir
Arthur Sullivan and Sir Edward Elgar proclaimed his genius,
which was a genuine one, but it was not a genius of an order
that could produce either a *Mikado* or a *Dream of Gerontius*.
Although his musical aims could not have been more different,
Coleridge-Taylor's status is probably equivalent to that of
George Gershwin. He was a natural melodist with no great
gift of Beethovenian development; he was a highly competent
colorist; he could appeal to the popular soul.

I learn now for the first time why he was named as he
was. His father was Daniel Taylor, who came from the Gold
Coast to England to qualify in medicine, duly qualified, grew

disgusted with the colour prejudice of patients in the practice in which he was an assistant, and left for Sierra Leone and biographical silence. He left behind in England an English wife, Alice Holmans, and a son of his own colour. This son had been born in the Lake District, and a sentimental association with the Lake Poets got him his name, not at first hyphenated. Coleridge-Taylor was later to make a cantata out of 'Kubla Khan', but the music could not rise to the words. He also set some minor lyrics of his namesake, but the songs are no longer sung. It is typical of Coleridge-Taylor's genius that it could cope with the simple trochees of Longfellow but not with more exalted verses. The list of his songs that his daughter gives us shows that he was typical of the British musicians of his age in having little literary taste.[2] Elgar was no better until some angel led him to Newman. It was only when Holst, Vaughan Williams and Delius discovered Walt Whitman that British choral music found its voice. The Victorian and Edwardian annals of provincial choral festivals make, from the aspect of libretti, distressful reading. Coleridge-Taylor spent two years on an opera that was doomed to silence because of its words. No British musician can afford to neglect his literary heritage, but too many alumni of the Royal College of Music were content with the effusions of provincial journalists who fancied themselves to be poets.

Coleridge-Taylor got to the Royal College having been observed by a kindly musician playing marbles with a violin case under his arm. A little black boy with a fiddle, remarkable. The talent was undoubted and it flourished early. Coleridge-Taylor was only thirty-eight when he died, but he left behind a lot of music. We should, perhaps, regretting that he never moved out of the Brahms-Dvorak orbit that Stanford kept spinning at the RCM, remember that he died in 1912, before he could absorb acerb and ironic impulses from the Continent, and that it was in order for a musician of his period to be content with harmonies that Stainer blessed. But consider that Dvorak, in his New World Symphony, dared consecutive sevenths and chords a tritone apart. Consider too that in 1909 Vaughan Williams set Housman in *On Wenlock Edge* and effected a quiet tonal and harmonic revolution considered by the late Hubert Foss to be quite as significant as that of Debussy's *Images*. Coleridge-Taylor, subjected to racial slurs in the streets and even from a jealous fellow-student, was a pioneer in the promotion of black rights and black art: he set negro melodies in the style of Dvorak; how much better if he had set them in the style of Vaughan Williams. There are black dances among his works, and an overture dedicated to Toussaint L'Ouverture, but he took no lessons in orchestral and harmonic colour from other British composers who could best teach him about the recovery of ancient styles and the development of exotic ones.

He is limited, then. There is hardly a sound in his works that you will not find in Brahms: *Tristan*, let alone Debussy, is too modern for him. But the melodic gift is remarkable. Amateur choruses, which like to enjoy their hobby and not serve progressive art with the *Gurrelieder*, find *Hiawatha* singable and the telling of the Algonquinian tale, however trivialized by Longfellow, dramatically moving. To produce genuinely popular music on a large scale is given to few. But expectations were different at the Royal College, when Holst merely played the trombone and Vaughan Williams the triangle in one of Coleridge-Taylor's youthful orchestral works. He was the hope of the British musical future, which meant he would carry the banner of a Central European art already outmoded by Richard Strauss and Mahler.

Avril Coleridge-Taylor – as on a larger scale, Imogen Holst – has divided her life between the exploitation of her father's music and the creation of music of her own. She gives a list of her works, but if I do not know any of them the fault must lie either in their quality or the crassness of concert promoters. Her life as an orchestral conductor, particularly of *Hiawatha*, has been distinguished by a residual sadness.

The daughter of a white woman (not, to judge from these pages, at all an exemplary mother) and a man half-black, she was destined to attain her greatest successes in South Africa until the whispers and threats began. It says much for her generosity of spirit that she loves that country. It is hoped that, stimulated by her advocacy of her father's neglected works (not so much neglected in America, one is glad to see), and intrigued by her admirable technical analyses of some of them, British conductors and chamber groups will consider bringing them back into the repertory. Benjamin Britten said in 1975: 'The gift of music which Samuel Coleridge-Taylor was born with is something to be remembered with gratitude.' Sir Malcolm Sargent asked, for a seventieth birthday present, that he be allowed to conduct a full-scale performance of *Hiawatha*. These are sizable tributes. For my part, I should like to hear again that orchestral 'Ballade' which once, when I was in short trousers in Bournemouth, made me thrill to the possibilities of orchestral colour. When I went back to school after the vacation we read *The Ancient Mariner*. I had no doubt that the black man had produced better art. Then, alas, I began to grow up.

Times Literary Supplement, 1980

1　The British conductor Sir Daniel Eyers Godfrey (1868–1939) founded the Bournemouth Municipal Orchestra in 1893 and remained its principal conductor until 1934. Sir Dan's father, Daniel Godfrey (1831–1903), was bandmaster of the Grenadier Guards; his son, also named Dan Godfrey, was the first full-time conductor of the BBC Wireless Orchestra (1924-1926) as well as station manager at BBC Manchester in the 1920s.

2　In a Letter to the Editor published in the *TLS* on 7 March 1980 (p. 266), Ralph Leavis of Lincoln College, Oxford, took issue with this judgment: 'Anthony Burgess in your issue of February 15 informs us that the composers of Coleridge-Taylor's time lacked literary taste. Whatever the faults of Parry's and Stanford's vocal music, lack of literary taste is not one of them. Perhaps Mr Burgess has confused his reviewing with his fiction?'

38. UNRAVELLING RAVEL

This year we commemorate the fiftieth anniversary of the death of Maurice Ravel, a very French musician (his father's background was Swiss and his mother's was Basque). Although the actual date of his death was 28 December, the French are starting their celebrations early. They think highly of him – far more highly than they think of their colossus Hector Berlioz. Perhaps Berlioz, with his vast orchestras, symphonic rigour, and epic conceptions, sinned against the French canon of good taste. Ravel was elegant, exquisite, and none of his works go on too long. Except perhaps for *Boléro*, which lasts little more than fifteen minutes but seems to go on for ever.

Conceivably, Maurice Ravel was the last of the twentieth-century composers to combine serious musicality with the ability to make himself popular. He disdained serialism, stuck firmly to the tonal, and actually produced tunes. *Boléro*, as nobody can deny, contains a tune – indeed, it contains nothing else but a tune, repeated *ad nauseam* on all the melodic instruments while the basses thrum out an incessant do sol sol and the drums hammer away in a slow crescendo at a figure which never once changes. Ravel himself disparaged the work. Having composed the tune, he said, all he had to do was to give minimal instructions to a group of music students and leave the construction of the score to them.

We, the mere listeners, tend to disparage *Boléro*. But when we hear that pianissimo rhythm on the side-drum and then the first statement of the theme on the flute (somewhat Basque, a filial tribute) we respond, against our will, to its curious magic. It is not, of course, a bolero at all. A bolero is fast. This is more like a sarabande danced in the desert. A hot wind blows through the work. We feel a burning sun on the back of the neck. I am not being fanciful. One of the curious aspects of Ravel's music is its capacity to evoke non-musical reality. It seems to describe things. Nobody can understand quite how this is done.

In the early days of the talking cinema there was a film called *Bolero* (no acute accent: the name of the work was quick to be degallicised). It featured George Raft and Carole Lombard and it was set in the Paris of the First World War, a long time before *Boléro* was actually written. Raft's great ambition was to open a night club in which, in partnership with Miss Lombard, he was to dance to *Boléro*. But the war got in the way. Raft in the trenches was accompanied by the rhythms of *Boléro* transferred to the guns. He survived, and his night club, which had no room for a symphony orchestra, resounded to his dancing feet and huge negroes battering jungle drums. You could, it seemed, do anything with *Boléro*, and Ravel never complained.[1] There was even a dance band arrangement in which I remember hammering away at the piano part until my fingers bled.

Ravel, although he wrote a good deal of abstract music, was happiest when he could evoke the outside world – the world of nature, ancient history, fairy stories. *L'enfant et les sortilèges*, with its libretto by Colette, is surely the one perfect opera of all time. The staging is fantastic – cups and saucers that dance, a whole forest that sings, Watteau shepherds and shepherdesses stepping down from their frame to rebuke the naughty child who treats things and animals badly and is taught, by Nature herself, the necessity of love and compassion. This could have been sentimental, but the citrous sharpness of the music keeps an ironic distance from the subject. There is wit. If there are any tears, they are ours, and they are compelled by the sheer beauty of the sound.

This concern with expressing the exterior world makes Ravel an impressionist. He is usually spoken of in the same breath as Debussy, the first and greatest of the musical impressionists, who used the orchestra to describe the moods of the sea and the wind, the passage of the clouds over the night sky, and, in his piano *Préludes*, a great variety of subjects, from Mr Pickwick to footsteps in the snow, from a girl with yellow hair to a firework display ending with an ironic echo of the *Marseillaise*. We may legitimately doubt whether music is capable of describing the outside world. It is, after all, only a succession of sounds which possess their own logic, withdrawn from reality. But give a piece of music a title – *La fille aux cheveux de lin* or *Poissons d'or* – and we are only too eager to see that outside world with our ears. What both Debussy and Ravel disdained to do was to express emotion. Emotion was Germanic, romantic, somewhat dangerous. It was too close to the id, condemnable by both St Augustine and Sigmund Freud. Wagner's *Meistersinger* Overture could excite an urge to fight for Germany, but nobody listening to Ravel's *La Valse* has ever wanted to fight for the Austro-Hungarian Empire. Or, hearing the baroque pastiches of *Le Tombeau de Couperin*, has shed tears for the demise of Louis XIV's France. Ravel's music keeps its distance from the didactic and the pornographic. It is exquisitely static.

And, as I say, it is popular. George Gershwin learned from it when writing his *Rhapsody in Blue*. The British composer-critic Constant Lambert condemned the *Rhapsody* as snobbish, disdaining the demotic roughness of the jazz on which it was based and proud of its French lessons. But probably both Ravel and Gershwin were right to see whether jazz themes could yield to sophisticated symphonic treatment. In the Hollywood film about Gershwin's life Maurice Ravel is actually portrayed nodding with approval at Gershwin's ragtime rhythms. It was a fairly accurate portrait – elegant, slight (he did not carry enough avoirdupois to get into the French army), something of the dandy.

My own knowledge of Maurice Ravel is somewhat limited, but I cherish certain stories told to me by our British composer, the late Ralph Vaughan Williams. Ravel was the most exquisite orchestrator who ever lived, and Vaughan Williams went to him in Paris to learn how to improve his own orchestration. Ravel said: 'Write me a little minuet in the style of Mozart', and Vaughan Williams replied: *'Monsieur,* I did not travel this distance to write little minuets in the style of Mozart.' Ravel was impressed by this British bluntness and taught his very mature pupil the technique of orchestral *pointillisme.* Vaughan Williams invited him to London to eat steak and kidney pudding in a restaurant near Victoria Station. Ravel was entranced by the dish and, every weekend, took the Channel boat to eat steak and kidney pudding. The heavy diet did not diminish his delicacy.

Shortly before his death, Cambridge University awarded Ravel the honorary degree of Doctor of Music. The French do not well understand doctorates. They think that the only doctors are doctors of medicine, and Ravel was extremely puzzled by his new distinction. In London his exquisite ballet *Daphnis et Chloé* was performed, and one or the dancers sprained her ankle. Ravel was distressed and said: *'Mademoiselle,* you have injured yourself dancing to my music. *Hélas,* I cannot cure you, complete doctor though I am.'

He was a man of great delicacy and large compassion. The piano concerto he composed for Paul Wittgenstein (brother of the philosopher) is an instance of this. Wittgenstein had lost his right arm in the First World War and it was evident that he would have to abandon his career as a concert pianist. But Ravel wrote his concerto for the left hand only, and Wittgenstein made a new name for himself. The work seems to me to be very difficult even for two hands.

It is right to think of Ravel fifty years after his death and to listen closely to his music. He is regarded by some – on the evidence of *Boléro* and *Pavane pour une infante défunte* and *Ma mère l'oye* – as a rather lightweight composer. He lacks

Beethoven's clumsiness (always a sign of sincerity) and is at the opposite pole to Teutonic portentousness. But he remains an exemplar of French culture at its best. He will not be played much during France's revolutionary bicentennial in 1989.[2] That was, when you come to think about it, a very unfrench event. From the French we expect delicacy, wit, refinement, artistic images of high civilisation. We get them from Maurice Ravel.

Corriere della Sera, 1987

1   Ravel was so taken with Larry Adler's rendition of *Boléro* on the harmonica (or mouth organ, as Adler preferred to call it) that he added a provision in his will exempting Adler from having to pay royalties on *Boléro* whenever he performed it. See Chapter 67 *Hand to Mouth*.

2   Burgess celebrated the *bicentenaire* by composing *Marche pour une révolution 1789-1989* and writing *1789: An Opera Libretto*, which Jean-Pierre Carasso translated and adapted as the libretto for a marionette opera titled *Le Bleu-Blanc-Rouge et le Noir*. See ACC, p. 352.

James Joyce's Chamber Music: *The Lost Song Settings,* edited by
Myra Teicher Russel
Bloomington and Indianapolis: Indiana University Press, 1993

The dead do not object to discourtesy, so, on their behalf, the
living must. It was extremely discourteous to leave off both
the cover and the title-page the name of the man who is the
occasion for this book's being published at all. Amends have
to be disinterred from a mass of introductory material, and
the ignorant eventually learn that the name of the composer
was Geoffrey Molyneux Palmer. He has disappeared from
Grove and other musical compilations, and his music remains
unknown. With the publication of these thirty-two songs, all
settings of poems from *Chamber Music,* any posthumous fame
he may garner must be solely as an appendage to Joyce.

   Palmer, like Joyce, was born in 1882, a fact that would have
been of superstitious import to the magic-minded master had
he known it. Though stricken by multiple sclerosis shortly after
gaining his degree in music at Oxford, Palmer died sixteen
years after Joyce. The ailment quelled his career as pianist and
organist, but he was able to compose innumerable songs, two
operas and three cantatas. These large-scale works are all on
Irish folk themes. For Palmer, though born in England, was
Irish, and was to emigrate to his ancestral land, where, tended
by his sisters, he lived close to the Martello tower in Sandycove
where the opening of *Ulysses* is set. Joyce guessed from his name
that he must be Protestant, and so he was, of Williamite stock
and clerical family. A temperamental kinship between the two
men is not easy to find. In 1907, the year of its publication by
Elkin Mathews, Palmer's mother gave him a copy of *Chamber
Music* as a present. He was, as they say, hooked.

He wrote to Joyce asking permission to set some of the poems. The ten settings that Joyce received, read, strummed and eventually sang were, in his view, as good as it was possible to get. The appendix to this book gives the names of other composers who set single poems or, recognizing the cyclical nature of the whole thirty-six, made major music of the little collection, and there seem to be (the list isn't complete: Antheil, for instance, is absent) about 150. Of all he heard, Joyce continued to adjudge Palmer's settings the best. He urged Palmer to publish, but he never did.

To his dying day, Joyce thought there were only ten Palmer settings. When Palmer himself died, it was revealed that there were thirty-two, neatly copied and bound, and that the inexplicable personal ban on publication had probably nothing to do with aesthetic dissatisfaction. It is possible that Palmer, in a prissy Protestant way, did not wish to be associated with Joyce after the scandal of *Ulysses*. I can think of no other reason. The songs, always publishable, are now published. They are highly professional; they even have a breath of lessons from Stanford at the Royal College of Music, whither Palmer went after Oxford. They have no flavour of, say, *On Wenlock Edge*, though they are occasionally modal – Dorian or Phrygian. The very first chord is a wide-stretching added sixth. There are isolated secondary sevenths but no real dissonances. They are mostly too high; tenors who have tried them recently have had to have them transposed a tone or more downwards.

The poems are mostly Elizabethan in flavour, and sometimes are mere pastiche: Joyce wanted the music to be pastiche too, but never got it. What he gets here is bland, pleasant, freely modulatory, and sedulous in clinging to Joyce's prosody: the effect is often that of recitative. Joyce's stanzas are too short to submit to Schubert-style strophic setting, with genuine tunes. It is the final song – 'I hear an army' – that is the true test of Palmer's musicianship. Ezra Pound and W.B.

Yeats heard modernism there, which Pound called imagism. It, and the song preceding it – 'All day I hear the noise of waters' – Palmer joins with a segue and thus makes an acceptable dramatic unity. We are in Edwardian England or Ireland, with no breath of futurism, but I think the Palmer style works. Unfortunately I am a drink-and-tobacco-ruined baritone and can make no auditory sense of the vocal lines. But throughout, I would say after long sessions at the piano with my son on the tenor recorder, these are of considerable sensitivity. Joyce, protecting his poor little verses, was right in his judgment.

Why did Palmer neglect to set XII ('What counsel has the hooded moon'), XXIX ('Dear heart'), XXXII ('Rain has fallen') and XXXIII ('Now, O now, in this brown land')? An editorial suggestion here is that Palmer was frightened of archaisms like 'ancient plenilune' and 'beauty raimented' and thought that 'comedian capuchin' (which, surely, everybody likes) might sound foolish. Edwardian song-writers were unduly timorous in their attitude to the legitimately settable. Vaughan Williams was wrong to cut the football stanza from 'Is my team ploughing?' Palmer was not a bold composer. That he was a highly competent one this volume makes clear.

Times Literary Supplement, 1993

Stravinsky: The Composer and His Works by Eric Walter White
London: Faber, 1979

Conversations with Igor Stravinsky by Igor Stravinsky and
Robert Craft
London: Faber, 1979

This is the second edition of Eric Walter White's book of
1966. The story has been brought up to Stravinsky's death, the
original text has been revised, and the Register of Compositions
now covers Stravinsky's last two works – *Requiem Canticles* and
The Owl and the Pussy-Cat. Publication of this indispensable
study coincided with the Stravinsky Festival of October and
November 1979, when the London Symphony Orchestra and
the London Sinfonietta played the entire canon, including
some brief compositions not previously heard. It was a noble
tribute to a great musician, probably the greatest of our
century. The noblest tributes are still to come. 1982 brings his
first centenary.

It also brings the first centenary of the birth of James
Joyce. It is not, perhaps, over-fanciful to see something cognate
in their respective contributions to modern art. Both began
with a scintillant post-romanticism, admitted (*Petroushka;
Finnegans Wake*) the rhythms of popular song, time-travelled
(a term used only derisively in Constant Lambert's *Music
Ho!*), explored a new language without entirely abandoning
the perspectives of the old. Technically they were without
peer. The ends of both were in their beginnings. The father
('with his broad and hairy face to Ireland a disgrace')
dominates *Finnegans Wake* and looks through a glass on the
first page of *A Portrait*.[1] The opening of *The Firebird* (1909)

– A♭ F♭ E♭ D♮ F♮ G♮ – recurs as the first hexachord of the series in the 1959 *Epitaphium*.[2] Stravinsky was a literary musician, Joyce a musical littérateur. They never knew each other, despite having Paris and George Antheil in common.[3]

The first part of White's book – 'The Man' – gives Stravinsky's biography accurately but frigidly. For a closer look at him we have to go to Craft's volumes of conversation, where the articulacy is, however, daunting and not really credible. We await the large synthesis of a biography which shall exhibit the talents of an Ellmann. But White's Register is remarkable. From it we learn that the opening folk-theme of the 'Princesses' section of *The Firebird* became, in 1946, a slow foxtrot with the words

> *Summer Moon, you bring the end of my love story;*
> *All too soon my love and I are apart.*
> *Summer Moon, why shine in Indian Summer glory?*
> *Summer Moon, while I'm alone with my heart?*[4]

The story we heard at the time was that Stravinsky was short of cash and needed, though he did not get, the transfusion of jukebox popularity. We hear also about that other strange flirtation with commercial pop, when 'in (or about) 1930' Jack Hylton's band is supposed to have played an adaptation of part of *Mavra*.[5] Hylton is said by Stravinsky to have conducted this in the Paris Opera House about 1932, and 'it was an awful flop'. White adds: 'It seems strange that the composer should have consented to such a travesty of his music.' The story as I remember it is rather different.

According to a news item in the *Daily Express* in, I think, 1932, Stravinsky when in London heard Jack Hylton's band and admired its precise ensemble work. He himself came up with a chunk of *Mavra* which the orchestra played accurately but uncomprehendingly. The composer's comment was 'Sveet.'

Hylton's was (bewildered): 'Yes, very nice indeed.' Hylton read music but would not have sought out the score of *Mavra*. Although at that period there was a dance band arrangement of Ravel's *Boléro* that Jack Payne's BBC orchestra played nearly every day about 5.15, contemporary serious music of Stravinsky's kind never got into the programmes.[6] Stravinsky's mixed-up reminiscence is, perhaps, significant. He wanted general acceptance, and, like, Joyce, he was fascinated by the popular and even banal (audi *L'Histoire du Soldat*). In *Petroushka* there is a banal cornet solo accompanied by bassoon arpeggios. These latter disobey the rules of harmonic decency by having the A of the dominant chord on F repeated. The German publishers of the score silently corrected the A to a bass F, making it orthodox. Stravinsky recorrected it to the incompetence he wanted.[7] The term 'wrong note harmonisation' was coined to describe his procedure in *L'Histoire du soldat*. Puzzled listeners, and even great musical experts, found 'wrong notes' in all his works up to the atonal phase (where, the unkind say, every note is wrong).

Ernest Ansermet, for instance. The end of the *Sanctus* in the *Mass* which he first performed is a chord of A major into which a G and D have been inserted. Ansermet said: 'This forms an agglomeration of notes which the ear cannot take in and which is literally cacophonous.'[8] If a logical justification is required for these two intruders, then we can find it in what comes immediately before, but Ansermet said that was sheer 'paper': the ear had to be satisfied. Stravinsky's tests for any chord or progression were, in fact, always aural. The ear *is* satisfied if it takes the chord as an anticipation of a change to the key of D, which Ansermet's ear was unwilling to do. It may be said that one of Stravinsky's aims in art was to open up ears to an acceptance of a new beauty of sonority, but new beauty always appears first as ugliness. If some composers (perhaps Schoenberg was one; Busoni was probably another) are best appreciated in the written score, Stravinsky's work was always intensely physical. We remember what he said about Bach's instrumentation: 'you can smell the resin on his strings and taste the reed on his oboe.'

Physical in more than an auditory sense, then: the entire sensorium has to be engaged – as it was in *Le Sacre du Printemps*, to the horror of so many of the Paris first-nighters of 1913. Stravinsky knew the *feel* of instruments, could associate the sound with what the fingers and/or lips were doing. Craft records his words about the playing of Shorty Rogers, a West Coast jazz trumpeter: 'His patterns are instrumental: half-valve effects with lip glissandos, intervals and runs that derive from the fingers, 'trills' on one note, for example, G to G on a B-flat instrument (between open and first-and-third fingers) etc.'[9] Stravinsky knew the possibilities of harmonics better than anyone: witness the *fleurissage* near the opening of *The Firebird*, where fingers lightly massaging a string produce the entire harmonic series (an effect also used in *Le Sacre*) to magical effect, and horns glissade on harmonics. Composing the Violin Concerto in D for Samuel Dushkin, he heard in his head a chordal motif (low D, E at the next octave, A an octave and a fourth above that) and asked whether it was playable. Dushkin said no, and Stravinsky said *'Quel dommage'*. But Dushkin went home and tried it out: 'to my astonishment, I found that in that register, the stretch of the eleventh was relatively easy to play, and the sound fascinated me'.[10] He telephoned Stravinsky at once, and the composer was not so much relieved as confirmed in a kind of auditory conviction: that chord he was to call his 'passport' to the Concerto.

Stravinsky, as the world knows, said he did not need twelve notes when he could do all he wanted with seven. But a study of Webern led him to his own highly idiosyncratic use of serialism. The concentration on segments of his twelve-tone *Grundstimmung*, rather than the whole stretch, was in accordance with his old love of diatonic folk-type motifs of a few notes. *Le Sacre* is made out of these – undeveloped 'symphonically' but varied in rhythm and colour, their rigidity, as it were, enforcing a flexibility of repetition that was new in music, though perhaps Mussorgsky had anticipated it. The fascination of these late brief atonal works, whose 'specific gravity' is out of all proportion to their size, resides in our awareness of the composer's awareness that tonality still exists. And Stravinsky's cherishing of his tone-rows as objects almost as tangible as new-laid eggs showed that the whole sensorium was still engaged; what seemed to the superficial ear a cerebral *tissage* was, and is, a solid object, a new addition to the physical universe which has to be judged not as 'expression' but as creation.

Any artist's importance can be gauged by the extent to which he modifies a world not much concerned with art. This world can see the truth in the line 'April is the cruellest month' without being too sure who wrote it. Hearing the musical equivalent – the opening high bassoon solo of *Le Sacre* (which Eliot seems to have had in his ears when invoking his own spring) – is to be conscious of prehistory.[11] *Le Sacre* can be regarded as a 'popular' work in that the untrained philistine ear accepts it as a just accompaniment to a cinematic presentation of prehistory. If Disney had not wanted that work for his *Fantasia* (he paid Stravinsky $5,000 but shrewdly pointed out that he strictly didn't have to pay anything, since *Le Sacre* had been published in Russia, hence outside the copyright covenant), its tonalities would still have found their way into the 'atmospheric' scores of films. The works that came after – neo-classical and neo-Webernian – disappointed lovers of the Diaghilev ballets and are still, for the most part, accepted uneasily by concertgoers who like to hear a thick brown sound and have their emotions engaged. But a surfeit of romanticism and even impressionism leads to a desire for musical space and light, and that is where the post-Diaghilev Stravinsky comes in.

Last summer, here in Monte Carlo (an appropriate place in which to discuss at least the earlier Stravinsky), we put on our evening clothes in great heat and climbed the hill to the Palais Princier to hear the final symphony concert of the season. The works played were Schumann's 'Rhenish' symphony and Brahms's First Piano Concerto. There was the thick brown sound, oppressive on a Mediterranean August evening, sour oboes mixing with horns like an Exeter stew.[12] At supper afterwards Frank Sinatra, whose ear is not to be despised, said that we should have had the tempering of a little late Stravinsky. Air, light, space, wit, immense intelligence, brevity – the properties of Mediterranean art. The success of the 1979 festival indicates that these aspects of Stravinsky are at last being appreciated. By 1982 the unity of Stravinsky's *oeuvre* may at last be understood.

Times Literary Supplement, 1980

1 See *A Shorter Finnegans Wake* by James Joyce, edited by Anthony Burgess, p. 107, for the quote, found near the beginning of Part II, Episode 2, which echoes the second sentence of *A Portrait of the Artist as a Young Man*: 'His father told him that story: his father looked at him through a glass: he had a hairy face.'

2 *Epitaphium* is a brief twelve-tone piece for flute, clarinet, and harp. As White explains in SCW (pp. 508-9): 'It is interesting that the first hexachord is closely related to the opening theme of *The Firebird*. If the notes are taken in the order 4 5 6 2 1 3, they will be found to spell out the initial phrase of the Introduction.'

When transposed down an augmented fifth (or up a diminished fourth), the reordered notes of the hexachord,

E C♮ B A♯ C♯ D♯, match the first six notes of the opening bass line of *The Firebird*, A♭ F♭ E♭ D♮ F♮ G♮.

3   As recounted in SCW (pp. 308-9), the American avant-garde composer-pianist George Antheil moved to Europe in 1922 and met his idol Stravinsky in Berlin that fall. Stravinsky encouraged Antheil to move to Paris, which he did, and even offered to arrange a concert to help launch his career, but severed the friendship upon learning that Antheil had boastfully exaggerated Stravinsky's esteem for him. Antheil and Joyce briefly collaborated in Paris on an aborted opera based on the 'Cyclops' episode of *Ulysses*; see Paul Martin, 'Mr. Bloom and the Cyclops: Joyce and Antheil's Unfinished Opéra Mécanique,' in *Bronze by Gold: The Music of Joyce*, and 'Cyclops' as Opera' by Timothy Martin in the *James Joyce Quarterly*, Vol. 38, No. 1/2. In *Earthly Powers*, Burgess's fictional composer Domenico Campanati spends part of the 1920s in Paris in the milieu of Antheil, Joyce, Stravinsky, Ezra Pound, and other historical personages of the time.

4   Lyric by John Klenner, published by Leeds Music Corporation. SCW, p. 191.

5   SCW, p. 307. Jack Hylton was an English pianist, composer, band leader, and impresario who rose to prominence during the British dance band era. Dubbed the 'British King of Jazz' by the musical press owing to his international popularity, polished arrangements, and use of unusually large ensembles for the time, he recorded with Maurice Chevalier and Paul Robeson. Quoting from Stravinsky's account in *Expositions and Developments* (p. 82n), White relates that Hylton made the arrangement 'with Stravinsky's agreement. He took the middle section of the opera, including the duet and quartet (nos. VI and VIII), replaced the voice by instruments and arranged the music for his jazz band (including saxophones).'

6   John Wesley Vivian 'Jack' Payne was another English dance music bandleader popular in the 1930s. He recorded a version of *Boléro* on the Columbia label. See *French Music and Jazz in Conversation* by Deborah Mawer, pp. 186-7.

7   In a Letter to the Editor titled 'The Bassoon in 'Petrouchka'',
    published in *TLS* on 28 March 1980 (p. 367), Professor Frederick W.
    Sternfeld of Oxford writes, 'I assume the reference is to the Lanner
    waltz quoted in the third picture (page 84 of the original score),
    alternately accompanied by the tonic and incomplete dominant
    seventh chords of E flat major…and the fact that the German
    engraver amended the D in the bass to B flat. Certainly, B flat is
    smoother, though to characterize 'D' as disobedient to the rules of
    harmonic decency is, perhaps, an exaggeration. In any event, may we
    assume that reference to 'F' and 'A' is due to an error, typographical
    or otherwise?'

    From his residence in Monaco, Burgess issued a courteous
    reply titled 'Petrouchka' that appeared in *TLS* on 18 April 1980
    (p. 441).

>   Sir. —Unfortunately, my music library is despersed, and I
>   am not sure exactly where my score of *Petrouchka* is. I admit
>   to an error in my article on Stravinsky, kindly spotted by
>   Dr Sternfeld of the Oxford Faculty of Music (28 March).
>   I put the Lanner waltz in B flat instead of E flat. One of
>   the peculiarities of my ageing memory is that I remember
>   musical passages a fourth lower or fifth higher than written.
>   This may also be a confusion caused by my taking up both
>   the alto flute and the horn. Anyway, I apologize.

    Music played on the alto flute sounds a perfect fourth lower than
    notated whereas music played on the horn (in F) sounds a perfect
    fifth lower (not higher); thus Burgess's waggish comment about
    these two instruments is only partially apt.

8   SCW, p. 450.

9   *Conversations with Igor Stravinsky*, p. 117.

10 As quoted in SCW (p. 369), Dushkin wrote, 'I had never seen a
    chord with such an enormous stretch, from the E to the top A,
    and I said 'No'. Stravinsky said sadly 'Quel dommage'. ('What a
    pity.')'

11 In his musical setting of *The Waste Land* (1978), Burgess quotes this bassoon melody (played by oboe) as the line 'April is the cruellest month' is recited by the narrator.

12 In the third novel of *The Malayan Trilogy* (published in the US as *The Long Day Wanes*), the fictional composer Robert Loo imagines 'the sudden citrous tang of the oboe', revealing, a quarter century earlier, Burgess's synesthetic association of the oboe with sourness. *Beds in the East*, p. 461.

Igor Stravinsky: The Recorded Legacy
CBS Masterworks GM31, 1982

It is unfair to Stravinsky that one should awaken to his
hundredth birthday (17 June) with a hangover engendered
by Joyce centennial celebrations or Bloomsday the day before.
And Dublin is not one of the Stravinskian cities. And Joyce
and Stravinsky never met. There is not one single line of
Joyce's that Stravinsky considered setting to music, and not
one bar of Stravinsky's that Joyce would willingly have sung.
Yet, sharing a centenary as they do, one has to, at least I have
to, look somewhere for a connection. Without doubt, the two
overwhelming artistic events of this century were the prémière
of *Le Sacre du Printemps* in 1913 and the publication of *Ulysses*
in 1922. Both artists enormously expanded the vocabularies of
their respective arts. Both have sometimes been considered to
have shot their bolts with those two works of early maturity
and to have wasted genius on fruitless experiments thereafter.
It is still too early to decide how good Stravinsky was as a
neo-classicist and, later, as a neo-serialist. The literary world
is still divided as to the validity of the oneiric experiment of
Finnegans Wake. But they are both, the Russian and the Irish
exiles, a hundred years old this year, and we ought to start
making up our minds.

I have been listening with great care, in the intervals of
rereading Joyce, to works like *Persephone* and *The Flood* and
such brevities as *Elegy for JFK* and *Aldous Huxley in Memoriam*.
CBS has sent me five albums of the 31-record set (we can
ignore the numbers: just knock and ask for the Definitive
Stravinsky). With Joyce in mind I have wondered about
Stravinsky's handling of words and at last decided that, except

when it's Latin, I don't much care for it. My friend Cathy Berberian sings *The Owl and the Pussycat* with great fidelity to the composer's wishes.[1] The atonal approach doesn't work with words so simple, and Stravinsky's wilful distortion of speech-accent turns a dream into a nursery nightmare. This was not intentional. Nor, I think, did he intend to make the comedy of the encounter between Noah and his wife (drawn from the York mystery cycle) so Schoenbergianly grim in *The Flood*. He either nursed a perverse desire to dominate words by destroying their natural prosodic features or else didn't understand them. This doesn't apply only to English; Gide, who wrote the text for *Persephone*, was appalled at the liberties the composer took with French stress. If, by some rare chance, Stravinsky had set the poems of *Chamber Music*, Joyce would have been horrified by the accentuating of synsemantemes like *the* and *in*.[2] Stravinsky is, first and last, an instrumental man.

The musicianship is always awe-inspiring, even when the artistic intention has not been exactly fulfilled (I don't think it ever was, after, say, the *Symphony of Psalms* and *Oedipus*). It is good to hear a whole side of Stravinsky at rehearsal. In his mid-eighties he retains a painful acuity of ear apt for the Mozart of four (when he fainted at the sound of a trumpet). He doesn't like the grace-notes of the clarinets and works on them like a watch-repairer. He doesn't like Cathy Berberian's Russian pronunciation and he gives a powerful phonetics lesson. He is expert in the mouth-music which conveys the exact rhythm he requires. On the other side he talks in very imperfect but charming English about composing *Le Sacre*. He tried it out on the piano, and a boy playing outside cried: '*C'est faux, c'est faux!*' That, of course, is what everybody said except Stravinsky. Diaghilev wanted to know how long a particular pounding rhythm was to go on for. 'To the end, my dear', said Igor the incorrigible.

The compositional problems Stravinsky encountered when it came to the writing of straight, as opposed to ballet, music find a parallel in the multistylism of *Ulysses*. God was dead, and with him died the omniscient fictional narrator. The impressionists had insisted on the limited point of view. Stravinsky deliberately, in the works of the twenties and thirties, found his point of view in the long-dead baroque composers. He was not imitating them, nor was he parodying them (as Joyce parodied dead styles in *Ulysses*); he was obscuring his own personality in their clothes and thus achieving the objectivity he felt the music of the new age required. He was right, one thinks, to be scared of the subjectivity the fashionable virtuoso or conductor brings to an 'interpreted' performance. He preferred the metronome to rubato and the pianola roll to the heirs of Liszt. As late as the 'Dumbarton Oaks' Concerto of 1938 the clockwork motion of a kind of surrogate Bach opposes the abhorrent notion of music as 'expression'.

It is both moving and amusing to listen to his version of 'The Star-Spangled Banner'. This is the tribute of a new-born American to his country of adoption. Its first performance in Boston brought in the police, who invoked a federal law establishing only one possible harmonisation, and that was not Stravinsky's. When we hear the chorus piously worshipping Old Glory, we hear harmonies acceptable enough, but only Stravinsky could have thought of them. It was his gift to be able to orchestrate a C major triad in a way all his own. It is perhaps finally the Stravinsky sound, not the Stravinsky structure, which holds the ear. There is nothing elsewhere quite like it.

Of Stravinsky's treatment of other composers – Tchaikovsky, Pergolesi, Gesualdo – one can only say that it is a kind of expert refocusing of the lights, a change of stance that turns diverse points of time into a spatial relationship. With Gesualdo, some of whose madrigals he interprets orchestrally, he goes terribly wrong. He reads the strange harmonies of the murderous prince (a character straight out of Webster, said

Huxley) vertically instead of horizontally, obscuring Gesualdo's linear justification of the harmonic heterodoxies.³ For all that, he never, anywhere, makes a false instrumental judgment.

He was a warm man but a cold composer, paying the price exacted by the aesthetic of objectivity. The romantics onanised on to music paper, but Stravinsky never confounded the toilet or bedroom with the all too public salon. Perhaps it was inevitable that he should end up as a serialist, but one often feels that the serialism is a mode as disjunct from his own personality as the clockwork or polyphony of the men of the baroque tradition. There is always, lurking behind the atonalism, an unkillable tonal certitude. A hexachord in one of his later tone-rows is identical with the opening phrase of *The Firebird* – A♭ F♭ E♭ D♮ F♮ G♮ – and the memory of *The Flood* is less of chaos (which atonality all too well expresses) than of the religious faith which tonality alone can convey.⁴ Browning was right when he wrote of 'the C major of this life' (*Ulysses*, ending with 'yes', has to end in C major).⁵ Stravinsky believed that serialism had to be the music of the future and, as his own serialist convictions come after so long an odyssey of formal searching, we have, though reluctantly, to believe him.

Anyway, here you have, if you can afford it, the entire corpus very handsomely packaged by CBS Masterworks.⁶ The range is astonishing – Russian dances and folksongs, ragtime, a work for Benny Goodman, austere theology, much ballet, eccentric word-setting, a polka for baby elephants, you name it. Stravinsky created modern music as Joyce created modern literature. One cannot enforce the duty of getting commemoratively drunk in Leningrad (all, alas, too easy in that bibulous city), but one can raise a vodka or two over a record or so. The whole collection is a distillery of a potent spirit we still have to learn to define.

Spectator, 1982

1   Cathy Berberian sings *Elegy for J. F. K.* (for mezzo-soprano and three clarinets) on Album 13 *Chamber Music / Short Pieces*. However, it is soprano Adrienne Albert, accompanied by Robert Craft at the piano, who sings 'The Owl and the Pussycat' on that recording.

2   Cf. Chapter 39 *I hear an army*.

3   Carlo Gesualdo da Venosa composed intensely expressive madrigals in a highly chromatic style unmatched by any other composer of that period. Upon discovering his first wife and her aristocratic lover *in flagrante delicto*, Gesualdo murdered them in a particularly gruesome manner that involved mutilation of the bodies. John Webster was a playwright and contemporary of Shakespeare regarded as the Elizabethan and Jacobean dramatist with 'the most unsparingly dark vision of human nature.' He remains best known for his tragedies *The Duchess of Malfi* and *The White Devil*, the latter of which is based on an Italian source and recounts the intrigue of an Italian woman who was assassinated at the age of 28.

4   Cf. Chapter 40 *Engaging the Sensorium*.

5   The twelfth and final eight-line stanza of 'Abt Vogler' by the English poet Robert Browning ends thus:

> Give me the keys. I feel for the common chord again,
> Sliding by semitones till I sink to the minor,—yes,
> And I blunt it into a ninth, and I stand on alien ground,
> Surveying awhile the heights I rolled from into the deep;
> Which, hark, I have dared and done, for my resting-place is found,
> The C Major of this life: so, now I will try to sleep.

Blooms of Dublin ends squarely in C major at the conclusion of Molly's soliloquy: 'yes I said yes I will Yes.'

6   In 'Creating a Stravinsky Monument' (*The New York Times*, 15 August 1982), Edward Rothstein describes the 'panoply of pastel colors…ranging from mauve to taupe, each coding one of the 15 record jackets.'

Mademoiselle: Conversations with Nadia Boulanger by Bruno
Monsaingeon
Manchester: Carcanet, 1985

I write this in Monaco, where philistine visitors scrawl on
picture postcards which are then, as like as not, stamped with
the image of Nadia Boulanger. It is a tribute from a very
musical principality to a great musician whom few of the
visitors (on the evidence of my desultory enquiries at café
tables) seem to have heard of. When huge hot air balloons
were released on her ninetieth birthday over Fontainebleau,
there was, apparently, a similar response of nescience. After all,
she was nothing more than a music teacher. But she was a very
exceptional music teacher and, without her, twentieth-century
music in the Free World might have lacked certain qualities
which, consciously or not, we prize. These include technical
rigour, sharp elegance and high seriousness allied to wit. That
we term these Gallic properties is primarily a kind of homage
to a great Gallic lady.

Nadia Boulanger died in 1979 at the age of 92. She was
always called Mademoiselle. She was married only to music.
Her long life had in it nothing to appeal to the biographer
who revels in externalities, and it has been possible to distil its
essence in a series of imaginary conversations. This does not
mean that this little book of 141 pages is a kind of pseudo-
fiction. Bruno Monsaingeon talked to Mademoiselle over five
years of intermittent encounters, asked questions, recorded
replies, and then structured the resultant material in the form
of an extended catechism. There is nothing about food, sex,
clothes or politics. Mademoiselle was conservative in the most
exact sense of the term: she held on to the past, never followed

fashion, lived in the same flat all her life and never changed the day and hour of her musical seminars. Republics changed their enumerations, the Nazis came and went, music remained as the daily miracle.

If Mademoiselle is, in the minds of those who care about modern music, most strongly associated with American composers, it is because of the enlightened sensibility of General Pershing, who, at the end of World War One, sent the conductor Walter Damrosch to Paris to investigate the possibility of developing musical studies in the American Expeditionary Force. Damrosch began by laying on a concert and asking Nadia Boulanger to play the organ part in that Saint-Saëns symphony which has an organ part. Then, impressed, he asked her to teach at what became the Conservatoire Américain at Fountainebleau. She knew no English, but music is an international language. 'We were very poor,' she said, 'like people who have splendid possessions but nothing to eat. We gave concerts and artists came to them for the pleasure of doing me a favour.' She inspired intense loyalty, as you can see from the reminiscences of artists like Aaron Copland (her first pupil), Virgil Thomson, Walter Piston and Roger Sessions. British aspirants who joined the Boulangerie included Lennox Berkeley and Thea Musgrave. But it was the Americans who needed her most.

What did she give them? Chiefly a sense of vocation, of the immense importance of the art, of the need to take composition seriously and to base it on the accumulated technical wisdom of the past. She has to be contrasted here with a British teacher like Granville Bantock, who encouraged his pupils to do what they damned well liked.[1] Mademoiselle demanded not sedulous imitations of Bach or Mozart so much as a thorough knowledge of traditional harmony and counterpoint, a firm foundation on which to venture into the avant-garde fields of planned dissonance, polytonality, serialism. Her Bible was the *Well-Tempered Clavier* of Bach. Everything, including the twelve-tone system (Fugue in B minor, Book One), is in those two magisterial volumes. If you could do what Bach did for Frederick the Great – write a canon that made sense backwards, forwards and upside down – you could be said to have mastered your craft.[2]

She was keen on solfège – a procedure which oppresses my oboist son and which is one of the academic heritages of Mademoiselle. You have to keep your ears clean and write down what you hear. In a sense she was building on a Gallic tradition of clean lines and sound logic. When she was herself a student she was astonished to find the great Maurice Ravel sitting next to her in a counterpoint class. He was already famous, but he believed in what he called a periodic house-cleaning – getting back to essentials again before a new modernistic venture. Erik Satie went to the Schola Cantorum in middle age to study fugue. This humility is part of the proud French musical heritage. Mademoiselle was humble enough to realise in her youth that she would never make a composer. She abased herself into a teaching rôle and, unable to write airs, never gave herself them.

The important thing to remember about her is her capacity to encompass the antique and the revolutionary. In 1937 she made some recordings which launched the revival of Monteverdi. But at the same time she was almost alone in understanding what Stravinsky was doing. In her last days she was a champion of Xenakis and Boulez, but she was still extolling the beauties of Beethoven and Mozart. She recognised, more clearly than any musician of the century, that music represents a continuous line from Gregorian chant to the electronic and the aleatory. She heard the past in the present and the present in the past.

Yehudi Menuhin, among others, found in her a fusion of Slav exuberance and French logic. Her mother was Russian.

She regretted in old age that she had never learned Russian. If she had learned only one word a week she would, in her eighties, have been able to read Tolstoy. This business of the arithmetical apportioning of time was part of her approach to the fundamentals of music: you could, she used to say, learn a new interval every day while waiting for a bus. But time was the servant of the eternity which music enshrines.

Leonard Bernstein asked her on her deathbed if she was hearing music in her skull. Mozart? Monteverdi? Bach? No. 'One music... with no beginning, no end... ' She was a great lady and she deserves that posthumous award of a postage stamp.

The Observer, 1985

1   Granville Ransome Bantock was a British composer, conductor and educator who became the principal of the Birmingham and Midland Institute school of music in 1900 and succeeded Edward Elgar as Peyton Professor of Music at the University of Birmingham from 1908 to 1934. Elgar dedicated his second *Pomp and Circumstance* March to Bantock, and Jean Sibelius dedicated his Third Symphony to him.

2   a reference to Bach's *Musical Offering* (*Musikalisches Opfer*), a collection of canons and ricercars composed for King Frederick II of Prussia on a theme that the monarch conceived and presented to Bach when he visited Frederick at his Potsdam residence in 1747.

The Days Grow Short: The Life and Music of Kurt Weill by
Ronald Sanders
London: Weidenfeld and Nicolson, 1980

Both the title and the dust-cover photograph – Weill
rehearsing *One Touch of Venus* with Mary Martin perched on
the piano – seem to promise or threaten the man of Broadway
more than the man of Berlin and Brecht. That may well be the
way Weill would have wanted it. When Walter Huston sang
'September Song' in *Knickerbocker Holiday* and brought the
house down, there was, in Maxwell Anderson's lyric, a quiet
celebration of change: the long long while or *Langeweile* from
May to December contradicted the composer's name, which
means short while. Weill wanted to be a man of the New York
musical theatre; he wanted to be an American. This entailed
ceasing to be the kind of subversive German who could write
a *Dreigroschenoper* or a *Mahagonny*.

When Louis Armstrong sang 'Mack the Knife' it was
with 'corrected' harmonies: the abrasive became bland.
Broadway did not exactly ruin Weill. To the end he remained
ingenious, inventive and highly professional, the only stage
composer who scored his own scores instead of giving them
to a hack.[1] Listen to one of those scores, however, and you
hear the Broadway sound more or less imposed by the
Musicians' Union. Then listen to the *Dreigroschenoper* prelude,
with its harsh wind and harmonium: that is the real Weill.
It is America more than the liberated Germanies that, since
his death at fifty in 1950, has vigorously promoted the real
Weill. There are no revivals of *Street Scene* or *Lady in the Dark*.
'September Song' remains a classic pop single (with the words
usually wrong: *I'll* instead of *I'd*) but its provenance is forgotten

and authorship disregarded.² Weill is, as he must be, bracketed with Hindemith, not Gershwin. His jazz is *schmutzig*, not *schmalzy*. He is probably one of the great twentieth-century European composers.

It is assumed, chiefly by those, meaning most of us, who have no chance to hear Weill's purely instrumental works, that without Brecht he would have been nothing. It is truer to say that Weill was essentially a vocal composer, a *Singspiel* man who adored *The Magic Flute* and needed strong lyricists and librettists. In Brecht he found the poet he needed: that Brecht needed Weill is less certain. Indeed, it is probable that, if he had promoted his own musical talent beyond mere guitar-strumming, Brecht could have composed the two major operas entire. He knew music: he delighted in such unfingerable guitar chords as C-sharp minor and E-flat major. The tunes of the 'Alabama Song' and the opening bars of 'Macki Messer' are his. But the increasing didacticism of his work for the stage demanded less music and more rant. The trouble with music is not merely that it cannot be political: it transcends faction and expresses abiding human situations which show up political propaganda as mere verbiage. Brecht saw the city of Mahagonny as the doomed capitalist state; to Weill it was merely a place where people were greedy.

Weill had already been long settled in America and was making application for citizenship when Brecht, after exiled sojourns in Prague, Sweden and Finland, suddenly appeared in New York and asked Weill's approval of a proposed all-black *Threepenny Opera*. Weill took fright at once. He did not wish his old communist associations to be known in the Land of the Free. He was a true musician in that he had no intellectual pretensions. If America held up to him the mirror it presents to all exiles, it was to show him that he was a Jew – something he had not much thought of before – and to remind him that he was the son of a cantor. Weill wrote liturgical Jewish music and a huge score for an American extravaganza about the sufferings of the diaspora, but Broadway taught him to be the kind of Jewish composer that Gershwin and Irving Berlin already were – drawn to the yearning music of black slaves, not the funkier jazz that fed the Berlin collaborations with Brecht, and very ready to deracinate and commercialize it. Hitler taught many renegade Jews to recover their heritage: such a recovery did not necessarily make for better art. It was a bad thing for Weill to wish to forget that he was a German.

Brecht's presence and even absence serve to supply the image of an intellectual rigour which would otherwise be lacking in this account of Weill's career. The American phase of it is altogether too showbiz. The source of *One Touch of Venus* is Anstey's Victorian novella, not Florilegus or *The Anatomy of Melancholy*.[3] Over Weill's grave Maxwell Anderson recited words that, along with the music, are inscribed on that grave:

> This is the life of men on earth:
> Out of darkness we come at birth
> Into a lamplit room, and then –
> Go forward into dark again.

– schmalzy, very inferior to the moving original of Bede's *Ecclesiastical History*.[4] Weill's American career was a kind of higher schmalz. Lotte Lenya, his brilliant wife, found as little to do in America as Brecht himself: only with the American rediscovery of the great early works was the magic of her voice appreciated; her skill as an actress found an outlet only in films like *From Russia with Love*. Brecht, having covered himself with glory as a witness before the McCarthy committee, went back to dirty decadent Europe. If Weill had lived to a reasonable age it is doubtful whether he would have yearned for the days of his greatness: it was more important to be a good American than to be a distinguished international composer.[5]

Ronald Sanders is a good American himself. A specialist in Jewish cultural history, he is well qualified to stress the ambiguous relationship between Weill and his cantor father and pick out the ancestral elements in the music. On the other hand, he is not able to do for that music what his subtitle seems to promise. The Busonian elements in Weill are important, but we have to be shown what they are in specific illustrations. There is nothing here set out in music-type; there is not even the most superficial formal analysis of any of the instrumental works. It is not, in fact, a book for musicians but for aficionados of Broadway. Nor is it well written. It is alternately ponderous and breezy and there are some very exotic syntactical structures. Mr Sanders is, however, kind enough to express a debt to the work of David Drew and the 'monumental study of Weill' that he has still to complete.[6] We must go on waiting for that work: Mr Sanders' book only serves to whet the impatience of Weillians.

Times Literary Supplement, 1980

1   Bernstein orchestrated *West Side Story*, albeit with assistance; the credit line in the score reads 'Orchestrations by Leonard Bernstein with Sid Ramin and Irwin Kostal.'

2   In the 1938 original production of *Knickerbocker Holiday*, the last line of 'September Song', as sung by Walter Huston, was 'These precious days I'd spend with you.' Those are also the words he sang in his 1938 and 1944 recordings of the song. Most later singers have altered the last line to 'These precious days I'll spend with you' along with other changes to Maxwell Anderson's lyrics earlier in the song.

3   Around 1950, Burgess wrote an opera libretto based on Burton and began setting it to music, but soon gave up, since the libretto

'was far too long – indeed, it would have been responsible for the longest three-act opera ever written.' He converted the libretto into a novella called *The Eve of Saint Venus*, thereby abandoning his ambition of being a composer in order to become a writer instead. Burgess claims that he was unaware of the existence of *One Touch of Venus* when he began work on his opera (*The Eve of St Venus*, 2006, pp. vii-viii). See also ACC, pp. 54-5; and Chapters 46 *A Writer and Music* and 72 *When Music Does the Talking*.

4   A quatrain from Maxwell Anderson's lyric for the song 'Bird of Passage' from *Lost in the Stars*. The lyric paraphrases a quote from the Venerable Bede, a medieval English monk best known for his *Ecclesiastical History of the English People*, who completed over sixty books and is known as 'The Father of English History'.

5   In a Letter to the Editor published in the 26 September 1980 issue of *TLS* (p. 1065), Patrick J. Smith takes issue with this view: 'The *oeuvre* of George Gershwin – or, for that matter, Harold Arlen – argues that the distance between a 'good American' and a 'distinguished international composer' may be more a matter of a received notion of an acceptable compositional life than of musical substance.' Smith also cites New York City Opera's 1979 revival of *Street Scene*, San Francisco Opera's 1980 revival of *Lost in the Stars*, and the popularity of *Down in the Valley*, which 'in the 1975-76 season was the fifth most performed American Opera'.

6   The British writer and editor David Drew, a long-time member of the Editorial Board of the Kurt Weill Edition, published many writings about Weill, most notably *Kurt Weill: A Handbook*. However, *Weill's Musical Theater: Stages of Reform* by Stephen Hinton, the first musicological study of Kurt Weill's complete stage works, is, at 569 pages, probably the most 'monumental' of the major studies of Weill published since this review appeared.

PART III
BURGESS AND HIS MUSIC

44. SYMPHONY IN C

Symphony in C, which was composed specially for performance in Iowa, is, I think 'English' in the way that the music of Holst, Vaughan Williams and William Walton is 'English'; it exemplifies the truth that a writer of words can to some extent disguise his cultural origins, but a spinner of notes never. It is tonal or modal or both; it has key centers, diatonic themes, secondary ninths and elevenths. Except for the presence of a pianoforte (as an orchestral, not a solo, instrument) and, in the last movement, a mandoline and a tenor and a baritone, the orchestra is the traditional one of the Romantic composers. The sonorities are not Romantic, however; they are twentieth-century 'English'.

The symphony began, in fact, as an 'English' dance rhapsody and developed into a symphony more or less against my will. It was begun in Siena, Italy, in December 1974 (one page of the score contains evidence of Christmas bibulosity – mild obscenities written in Arabic script) and completed in early April this year in a Holiday Inn bedroom in a small town in Georgia (U.S.A.).[1] A good half of the work was written during a lecture tour in the United States, along with the draft script for the next James Bond film, *The Spy Who Loved Me.*[2] I do not think there is any evidence of interinfluence. The score was sent to James Dixon from Oshkosh, Wisconsin, without my having checked a note of it aurally (Holiday Inns have muzak but no pianos).

The first movement, which is more or less in traditional sonata form, has an opening theme which combines the minor tonal mode and the Phrygian mode and is characterized by a climb of superposed fourths and a descent in fourths a tritone apart.[3] I hope this means something to the reader. The other subjects are, respectively, a slow folk theme which first appears in combination with a rather 'jazzy' theme (viz., it uses minor intervals where major ones would have done as well), and a very 'English' pendent theme which suggests a jig gone wrong.

This movement, which ends in C minor, ends slowly, to provide a minute or so of repose before the Scherzo (in G Major) begins. This is a kind of mock pastoral, full of themes, many of them presented in combination with each other and never separated out, and it is very brief.[4] The slow movement, which I wish now to dedicate to the dear memory of Dmitri Shostakovich, whose influence may occasionally be heard here as a foil to the Englishry, is very modal but is not very well aware of its center.[5] As the music of Vaughan Williams reminds us, some modal cadences can be harmonized in consecutive major triads, and one major triad easily leads on to another major triad so that there is no real final one. There is an elegiac theme in the middle suggesting a kind of deformed bugle call, and the movement ends with this on a trumpet.

The final movement betrays that I am a literary man more than a musician, but it may remind listeners that there was once a time when a man could be both without being sneered at as a Johannes Factotum.[6] In Shakespeare's *Love's Labour's Lost*, the pedant Holofernes, who was probably played by Shakespeare himself in the first presentation of the comedy, has a very interesting speech, in which he praises the old poet Mantuan, quotes a line from him, sings a snatch of Italian song – *'Venezia, Venezia, chi non ti vede non ti prezia'* – and also warbles the notes *do re sol la mi fa*. This snatch is, I believe, the only tune that Shakespeare wrote, and it has been unaccountably neglected by Shakespeare scholars.[7] My finale pays homage to *Love's Labour's Lost* by basing itself on that brief Shakespeare motif – forward, backward and upside down – and setting the *Venezia* words to an appropriate Adriatic- or Neapolitan-type melody, corny, full of schmalz, and with a mandoline tinkling away in the background. After some rather grim-sounding development, the solo singers, tenor and baritone, decide to take over. They deliver the two songs that end *Love's Labour's Lost*, using the two main chunks of musical material already presented, and allow winter and spring, the owl and the cuckoo, to become mixed together, to appear – to use a Holofernian kind of pedanticism – synchronically instead of, what nature decrees, diachronically. Which is absurd. But the singers do not mind. Having sung, they wish to finish the proceedings as quickly as possible, so the movement ends as *Love's Labour's Lost* ends – with these spoken words: 'The words of Mercury are harsh after the songs of Apollo.' The orchestra plays a single fortissimo chord of C Major, and everybody goes off for a drink.

This, I may add, is my third symphony but my first to be performed in the United States. The first one was written when I was about twenty and is so 'English' as to make even me sick. The second was composed in Malaya in 1957 and was intended to form part of the celebrations of Malayan independence. In the last movement, as an infinitely extensible coda, the timpanist rolled indefinitely on C and the crowd was encouraged to shout '*Merdeka!*' which means freedom, liberty, the yoke of the tyrannical white man has dropped from us, etc. The crowd could not be dissuaded from turning this shout into a free fight, so the timpanist stopped rolling and the whole orchestra went home in disgust. Thus, the symphony never really ended. It is still, in a kind of Platonic sense, waiting for its final chord.[8]

Programme note, 1975

1   See Chapter 45 *How I Wrote My Third Symphony* and ACC (Chapter 17 *Symphonic Shakespeare*) for further information about the symphony's genesis, development, structure, and thematic origins. Transliterations in Arabic script of 'And fuck you too' and 'schlock' appear in the first movement.

2   Produced by Albert R. Broccoli and released in 1977, *The Spy Who Loved Me* was the tenth James Bond film and third to star Roger Moore as the debonair secret agent. Burgess's script was rejected in favour of a screenplay by Christopher Wood and Richard Maibaum (with an uncredited rewrite by Tom Mankiewicz).

3   The discovery in 2015 of the long-lost score of Burgess's Concerto for Flute, Strings & Piano revealed that the symphony's first movement is closely modelled on the opening movement of that concerto. Composed in Adderbury in July 1951, the concerto opens with the theme that Burgess describes here – the same one that opens the symphony. In the concerto, the theme (beginning on D) is played by the solo flute; in the symphony, it is introduced by a pair of flutes (transposed a tone lower, beginning on C). A close correlation between the symphony and concerto prevails throughout the rest of the movement.

4   The symphony's second movement later served as the model for the first movement of Burgess's first guitar quartet – *Quatuor (No 1) pour Guitares: Quatuor en hommage à Maurice Ravel,* composed in 1986.

5   In TMM, p. 64/85, Burgess writes that his intention in composing the slow movement of the symphony 'was to express regret at the death of Dmitri Shostakovich' despite having composed the movement four months before Shostakovich died on 9 August 1975.

6   Jack of all trades

7   In *King Lear* (I.ii, lines 132-3), one of Edmund's lines also includes a short solfège melody: 'O, these eclipses do portend these divisions. *Fa, sol, la, mi.'* In *Love's Labour's Lost,* each

attempt by the pompous pedant Holofernes to display his erudition results in a botched misquotation or misunderstanding to comical effect. Even his rendition of a simple musical scale – *Ut, re, mi, fa, sol, la* – comes out wrong as *Ut, re, sol, la, mi, fa*. Holofernes's ineptness thus produces the theme that Burgess uses as the basis of the symphony's final movement. See ACC, pp. 190-5.

8   Burgess contradicts this account in his autobiography, asserting that his *Sinfoni Melayu* was never played. See Chapter 45 *How I Wrote My Third Symphony* (where he calls it *Sinfoni Merdeka*); also LW, p. 416, and ACC, pp. 66-7.

Iowa City, Iowa

I'd had a long-standing invitation to visit the University of Iowa, internationally known for, among other things, its Writers' Workshop, but something always got in the way of acceptance. Then I received a letter from Jim Dixon – not the hero of Kingsley Amis's *Lucky Jim* but the conductor of the Iowa University Symphony Orchestra – asking me if I had anything in stock, musical of course not literary, that the orchestra might perform when, if, I came there.[1]

This seemed too good to be true. Neglect of my music by the orchestras of the Old World was what mainly turned me into a novelist, but most of this music had by now been blitzed, lost, torn up, and I had nothing in stock. So just before last Christmas I bought myself a half-hundredweight of scoring paper and started writing a symphony – my third. I'd written the first in my late teens and shudder at the memory of its Vaughan Williams folkiness.[2] The second had been called 'Sinfoni Merdeka' and had been intended as a celebration of Malaya's independence in 1957, and the less said about that the better. The third represented a fresh start, an attempt to see if – after twenty years spent on the strenuous manipulation of words – I could compose something for large forces on a largish scale that should not be total musical nonsense.

The work was started in Rome and then it moved to Siena. Part of the first movement was evidently composed drunk, probably on Christmas Day, since there are obscenities written in Arabic script between the harp part and the first violins, though the music seems sober enough.[3] Then, in late February, I embarked on a lecture tour of the United States, continuing the work in Holiday Inn bedrooms or attempting to continue it in airports while waiting for a plane.

Airports, however, are infested with muzak, as are most public places in the United States. Do the people responsible for this bland abomination realize that there are people around desperately trying to compose music of their own? What on one level is mere auditory pollution is, on the other, brutal and, I should have thought, illegal and unconstitutional sabotage of the act of creation, which is one form of the pursuit of happiness. However.

During my brief time working as librettist and lyricist of a Broadway musical, though, I noticed that professional orchestrators were never quite sure what they'd written until they'd heard it, and were always tinkering until another orchestrator was called in, and then another. I was pretty sure that what I'd written would sound at least literate, but there are always imponderables. When the score safely reached Iowa City, Jim Dixon told me that it would cost $1,200 to have the parts copied. This I expected. Becoming a novelist was, I suppose, one way of earning enough money to have my music performed.

When, last fall, I got to Iowa City I started lecturing with a fair amount of confidence on the Contemporary Novel. Fear, doubt, trembling, humility were reserved for the other art. I attended the first rehearsal and was awed at the large competence of all those delectable kids in blue jeans. Some things went wrong, of course. Young people do not take kindly to pianissimo markings: they like to saw or blast away. Woodwind was near-drowned and had to be rescued. The copiers had ignored an important solo violin passage. The harpist complained that the note-content of her glissandi had not been specified. And so on.

But it worked. The work worked. I was, and remain, overwhelmed. I had written those noises. That was me, that great web of sonorities being discoursed by those hundred handsome kids under that big man on the rostrum. I had written over thirty books, but this was the truly great artistic moment. Evanescent, of course.

The work went on to tape, to be blurred by the magnetic apparatus used in airport security checks, eventually to be snarled up or to wear out or to be accidentally wiped off, while the thirty-odd books would sleep solidly on their shelves. But how blessed the opportunity, however brief, to communicate without preaching, without being groused at for delivering no or the wrong message – to communicate in pure sound, form, pattern. And, even in terms of the art by which I try to earn a living, the experience was overwhelmingly salutary.

Music, though it conveys nothing but itself, has a precision which I, the word-man, had forgotten existed. You can't get away with a sloppy sentence in music, or an ambiguous syntagm. Either you mean a sforzando or you don't. You may doodle on your typescript, but a curve or a dot or a line or a hairpin on a sheet of music is a suprasegmental signal.

Richard Strauss, supreme weaver of sound as he was, was harmfully influenced by literary vagueness, thinking he could get away with a blurred background imprecision but finding that the new precise technicians of the new orchestras were all for dotting i's and crossing t's. You can write a paragraph that you hope the reader will skip, but there's no skipping in a musical performance. And as for shape and duration, you can't bring ten thousand pages of score to a kind of musical Max Perkins and expect him to cut it down to size. There's no room for a Thomas Wolfe in music.[4] Your errors are painfully evident in the concert-hall; in a book they may be forgiven as a mere *lapsus calami*.[5] If your pen slips in the score you're in trouble.

It follows that all novelists should also be symphonists and that their works should be performed in Iowa City. Good for their souls as well as for their primary craft. And it might also give them a chance to write gratefully about people like Jim Dixon and orchestras like the one he trains and conducts up there. Not long ago they did Scriabin's *Prometheus* complete with (laser) color projections, as indicated in the score but only once previously fulfilled in practice.[6] This sort of thing doesn't happen in New York.

And the prospect of a new life for a middle-aged British novelist came in farming country, not in topless Manhattan. I have two choices now. I can continue to try to make a living out of novels and subsidize the Iowa City performance of the most rarefied musical works. Or I can write the most rarefied novels, subsidized by music. Is there anyone who will give me a job as a writer of music for films, or is it a closed shop?

Closed shop or not, there are some of us who are growing tired of the compartmental spirit that nowadays doubts the capacity of the artist to do more than one thing. It wasn't like that in the Renaissance. The biographies of artists seem to show that nobody is born to be a novelist (unless he is Flaubert or Henry James) or an architect or a composer; it is rather a matter of the creative impulse trying all, or most, or many channels and then settling, because life is short, for one only. But if the musician writes novels or the novelist music does he have to be grumbled at for biting off too much? There may have been reservations about my symphony in Iowa City, but I didn't notice too many grumbles.

The New York Times, 1975

1   Reading *Napoleon Symphony* and its addendum ('An Epistle to the Reader', in which Burgess wrote, 'I was brought up on music and compose / Bad music still') prompted the American conductor James Dixon to contact Burgess to ask if he had any orchestral works that Dixon could perform with his orchestra at the University of Iowa. That inquiry led Burgess to compose his Symphony in C, which Dixon premiered in Iowa City in 1975. See Chapter 44 *Symphony in C* and ACC, pp. 185-6.

2   See ACC, pp. 24-6, for discussion of this symphony, including musical examples.

3   See Chapter 44 *Symphony in C* and ACC, p. 188.

4   William Maxwell Evarts 'Max' Perkins, the legendary book editor at Charles Scribner's Sons, helped discover and promote F. Scott Fitzgerald, Ernest Hemingway, and Thomas Wolfe, among others. The latter wrote voluminously and strenuously resisted all cuts to his writing. Perkins is credited with enhancing Wolfe's literary success by persuading to him to cut copious amounts of prose from his novels, particularly *Look Homeward, Angel* and *Of Time and the River*.

5   slip of the pen

6   In 1975, the University of Iowa Symphony Orchestra and Kantorei, Iowa's premier choral ensemble, performed Scriabin's *Prometheus* with visuals provided by the VIDEO/LASER III. See *A History of Electronic Music at the University of Iowa*, published online by Cambridge University Press, for further information.

46. A WRITER AND MUSIC

Harmonie: In your books, music and the musical environment play an important role: the composer is consistently present behind the writer.

Anthony Burgess: I must say that I had been a musician before I became a writer. I used to compose on a regular basis and I can say that this was my major activity until the age of thirty-six. At that point, being slightly discouraged by the obstacles I encountered when trying to get my works performed, I wrote a little book, almost for fun.[1] Thus, I became a writer by accident.

Subsequently I took pleasure in writing by using certain musical forms; I tried to combine music and literature. In so doing, I took Beethoven's *Third Symphony* as a model for *Napoleon Symphony* and arranged the facts of Napoleon's life into the four movements of the *Eroica Symphony*. I admit, this was a bit artificial. But I was the only writer – since also a musician – who was able to attempt such a feat.

I was struck once by a remark of Lévi-Strauss, who believed that the elements of human structure could be found in music. They can be found in language as well. As a result, when I map out a book, I always visualise a musical form – symphonic, operatic. In order to write, I have to keep the image of a musical work in mind.

H: Which one of your books do you think corresponds to the form of a concerto, for example?

AB: In the trilogy *Enderby I*, *Enderby II*, *The Clockwork Testament* – of which the first two parts, unfortunately, have not yet been translated into French – my hero, the poet Enderby, is the soloist of a concerto in three movements. And the orchestra is the world that does not understand him very well and which he does not like very much. He chooses solitude in order to write his poems. One could call it a concerto for violin and orchestra.

H: What place does music have in *A Clockwork Orange*?

AB: In this novel, rather than providing a structure or a series of structures, music comes in as a philosophical concept: the idea of Beatitude beyond Good and Evil. Music is merely an image, a symbol of the ultimate reality of the divinity.

H: Did you choose the transposition of the Ninth Symphony as musical accompaniment for the filmic adaptation?

AB: No, that was not me. I was at Princeton University at the same time as the composer, but – and this is typical of the departmental divide at Princeton – I did not even know he was there.[2] I did not intervene. My only contribution, so to speak, was mentioning the name of Beethoven in the book (all the other composers' names in *A Clockwork Orange* are fictitious).[3] I guess Kubrick was the one who suggested using the *scherzo* and *finale* from this symphony.

H: Most literary critics stressed the fact that the musical quality of language played an extremely important role in your work.

AB: Yes, that is true, but it is not easy to create an exact relation between a musical sound and the sound of my own language. I realised that Joyce, my master, composed his phrases like songs: repetitions, variations. I followed him in composing my phrases by ear like things to be heard, and not like things to be read by the eye.

Indeed, there are two types of literary procedures: literature for the ear and literature for the eye. Most of the books we read are written for the eye. Mine are not. In order to translate my books properly, one has to render not only the sense of the phrase, but its music, its rhythm. For that reason I can say that the translation by Georges Belmont and Hortense Chabrier of my new book, *Earthly Powers*, is a masterpiece. It is a new creation. This I affirm in complete sincerity.

H: Do you think poetry allows for a music/literature interaction which plain prose does not?

AB: I wrote a little book – called *Blest Pair of Sirens* – about this question.[4] To begin with, one has to realise that English prosody is completely different from French prosody. At worst, one cannot migrate to the other language. English poetry is based on musical periodicity; French poetry is based on the number of syllables. As a result, English poetry is very close to music and French poetry is very distant from it. In French literature, there has been nothing comparable to Gerard Manley Hopkins: in his verses, one finds the same movement as one finds in Wagner (nevertheless, I think I know that Hopkins, who was a priest and even a Jesuit, never heard a bar of Wagner!). In any case, his lengthy poem *The Wreck of the Deutschland* is completely Wagnerian.[5] His verses transport the very sound of orchestral music. That is very strange. I composed a symphony in which I tried to transpose Hopkins' rhythm into musical language.[6] I failed. I did it to prove that it was not possible. To succeed in making a book perfectly musical, one would have to renounce all psychological continuity. Imagine that I chose to imitate one of Mozart's symphonies.[7] The first movement contains the exposition: a tea-party, a reception on the lawn of the parish priest. The gentlemen and the ladies. Everybody is friendly, everybody is polite. Then, suddenly, in the second movement, everything changes: manifestation of unbridled sexuality, exposition of sadism. No preparation, no modulation. Then, we return to the reception on the lawn, the gentlemen and the ladies quite polite and well-behaved. That would be the authentic imitation of a symphonic movement, but it is very dangerous to blend the Marquis de Sade with Madame de Staël.

H: Anthony Burgess, what has been your musical education?

AB: My education? I am a complete autodidact. Like Wagner.[8] Anyhow, my father played the piano in a pub and my mother was a singer and a dancer.[9]

H: Did you never take lessons; did you never have a teacher?

AB: As a very little child I had a violin teacher. But I was a very bad pupil. I repeat, I am a complete autodidact. I found the note C on the piano, and I found the same note on a musical score. After that, everything was easy, because after C comes D, E, etc.

H: It obviously is very simple! One might wonder what's the point of conservatories. But you have just presented the manuscript of one of your scores for orchestra; how did you solve the problem of transposing instruments?

AB: There is no problem. If one inwardly hears the note C, one knows by instinct this is a [written] G for the F horn.

H: So, you are educated as an autodidact, or rather, you have not got any education at all. How did you find your way?

AB: I owe everything to Debussy. I was living in Manchester, I was fourteen years old and I had a radio which I had made myself. I listened to *L'après-midi d'un faune*. The flute! This was the revelation.[10]

H: And today, how many opus numbers do you have to your name?

AB: I have never numbered my works. But I composed three symphonies and I am in the process of composing a fourth one, for baritone, chorus and orchestra.[11] I wrote a concerto for Yehudi Menuhin, who has not yet played it, a concerto for piano, some works for string quartet, etc. I also composed a lot for the theatre, incidental music, mainly in America. The difference between my own country and America is that, over there, I am accepted as a composer. In the UK, this is beginning, too, but very slowly.

H: By the way, your career might be compared to Charles Ives'.

AB: I admire him a lot. I was somewhat affected by his influence. Since he was an autodidact, like me, he composed like a poet: all of his works have literary qualities. His symphonies are novels, they are very visual. His innovations were only possible because he did not attend academies.[12]

> *Anthony Burgess interrupts the interview to play a tape on the reel-to-reel tape recorder, containing a concert delivered by the BBC orchestra executing the premiere of his ballet 'Mr W.S.'. This work contains a relevant part for violin, which in this recording is played by Yehudi Menuhin.*[13]

H: What does 'W.S.' stand for?

AB: William Shakespeare, of course!

H: The work we have just heard is completely tonal, mainly in C Major. That is not, how shall I put it, very contemporary music.

AB: Remember that we have had some problems in the UK. We have been influenced for a long time by Handel, by Mendelssohn. This influence lasted up to World War One. Our great composers of the time – Elgar, Vaughan Williams, Holst – have not been touched by the continental wave.

Even Stravinsky did not gain fame in Great Britain but with delay. And of course, I have mainly been affected by the influence of my fellow countrymen. Do not let us speak about Schoenberg; he was practically unknown. It was only afterwards that British composers were able to find an international style. And I found that style only very late myself. Today I compose works which are in a way traditional like the ballet you have just heard, at the same time as vanguard works, which are closer to Boulez, for example.[14] I pass from one style to another, without being emotionally attached, just according to what is necessary.

H: Your musical approach can be compared to that of a painter who holds with abstraction and realism, simultaneously.

AB: But what does realism mean in terms of music? Is music a real language? Is it possible to use music like a language? Music contains the images of a certain society, of a certain social structure: if one wishes to transcribe this image of our society in a musical way, yes, it is necessary, it is indispensable to employ the Schoenbergian or Boulezian forms. But if one returns to speech, to reality, one has to be able to make use of the whole palette of compositional means. It is impossible, and Boulez recognised it, to put the word 'God', the word 'Credo' onto a dissonance. It is very easy to compose like Boulez, but this style of music has immense limitations.

H: Anthony Burgess, throughout the world you are recognised as one of the greatest contemporary writers, as a professional of the highest level. When it comes to music, do you consider yourself as being a professional or an amateur?

AB: I am obviously an amateur since I do not earn my living from composing! Apart from exceptions. Nevertheless, I have been offered £2,000 for the operetta I am working on, based on Joyce's *Ulysses*!

H: An operetta?

AB: An operetta. That will be in 1982, the centenary of Joyce's birth.

H: Does it hurt you that you are played so little?

AB: As I told you, this is progressing little by little. Some of my symphonies have recently been performed in Baltimore, in Buffalo.[15] The UK is following. But I share the fate of every British composer, especially in France. France ignores, despises British music. What makes it even more heart-rending, unjust, is that we British are constantly playing Ravel, Debussy, Roussel and even Franck or d'Indy.

Thanks to Hortense Chabrier and Georges Belmont, I am read in France. Thanks to Philippe Caloni, the French could hear extracts from my *Third Symphony* performed by the University of Iowa Orchestra – 120 musicians – conducted by James Dixon.[16] This was a real premiere for me. But it is not up to me to complain about the fact that, here, they refuse to admit that Elgar is as great a composer as Mahler. Of his works, only *Pomp and Circumstance* is known!

This ostracism does not keep me from adoring French music: Debussy – Debussy first of all –, Ravel, Satie, Milhaud,

Messiaen. And Berlioz, of course! It's Sir Colin Davis, an Englishman, who is the greatest Berliozian orchestra conductor at the moment. Did you know that I made an English translation of *L'Enfance du Christ* for the BBC?[17] It was very difficult, it is the most challenging work I have ever faced. And I also have something else in common with Berlioz. Like him, I write directly for the orchestra: I compose far away from the piano. I only need ink and paper. I never do drafts. As with my novels, I never revise. I hear inwardly the orchestral sound. In any case, I could never, as did Ravel, write *Ma mère l'Oye* for the piano and afterwards for the orchestra. The only thing I cannot hear inwardly is the harmonies. That is the only superiority which reality provides us with. The equilibrium between orchestral sections is also difficult to conceive by the inner ear. It was a big problem for Beethoven. It is, for me, too.

Harmonie hi-fi conseil, 1981

1   *The Eve of Saint Venus.*
2   Wendy Carlos, the person referred to, worked at her New York studio and not at Princeton the year that Burgess taught creative writing at Princeton and Columbia. His confusion evidently arose from the name of the Columbia-Princeton Electronic Music Center (now called the Computer Music Center at Columbia University), located in New York City, where Carlos had carried out graduate studies in music composition at Columbia. In 'Princeton's Small World of Big Writers' (*The New York Times*, 20 May 1983), Glenn Collins wrote: 'The novelist Anthony Burgess loathed Princeton. "Just about the only pleasure I got in Princeton was leaving each week and going to Columbia University to teach creative writing to the students there," said Mr. Burgess who is living in Monaco.'

3   J.S. Bach, Handel, and Mozart – or pieces composed by them – are also mentioned in *A Clockwork Orange* along with veiled references to Debussy, Mendelssohn, and Britten. Fictional composers mentioned in the novel are Friedrich Gitterfenster, Otto Skadelig, Geoffrey Plautus, and Adrian Schweigselber – the latter alluding to another fictional composer, Adrian Leverkühn, the protagonist of Thomas Mann's *Doktor Faustus*. Claudius Birdman, the composer of 'a very nice malenky string quartet', represents Claude Debussy; see ACC, pp. 84-8.

4   published as *This Man and Music*. See Chapter 15 *Blest Pair of Sirens?*

5   In Burgess's novel *The Clockwork Testament*, a lurid film version of *The Wreck of the Deutschland* converts F.X. Enderby's prim film treatment into a disaster flick filled with sex and violence, overturning Enderby's life just as Kubrick's film of *A Clockwork Orange* had upended Burgess's.

6   a reference to his setting of *The Wreck of the Deutschland* for baritone solo, SATB chorus, and full orchestra in the early 1980s, which was in progress at the time, as asserted later in the interview. At this point, Burgess considered the work to be a symphony rather than an oratorio. He completed the score on 8 March 1982 according to the date on the manuscript. See ACC, pp. 288-9.

7   which he later did in *Mozart and the Wolf Gang*, pp. 81-91, with a literary imitation of Mozart's Symphony No. 40 in G minor, K. 550.

8   Richard Wagner was not self-taught. He studied piano from the age of 7 and, along with study at the University of Leipzig, took composition and conducting lessons from the cantor of St. Thomas in Leipzig.

9   Burgess's mother was neither a singer nor dancer, as Simon Johnson has established. See Commentary on Chapter 47 *The Making of a Writer*.

10 See Chapter 3 *Music at the Millennium*, where this incident is said to have occurred in 1929, when Burgess would have been twelve years old.

11 See note 6 above.

12 Charles Ives was an iconoclast, but no autodidact. As a boy, he was instructed by his father George Ives, a professional musician who taught music theory and several instruments, directed bands, choirs, and orchestras, and had been a U.S. Army bandleader in the Civil War. George provided Charles with instruction in harmony and counterpoint while introducing him to polytonality and guiding his first efforts in composition. Charles became a professional church organist at the age of fourteen and, at twenty, entered Yale University, where he studied composition with Horatio Parker, one of America's leading composers at that time. Under Parker's supervision, Ives composed his Symphony No. 1 as a senior thesis.

13 This would have been a tape of the recording that the BBC made and broadcast in 1979. In 1980, Burgess played an excerpt from this recording at the conclusion of his T.S. Eliot lectures, *Blest Pair of Sirens*, at the University of Kent; see YH, p. 360. Yehudi Menuhin did not play on that recording and had no involvement with it. Burgess's recording was apparently an unauthorized copy, since, as he asserts earlier in YH (p. 309): 'The BBC broadcast it twice and then, in obedience to Musicians' Union regulations, destroyed the tape.'

14 Except in a few early twelve-tone works that are lost, Burgess eschewed serialism in his music. Although some of Burgess's compositions, like *The Brides of Enderby* and *Mr Burgess's Almanack*, are in a more modern style than *Mr W.S.*, none of them are particularly avant-garde or similar to Boulez.

15 There is no evidence of performances of Burgess's music in Baltimore or Buffalo prior to 1981, and certainly not of his symphonies. In the spring of 1976, during a six-week residency at SUNY-Buffalo, Burgess played a tape of his Third Symphony in the Department of Music, where it was disparaged; see YH, p. 335; ACC, p. 195. Following its premiere in Iowa in 1975, Burgess's Third Symphony was not played again until 1997, when it was performed in Providence, Rhode Island, and Cambridge,

Massachusetts, by the Brown University Orchestra under my direction.

16 Philippe Caloni was a French journalist and radio producer of classical music programs.

17 Burgess wrote a singable English translation of *L'Enfance du Christ* in 1966 for a Christmas broadcast on BBC-2. Colin Davis, who conducted that production, pleaded in vain with the BBC to allow it to be sung in French and 'grumbled at every line I wrote'; see YH, p. 122, and ACC, pp. 103-4. Three years after this interview, Burgess was commissioned a second time to produce an English version of *L'Enfance du Christ*, this time for Thames Television. Essentially, he repeated his 1966 translation; see YH, pp. 123-4, and ACC, p. 298.

Anybody can be a writer; all you have to do is to write. But not anybody can compose music; to do that you have to learn a rather exacting set of techniques. True, with the spreading of the stain of democracy into the arts – which used to be healthily autocratic, as though run by Nabokov – a lot of people have been alleging that they can compose music, unembarrassed by the shit or crap or whatever the popular democratic word is of what Beethoven had to agonise over before he wrote his first sonata. Some years ago a young American pop promoter said he was one of the best arrangers in the business, even though he couldn't read or write a note: 'I say right man you give me a Spanish sound and then like give me like a trumpet sound man and you get the best fucking arrangement you ever heard.' Let me amend my first statement in the light of this last. Any illiterate with a cassette recorder can write a book: all you need is a transliterative hack who did not drop out of primary education.

I say this about musical composition because I began my career as a writer as a composer. My family, being Lancashire Scottish Irish Catholic, had no tradition of higher education. Until 1829 Catholics living in England had no right to enter universities and become professionals in the liberal arts, and the habit of buying books was not so entrenched in the Catholic population as in the Protestant. If a Catholic had talent, it rarely found a literary outlet, any more than it found a legal or pedagogic or medical one. Talent in the Catholic North of England expressed itself in the popular arts – singing, dancing, being a comedian. That tradition still subsists. The Beatles were only one of the many Catholic Irish Lancashire manifestations of popular musical talent. Gracie Fields was greater than the whole four of them; Sir William Walton is greater than Gracie Fields.[1]

My mother was a singer and dancer, and my father played the piano for Fred Karno, the impresario responsible for *Casey's Court*, an extravaganza in which Charlie Chaplin and Stan Laurel performed.[2] I learned nothing about books from either of my parents, and any talent I possessed as a boy was pianistic and, later, compositorial. It was when I was already in my middle thirties that I was led into literature through the ambition of composing an opera. At school I had had to read the poems of John Keats, and I was encouraged to look up in Burton's *Anatomy of Melancholy* the source of his narrative poem *Lamia*. On the same page I also found a story taken from Florilegus, the one about the young man who, putting his ring upon a finger of a statue of Venus, found himself married to the goddess.[3] This is a tale which circuitously got itself made into the Kurt Weill musical *One Touch of Venus*. I made a libretto out of this story, and I tentatively called my opera *The Eve of Saint Venus*. Being poor, I could not afford the several hundred sheets of manuscript music necessary for the writing of the full score of an opera, so my libretto remained as a kind of unwished piece of literature.

I had learned to enjoy the putting of invented words into the mouths of invented characters, and I found literary composition a relaxation in the intervals between composing unplayable, or certainly unplayed chunks of music. I did not, of course, take at all seriously this literary hobby. It was so much easier to practise than the musical craft. For five seconds worth of music in quick tempo you needed to spend hours on a thirty-stave sheet of scoring paper; the writing of a piece of fiction was a matter of single lines of uncomplicated monody. A gift. Nothing in it. The horrible irony was that, while I could not get my music performed, I had no difficulty in placing my hobbyish narrative compositions. The writing of fiction would have remained a mere diversion if I had not been pronounced mortally ill of a cerebral tumour and faced with the problem of earning a living in my terminal year. I lived and still live, and writing was, and still is, the only job I could get. I regard myself as one of the unemployed who pays the bills by doing a bit of writing.

I have published, I think, forty-odd books, and I rather despise the craft I practise because it is not the craft of the musician. Most musicians know about literature, but few littérateurs know about music. I have read already, from other writers who have contributed to this series, expressions of mystical devotion to the literary art, a sense of elation at having joined the pantheon to which Hawthorne and Henry James belong (or is it rather more frequently Updike and Vonnegut and Ken Kesey?). I do not feel this elation. I thank America, or rather part of the cornbelt of America, for granting me the only true artistic exaltation I have ever experienced. In Iowa, some seven years ago, there was a performance of my Third Symphony. My father would have been proud. He ended up as a cinema pianist. I remembered this at Iowa very sharply. There was a presentation of Fritz Lang's masterpiece *Metropolis* and I did what my father had done – played the piano accompaniment. This was a mystical identification of paternity and filiality of the kind developed in James Joyce's *Ulysses* – the only novel I have ever really admired. It was, of course, written by a musician.

I have, by steady application of such literary talent as I possess, managed, at the age of sixty-five, to make myself financially independent – that is to say, I can pay some of the bills so long as I smoke cheap cigars and avoid alcohol. Any margin of my income has to go to the copying of orchestral parts. Being known as a writer of words, I am tentatively accepted as a musical composer by such bodies as the British Broadcasting Corporation. There is no money in it, of course. The point about music to me is that it is art, the manipulation of pure form, whereas writing is too easily drawn to the level of the utilitarian. There is nothing utilitarian about music, which offers no information and doesn't even know what it means.

Let me not read, in future contributions to this slot, about the joys of writing. Let me hear instead about the joys of art – which, on occasion, can include the crafty manipulation of words. But I feel uncomfortable here, since I am surrounded – in reviews and in advertisements – by what I know not to be art – film stars pontificating about physical health, cat cartoons, guides for job hunters, regimens for the overfed, houses of horror in New York suburbs, resolutions of the identity crisis, the comforts of sex. God help you Americans, do you consider these things to be worth reading or reading about or, save the bloody mark, *buying*? It is because the authors of these works call themselves writers that I am not too happy about being called one myself. Still, so long as bills have to be paid, I will push on. I would even father the Garfield books or *Color Me Beautiful* or the *Jane Fonda Workout Book* if I could thus subvent the composition of another unplayable symphony.

The Times, 1983

1   Gracie Fields, a native of Rochdale, Lancashire, was an English actress, singer, comedian, and music hall celebrity whose theme song 'Sally' was featured in her first film, *Sally in Our Alley* (1931). She became one of the top movie stars in Britain during the 1930s and is said to have been the highest paid film star in the world in 1937. Sir William Walton (1902–1983), born in Oldham, Lancashire, was one of the most prominent English composers of the twentieth century; because he died eleven days prior this essay's publication in *The Times*, the last phrase was changed from present to past tense. See Chapter 61 *Enjoying Walton*.

2   In his research paper *'The Beautiful Belle Burgess': A Biography of Elizabeth Burgess – The Mother Anthony Burgess Never Knew* (2015), Simon Johnson presents compelling evidence that Burgess made up a false version of his mother, who was neither a singer nor dancer and was never a music hall performer, based on a Lancastrian opera singer with a similar name. See Commentary.

3   See Chapter 43 *A Berliner on Broadway* and ACC, pp. 54-5.

48. MUSICALISING *ULYSSES*

On the eve of 2 February 1982, the hundredth anniversary of James Joyce's birthday, the BBC devoted three hours to the transmission of a musical version of *Ulysses* written and composed by myself. My title was *The Blooms of Dublin*, but the definite article got lost somewhere. Still, I do not object strenuously to *Blooms of Dublin*, which emphasises the blossoming of things on a June day in Ireland's capital. The things that blossom are perhaps trivial in Tolstoyan or Dostoevskian terms – the awareness of the hero Leopold Bloom that he is a cuckold, the insults he suffers because he is partly Jewish, his sense of the need for a foster son to replace the true son he has lost. He sees bloom also a tiny victory: he finds a spiritual son in the young poet Stephen Dedalus, and he is given thus the confidence to assert himself at home and perhaps stand no more nonsense from Irish antisemites. The novel is very long, and it is a great blooming garden of literary experiment. A musical version had to be short, and there was no room for linguistic cadenzas.

I was told, while first meditating the notion of putting *Ulysses* on the American musical stage, that this was the one novel that totally resisted such popularisation. I failed to see why. The book is about ordinary people. As for musicalisation, two of the three main characters are singers – Stephen a tenor, Molly Bloom a professional soprano; Bloom seems to be a potential baritone. I doubt if many of the scholarly Joyceans would have objected to an operatic version – like *Lulu*, though with fewer acerbities. The fact that I have produced a work whose idiom is mostly Broadway has already displeased a number of the professors.

I had better say at once though no scholar has a right to consider himself a Joyce specialist unless his knowledge of the art of music matches Joyce's own. There are too many tin-eared Joyceans around, just as there are too many Joyceans more interested in literary symbolism than in the quotidian physicalities that Joyce relished so much. I have met Joyceans who have never tasted Guinness. At a meeting of scholars I addressed in a year when the Ascot Gold Cup, as in 1904, was run on 16 June, I could find none who were even aware of the event.[1] There is also a kind of closed-shop jealousy which would deny the enjoyment of Joyce to the sort of common people he wrote about. The conversion of *Ulysses* into a Broadway musical is a pedagogic act – a device for introducing the original to those who have been scared off it. That is justification enough for what too many would call flagrant vulgarisation.

But so many of the emotions expressed in *Ulysses*, as well as the actions, are vulgar, crude, or sentimental. Bloom's mooning over a dead son, Molly's concupiscent excitement at the prospect of getting a new young lover, Mr Deasy's antisemitism, Buck Mulligan's talk of 'Hellenising the island', the Citizen's blatant chauvinism, the masturbation on Sandymount Strand – these, turned to song, exhibit at least Joyce's raw, all too raw, material. There is certainly more Dickensian mawkishness in *Ulysses* than some scholars will admit. If song brings all this out, yet there is behind or underneath the song a more complex entity than the tin-eared will catch. I refer to the orchestral accompaniments, which can be as multi-referential as Joyce's own prose. How many will notice that the closing cadence of a very vulgar song called 'Copulation Without Population' is based on the opening bars of *Tristan und Isolde*; or that Bloom's song in Glasnevin Cemetery, exalting the vulgarity of 'warm, fullblooded life' (Joyce's own words), has orchestral quotations from *Martha*, *The Bohemian Girl*, Puccini's *La Bohème* and Beethoven's Fifth Symphony?

Joyce, being a musician, knew that there are certain phases of the mind which will not yield to verbal expression but can convey some of their essence in organised sound. *Finnegans Wake* moves towards the condition of music but cannot reach it. Certain of Bloom's interior monologues in *Ulysses* ask for the enrichening of background music which can, at a certain point, take over entirely the expression of mood. Joyce knew that Molly's final 'yes' is a verbalisation of acceptance of the universe ('By God, she'd better', said Carlyle) which can be better conveyed in an orchestral C major triad.[2] It was my early realisation (at about the age of seventeen) that *Ulysses* ended in C major which led me eventually to wish to turn the whole thing into music. And, if both Stephen and Molly are singers, why should we not be permitted to hear them singing?

I catch a defensive note in the above, and yet, considering the work that had to go into the orchestration alone, aggression might be more in order. Purely literary people have no conception of the physical labour involved in putting a score together, and it is time they learned. Making flutes, oboes, cor anglais, clarinets, bassoon and double bassoon, horns, trumpets, trombones, masses of percussion, harp, piano, celesta, strings and human voices produce a multiple paranomasia of sound relevant to the themes of *Ulysses* is a little harder than penning lines about symbolism. Consider then the work of copying and correcting parts, of rehearsal, of recording. Literature and especially literary criticism are, in comparison, a little too easy.

I make the comment about the labour of creating a musical version of Joyce's novel chiefly because such labour is a correlative of seriousness of intention preceded by prolonged meditation. One does not undertake such a task lightly, and I would not have undertaken it at all had I not been convinced that Joyce, however unconsciously, planted the materials of a musical in his book: being a musician – though not a Schoenbergian or Boulezian one – he could not help it; being a man of the people, he had to have popular music in mind. Ah, the intellectual Joyceans will say, but consider that the only specific use of musical form in *Ulysses* relates him to Bach rather than Irving Berlin (with whom Professor Denis Donoghue has unfavourably compared me).[3] True, and if you want a double fugue in *Blooms of Dublin* you will find it in the Overture: it does not work in the context, any more than Joyce's own *fuga per canonem* works in the Ormond bar and restaurant. In both instances the structure was not intended to work.

Finally, a musical of *Ulysses* clearly had to be done sometime, and I have done it. Any other sufficiently equipped lover of Joyce is welcome to supersede my own effort. *Pygmalion* remains after the lucrative illiteracies of *My Fair Lady* ('I'd be equally as willing for a dentist to be drilling than to ever let a woman in my life'), and *Ulysses* will continue to stand as a great monolith when all the incrustations of adaptation to stage and film and radio musical have been washed away by the rains. But the scholarly complainants might care to consider sometime that a popular musical version is as legitimate an act of criticism as a doctoral thesis, and if even one door to the better appreciation of the book has been opened, then the fingers of the composer have not been abraded in vain.

Typescript, 1982

1 The Ascot Gold Cup was run on June 16 in 1977.
2 As the story goes, when Margaret Fuller stated, 'I accept the universe,' Thomas Carlyle said, 'By God! She'd better.' Sarah Margaret Fuller was an American journalist, editor, critic, translator, and women's rights advocate associated with the American transcendentalist movement. Thomas Carlyle was a Scottish historian, satirical writer, essayist, translator, philosopher, mathematician, and teacher, known, among other things, for the

'Great Man' theory of history and for dubbing economics 'the dismal science'. As a correspondent for Horace Greeley's *New-York Tribune,* Fuller traveled in 1846 to Europe, where she interviewed many prominent writers, including Carlyle, whose reactionary political and social attitudes were contrary to Fuller's liberal views. See Chapter 41 *Stravinsky's Potent Spirit,* note 5

3   The prominent Irish literary critic Denis Donoghue held professorships at University College Dublin, his alma mater, and later at New York University, where he held the Henry James Chair of English and American Letters. A gifted singer, he studied voice at the Royal Irish Academy of Music and served for a year as music critic of *The Irish Times.*

Phoneydom
by Hans Keller

Blooms of Dublin (Radio 3), *Haydn's First Quartet* (Radio 3), and *Berg, Schoenberg and Brahms* (Radio 3)

Priding itself on its permissive ability to call a spade a spade, our uninhibited civilisation fails to notice its multi-dimensional cultural phoniness, its highbrows' readiness, for instance, to see spade-work in your spare time's doodles – or Anthony Burgess's, anyway. In *The Times* the other week, he announced music's death after Mozart, turning Beethoven – arguably the most selfless thinker ever – into a post-musical egocentric.[1] Now, as Burgess's moribund 'musical for radio' showed last week, he should have spoken for himself, but then he no doubt did, under the unerring direction of his unconscious. Had that unconfessed musical autobiography been shown to *The Times*'s chief music critic, it would not, I am sure, have been inflicted upon us. Nor, for that matter, would the much-heralded *Blooms of Dublin* have been, had it been shown to any of the BBC's musicians.

As it was, close on three hours of the BBC's culture time were devoted to music, intended for 'ordinary people' and 'a wide audience', which would have flopped on Radios 1 and 2. In order to sustain the illusion of its own post-natal health and survival, then, the phoney show needed every phoney listener available – every highbrow practising lowbrow snobbery, ready to respect sheer musical stupidity, delightfully accessible gas, especially in the shape of the leading event of the Joycentenary.[2] In the event, Burgess's pathetic pastiche evinced a centrifugal incompetence which pervaded its entire orbit, so that continuous listening became impossible for any naturally musical ear, professional or naive.

The score teems with tuberculous attempts at updating it all, at enlivening both its harmonic progress and its rhythm with the help of unmotivated, aimless dislocations and distortions. An early 5/4-time (3 plus ill-assorted 2) makes it easy for all but the tone-deaf to find out how the whirlwind blows: in the more modern manner but without the slightest formal justification, the number 'progresses' from F major to E flat major, though a conventionally concentric tonality would at least have accorded with the structure's primitive terms of harmonic reference. Thenceforth, what is most predictable about the score is its surprises.

Senseless tonal and rhythmic antics, then, take the place of even the most elementary invention – as do, in search of tunes, such mouldy, folkloristic devices as Scotch snaps on 'mo-ther', flat leading-notes, and normal leading-notes after flat sixths; the twin sister of this augmented second is, of course, the one between the minor third and the sharpened fourth degree. Burgess's models, close yet unreachable, are one genius and two supreme talents – George Gershwin and, surprise, Irving Berlin and Cole Porter. Mind you, he didn't mention them on *Kaleidoscope* – where, instead, he talked about the 'rather Debussyan way' in which he had orchestrated a set piece; in reality, his scoring would be wide open, not yet to criticism, but to a teacher's corrections.

However, instrumentation apart, wasn't Burgess very modest on *Kaleidoscope*? You can't be modest about nothing. Later in the programme, the former music critic of the *Irish Times* tore the score to shreds, suggesting that the 'nightmares' about this 'musical adaptation of *Ulysses*' which Burgess had reported seemed altogether justified. Nightmares about nothing? And incapable of a tiro's self-criticism, was Burgess in a position to criticise, in public print, Beethoven, Mahler,

Schoenberg – to sign their music's death certificate after diagnosing the cause of death?

That, admittedly, is *The Times*'s problem, but *Blooms of Dublin* is Radio 3's: inquest, please. An enormous amount of talent was wasted on this co-production with Radio Telefís Eireann: John Tydeman, who co-directed, is one of the most independent minds amongst the BBC's drama producers, and on the Irish side, the thoughtful musicianship of Colin Mawby, the choral director of the well-rehearsed RTE Singers, could have been far more fruitfully employed.

Another mind full of independent thought is, it so happens, Ian McIntyre, the Controller of Radio 3 himself. What, I wonder, will he call my spade? On behalf, I feel, of all music-loving listeners to his channel, may 1 ask him how it could have happened and, yet more importantly, whether he will kindly make sure that it won't happen again? There's a case for imaginative amateurishness and, sometimes, there is no escape from unimaginative professionalism – but Radio 3's musicians must be enabled to identify unimaginative amateurishness posing as popular art before plenty of talent, time and tin has gone down the drain.

It was, in fact, quite a week for our culture's phoney urgers – the exploitation of Haydn's doodles not excepted. Sharply defined performances of his great Symphonies No 83 (RLPO under Howard Williams) and No 87 (Bournemouth Sinfonietta under George Hurst) might have been missed by the casual reader of the *Radio Times* – who, however, cannot possibly have failed to notice this downright fanfare of a title: *Haydn's First Quartet.* So, what's wrong with it? It's truthful, isn't it? Yes, and utterly phoney to boot – because of the ineluctable implication it proudly carries. For this was not the first of those forty-five-odd quartets which established both *the* sovereign instrumental form and Haydn himself as its first, unsurpassable master.

It was Op. 1, No 1, whose interest rivalled that of *Blooms of Dublin*: not specifically written for solo quartet, it is a wholly uncharacteristic, consistently conventional, uninventive composition which Haydn the genius (who had not then been born) would never have allowed to be broadcast at all.

But let our final words honour the exceptionally unphoney – the first performance of Edward Cowie's concretely conceived, conscientiously heard Concerto for orchestra; the BBCSO strings' technical application in a Berg Piece which, normally, has to suffer technical brilliance at its most bogus; and Phyllis Bryn-Julson's equally decided abstention from the usual utility intonation in Schoenberg's *Erwartung*: she is prepared to risk a wrong note or two, instead of playing safe with demi-semi-*parlando* pitches. Michael Gielen himself, too, is an exception – in touch with our time, and out of touch with its ubiquitous intonational, harmonic, and rhythmic sham.

The Listener, 11 February 1982

Unsent response
by Anthony Burgess

To the Editor, *The Listener*

Dear Sir,

Fourteen years ago I left England, taking with me memories of various minor joys, among which was the televisual spectacle of Mr Hans Keller making a fool of himself with pop-groups. He also, as I recall, produced a kind of musical journalism which endeavoured to force shoddy grandiloquence on his readers as a substitute for aesthetic analysis and appraisal. It was with special small pleasure that I found Mr Keller recently swimming back into my ken when, in a letter to *The Times*, he demonstrated his incapacity to avoid the easy trap of an attack on Beethoven I had published in the same newspaper.[3]

I have long worried about musical critics, and for two reasons. They are, first, not forced by their craft to show their competence in the art which sustains that craft. A literary critic has at least to show literacy, and is thus drawn into the orbit of the art he evaluates. A music critic has no parallel obligation. Second, the impossibility of conveying the effect of music in words makes him indulge in verbalism which resembles music only in not possessing a separable semantic content. I attacked Beethoven, who, I alleged not altogether sincerely, had brought the ego into music and prepared the way for its destruction, because I was curious to see how Beethoven-lovers would reply. They either did not reply or else, like Mr Keller, vituperated.

I smiled secretly at Mr Keller's demand for my suppression as a mere man of letters claiming the right to initiate discussion of an art which, I now learn, is the province of musical functionaries like Mr Keller. I knew that he would leap at the chance of denigrating music of my own and that I would not have long to wait for this denigration. His article on my *The Blooms of Dublin* makes entertaining reading but, like his letter, lacks a separable semantic content. True, Mr Keller is drawn to the display of technical knowledge (which Bernard Shaw said he could impart to his dog in half an hour), the blinding with science which is the last resort of the critically incompetent. But his own application of science to my pit-orchestra score is impertinent. Since when has a semiquaver-duplet in slow time been a Scotch [snap?][4]

Typescript, February 1982

Letter to the Editor
by Anthony Burgess

February 16 1982
To the Editor, *The Listener*

Dear Sir,

My attention has been drawn to a notice by Mr Hans Keller of my radio musical *The Blooms of Dublin*, in which he refers to me as having set the word 'mother' to a Scotch snap. I set that word to a semiquaver duplet in slow time. Mr Keller ought to have listened more carefully or else looked up 'Scotch snap' in some musical dictionary or other. Such inaccuracy is not really tolerable in a musical journalist of, I gather, some reputation.

Yours very truly,
Anthony Burgess

The Listener, 25 February 1982

1   See Chapter 11 *The Ruination of Music*
2   Keller's book *Criticism*, published posthumously in 1987, demonstrates his fondness for the word 'phoney'. Part I is titled *Phoney Professions: The Element of Criticism* and includes 'Phoney Musical Professions' (such as 'The Conductor', 'The Music Critic', and 'The Musicologist') and 'Other Phoney Professions' (including 'The Editor', 'The Psychoanalyst and Psychiatrist', and 'The Teacher').
3   See Chapter 11 *The Ruination of Music*
4   The last word on the page is 'Scotch'; 'snap' and the question mark that follow are editorial additions.

I'm a novelist and literary critic by profession, but my first ambition was to be a great composer of music. This ambition has not entirely died but it has undergone a decent modification: I merely want to compose music occasionally and don't much care if it's considered great or not. Some of this music has been, and still is, for the guitar, and this implies that I know something about the instrument. It is well known that a composer can write for the bowed stringed instruments without ever having handled them – all he needs to know is something about the technique of multiple stopping; this he can learn theoretically. But the guitar presents problems which can be solved only by getting the damned (blessed, really) machine on to one's knee and seeing how it works.

I bought a second-hand guitar back in 1950s and did badly with it, chiefly because the instruction manuals were so discouragingly dull. It seemed to me that the only way I could learn to play it at all was by composing little pieces with plenty of open-string work (a minuet in E minor, for instance, and a two-voice fugue of excruciating simplicity with a subject built on E A D – answer A D G). I did not do well and I have ended up as a strummer of accompaniments to my own hoarse and dirty songs. I have often wondered how well Hector Berlioz played it. He was the first orchestral composer to warn non-guitarists away from the hexachordal hell of trying to write chords for it that can be played. By the way, did Shakespeare play it, meaning the lute? 'Screw your courage to the sticking-place' in *Macbeth* sounds to me very much like the metaphor of a lutenist. Of course, he was probably friendly with John Dowland and watched him when he was screwing.

I was forced into composing fairly seriously for the guitar when John Sebastian, the late great American harmonica player (not mentioned in *Grove*, though Adler and Reilly are), proposed going on tour with a guitarist – admirable idea: could any duo be more compact? – and needed original works for the combination. I wrote him first a little Pierné-like fantasy called *Faunal Noon*, with a cautious guitar part that proved awkward to finger but didn't have to be substantially changed by the player.[1] More ambitious, I then produced a sonatina in three movements whose guitar part didn't have to be changed at all. I was proud of this. Most recently I wrote a musical version of Joyce's *Ulysses*, in which Molly Bloom's lyrical reminiscences of Gibraltar call for some flamenco-style spread chords, and this too offered no problems. But I still can't play the guitar. If I have an instrument at all it is the keyboard, and I'm not as good at it as, so I'm told, Robert Browning and George Eliot were.

Still, I find it hard to leave the guitar alone. If I enter a house and find a guitar lying around in it, I immediately, and without invitation, start tuning it and, to everybody's surprise, start playing my little Minuet in E Minor. In Italy I discovered, lying on top of a locked piano in a trattoria in Cremona, a mandolin, and I have had more success with that because of the mere tetrachord and the violin tuning. James Joyce played it quite well. In the symphony I wrote a few years ago for performance in Iowa City I introduced a mandolin part among the second violins. But it can't touch the guitar, an instrument which has the difficult nobility of a great disease. I can fake flamenco, and I can strum, but I can't ever hope to be a guitarist. I sometimes wonder why. After all, I have ten strong fingers, a musical sense, and a delight in the sounds it makes. I can make some kind of a showing on most of the wind instruments, but an indefinable barrier lies between me and nylon or wire or catgut. I am just not a stringman.

Classical Guitar, 1983

1   The piece Burgess calls *Faunal Noon* is actually titled *Panique*. See Chapter 68 *John Sebastian – A Personal Reminiscence.*

I was born in the city of Manchester, in the North-West of England. This city had one of the finest orchestras in the world – the Hallé – and its most distinguished conductor was Hans Richter, who introduced Wagner to England; a later conductor, the Irishman Sir Hamilton Harty, taught England, if not France, to appreciate Hector Berlioz. My early environment was totally musical, and my boyhood ambition was to be a great composer of music.

The ambition was thwarted, chiefly because of the poverty which forbade a course of academic instruction at the Manchester Royal College of Music. I taught myself the elements of music, including the piano, and worked for a time as a pianist in a jazz sextet. I also learned orchestration and composed my first symphony at the age of sixteen.

I was, however, led to the career of literature and have, for the last thirty years, earned my living as a novelist and critic. Music has been a part-time occupation, though the impulse to compose has been fired by the practice of literature. When I published my novel *Napoleon Symphony*, which attempts to present Napoleon's career in the form of Beethoven's *Eroica* Symphony, I received an invitation to compose, for the Iowa Symphony Orchestra, a symphonic work of some length. The conductor who commissioned the work had read *Napoleon Symphony* and divined that it was the work of a musician. Composing a symphony for Iowa brought me back to an art I had more or less neglected, and I have composed other works since then.

Living in Rome, I was asked by the American harmonica virtuoso John Sebastian to compose works for harmonica and guitar – the most portable combination imaginable – and this led me to the study of the guitar – an instrument which, as Berlioz rightly said, one has to be able to play before one may dare to write for it. I cannot play the guitar, but I have learnt what it can do and what it cannot do, chiefly through my acquaintanceship with Philippe Loli, a master of the instrument. For him I have composed a concerto.

Of the works for guitar and orchestra composed in our day, I note that some are Spanish and have a strong Spanish flavour, while others are progressive and atonal. In other words, some smell of Andalusia and others of Schoenberg's Vienna. But there is in my native country a tradition of guitar-playing which dates back to the great John Dowland, whom Shakespeare admired, whose instrument was the lute, ancestor of the modern guitar. My aim was to compose a guitar concerto which should be in the English tradition – tonal, melodic, formally orthodox. It should also provide an opportunity to display the exceptional skill of Philippe Loli in extended cadenzas. Here is the work – in three movements and of thirty minutes duration. At one point, with British irony, I allow a Spanish flavour to intrude, but that is only to emphasise how fundamentally non-Spanish the work is.

It is Philippe Loli's Concerto, and he brings out of it all I put into it. Perhaps more.

Undated typescript [ca. 1987]

52. CONCERTO GROSSO FOR GUITAR QUARTET AND ORCHESTRA

A Concerto Grosso is a traditional form, quite well known in Baroque music, which presents a kind of dialogue between a combination of instruments and an orchestra. I invoked this tradition with a concerto for a guitar quartet and a modern orchestra, not a baroque one – that is to say, all the Stravinskian or Straussian sonorities, trumpets, trombones, timpani and all the vibrations. It is not an avant-garde composition, because, in my opinion, the nature of the guitar, an essentially tonal instrument, clashes with musical innovations and blends with traditionally melodic phrases and harmonies based on the arrangement of the strings. Thus my little concerto is more nostalgic than futuristic, evoking the past of the great Englishman John Dowland (William Shakespeare's contemporary) and the tonalities of the Andalusian guitar – admittedly a rather bizarre mixture. Perhaps no other instrument is more capable of asserting these historical and geographical associations.

I said 'small concerto', which seems a contradiction to the 'grosso' of the title, because the guitar has some limitations which prevent the longueurs found in concertos for violin or cello. The alternation of 'pizzicato' and 'arco' is impossible and the range of the instrument is not large. If the composer uses four guitars, there is not much tonal variation: the combination is not analogous to a quartet of two violins, viola, and cello. The effect is that of a gigantic instrument with twenty-four strings, capable of amazing harmonies and counterpoint, even polytonal polyphony, but not the tonal variations found in a single violin. It goes without saying that the quartet for which I expressly composed this concerto is of virtuoso quality. Anything that can be done with four guitars, it can do.

At this time, the repertoire for this combination is very limited and this concerto grosso is a gesture of expansion. I have already composed two classical quartets as well as a concerto for solo guitar, and this new composition tries to explore the possibilities of contrast between two 'sonic' masses, because the guitar quartet has the qualities of a small orchestra. The quartet asks and the real orchestra answers, and vice versa. But, ultimately, I tried to give a little pleasure to both the players and listeners. There are no big shocks: these are reserved for the music of Boulez or Berio. But there is, I hope, a demonstration of the possibilities of the loveliest and most beloved instrument of all.

Programme note, 1988

53. THE AÏGHETTA QUARTET

Most of us meet the guitar in four genres – the electronic travesty of the rock group, the strummed chords of the blues or folk singer, the flamenco improvisation of southern Spain, and the classical form ennobled by such masters as Segovia. The classical guitar has a long history, but there have never been many great classical guitarists. To turn the instrument into a kind of one-handed clavichord requires rare skill, strength, and long application. It is perhaps the simplest instrument in the world to play badly and the most difficult to play well.

The guitar has its limitations, most evident when it is compared with the violoncello, its cousin in pitch. It cannot be bowed, only plucked, and it is slower-speaking. Multiply the guitar and produce a quartet, and these limitations are not removed. The guitar remains the guitar, and there is no analogy to violin, viola and 'cello, no extension of tonal range. But there are new possibilities of counterpoint, antiphony, dynamic. The guitar quartet can sound like an orchestra, while a string quartet is still what Sibelius called his sole work for the combination – *voces intimae*. The quartet is still something of an innovation, but, when composers become alive to its possibilities, it will be seen to have a future.

The Aïghetta Quartet was formed in 1979 in Monte Carlo. Its members – André Michel Berthoux, Alexandre Del-Fa, Philippe Loli and François Szönyi – studied at the Académie de Musique Rainier III of Monaco with Pier Domenico Amerió, a pupil of both Segovia and Alirio Diaz. It was first heard in public in February 1980, but its career as an international ensemble may be said to have been launched with its performance of the *Concerto Andalou* by Joaquin Rodrigo, with the Philharmonic Orchestra of Monaco, at Monte Carlo's Salle Garnier in 1982.[1] Tours of France, England, Italy,

Hungary and the German Federal Republic have followed, as well as numerous television and radio broadcasts. The appeal has not been one of sheer novelty – the song of a four-headed bird – but rather of the recognition of a new and compelling sound.

What has naturally been lacking is a repertoire to exploit this sound, but composers have already been sufficiently attracted to it to produce works specifically for the Aïghetta Quartet – Willy Merz in Switzerland, Fréderic l'Epée in France, Federico Moreno Torroba in Spain, Stefan Rouk in Czechoslovakia, and John Duarte in England. There are already two concerti grossi – Rodrigo's *Concerto Andalou* and Torroba's *Concerto Iberico*. A third has just been completed by the author of this sleeve note. It has no exotic title.[2] The works performed on this disc are intended to demonstrate the musicianship of the quartet with no exterior aid from an orchestra.

Johann Sebastian Bach: Concerto in B Minor
This work will be recognised as the Concerto for four harpsichords in A minor, itself an adaptation of Vivaldi's Concerto for four violins in B minor. François Szönyi, a member of the Quartet, has restored the work to its original key in adapting it for guitars. Vivaldi needed a string orchestra to provide his soloists with the tonal body they lack, Bach to offset the sharp pecking of the quills of his harpsichords. Here we are made aware of the resourcefulness of the guitar, which needs no extra strings. Here too we hear the contrapuntal possibilities of a guitar ensemble in a work of great geniality and verve.

Ferdinand Carulli: Quartet in G Major
A Neapolitan who died in Paris, Carulli (1770–1841) was known in his own day as a guitar virtuoso and also an influential pedagogue. His *L'Harmonie appliquée à la Guitare* was widely translated and

helped to promote the serious revival of an instrument too often debased into a device of easy accompaniment. He composed about 330 works for the instrument, solo and in ensembles, and the present work, his Opus 21, exists also in a version for soloist and piano. It is not a work of large profundity, but it exhibits the capabilities of the instrument. Hector Berlioz rightly said that only those who know how to play the guitar know also how to compose for it. Carulli had a thorough knowledge of the instrument to which he dedicated his life.

Antonio Ruiz-Pipó: Cuatro para Cuatro
This Spaniard, born at Granada in 1934, became a naturalised Frenchman in 1979.[3] He studied at Barcelona and, in that city, became a member of the Circulo Manuel de Falla, a group of young composers in whom, following the example of the great dead Spanish composer who was their patron saint, there was as much interest in the musical heritage of Spain as in the European influence, especially as manifested in France. Ruiz-Pipó made his name primarily as a pianist and as a composer, as well as the director of the Festival of Bonaguil. He gained an international prize at Zaragoza for *Cuatro para Cuatro* – four brief pieces for four guitarists, presented on this disc. He is without doubt the most prolific of contemporary composers for the instrument, with the possible exception of Joaquin Rodrigo. He is a post-tonalist with charm, a rare commodity in the avant-garde field.

Robert Delanoff: Ein Türkisches Volkslied
Delanoff was born at Troppau in Czechoslovakia in 1942 and studied at the Richard Strauss Conservatory in Munich from 1961 till 1968. Since 1970 he has played as clarinettist in the Grauke-München Symphony Orchestra, interrupting this career for a five-year stint with the National Symphony Orchestra of Istanbul. A life given to a wind instrument has stimulated an interest in works for strings, bowed and plucked,

as well as in the possibilities of electronic music. The popular Turkish song here recorded comes from a suite for four guitars, of which the two other movements are a 'tango sentimental' and an impromptu. This little piece is piquant, modal in the Near Eastern manner, and prepared to exploit the possibilities of the guitar as a percussion instrument. Not only flamenco players are permitted to slap the body of the instrument.

Anthony Burgess: Quatuor en hommage à Maurice Ravel
The author of this sleeve-commentary is now writing about himself. Born in 1917 in Manchester, Burgess, known chiefly as a novelist and critic, had early ambitions to be a composer and spent the first thirty-five years of his life trying to establish himself in the field of popular as well as serious music, without success. The publication of his novel *Napoleon Symphony* in 1974, a work which presents the great Corsican's career in the shape of Beethoven's *Eroica Symphony,* led to a resumption of a spare-time musical career, since an American conductor read the book and suspected that Burgess was a composer in disguise as a novelist.[4] In the 1950s Burgess took to study of the guitar but found the instrument too difficult. Nevertheless he learned, in the Berlioz manner, both the limitations and strengths of the plucked six strings, and required little encouragement to write for them. He composed two works for harmonica and guitar and, on meeting the Aïghetta Quartet in Monaco where he lives, was stimulated to write this present Quatuor. It is a straightforward work in orthodox sonata form which is intended to be a homage to Ravel. It flirts with the polytonality of Darius Milhaud but in other respects may be regarded as very British. The slow movement is a passacaglia inspired by the example of Henry Purcell, a master of the form.

Liner note, *Oeuvres pour Quatuor de Guitares*, 1987

1   This work is more often known by its original Spanish title *Concierto Andaluz.*

2   Burgess completed his *Concerto Grosso pour Quatuor de Guitares et Orchestre en La mineur* around May 1987. See Chapter 52 *Concerto Grosso for Guitar Quartet and Orchestra* and Commentary on that chapter, and Chapter 68 *John Sebastian – A Personal Reminiscence.*

3   Antonio Ruiz-Pipó died in Paris in 1997. He was a composer and piano virtuoso who studied with Alicia de Larrocha. In later life he resided in France, where he taught at the École Normale de Musique de Paris and Conservatoire de Musique.

4   See Chapters 44 *Symphony in C* and 45 *How I Wrote My Third Symphony.* The publication of *Napoleon Symphony* is given incorrectly as 1971 in the typescript.

Remarks at a Celtic festival

I'm half-Irish, half-Scottish and lived (legally) for twenty-six years with a Welsh woman with whom I spoke Welsh every day. I believe I am qualified to be considered truly Celtic. I have composed a concerto grosso for four guitars and orchestra. Despite the guitar being Spanish (or Arabic – a Moorish instrument adopted by a nation of Celtic heritage), the concerto grosso has Irish and Welsh qualities – for example, themes in a Welsh tonality, rhythms of Irish dance. My musical participation in this festival is therefore legitimate: the Celtic blood flows, I hope, with vigor in a work for a rather rare combination of instruments. You will hear the beating of a very Celtic heart in the vibrations of the guitar strings and cries of the orchestra. Listen well!

Typescript, 1987

Introduction to a concert of Burgess's music for guitar quartet at the Princess Grace Irish Library in Monaco

It seems appropriate, though some will think not, that the Princess Grace Irish Library should sponsor an evening of music for four guitars. Anything less Irish than the guitar is hard to imagine. James Joyce alone can bring them together in the person of Molly Bloom, half-Spanish and half-Irish, who spent her well-remembered girlhood in Gibraltar and was kissed under the Moorish Wall. But Anthony Burgess, whose grandmother was Mary Ann Finnegan of Tipperary, who lives in Monaco and was one of the founders of the Irish Library (and also spent some of his war service in Gibraltar), may help in a sub-Joycean way. As a writer of novels he has earned his living and some praise, but he began his artistic career as a composer and, in old age, has returned to the craft. It was partly the desire to expand the repertoire of the harmonica and the guitar quartet – an instrument and an instrumental group that Beethoven never thought of – that brought him back to composition while living, pianoless, in Monaco. He has written works for the three great harmonica-players of our time – John Sebastian, Tommy Reilly, and Larry Adler – and for the admirable and already famous Aïghetta Quartet of Monaco. The late John Sebastian expressed the desire to travel the world with the minimal musical equipment of his own harmonica and an accompanying guitarist (nothing less weighty can be imagined), and this forced Burgess into studying the guitar – an instrument, as Hector Berlioz said, for which nobody who doesn't play it can write. And so tonight the music of Burgess demonstrates what four guitars can do. Although the twang of the strings recalls Spain, the musical content will be found to be not un-Irish. As a *bonne bouche*, a brief recording is proposed – that of the finale of Burgess's *Blooms of Dublin*, a light opera based on Joyce's *Ulysses*. Burgess will say a few words also on the struggle between music and literature in his own life and on the works that will be played. He will be too scared to handle a guitar himself.

Concert programme, 1989

55. THE TWENTY-FOUR-STRING GUITAR

I have achieved my first professional recording – of a quartet for guitars played by the Quatuor Aïghetta of the Principality of Monaco. As I wrote in this magazine some years ago, I think I know how to compose for the guitar without actually being able to play it. Well, not exactly: I can play 'Greensleeves' in G and a Bach minuet at the speed of a sarabande. As my son has been studying the oboe at the Monaco Academy of Music, I came into contact with some of the instructors there, and among them was, is, Philippe Loli, a member of the Quatuor Aïghetta. This group has made a name for itself in Europe, but it necessarily has very little of a repertoire. One of my little hobbies has been to arrange and compose for it. When my new version of Weber's *Oberon* was presented at the Fenice Theatre in Venice a year ago, the Aïghetta group came along to play my arrangement of the *Oberon* overture and the *Quatuor en hommage à Maurice Ravel* (whose centenary we were celebrating).[1] The possibilities of the ensemble fascinate me. Its only trouble is the lack of a bass lower than that low E. It can take, with some inevitable fiddling, a fair number of reductions of orchestral works in its stride. I have just arranged the 'Mercury' movement from Holst's *Planets* for it. What it lacks, apart from a good low bass, is the kind of tonal variety that subsists in a string quartet.

Still, the combination has a future. I have written a three-movement concerto grosso for it, with a full orchestra at the back (three trumpets, three trombones, tuba, a good deal of percussion). While my hand was in, I composed a concerto for the solo guitar of Philippe Loli, which he has recorded with the orchestral score reduced for piano. There seems to be a certain reluctance on the part of orchestral societies to present either work, an unspoken sense that a guitar concerto is a mere 'novelty', unworthy to be sandwiched between an overture and a symphony.

How, in these late 1980s, should one compose for guitar – solo or ensemble? It will accept atonality well enough and, with four, it possibly enjoys polytonality, but a composer is right, I think, to cling loosely to tradition. I was aware that my quartet in homage to Ravel was far too tonal, too glibly melodic, to please the young Turks of the avant-garde, whatever the avant-garde is these days, but one ought to be aware, however modernistic the music, of how the guitar is tuned, of the readymade fourths, the minor triad up there and the major triad in the middle. To evade triads, which is to evade tonality, is a kind of perversion. When Alban Berg composed his violin concerto, he almost threw into the faces of the auditors the abiding truth of the GDAE of the fiddle. His *Grundstimmung* is a wonderful compromise – G B♭ D F♯ A C E G♯ B C♯ E♭ F – that shows tonality sitting happily with serialism.

I make no great claims for my *Quatuor*. Though dedicated to the memory of Ravel, it is closer to Poulenc than to that half-Basque master. Written on Monegascan ground, it is aware of the vast stretch of French territory all around (except for the Mediterranean) and of the fact that you can get on the train at Monte Carlo and cross the Pyrenees in a few hours. In the last movement I had a very clear image of the lean knight and the fat squire taking the road. It is hard to expunge the Spanish, since one has so many clear memories of the illiterate flamenco masters just north of Gibraltar. The second movement is a passacaglia. I was thinking there more of our own English tradition – not the lutenist one but the Purcellian one, since Purcell was the great master of the passacaglia (I have just been hearing the new compact disc recording of *King Arthur*).

I think, and this may be aesthetically unworthy, that the guitar is the one instrument whose physicality one cannot ignore. Stravinsky said that he loved Bach because you can smell the resin on his strings and taste the reed of the oboe. You cannot, as some atonalists have tried to do, convert the guitar into plastic. The physicality of the guitar is matched by one's sense of its history – from the Elizabethan lutenists to the greasy-haired flamenco thugs. Spain cannot help getting in, even in a transcription of Vivaldi. At least, this is true of myself as amateur composer for the instrument. There comes a point in my composing when my back hair bristles at the imagined sound of a fourfold thrummed E major chord alternating with a Phrygian EADACE. This is the vulgar streak in me. But it is responding to something vulgar, or shall we say demotic, in the guitar itself.

Classical Guitar, 1988

1   Actually the semicentenary (of Ravel's death in 1937).

Your honour, ladies and gentlemen, good evening. I hope you will forgive my ugly French. Unfortunately I am Anglophone almost since birth and cannot ameliorate the situation. This evening I can express, in general, the difficulties I have at my age with all foreign languages...perhaps for this reason I've returned to the world of music.

I began my aesthetic career as a composer and have returned to this vocation to pay a small homage to your great city and to you, its citizens. I have composed a little symphony that is not too avant-garde. It's rather conventional and not too difficult, and you are going to hear it twice. Perhaps because his honor, the mayor, has another appointment, he cannot stay with us the entire evening, yet he knows that it is fitting to hear a new work twice.

The work itself is in three movements. The duration is about fifteen minutes. Three movements: *Toccata, Serment* and *Fugues*. In the *Toccata*, a very quick movement, I have tried to present your city's liveliness as well as its sufferings. One ought not to forget the sufferings during World War II and throughout history. In the second movement, I have tried to pay homage to the great Oaths of Strasbourg with which, one might say, the French language truly began. And finally, there is the movement titled *Fugues*, which presents impressions of the city, the city's daily life, fleeting glimpses of the cathedral.

And finally the glory! The slightly qualified glory of Strasbourg. I hope that the work will not upset you. Perhaps you will even like it a little. We begin with it. Thank you very much.

Spoken remarks at the premiere, 25 November 1988

PART IV
PERFORMERS AND PERFORMANCES

57. BRITTEN, ADLER, JAZZ

One of Major Walter's epigraphs is from Sir Arthur Keith: 'It has to be remembered that the characteristic of an impulsive or instinctive action is that it is done for a purpose of which the doer is unaware'.[1] His other is the profoundest piece of demotic poetry that the First War produced: *We're here because we're here because we're here because we're here.* I was glad to see this latter prominently featured in the excellent *Songs for the Times* (BBC-1, August 4), which was a model anthology, with first-rate narrative links, of the two kinds of song that came out of that war, or rather the kind that came out of it and the kind that was imposed upon it. *We don't want to lose you but we think you ought to go* – the old men put that into the mouths of the women. The young men sang *We are Fred Karno's army* and *Always bloody well raining*, instinctively, by giving words of sacrificial resignation a hymn-tune setting, deferring to the Father.[2] Then over the top, millions of spermatozoa spent so that one or two might live. Our awareness of the mythical frame that encloses these songs seems to turn them to a form of art, of a terrible poignancy. Nobody put words to hymn-tunes in the last war, and we had no real songs except *Lili Marlene*, which was a song of the enemy.

We had no poets either, and Cecil Day Lewis explained why:

> It is the logic of our times,
> No subject for immortal verse –
> That we who lived by honest dreams
> Defend the bad against the worse.[3]

But the First War had Wilfred Owen, and Mr Day Lewis was the right man to present him to us in (on this same jubilee evening) *The Pity of War* (BBC-2). Great war-poets only spring out of useless wars: it is their task to try to understand the myth that surrounds them. Owen's gift – in music, at least – approached Dante's; some of his lines are as close to Dante as English poetry is ever likely to get. The excellence of this tribute to him rested not merely in the fine readings (by Peter Wyngarde and Alan Dobie) but in the wedding of word and film image to create a transcendental series of symbols which, as it were, showed war *sub specie aeternitatis*.[4] Owen purged his own war of its particularity and there was no other poet Benjamin Britten could properly choose for his *War Requiem*. And yet, very curiously, I felt in the performance of the *War Requiem* that followed the Owen programme (this was an evening of inspired planning) that the Owen words soared above their settings, that they were about reality and that Britten's music was not. I have admired this music intensely ever since Coventry, but I am beginning to feel that it is more decorative than expressive.

The *War Requiem* came to us from a Promenade Concert, and television is doing the right thing in giving us those concerts which gain from an exploitation of the eye.[5] The first night (July 25, on BBC-1) was full of fresh faced youngsters waving things, joyfully gregarious, a salutary inoculation against the desire to exterminate all youth which came over me, hobbling through Hastings, the following weekend. I can't say I like the party atmosphere – everybody giving the A, Sir Malcolm greeted like Dusty Springfield – because I don't think it's conducive to good playing, and I think the performance of Bach's E-major violin concerto was the most perfunctory I've ever heard. The performance of Ravel's *Boléro* on August 11(BBC-1) wasn't much better – not enough ictus, the row at the end insufficient – but there's a certain divine cheek about the opulence of the orchestral lay-out, the expense of spirit in a waste of sham, and one grins with satisfaction at the sight of an E-flat clarinet and an oboe d'amore and a bank of saxophones all waiting to tackle that tune which is not a bolero-tune at all. It is the ultimate consort in the service of anti-music, all the daughters of music brought low.

We've done well enough for real music lately. *Festival in Provence* (BBC-2, August 9) was a delight, and it was wrong that it should have been hugged to the 625 belt. There was a civilized piquancy in seeing and hearing excerpts from *Don Giovanni* in latitudes which, though far north of Seville, suggest life running very high. A statue singing *Tu m'invitasti a cenar teco* makes sense in a rococo world, as do hot blood and a formal chorus telling of the horrors of a baroque hell. I'm happy also about the two recent *Workshop* programmes. It was a fine stroke to hand over a whole programme to Larry Adler (BBC-2, July 18), intellectual, serious musician, harmonica-player who has exalted that most desolate of first-war trench instruments to nobility. That important composers rush to write concertos for Mr Adler is less a tribute to the musical potentialities of the harmonica than a recognition of his skill. Mr Adler is the only man who, since the sight of his instrument frightens no one, could get away with Stravinsky in a variety show. The very limitations of the harmonica encourage an unlimited repertoire, from Alban Berg to *Three Coins in the Fountain*. This was a most stimulating and entertaining programme.

So, for that matter, was, in the same series, *Brecht on Music* (BBC-2, August 15). What I don't like about Brecht is his authoritarianism, his old-fashioned expressionist insistence that all the arts of the theatre should bow to an idea, and that music should be gelded into 'misuk'.[6] I think it was Brecht who made both Hindemith and Kurt Weill say the silly things they once did ('Omissions, inversions, and additions are practicable. Musical portions may be left out...passages from other composers may be introduced if necessary, provided they conform to the general style of the original' – Hindemith, on his score for Brecht's *The Lesson*). Still, this is not the point. The point is that Martin Esslin made his points very well, and it was bracing to hear Dessau, Eisler, and, above all, Weill in the context of a doctrine which is essentially anti-musical. It all proved how neatly music will outlive ideology, bending to the doctrinaire as a bough will bend to the snow on it and then, when bent enough, dislodging the powdery burden.

Which brings me, for some reason, to jazz and my own guilt at having, so far, said nothing about BBC-2's *Jazz 625*. I think that this new channel has been kinder to jazz than to anything, and that the quality of the presentation of jazz, apart from the performances, has been consistently high. What I find hard to understand is why so many people are able to listen to jazz without themselves ever having played it. I once played jazz (as well as pop) and my interest in listening to the 'great' performers was primarily technical, it sprang out of a preoccupation with the possibilities of my own instrument (piano) in an essentially limited medium. Jazz is not expressive, nor is it concerned (unless it is played by Brubeck, who I am told is no jazzman) with extending its melodic, rhythmical, or harmonic scope. It is narcissistic and, far from rejoicing in true improvisation, it will slyly hoard effective tropes and bring them out again and again. If *Jazz 625* has done nothing else, it has convinced me of the ultimate auditory aridity of a medium whose true appeal is to the effector organs.

The Listener, 1964

1   The article opens with comments on a book titled *The Sexual Cycle of Human Warfare* by Major Norman Walter.
2   Burgess claimed that his father played piano for Fred Karno. See Chapter 47 *The Making of a Writer*.
3   the final quatrain of 'Where Are The War Poets?'
4   'from the perspective of the eternal'
5   Cf. Chapter 60 *Reflections on a Golden Ring*
6   For more on Brecht and Weill, see Chapter 43 *A Berliner on Broadway*.

Coming now to Gilbert and Sullivan, I go back to Ibsen, making him and Gilbert link arms as the two supreme poetic dramatists of the nineteenth century.[1] Ibsen's bad dreams found tragic expression; Gilbert's were cathartized in farce. Sado-masochism, gerontophily, a whiff of incest – the Savoy sweetened them all. It is the rankness beneath the sweetness and fun that turns pure fascination into obsession. But the Sadler's Wells production of *Iolanthe* (BBC-1, October 1) could, if anything could, greatly qualify the obsession, though it's difficult to say what was really wrong with it. The clumsy lumpishness of the opening fairy chorus looked less like fun than real ineptitude – aleatoric, as we now say, not designed. Of course, a lot can be blamed on television, a medium which has inured us to naturalism. Listening to the Weberian music of the first act, I wondered what the cameras would do to *Der Freischütz* and *Euryanthe*, all trapdoors and greasepaint. Until the screen spreads all over the drawing-room wall, perhaps television had better leave the stagey to the stage (though see below). Gilbert's Arcady and Palace Yard don't take kindly to being grid-lined like a map, the camera pointing now to this square, now to that; that way visual dullness lies and, in this presentation, lay. The singing was another thing entirely, though I was uneasy about standards of verbal clarity – less stringent here, surely, than in the older (Gilbert's directorial influence still alive) tradition?

The Magic Flute came from Salzburg in two instalments (BBC-2, September 25 and October 2), and here the cameras, by standing decently back, caught some of the opera's essential staginess. The music is so ravishing that we are persuaded to accept everything of the preposterous Masonic parable – the Queen of the Night looking younger than her daughter (but we can take that as an *Iolanthe* touch), the jingling bells that don't jingle, the Christmas pantomime Moors, the disastrous serpent of the opening scene. It was a privilege to meet a Papageno (Walter Berry) of the true Viennese mould, his humour of the most delicate shoulder-shrugging kind, dead on cue with his pan-pipes. Roberta Peters was a wonderful Queen of the Night; Walter Kreppel as Sarastro was, as he should be, a mellifluous bore. This strange work depends on the sustaining of a mood of enchantment conjured in the very first bars. It was a pity that Richard Baker had to break it with his narrative links, though I know such things have to be. If we could have been allowed to hear, however faintly, the voices still at work during these intrusions, instead of just watching silent mouthing, the temporary disenchantment might not have been so painful.

It is a good thing for critics to have moments of self-doubt. Immediately after *The Summer in Gossensass*, BBC-1 gave us a repeat of a two-and-a-half-year-old *International Concert Hall* – Yehudi Menuhin playing the Beethoven Concerto, Colin Davis conducting the London Symphony Orchestra. I was not happy about this performance, though I should have been. Mr Davis seemed to be lashing out a life that would not emerge; Mr Menuhin played beautifully but failed to move me. Can it be that the work itself is not good enough for these great combined talents? I ask diffidently, in self-doubt. I've bowed down for thirty years to the general acceptance of this concerto as one of the supreme works of the repertory. Now, too old to worry about sticking my neck out, I declare it a bore. But still diffidently. The other memorable orchestral experience of the month was the 'Last Night of the Proms' (BBC-1, September 19), though, as always, it was more of a social occasion than a musical one, I don't think even the words count, let alone the music. How many of the youthful roarers of Parry's *Jerusalem* know that Blake's 'dark satanic mills' are not factories but churches? (And, before I forget, can anyone spot the rude word in Britten's *Spring Symphony*?)[2] But the whole evening was warmly phatic, providing an image of British teenagers as less delinquent than jingoistic.

The Listener, 1964

APPLEGARTH,   24, GLEBE STREET
ETCHINGHAM,   CHISWICK,
EAST SUSSEX.   LONDON, W.4.
ETCHINGHAM 262.   *CHISWICK 1411.*

here now   here in January

December 16th[3]

Dear Diana Menuhin,
Forgive typing: my handwriting is a kind of cacography, so to speak. It was delightful to hear from you, and at such length too, and this in spite of the trepidation I felt when I saw that the major theme was to be about what it was about. I still can't make up my mind about the viability of my new and middleaged attitude to the Beethoven. I've listened again and again since to my record of Menuhin (who else?) doing it, and I DON'T THINK I REALLY LIKE THE WORK, but there may be a tangle of extra-musical factors working against a pure aesthetic response. I don't think I can get over what I regard as the near-vapidity of that first subject. I mean, contrast it with the Elgar. I mean, contrast it with the Brahms. But I'm aware again that this may have nothing to do with the music. Was I once brutally assaulted as a child to a tune

with the same rhythm as the Beethoven? I don't know, and I remain worried.

What you say about the visual business I recognise as all too true. I still can't understand what television really is, and I can't see why music isn't enhanced by the sight of the performers. But it evidently isn't. The trouble is that when I write about music-on-TV, as I have to, I have to find some gimmicky approach which doesn't get in the way of what the pure music critics are doing, and it usually ends up as one of these nexus things – viz., WHAT THE MUSIC MEANT TO ME VISUALLY. This may mean a subtle and unconscious twisting of approach which inhibits willingness to listen to the music alone. I don't know. I don't don't know. The whole thing's wrong somewhere, and I suppose I should be less lazy and try to find out.

No more unseasonable brow-knottings. I enjoyed so very much meeting you two on that memorable occasion of the

if that's the way it goes. I look forward to a renewal of that meeting. And I wish you both (all, though I've not met all) a very fine and undisturbed Christmas and a remarkable New Year. It was nice of you to write. My fond regards (one may be impelled to send such, even after a single meeting, since your joint myth has been part of one's life for a long time) and admiration from

always,
Anthony Burgess

1   This 'Television of the month' column begins with a review of *The Summer in Gossensass*, a programme about Henrik Ibsen by Casper Wrede that Burgess deemed 'one of the finest literary documentaries that television has yet given us.'
2   Reference to the phrase 'bucke uerteþ', which means 'the billy-goat farts'. It occurs in Britten's setting of 'Sumer is icumen in' (Summer has arrived).
3   Evidently 1964, although the year does not appear on the letter.

I was particularly anxious to see and hear the repeat of Britten's *War Requiem* on November 5 (BBC-1), since I felt that the illusion of one more live performance would help me to make up my mind as to what I really think about the work. Playing it over and over in a monophonic recording has not seemed really to be enough: it's been rather like attending High Mass by the proxy of a transistor radio, which (though I've not yet heard any definitive pronouncement on this) cannot transmit the Real Presence. But the work seems to lean heavily on certain extrinsic factors – the visual bombardment by the vast forces employed, the sense of space in the physical disposition of these forces, the reverence to which we're predisposed because of the poignancy of the theme, the majesty of the liturgy, and the aura of sacrificial hero – apart from intrinsic poetic greatness – which surrounds Wilfred Owen. To offer a critical assessment of the *War Requiem* has, at this stage, become a sort of blasphemy. Every performance is a ceremony. If I may vary T.S. Eliot's epigram, devotional choral works are now a substitute for religion, and so is our religion.[1] It's dangerous for art to become greater than itself.

As things turned out, I saw the *War Requiem* without hearing much of it. There were fireworks all round my house, an ironical simulacrum of war, and in my house was my border collie, made mad by the din. We gave him, at well-spaced intervals, two tranquillisers and a sleeping tablet, but these merely made him turn inwards from the fireworks to the television screen. He barked at Britten's brass and percussion and, for some reason, whined at Peter Pears. Eventually, just as Messrs Pears and Hemsley got to 'Let us sleep now', he slept.[2] So my judgment on the *War Requiem* has to remain very tentative.

I remain convinced, though, that it has to be seen as well as heard, but that the screen cannot really swallow it, and that its effect derives more than in any other of Britten's works, from elements not intrinsically musical. Britten seems hardly able to start a movement without a percussive exordium; when we hear his own voice it is in those arpeggios of the thirteenth which have become too much of a habit; the style is too eclectic; to set Owen is supererogatory.[3] Let us accept the work as a most moving ceremony and hope that BBC television will make a regular commemorative service out of it. It remains to add that Richard Baker's introduction, links, and conclusions were tasteful and, indeed, moving in themselves.[4]

A slighter musical occasion which gained much from the cameras was the performance of Mozart's concerto for flute, harp, and orchestra which came from the Palais Schaezler, Augsburg (BBC-2, October 16). We ought not to pretend that this work pours the headiest Mozartian wine, since the composer knew little about the harp and had a devotion to the flute more symbolic than musical. In any case, the harp was still a bit clumsy in 1778, waiting for that man Cousineau to improve it – more of a keyboard instrument without keys, really; very remote from the sumptuous Erard ships which sail through our modern orchestras. This music, which breathes the commission and the occasion, gains from odd little visual distractions like views of fat-bottomed rococo cherubim – a kind of apotheosis of the Palm Court. The Rostropovich performance of the Bach Suite No. 3 (BBC-2, October 23) was, and had to be, a very different matter – plain, pure, austere, nothing between us and the music. Why bother to televise it then? Perhaps to remind us how easy it is to be seduced by a performer's personality. Perhaps we've seen too much of Tortelier as a teacher – though I don't see how that's really possible – and, when he merely performs, we tend to watch that most expressive face for clues as to the music's meaning. With Rostropovich there's nothing to watch except the engine that produces the sounds. And what sounds.

Anyway, all the Bach visual stuff had to be saved up for the after-dinner conversation about him in *Music Forum* (BBC-2, October 30). This, if you like, was a waste: there was everything except enough time. Figure to yourself, as they say – Leopold Stokowski, Michael Tippett, William Mann, John Amis, port on the table, most efficient putters-on of records, fine blown-up Bach portraits, and all we got was a mean, a criminal, half-hour. This cries to heaven for vengeance. Some of the most intriguing lines of approach were snipped cruelly – that opening business about Stokowski's orchestration of the toccata and fugue in D minor, for instance, and the question of what non-Bach instruments it was permissible to use in a modern redaction. But some things of value squeezed through the press of time. Dolmetsch's 'whooshing' interpretation of the first prelude of the Forty-Eight was rightly condemned because it could not show the organic not-quite-identical-twinhood of each arpeggio and its repeat. When we heard a jazz version of the same piece the response was prompt and unanimous – good fun but nothing to do with Bach. John Amis was determined to let us hear as many Bach fragments as possible, as though it was likely that we should never be allowed to hear any Bach again, but the ultimate effect was of the raising of children's 'flash-cards': what do you think of this? – two seconds to answer. I note that the same ghastly limitation of time is to be imposed on all programmes in this series. Please. Humphrey Burton, do something about it.[5]

Andrew Cruickshank looked surprisingly embarrassed in his role of compère in *Gala Performance* (BBC-1, October 23), as though he had just been caught out in a breach of medical etiquette. He told us that Benny Goodman strode both his musical worlds like a Colossus, which is perhaps going too far. There is no doubt that Mr Goodman's technique remains brilliant in both jazz and the other stuff, but the other stuff, in this little concert, consisted of the Weber concertino, mere gymnastics, a kind of earnest that he could play anybody off the platform if he wanted to, therefore don't take the jazz that follows as the mere doodling of the musically illiterate. It was, in fact, very good jazz and far more interesting than the Weber. We also saw the Moiseyev Dance Company and, on October 29, on BBC-1 also, saw them again. It will take a good deal of psychiatry to locate the trauma which blocks my appreciation of boisterous folksiness: I often dream of being trampled to death by riding-booted lines of roaring country Venuses. Some of the titles of some of the dances still, by some synaesthetic quirk, bring a whiff of sweating horses – 'Moldavian mass dance', 'The football match', 'The partisans'. But one cannot deny either the energy or the skill. Snow would not stick long to these boots.[6]

1   'Our literature is a substitute for religion, and so is our religion.' T.S. Eliot, 'A Dialogue on Dramatic Poetry' (1928)
2   Britten composed many songs, concert works, and operatic roles for Peter Pears, his lifelong partner from the time of their first meeting in 1937; together, they co-founded the Aldeburgh Festival in 1947 and the Britten-Pears School in 1972. Thomas Jeffrey Hemsley was an English baritone renowned for his performances of German and English repertoire, especially the music of Richard Wagner, Frederick Delius, Benjamin Britten, Michael Tippett, and Iain Hamilton.
3   Burgess often cites chords and 'arpeggios of the thirteenth', i.e. strings of seven thirds that extend as far as possible before returning to tonic, to characterize Britten's harmonic language.

4   Richard Douglas James Baker was a presenter of classical music on BBC radio and television for many years and a well-known newscaster for BBC News from 1954 to 1982.

5   Humphrey McGuire Burton is an English classical music television presenter, broadcaster, director, producer, impresario, lecturer, and writer. He began working for BBC Radio in 1955, was the BBC's first Head of Music and Arts (1965–67), and, after a stint in commercial television, resumed his former position in the mid-1970s, remaining with the BBC until 1988. After the broadcast premiere of *Blooms of Dublin* on 1 February 1982, he sent Burgess a letter the following day, writing, 'I enjoyed your musical version of *Ulysses* very much indeed and I hope it has a long life and a varied one; I hope somebody from the R.S.C. was listening.'

6   This 'Television of the month' column continues with a review of an interview on *Encounter* with theatre director Peter Hall.

Music-wise (this is self-evident), radio is a transparent and television an opaque medium. Or, to put it another way, radio can *become* music while television can only use it. No matter how great the intended homage to the art of sound, the craft of vision always brings the daughters of music low. Strictly speaking, there is no great harm in this, since the divinest of noises are made out of spittings and scrapings and we ought sometimes to be reminded of that gross reality: to see a beery flautist doing a Debussy faun-call is to watch a kind of allegory of the mystery of hypostasis. But that's a mere by-product of the business of looking at music being made, and it ought never to go on too long. Admirers of Eric Linklater will remember that terribly ugly orchestra in *Juan in America*.[1] To be presented with such an orchestra – fat men, strabismic men, portraits out of Lombroso or Garofalo, cretinous leerers, dwarfs – playing Mozart divinely while the cameras dwelt successively and lovingly on every telegenic deformity – would not that be selling the daughters into the kinkiest kind of whoredom?[2]

It has never happened, and musicians – being at least as comely and intelligent as their antitheses, the pop-singers – are unlikely to realise in any one body that fantasy of Linklater's. But one remains disturbed and embarrassed by this question of what we ought to be looking at when an orchestral concert is presented on television. In the first place, I don't think we ought to be looking at the conductor. Bernstein, exalted, balletic, lips parted in rapture, crafty, miming vibrato to squeeze the last drop of sonority out of the strings, Bernstein swallows up in his personality the personality of Mahler, Shostakovich, Sibelius. It is in the nature of the man, as the admirable *Young People's Concerts* have been showing (BBC-1 on three successive Sundays), to impose his personality, and that is fine in a teacher or leader. But it is the concern only of him and the led or taught, and we are the listeners. When I think back to Bernstein's conducting of Sibelius's Fifth Symphony, many months ago, I find I remember very little of the music. Worse, when I put that symphony (conducted by Karajan) on my record-player, I keep seeing Bernstein capering and smirking between me and it.

Should we see only the orchestra? This depends a great deal on the music. There's no thrill in watching the orchestra of Haydn, Mozart or even early Beethoven at work. The late romantics are different: the Strauss orchestra is a superb thing to look at, especially in *Don Quixote* and *Ein Heldenleben* – eight horns, Wagner tuba, wind-machine and so on. An orchestra as an army is supremely visual, and I wonder if that was one of the points of BBC-2's *The Golden Ring*, which let us see what we never see in the opera-house – the *Götterdämmerung* orchestra in all its mad Ludwigian opulence. In a sense, this programme (which I felt, probably mistakenly, that I was seeing for more than the second time) was not about music: it was about the machinery that produces music. Birgit Nilsson, Gottlob Frick and Dietrich Fischer-Dieskau were part of the machinery, and the orchestra shone and glowed like an Edwardian locomotive. There came a time, towards the end, when some of the obscurer machine-minders seemed to revolt against the whole mechanistic process (the opera was being recorded) and brought in a horse that was supposed to be Grane. Brünnhilde Nilsson laughed; Solti said, unsmiling, that it was very funny; and everybody had another *Zigarettenpause*. The horse was led back to its stable, the ghost of Wagnerian glamour faded again, and the machine resumed its sway. This musical programme, then, was doing nothing except grope after a nexus between eye and ear, trying to justify television's concern with music. But it was really all eye.

Orchestral soloists – flute in *L'Après-midi*, cor anglais in *The Swan of Tuonela* – distract from the image of the whole work: there are, after all, other lines going on in the score, it is wrong to suggest a factitious concerto element. Score-following producers, eager to show a new instrumental entry, can often be led astray – especially when composers like Elgar bring in, say, a bass clarinet some bars before it's really needed, to enable the player to warm up his instrument. It is only on the concerto soloists that the cameras can justly gorge themselves – especially when they're glamorous like Jacqueline du Pré, though personal glamour can be a terrible distraction. Strictly, there's only one true visual correlative of the music heard, and that is the music seen. We have (as in a recent performance of Ravel's Piano Concerto) been permitted occasionally to see the score, but I think the time has come for some enterprising producer to give us the televisual counterpart of score-reading.

I mean something like this. Take *L'après-midi d'un faune*. We hear the opening flute and travel along the flute-line in the score. Oboes, clarinets and one horn enter on the flute's A sharp, and the first harp glissandos up and then down. A shift of vision, a longer shot, shows this happening. When, on page three of the score, the flute repeats its theme over clarinets and muted strings trembling *sur la touche*, the camera shows the four bottom lines of the page, taking the flute part for granted, but, as the horns re-enter and we're ready for the oboe to take over from the flute, we shift up to the woodwind section (Fl., Hauts, Cl., Bons.) at the top of the page again. Too much of a musician's thing? Well, tell me what else we can look at.

For this particular work, Ken Russell gave us balloons in a garden and Pierre Loti lying on a studio couch. I know that the aims of his Elgar and Debussy films represented the ultimate bringing low of the daughters – music in the service of biography. This is, of course, very much in televisual order so long as we don't seduce ourselves into thinking that we're learning anything about either music or the making of music. The Elgar film, beautiful to look at as it was, had little to say about the great Elgar – the Elgar of the symphonies. The Debussy film was, though a technical *tour de force*, a genuine traducement of the composer. It was also perverse, using *La Mer* to accompany Debussy's dream about himself as Roderick Usher instead of *Ce qu'a vu le vent d'Ouest* (originally intended as a prelude to the unwritten opera based on Poe's story). But these are the music productions that are praised, and it seems probable that television has little real room for either the straight presentation of music or its scholarly interpretation. Radio is the only substitute for the concert-hall experience.

Perhaps commercial television is being truer to the medium, as well as to the taste of its viewers, in totally ignoring music – except, of course, for the off-peak highbrow concessions of *Tempo*. Still, the BBC at least possesses the courage to attempt the reconciliation of self-sufficient sound and the fidgety eye. This end of the year is an appropriate time for noting, with a kind of awe, the steady diminution of any interest in the arts on Independent Television. I'm not concerned with a pious duty to bring, to other than schoolchildren, the undiluted transports of great drama, opera, orchestral music. It's rather that ITV's neglect of these leads infallibly to a lowering of sights in what is known as 'entertainment' (as though the purpose of art was not to entertain). I've not seen a single important film, let alone play, on either Rediffusion or Southern during the past year. In all but news and documentary programmes, the standards have become smugly mediocre, and I don't expect the stirring of any progressive spirit in the New Year.

There are a few minor exceptions. I've already instanced *The Prisoner* – which I'm sure is highly unpopular. A new comedy programme called *Never Mind the Quality, Feel the Width*, despite its revival of that ancient Cohen-Kelly mock-hostile symbiosis which originated in New York, does for religion what *Till Death Us Do Part* did for demotic social prejudice.[3] An Irish Catholic and a London Jew, partners in tailoring, bang away at each other's religious taboos, and our shock is expressed in laughter. Would it work with a Jew and an Anglican? Probably not: you have to assume a vaguely C of E audience to whom both Jews and Catholics are a bit exotic and hence not to be taken seriously.

To see BBC-2 colour I have to visit the Earls Court flat of a young novelist who has spectacularly made the grade. I don't pay too many of these visits, since the drabness of black and white thereafter is, until the coloured after-image fades, so depressing that it colours (inept word) my attitude to the, as it were, unorchestrated programmes.[4] Chromatic *Vanity Fair* is particularly delightful and, coloured or not, it is a superbly vigorous and thoroughly Thackerayan adaptation. One minor niggle, and this is to do with music. In the first instalment Becky sang 'Passing By' to her own accompaniment. Unfortunately, her setting was the Victorian one by E.V. Purcell, made to appear about fifty years before its time. Somebody obviously saw the name 'Purcell' and thought it was Henry – very old and safe.

Musical anachronism, Victorian literature, Ken Russell. It's nice to be able to round off with a postscript in which these three themes combine. *Dante's Inferno* (BBC-1) was Russell's attempt to make pop art out of the Pre-Raphaelite Brotherhood, with Rossetti capering to 'There's no business like show business' and Holman Hunt posturing in a mock-Egypt to 'In a Persian market'. The unfunny parts were horror-comic that sadly diminished the post-Poe Gothic realities of Rossetti's life, and they showed that the Russell bag of tricks had been emptied in that Debussy programme. It was only Oliver Reed again, guilt-ridden over a slut, his John the Baptist head served up with necrophilic forces. As a study of the PRB this over-long programme was unspeakable. Even the meanest member of that brotherhood could have eaten an artist like Russell before breakfast.

The Listener, 1967

1   Eric Linklater was a Welsh-born Scottish poet, novelist, military historian, and travel writer. His third novel *Juan in America*, a best-seller published in 1931, is a picaresque tale set in 1928 that recounts the mania and absurdities of Prohibition through the eyes of his antihero Juan, a bastard descendent of Byron's *Don Juan* who is drawn to the more grotesque and ridiculous aspects of that outrageous era.

2   Cesare Lombroso was an Italian criminologist whose study of physiognomy helped him develop his theories of anthropological criminology and criminal atavism, which posited that someone 'born criminal' could be identified by congenital defects and physical anomalies. He collected skulls, crania, skeletons, brains, and various other specimens that have been displayed in the Cesare Lombroso Museum since it first opened in 1892. Raffaele Garofalo, a student of Lombroso, was an Italian criminologist whose approach reflected a more sociological and psychological orientation than Lombroso's emphasis on physical characteristics.

3   *Abie's Irish Rose* is a comic play about a Jewish man and Irish Catholic woman who fall in love and marry despite their different backgrounds and religions, and over the objections of their families. It premiered on Broadway in 1922 and was a huge hit that ran until 1927. Many later stage, radio, and television productions followed, as well as imitations like the 1926 silent comedy film *The Cohens and Kellys*.

4   Burgess was a Daltonian. See LW, pp. 41-2.

Waking crapulous and apothaneintheloish, as I do most mornings these days, I find a little loud *British* gramophone music over the (a) bloody mary and (b) raspberry yogurt helps me to adjust to the daily damnation of writing.[1] Among the records I play most frequently are Walton's *Portsmouth Point* Overture and *Crown Imperial* march. The therapy is formidable. Why? It isn't just the cold-shower impact of diatonic dissonance and Chianti-rough orchestration. It's something to do with being swallowed up in a healing world (Goethe, unfeelingly, told a toothache-sufferer to meditate on the All – the advice would have been better for hangover). Walton evokes various allotropes of Old England that are (pursuing not so much that Chianti suggestion as the biographical facts) gently sauced with the Mediterranean. The Walton flavour is unique, and the Walton detractors who sneer at sub-Elgar have missed many points. Yet, so potent is fashion – meaning Cage (whose life is devoted to living down the 'sphinx' of his name), Boulez and Stockhausen – that I am sometimes as ashamed of enjoying Walton as I am of sharing the Prime Minister's liking for a certain brand of sauce.

One of the virtues of John Warrack's BBC-2 *Workshop* profile was to bring out the sharp Latin qualifiers of Walton's romanticism.[2] All the best British composers are romantic: they have to be, since our music is chiefly an extension of our literature, and that extension comes from the area of feeling, not of form. Without literature, Britten would have only an arpeggio of a 13th to exhibit. Having no literature, a man like Fricker is nothing.[3] Now Walton's richness is a literary one, but he was lucky early in life to come under the influence of something better than the poets of Elgar's *Sea Pictures*. Warrack was right to stress the importance of *Façade*, the releasing quality of the Sitwell imagination, but he was not right to let Walton conduct 'Popular Song' (a work which, anyway, as Walton exhibited, doesn't have to be conducted) and thus demonstrate that without the Sitwell words *Façade* is only half-alive. As for the *Façade* items recited by Peter Pears and Cleo Laine, these were not quite right, either. The work was intended for speakers (Constant Lambert did a good recording with Edith Sitwell) and not for singers who have temporarily cut out voice.

On the whole, I think that Warrack's insistence on making us hear studio performances of whole symphonic and concerto movements was misguided. There is always time for concert presentations of Walton: what was wanted on this occasion was plenty of background – workshop stuff, in fact, with carved chunks of illustrative music. The filmed barbaric march sequence from *Belshazzar's Feast*, with its strong visual emphasis on the brass bands to right and left of the orchestra, was, perhaps unfairly, far more thrilling than what was played live in the studio. This was because the primal fact of the whole programme was Walton himself, and Walton appeared recorded. *Belshazzar* belonged to the same area of presentation. No more grumbles, though. This was a fine and greatly needed tribute to a composer who has meant more to some of us than anyone since Stravinsky. And there is at least one treasurable anecdote. When Walton was coming to the setting of *Mene mene tekel upharsin,* he read Beachcomber, who said that the true writing on the wall was 'Aimee Aimee Semple Macpherson'.[4] Walton had to take a holiday.

The Listener, 1968

1   The Greek phrase *Apothanein thelo* ($A\pi o\theta\acute{a}v\epsilon\iota v\ \theta\acute{\epsilon}\lambda\omega$), meaning 'I want to die', concludes the epigraph of *The Waste Land*: 'Nam Sibyllam quidem Cumis ego ipse oculis meis vidi in ampulla pendere, et cum illi pueri dicerent: $\Sigma\acute{\iota}\beta v\lambda\lambda\alpha\ \tau\acute{\iota}\ \Theta\acute{\epsilon}\lambda\epsilon\iota\varsigma$; respondebat illa: $\acute{a}\pi o\Theta\alpha v\epsilon\tilde{\iota}v\ \Theta\acute{\epsilon}\lambda\omega$.' This quote from Petronius's *Satyricon* can be translated as: 'For once I myself saw with my own eyes the Sibyl at Cumae hanging in a cage, and when the boys said to her "Sibyl, what do you want?" she replied, "I want to die."' The Cumaean Sibyl had asked Apollo for long *life*, which he granted her, but had neglected to request long *youth*. Thus, the meaning of 'crapulous and apothaneintheloish' corresponds to 'suffering from grossly excessive drinking and feeling like I want to die'.

2   John Hamilton Warrack is an English oboist, music critic, and writer. His biography of Carl Maria von Weber is considered the standard monograph in English on this composer. He also wrote books on German opera and great composers, and co-authored *The Oxford Dictionary of Opera* and *The Concise Oxford Dictionary of Opera*.

3   The English composer Peter Racine Fricker – a direct descendant of the French playwright Jean Racine – composed in an atonal, dissonant style related to Schoenberg, Bartók, and Hindemith while retaining a basis in tonality. After succeeding Michael Tippett in 1952 as director of music at Morley College, in 1964 Fricker joined the music faculty at the University of California, Santa Barbara, where he spent the remainder of his career. Burgess's disdainful comment implies that Fricker composed mainly programmatic music based on literature, but aside from one oratorio, none of his major works – five symphonies, five concertos, three string quartets, and several other instrumental compositions – bear descriptive titles from literature.

4   Aimee Elizabeth Semple McPherson was a Canadian Pentecostal

evangelist, faith-healer, media celebrity, and church founder who was a household name in the US by the mid-1920s. Her legacy includes a controversial disappearance for five weeks in the spring of 1926 while she is believed to have indulged in an adulterous affair that she subsequently tried to cover up as an abduction.

Unfinished Journey by Yehudi Menuhin
London: Macdonald and Jane's, 1977

I used to play sonatas with an old fiddler who spoke of Yehudi Menuhin as though he were the Son of God. 'Sent down is my belief,' he would say, 'just to set us violinists an impossible example.' In other words, a genius, and genius, as George Steiner reminds us in his 'Not a Preface, but a Word of Thanks', remains a mystery.[1] Creative artists grow a little disturbed at this regular attachment of the term genius to mere executants. I never heard the word applied to Holst, Vaughan Williams or even Elgar, but there is hardly a concert performer around who is not called a genius by someone. The genius of Yehudi Menuhin has been rewarded very amply. The blurb of his autobiography *Unfinished Journey* says that his 'honours are too many to enumerate but among them are the Knight Commander Order of the British Empire, the Nehru Award for International Understanding, the Freedoms of the Cities of Bath and Edinburgh and honorary degrees from 12 universities including the first to be awarded to any musician by the Sorbonne.' One is naturally very glad to see musical ability so widely acknowledged, but the shining light round Menuhin serves also to illustrate the figure of Béla Bartók, starved in his American exile, dying in poverty of leukaemia.

Menuhin, of course, would be the first to admit the ghastly disparity between the reward of the maker and that of the mediator. He strove to help Bartók, who refused to be helped, but succeeded in commissioning a concerto for which, especially as played by Menuhin, one is very grateful. And if Menuhin has genius, it might be more appropriate to find it in his character and his way of life and speak of saintliness, which

Steiner might also concede to be a mystery. Few men have done more for the cause of international brotherhood than Menuhin, few have shown more genuine loving-kindness, none has done more to transmit to the future the arcana of fine practical musicianship. Add to all this a respect for the human frame which springs out of the physico-spiritual nexus of his primary vocation and has been nourished by contact with yoga, and you have a personality that puts to shame those of us who smoke, snarl, drink and cherish ill-health as a supposedly necessary ground for creativity.

Menuhin – or Mnuchin – had remarkable parents. His father was from Gomel, a thousand miles equidistant from the Baltic and Black Seas, his mother from the Crimean peninsula. Moshe Mnuchin was of the stock of Chassidic rabbis, Marutha Sher was brought up on Circassian chivalry. They became Americans and looked for lodgings in New York. A prospective landlady said: 'And you'll be glad to know I don't take Jews.' Marutha's response was to vow that her unborn child would proclaim his faith to the world in his very name – Yehudi, or 'The Jew'.

> Their appearance astonished everyone. So young, fair, free and self-assured, my handsome father and lovely mother (her hair scandalously bobbed) might well have given their elders pause and made them wonder if such Jews did not render gentiles superfluous. If the adults looked for *gravitas* and didn't find it, the children rejoiced to find the impromptu, the messianism and the energy of youth.[2]

The family settled in San Francisco. Yehudi had precisely one day at school; his parents undertook his education and respected his infantile desire for a violin (the first one was a tin toy which he promptly rejected). As a prodigy he had powerful parental discipline imposed on a love of music which, like all love, is never enough. He was taught languages thoroughly. He handles English in the manner of one who has read much, but he never deviates into fancy or, often, into humour. His education seems to have been quite unliterary: his prose is that of a Scottish engineer.[3]

The story is not wholly a success story. I am Menuhin's almost exact coeval and I remember, as a schoolboy of little talent and few prospects, seeing in the newspapers this well-fed young fiddler in kneepants, reading of his masterly performance of the Elgar concerto and his views on ice-cream and international politics, and wondering what happened to prodigies when they grew up. In *Unfinished Journey* we are told. What a child does by instinct and imitation the adult must relearn through imagination and intellect. Menuhin's initiation into the mature processes of music-making began with the detailed analysis of a quite minor violin composition (by a composer well known to violinists but certainly not to me) and continued with a close examination of the Beethoven concerto.[4] He became, in fact, a serious musician and was already on the road to orchestral conductorship. Recently, he achieved an interpretation of the 'Eroica' which owed nothing to the great Beethoven masters but much to his playing through of the first violin part. His future undoubtedly lies in the fields of conductorship and teaching. He is a great teacher and has the time to become a great conductor.

Cognate with his need to grow up as a musician was his need to become a mature human being. His first marriage failed through, he believes, his lack of humanity. A home education, an exposure only to his teachers (like the remarkable Enesco) and his adulatory audiences cut him off from ordinary people until the war came and he played for troops whose musical background was limited to jukeboxes. He was able to achieve a radiant marriage to the talented, exquisitely beautiful fireball

Diana Gould.[5] His children are as gifted as the rest of his family. He is the happiest of mortals.

Unfinished Journey records discoveries but is mainly, owing to the nature of the virtuoso's life, a chronicle of working tours, the purgatory or limbo of airports, railway stations and one-night hotels. But, in the post-war age which has made everything political, Menuhin has had to use the concert platform to make statements of belief before dragging horsehair across catgut. He had, for instance, to defend himself against his fellow Jews for his exoneration of Furtwängler, as much a Nazi as P.G. Wodehouse was.[6] His knowledge of Russian and his Russian background have lent weight to his attacks, on Russian soil, on Soviet intolerance. But his ultimate weight has been that of a superb and internationally acclaimed musician. Men like Menuhin, Paderewski and Casals, communicating sub- or super-linguistically, remind us that the cause of political liberty can be very well served by a kind of speech that lacks semantic content.

There are things I should like Menuhin to have written about which he is well able to write – the actual quiddity, the whatness of the violin-playing experience, how one *knows* one is going to play the right note on string unfretted and unjacked. Menuhin, it is true, once said to me that a violinist trusts somewhat to God on those upper wastes of the E string, but I want more than that. I wanted something on the mystery of tone ('Where does he get his tone from?' asked my fiddler friend. 'It can only come from heaven.'). I should like an account of what a virtuoso violinist earns, how much he pays his agent and the taxman. From every artist's autobiography one looks for the immediate artistic problems and their solution; one is always given mainly a journey, unfinished or otherwise.

There is, finally, a limitation of taste or ability which, in mv view, invalidates the claim of violinistic supremacy which has been made so often by Menuhin's admirers (though Menuhin is too humble to make it himself). He has never, apparently, played the Alban Berg concerto.[7] If this is, as some think it is, one of the ten great violin concerti of all time, there must be very cogent reasons (not given in this book) for Menuhin's rejection of the work. That he does not like the dodecaphonic schools he makes quite clear, failing to see (like Bartók himself) any strong reason for the stringent limitations of the tone-row; but one would have thought that the Berg concerto mediated remarkably between the human and the academic and, with its almost ingenuous insistence on putting all four open strings into the *Grundstimmung*, was a work that would draw a violinist even if only out of curiosity. But Menuhin has deviated from the standard repertory only to explore Indian music which, since he lacks a talent for improvisation, he can merely regard as a hobby. The same goes for jazz. Menuhin admires Stéphane Grappelli and has played with him, but his riffs, presumably, had to be written out first.

This is a fine book by an American who is a citizen of many cities but whom British admirers may take pride in seeing finally as an adoptive Englishman. England is the country, Menuhin says, of teamwork and quiet discipline (Elgar's control of the orchestra having much to do with his ability with dogs), the country of the viola, of the best sight-readers in the world (not enough rehearsal time). The preface (sorry, word of thanks) of George Steiner, himself a fine musician, rightly points to Menuhin's 'two proud mottos' — 'I have never resigned myself' and 'My life has been spent in building utopias'. In Britain's present cacotopia may he continue to rule an enclave of virtue and beauty.

Times Literary Supplement, 1977

To the Editor

Times Literary Supplement, 22 April 1977, p. 488

'Unfinished Journey'

Sir, – I read Anthony Burgess's review of my *Unfinished Journey* (April 8) with appreciation and hope I shall live up to the future he confidently predicts. May I be a allowed correction? I have played the Berg Concerto quite often and have recorded it with Pierre Boulez. I have deviated from the standard repertoire, incidentally commissioning a new work for each of my ten Bath festivals. I would like to be able to claim Bartók's Violin Concerto, but it was on playing this marvellous work, dedicated to Zoltán Székely, that I plucked up courage to ask him to write the Sonata for Solo Violin.

It is suggestive and no doubt appropriate that my literary style should be likened to that of a 'Scottish engineer'. I have tried to build bridges all my life; alas! none as successful as those of the Scottish engineer!

YEHUDI MENUHIN
2 The Grove
Highgate Village
London N6 6JN

44 rue Grimaldi
Monaco
April 16, 1977

Dear Diana and Yehudi M.,

Many thanks for your delightful letters and mea maxima culpa about my allegation that the Berg concerto had never been played. Because there was no whisper about it in the autobiography I assumed etc. Here I have few records. The only one of Yehudi's I have is of the Elgar. I am ignorant and improvident. But I did like the autobiography and I admire it for very personal reasons as well as impersonal ones, the personal ones having much to do with my own inability to write one myself. I tried last year to start, and it was all lies – the novelist's inability to know what really happened as opposed to what he thinks ought to have happened. Also I couldn't generate a *style*. When I say that Yehudi writes like a Scottish engineer it's meant to be high praise, but many readers of the review may think otherwise. If you've seen how Scottish engineers write you'll know I mean objectivity, exactitude, tough elegance, not the kind of false artiness you get from many autobiographers who consider they have an aesthetic duty, whatever that means.

How you manage to cope with the fiscal cauchemar of living in England I don't know. I feel guilty sometimes at having left, and I've cut myself off from the basic material a British novelist is supposed to need, but it had to be done. Now all the governments of the world take revenge by taxing anything I publish within their domains. How does one save up for one's old age? Apart from tax, though, I began to feel that the preoccupation of English people with trying to subsist wasn't the best material for novelising about. I wish Yehudi had said something about the situation of the artist in a country or countries where the artist, unprotected by tough unions, is a soft body to be chewed at by the State.

Fireball was not perhaps the right word, though the qualifying epithets of course stand. Fireball is round. Tongue of flame, pillar of flame? Too biblical, NT and OT respectively. However, my admiration continues. You have been here recently, I know. Indeed, they made a film of it. It is a musical place, though quite unliterary. I have responded to the musical ambience by buying Josephine Baker's old piano and starting to write music again. I had a symphony performed in Iowa City by 120 young musicians, I have written a film score, I have completed a piano concerto. Getting back to orchestral composition means, mainly, studying the technique of stringed instruments again, and I am starting, old as I am, to play the violin and *am* doing it by writing little pieces on a system which may work. I mean this sort of thing:

Fondest regards to you both
— Anthony Burgess

---

2 The Grove
Highgate Village
London N6 6JX
28th April 1977

Dear Anthony Burgess,

Diana and I loved your letter. When I next write, I may say something about the situation of artists generally, both where they are appreciated and not protected, and where they are protected but not appreciated; where they are appreciated and protected and where they are neither appreciated nor protected.

How extraordinary of you to find Josephine Baker's old piano. I am sure it will be most inspiring, and you seem to be doing a lot of composing, not to speak of playing the violin. We will be in Monte Carlo in the summer of '78, and if I may give you a few tips on the violin I shall be delighted! What is your new system all about? At least the Barcarolle is not on open strings. Is that part of the system? And it could be played fairly well in tune by using only the first and second fingers.

With all my thanks and best wishes,
Yours,

Yehudi Menuhin

affectionate thoughts from

Diana, too

------

2 The Grove

Highgate Village

London N6 6JX

Dear Friend

I was amazed to receive so excellent, professional and viable a violin concerto from you – and dedicated to me!

I should not really be amazed because I should have expected no less from a man of your musical experience, erudition and general standards but human nature is such that it is willing only to accord one particular excellence to any given person. It is our one-track-mindedness which is so reluctant to see the whole – but you have, in fact, revealed yourself as a very whole human being.

The concerto has flow, impetus, thematic construction, a good cadenza and an interesting slow movement in its development and its gradual acceleration of pace.

When time permits, which is unfortunately not this year – or possibly even next, I should like to suggest that I should one day perform it in Monte Carlo; but please don't hold me to this too absolutely or too soon. You have no idea how much I have to accomplish and am already committed to. One consolation is that the dates on your excellent orchestral score are 'Gibraltar Summer 1945' and 'Monaco July 27th 1979'. This is a span of 34 years! I promise that in the performance of the work I shall try to do better.

With all best wishes

Your
Yehudi

22nd August 1979

1 *Unfinished Journey*, p. xv
2 Ibid., p. 12
3 See Menuhin's Letter to the Editor.
4 Violin Sonata in G major by the Belgian composer Guillaume Lekeu. Menuhin was introduced to this work by the French pianist Alfred Cortot. See *Unfinished Journey*, pp. 135-6
5 See Chapter 58 *Beethoven Violin Concerto*
6 The English comic author Pelham Grenville (P.G.) Wodehouse was vilified in his native Britain for taping humorous anecdotes about his experiences as a prisoner of the Nazis during WWII. When Germans began advancing through France in 1940, the Wodehouses, who had moved to France in 1934 to avoid high British taxes, made an unsuccessful attempt to flee from their home in the French

village of Le Touquet and were captured the following day. After nearly a year of captivity, Wodehouse taped several apolitical, comic broadcasts titled *How to be an Internee Without Previous Training*, which were broadcast on US radio during the summer of 1941. Wodehouse's biographer Barry Phelps maintains that the humorist was 'cleverly trapped' into making the broadcasts as the price of freedom, but he and his wife were forced to remain in Berlin until 1943, when they were allowed to move to Paris. Still reviled in the UK, and believing himself in danger of facing serious legal charges there, Wodehouse emigrated with his wife to the US in 1946 and spent the rest of his life there, never returning to England. The case of Wilhelm Furtwängler, the most prominent German conductor to remain in Germany throughout the Nazi regime and conduct concerts attended by Hitler and other Nazi leaders, is much more controversial. Menuhin's decision to record the Beethoven Violin Concerto with Furtwängler and the Lucerne Festival Orchestra in August 1947, shortly after the post-war prohibition of Furtwängler's conducting activity was lifted, was a bold statement at the time. Menuhin recorded the same concerto with Furtwängler and the Philharmonia Orchestra in April 1953, and recorded other concertos with Furtwängler after the war, including the Mendelssohn and Brahms concertos, and the Brahms Double Concerto.

7   See Menuhin's Letter to the Editor.

63. THE PRINCE OF PERCUSSION

*Drum Roll: A Professional Adventure from the Circus to the
Concert Hall* by James Blades
London: Faber, 1977

Jimmy Blades has been heard by nearly everybody in the world.
It was he who, on African drums, beat the V for Victory signal
of BBC radio during the war. It is he who makes the noise
when, at the start of a J. Arthur Rank film, Bombardier Billy
Wells is seen striking a gong.[1] Serious musicians know his
Percussion Instruments and Their History (Faber & Faber), the
definitive work on the subject. After fifty years in the business,
he is the doyen of British percussionists. His autobiography
goes, wisely I think, unedited. An American editor would have
tidied up the solecisms and destroyed an ebullience very rare
these days in the memoirs of showbiz personalities, who often
think they have a duty to literature. This story of the life of
one of four brother drummers, from rags to circus to cinema
pit to, at length, virtuoso of the Bartók sonata for pianos and
percussion and special effects adviser to everyone (including
Benjamin Britten), is a great delight.

Orchestras are built on injustice. The flautist carries a little
case around, while the percussion player has to be responsible
for four kettledrums, bass drum, side drum, tubular bells,
xylophone, marimba, vibraphone, triangle, tam-tam, Chinese
blocks, whip, tambourine and, if he is playing in Hindemith's
News of the Day, typewriter, anvil for Wagner or the *Gurre-
Lieder*, wind machine for *Don Quixote* and the *Sinfonia
Antartica*, and many more. I recognize that, in full symphonic
orchestras, there is some division of responsibility in the
kitchen department, but the burdens are still heavy enough.[2]
In chamber orchestras, like those used by Britten in his later

operas, the weight of providing a great deal of the 'colour' falls on one man. It has usually been Jimmy Blades, a Puck-like figure, non-smoker, teetotaller, vegetarian, a demon for work.

Beethoven, until he arrived at the 'Turkish music' in the finale of his Ninth, was content with a tonic and dominant on the kettledrums.[3] There are many who say that the multiplication of percussive colour that came in with Wagner and, more so, with Richard Strauss has done music no good. This view is based on a very primitive notion of what percussion is about: it is not pure punctuation, italicizing, the adding of exclamation marks; it is a mode of expression as old as music itself, and some of the 'new' refinements we find in Boulez and Stockhausen are really returns to old, and very subtle, percussive devices from civilizations that the music of the Enlightenment chose to ignore. The percussion department may be at the back of the orchestra, but the importance of Jimmy Blades's department is frontal enough, and his autobiography ought to be accorded at least as much respect as Yehudi Menuhin's.[4]

His story covers the whole musical field, from the Saturday-night gig to grand opera, and its evaluation of the musicians met on the way is highly democratic. The composer of *The Dream of Olwen* is a fine musician, and so is Stravinsky (whose *L'Histoire du Soldat*, thinks Jimmy, has a really admirable percussion part).[5] Charlie Kunz, with whom Jimmy often played, is another fine musician, and thus a myth which has baffled me from the start is perpetuated. The tale was told in Manchester of Artur Schnabel's being refused admission at the artist's entrance of the Free Trade Hall and, on saying who he was, being told: 'I don't care if you're bloody Charlie Kunz, you can't come in here.'[6] Charlie Kunz, by all accounts a delicate, delightful, generous man, was a schoolgirl-type player of popular sheet music as written. His popularity was immense. He is duly here, among the giants.

But it is not Jimmy Blades's job to evaluate according to the higher aesthetics. A practical musician has to think of the end with which he is presented, and for which he is paid, and to judge musicianship in terms of how efficiently that end is attained. A professional player will do as well for the eight bars of 'tabs' music he is given in the music-hall pit as he will for *Wozzeck*, and his judgements on the music will have more to do with practical playability than with spiritual transports. Some of the musical problems with which Jimmy Blades has been faced – chiefly in the devising of expressive sounds for films or for Britten's later operas – may strike the highbrow mere listener as trivial, but of course, from the view of a serious professional, they are not. When Chaplin was affixing soundtracks to his newly edited early films, he wanted 'a "tick tock" effect to dramatise the situation where an officer was intently watching the second hand of his wrist watch awaiting zero hour'.

> 'Not wood blocks – something really sinister', I was told. The sound that most pleased C.C. was when I placed a small cymbal on a small kettledrum and a larger cymbal on a large kettledrum, and struck the cymbals gently with coins. The difference in the size of my cymbals and the resonance of the drums produced a rather uncanny tick-tock. 'I'll have thirty seconds of that,' said the maestro.[7]

Jimmy is equally fascinating when he describes the contrivance of that memorable heart beat which is to be heard in the battlements scene of Olivier's *Hamlet*. A stethophonic recording of a real heart was 'like someone consuming thick soup with a rhythmic intake', so finally Vivian Leigh's fur coat was draped over a bass drum and Jimmy prodded with his fingertips.[8] In one of the first TV commercials, Jimmy earned

£12 by crinkling a five-pound note in his hand in rumba rhythm, successfully simulating the sizzle of sausages. For the ultimate in fascinating triviality, take the progressive inflation which has overtaken the coin throb on kettledrums in the penultimate variation of the *Enigma*. It used to be pennies, then it went up to half-crowns, now it's 50p pieces. Jimmy does it with guilders given to him in Holland by an Old Fagin-like man who remembered his wartime V signal.[9]

The non-musical reader of these memoirs will be amazed by the amount of work done – in the days when the tax situation made hard work worthwhile – by the professional musicians of England. The average working week of Jimmy Blades – film studio to dance-band dais to recording studio to symphony concert – called for a stamina and a devotion to duty that are now probably outlawed by the unions. Ending his book at the age of seventy, Jimmy asks for another twenty-five years to do the things he still wants to do. I would like to hear him play the percussion score I wrote for the Minneapolis production of *Cyrano de Bergerac* – sizzle cymbal slowly raised out of water, kitchen-utensil glockenspiel, cymbal placed on chromatic kettledrum and soft-rolled while the drum emits a slow glissando.[10] He has probably done these things, and more. He has also banged out a melodious book.

Times Literary Supplement, 1977

1   Beginning in the 1930s, each film produced by the Rank Organisation started with the sound of Blades striking a tam-tam while a musclebound man appeared to hit an enormous gong that was actually a papier-mâché prop. The first 'Gongman' was Carl Dane, a circus strong man; the second was the heavyweight British boxing champion William Thomas Wells, popularly known as Bombardier Billy Wells. See *Drum Roll*, pp. 150-2.

2   The extensive assortment of instruments and accessories included in a fully equipped percussion section is sometimes called the kitchen sink or kitchen department.

3   Except for *Wellington's Victory*, composed and premiered in 1813 about a decade before the Ninth Symphony. Beethoven composed *Wellington's Victory*, or *The Battle of Vitoria*, Op. 91, to commemorate the victory in Spain of Arthur Wellesley, then the Marquess of Wellington, over the army of King Joseph Bonaparte. Hailed in Britain as a conquering hero, Wellington was elevated to Duke in 1814 and on 18 June 1815 commanded the army that defeated Napoleon Bonaparte's forces in the Battle of Waterloo. *Wellington's Victory* includes triangle, cymbals, bass drum, and timpani – the same percussion instruments later employed in the Ninth – plus two ordinary snare drums on each side of the stage, ratchets to imitate the sound of small gunfire, and two large bass drums, positioned off-stage, to produce the sound of cannon shots.

4   *Unfinished Journey*, also published in 1977. See Chapter 62 *The Vocation of a Virtuoso*.

5   The British composer-conductor Charles Williams composed the 'The Dream of Olwen', the musical theme of the 1947 British film *While I Live*.

6   Charles Leonard Kunz was an American piano prodigy from Allentown, Pennsylvania. In 1922 he traveled to the UK as a dance band pianist and never left. His popularity led to countless engagements in variety theatres throughout the UK and continental Europe, and a long series of solo records titled 'Charlie Kunz Medleys'. It is said that at the height of his fame he was the highest paid pianist in the world, earning up to £1,000 a week.

7   *Drum Roll*, pp. 230-1.

8   ibid., p. 200.

9   The kettledrum rolls in Variation XIII (***), *Romanza*, are marked to be played 'with side drum sticks', but timpanists have traditionally played them with coins to better emulate the sound of an ocean liner's engine. See *Drum Roll*, pp. 215-6.

10 'The score's most imaginative number is 'Music for Ragueneau' (I:ii), which augments an ensemble of flute, clarinet, trumpet, and cello with a battery of whisks, spatulas, and other baker's tools.' (ACC, p. 131). Burgess's incidental music, which featured his new translation and adaptation of the play, elicited this comment from the prominent theatre critic Clive Barnes in his rave review in *The New York Times*: 'I was fascinated to note that Mr. Burgess, in addition to everything else, composed his own attractively flamboyant music.'

The Counter Tenor by Peter Giles
London: F. Muller, 1982

Alfred Deller, the counter-tenor whose artistry has done much to rehabilitate a reach of the male voice too long neglected, was, in the 1950s, waiting to go on at the Royal Festival Hall. He was standing near Sir Malcolm Sargent and the leader of the orchestra. The latter, who had better remain anonymous, said to Sargent, all too audibly: 'I see we've got the bearded lady with us.' Sargent, according to Peter Giles, 'the epitome of the English Gentleman, affected not to hear and is said to have brushed some imaginary dust off his sleeve.' The anecdote indicates a prejudice against the high male voice which is based on the pitch of the speaking voice as an index of sex. As James Bowman (himself a distinguished follower of Deller) says in his foreword to this book, 'The fact that we sing at a higher pitch than the other adult male voices does not instantly make us a peculiar breed apart – distant relatives of the castrati. There is no "mystique". We are just singers who, for one reason or another, have preferred to develop the upper reaches of our voices, and this has become a natural means of vocal expression.'[1]

Mr Giles, rightly, spends some time in his book – the first ever on the counter-tenor – dealing with the phenomenon of the castrato or *everato* (properly *evirato* – devirilized or emasculated). The image of papal shears snipping off testicles to ensure the continuation into adulthood of a fine boy's voice is not strictly accurate. Kingsley Amis's novel *The Alteration* is historically correct in presenting the owner of the voice as possessing the legal right to accept or reject the proposed operation, right too in his ironical dénouement, where the hero becomes what he has voluntarily rejected through a disease of the testicles. A lot of Italian castrati swam into fame through a morbid accident. As for those boys who put music before the joys of sex, it was usually a matter of dosing them with opium, placing them in a warm bath, then snipping the lifelines, so that the testicles eventually shrivelled away. It was a voluntary matter, and the *potestas clavium* never came into it.[2]

It is necessary to spend some time with the castrati before dealing with the counter-tenor, since those 'brilliant artificial voices' eclipsed for a long time the natural falsetto or counter-tenor. There was a castrato in the papal choir as early as 1562, but the last of the Sistine falsetti, Giovanni di Sanctos, died in 1625. England clung to the counter-tenor until the castrato, with all things musically Italian, became popular in the time of Handel. Henry Purcell was himself a fine counter-tenor. Incidentally, the last of the papal castrati, Alessandro Moreschi, who died in 1924, made some gramophone records in 1903–4. It is not a great voice, and the quality of the recording is inevitably poor, but the castrato sound is at least available to those interested or, like Mr Amis, fascinated by the phenomenon.

There is not, despite the stupidity of that orchestral leader, as much prejudice against the counter-tenor today as there would have been in, say, the Victorian era. Pop singers favour the higher, or even falsetto, reach of the voice; unisex has been, in some ways, a healthy solvent of a crass and brutal polarity. When Alfred Deller's voice erupted on the air or the concert-platform, it was an older generation of musicians that was disturbed, not the possessors of an innocent ear. The exploitation of the higher reach of the male voice springs from no mental or physical morbidity. In theory, anyone can restrict the vibration of his vocal cords to a single segment, thus ensuring a high range which can take advantage of the vibration of an adult sounding chamber – not possible to boy altos.[3]

We accept the four-part mixed chorus – S A T B – without being altogether satisfied with it. Female and male voices do not blend well, any more than (to push the range downwards) trombones blend well with the bass tuba. Wagner saw or heard the need for total homogeneity in his wind sections – hence the development of the heckelphone to complete the family of oboes, and the bass trumpet and the contrabass trombone to ensure a uniformity of tone in the brass. The church choir, with its trebles and male altos, may be regarded as one of the fruits of St Paul's misogyny, but the oratorio tradition, related to the operatic, accepts the two sexes not only because drama involves sex but because female voices are adult and hence powerful. Yet the female alto has an unfortunate woolliness and the counter-tenor, which theoretically could replace it, is probably the sound which composers hear in their brains when they pen the second choral line. Unfortunately, there are not yet enough counter-tenors around to be massed chorally. The counter-tenor, like the castrato, is a rare and brilliant solo phenomenon, and it might have been even rarer had not Michael Tippett heard the late great Deller in Canterbury and given him the encouragement he needed. We are thankful to have his voice preserved for all time, granted perhaps its finest exploitation in the Oberon role of Britten's *Midsummer Night's Dream,* written specially for Deller. And we are thankful that he has followers like James Bowman, John Whitworth, Paul Esswood and Mr Giles himself.[4]

Giles's book is brief, but it has some of the qualities of a comprehensive guide to counter-tenordom or -ship. There are photographs and a discography, an account of the counter-tenor in history, and an admirable appendix on 'The Counter Tenor as an Artistic Phenomenon'. He considers the essential 'Englishness' of the type of voice and relates it to the 'love of *line*' which Nikolaus Pevsner extols in his Reith Lectures collected as *The Englishness of English Art,* the cult of idiosyncrasy, and the persistent conservatism which, by some paradox, emerges occasionally as the new and even shocking.[5] Dunstable showed European composers of the fifteenth century how to accept thirds and sixths, officially dissonances, as an aspect of the native love of the independent vocal line, a traditional contrapuntalism which persisted while Europe was trying to think horizontally. Giles finds an 'ultra-linear' property in the high male voice:

> It is decidedly otherwordly, inhabiting a strange unreal world somewhere in the head, indefinably more than falsetto. It is eccentric and irrational: men do not normally sing as high as women, therefore who but the English would favour over many centuries a purely natural voice which does? The counter tenor is itself the result of English conservatism. Its continued existence stems from English reluctance to embrace the new or recognise when the game is up, the battle lost![6]

Shaw, in *Man and Superman*, has a counter-tenor in his infernal quartet. 'Ah, here you are, my friend,' says Don Juan to the Statue. 'Why don't you learn to sing the splendid music Mozart has written for you?' The Statue replies: 'Unluckily he has written it for a bass voice. Mine is a counter tenor.' Should we take that 'unluckily' seriously? For a decidedly otherworldly visitant a decidedly otherworldly voice might have been in order. Let us imagine that invitation to supper soaring over the trombones. But, alas, Mozart was historically unable to think in counter-tenorly terms.

Times Literary Supplement, 1982

1   *The Counter Tenor*, p. vii.

2   *power of the keys*, an expression signifying the supreme authority of the Church. It derives from Christ's words to St. Peter in Matthew 16:19.

3   This explanation of the physical process used by counter-tenors to produce their characteristic sound triggered a spirited exchange of Letters to the Editor on the subject by Milo Keynes (University of Cambridge) on 28 May, Frances Killingley (University of Essex) on 18 June, and Peter Giles himself (Canterbury Cathedral) on 2 July 1982.

4   In his Letter to the Editor of 2 July, Peter Giles points out that John Whitworth's name was misprinted as John Bowman in Burgess's review.

5   Nikolaus Bernhard Leon Pevsner was a German-British art historian and architectural historian best known for *The Buildings of England* (1951–74), a 46-volume series of guides to the notable architecture of each county. Beginning in 1946, Pevsner began a series of broadcasts on the BBC Third Programme about European art; eventually he would deliver 78 of these broadcast talks by 1977. Among these were the Reith Lectures – a series of six broadcasts in 1955 titled *The Englishness of English Art* in which he discussed the qualities of art that he regarded as particularly English.

6   *The Counter Tenor*, p. 204.

I know what the notes mean just by looking at them. I can read an orchestral score with as much pleasure as a novel – probably more. Probably more because the eye has more to do, the seat of human engagement is sealed off, I'm away from the world of sex, violence and politics, I'm into an empyrean of pure form. Being a sort of musician, I am, I think, immune to the heresy which afflicts the pure music lover – that of making the mere interpreter of music into a god. Opera singers from Tetrazzini to Maria Callas and beyond have been called *diva* – goddess. This indicates the scope of the heresy. The rewards for the *diva* have been manifold and extravagant – the harnessing of her coach to the adoring shoulders of those made delirious by her high Cs, the drinking of champagne from her sweaty slipper, the fan club and the private jet. Then there are the conductors, of whom Karajan may be taken as the prime living, though aging, example: While the applause deafens, body servants await, ready with beef tea and a change of shirt; the airport has been warned, the police are ready to keep the roads to it clear. All this for the man who wags the stick. All that for the vocal machine which doesn't understand all that well what it's doing. Meanwhile the composer, who is, if not a god, at least married to the Muse, is elbowed out of the way by the photographers.

We celebrate this year (1982) the centenary of the birth of Igor Stravinsky. He was a very great composer who feared the cult of the interpreter. There was a time in his career when he wanted to hand over his piano music to a mechanical instrument to keep the interpreter out. He insisted that his tempi be sustained mechanically, without expressive rubato, that his dynamic marks be scrupulously observed, that 'expression' as a superadded spice be omitted from the plain meal of his music.

He adored no singer, violinist or conductor – these were the mere necessary conditions for turning musical thought into physical reality. When I was a boy I used regularly to go to the concerts of the Hallé Orchestra in Manchester. This orchestra was, at that time, one of the finest in Europe, though concert subscribers prevented it from giving of its best by denying it such expansive experiences as playing Stravinsky's *Le Sacre du Printemps* or Schoenberg's *Five Orchestral Pieces*. The orchestra was forced to stick to the two Bs, Beethoven and Brahms, with occasional bloody chunks of butcher's meat out of Wagner – otherwise audiences would stay away.

On one occasion, to my joy, a performance of an advanced work by the Russian Alexander Mossolov was announced. I turned up and, to my chagrin, could not get in. Artur Schnabel was playing Beethoven's 'Emperor' Concerto, and the Mossolov had been merely sneaked into the program because, with Schnabel playing, it would not harm the box office. But I did not wish to hear Schnabel and the 'Emperor': I knew that damned concerto by heart. I wanted Mossolov, though those who got in did not. There was another occasion when a student from the Royal Manchester College of Music played, to a near-empty house, the little-known piano concerto of Frederick Delius. That, to me, was worth all the visits of Schnabel and Horowitz and Rubinstein put together. I became convinced that the adorers of the great interpreters were philistines, and I have not since been seriously shaken in that conviction.

Let me be honest and admit that it is not enough just to read the music of a symphony or oratorio or song cycle and, hearing a kind of ideal performance inside one's skull, consider that one has had a genuine musical experience. Beethoven was limited to this purely cerebral audition, and a stupid school of musical thinkers once existed, headed by the critic Ernest Newman, which asserted that what was good enough for Beethoven was good enough for the rest of us. Music, said Newman, should be what John Keats called a matter of hearing ditties of no tone: the sensual ear was a labyrinthine snare which vitiated the purity of what the composer had put on to paper.

There was a music critic in England named Cecil Gray who wrote a cantata based on Flaubert's *La Tentation de Saint-Antoine* which he did not wish to have performed, lest gross external sound should sully the ghostly purity of it.[1] There was a very well-known work by the Dutch composer Bernard van Dieren, the 'Chinese' Symphony, which every London musician knew from the score but no one ever heard and, so far as I know, no one has ever heard in the sixty years since its composition.[2] It used to be thought that Bach wrote most of his works for the sake of writing them and, without the benefit of performance, shoved them into a drawer to be forgotten. All this goes too far. I would be foolish not to wish to go to a recital of Schubert Lieder by the German baritone Dietrich Fischer-Dieskau.[3] Schubert's cycle *Die Schöne Müllerin* has to be heard. We need the physical impact of the sounds, and emotion will not be easily stirred otherwise: the notes on the page cry out for incarnation in the vocal cords and the chords of the keyboard. But why Fischer-Dieskau and not some well-meaning tyro from a music school? Because, we believe, Fischer-Dieskau has a profound insight into the structure of the music and the manner in which this relates to the meaning of the words. Because he possesses a superb physical instrument and the intelligence to control it. Because he subdues his personality to those of the poet and the composer, concerned only with presenting a generalized emotional complex which each of his hearers will recognize as part of his own actual or potential human experience. But the fact remains that he is no more than the discardable medium through which Schubert is made flesh. Compared with the composer, he is nothing.

It is conceivable that a vocal machine could be programmed to deliver a Lied with scrupulous adherence to the written expression as well as the written notes; no *Schubertmaschine* is remotely conceivable.

But what admirers of Fischer-Dieskau get from his performance is, of course, the personality of the singer himself – warm, intelligent, *sympathisch*, recognizable – yet I doubt whether one is justified in saying, 'Let us go hear Fischer-Dieskau sing,' rather than 'Let us go hear some Lieder – ah, I see Fischer-Dieskau is singing them; good.' For there will come a time, even with the most intelligent and modest singer, when he will feel a certain superiority to his composer and start taking liberties with him. He will consider that, knowing more about singing than the composer ever did, he can put the composer right on certain points; that the composer, living and dying in the pre-Freudian age, did not understand himself as well as he thought.

As the Lied represents a kind of house halfway between music unapplied and music attached to the service of the opera house, a speck of forgiveness is possible for the personality cultist. For opera, above all the other branches of music, has depended on the singer's capacity for projecting elements beyond the mere words and notes. But, before going to worship a particular Heldentenor or diva, we ought to remember Mozart's attitude to the singers he had waiting for him in Prague when he went thither with the scores of *Le Nozze di Figaro* and *Don Giovanni*. These were to him no more than imperfect instruments, childishly self-assertive, not so talented as they thought they were, swollen by applause, ready to tolerate the composer only because he gave them the materials for self-glorification. They were to be coaxed sometimes, sometimes bullied, but the great thing was to subdue their egos without their being aware of it. For to a sighing Mozart, singers were only necessary evils.

It's inevitable that I should want to diminish the glory of the mere interpreter, since I have for the last thirty-odd years practiced an art which doesn't depend on interpretation at all. With the novel, nothing – save the printer's errors – stands between the giver and the taker. The critics are, of course, ready to interpret for the reader and tell him what he is really reading and what the author, without knowing it, really meant, but there's no obligation to read the critics. As soon as I have brought such narrative gifts as I have to a medium – such as film, stage or television – which depends on interpreters, then I have gone through hell. It is bad enough to have to cope with the ill-informed egos of actors, but there is that new, very twentieth-century phenomenon to deal with – the director, who has produced the 'director's theatre' and the *cinéma d'auteur*.

Some years ago, I remember, I was asked to write a definitive essay on Stanley Kubrick, who had made a film of one of my novels. It was assumed that I would be honored to follow around my own interpreter with a tape recorder, conceding that he was more important than the primary creator: no insult was intended, but umbrage was taken. If Shakespeare were alive today, he would be asked to take time off from *The Tempest* to write an epic poem on the first interpreter of Hamlet – Richard Burbage – or even on the clown Will Kemp.

But back to music and a word about conductors. The conductor was once a man who kept time from the harpsichord. With the development of the romantic orchestra he acquired a dais, a stick and limitless authority. But the Russian Revolution showed that he was not indispensable: the first Soviet orchestras did well enough without an imperious stick-wagger. For that matter, even in the democracies, there are seasoned orchestral players who find it safer to ignore the beat and perhaps give only a little attention to the expansive gestures which mean *stringendo* or *allargando*. The music, they feel, if accurately played, will make its own impact. A conductor is, properly, a man who has little to do after rehearsal: he should no more take the center of the stage than the theatrical director. Pierre Boulez, whom I admire, demonstrated the truth of this with *Le Sacre du Printemps*. His gestures were minimal and served as mere reminders of what had been decided in rehearsal. His concert performance had none of the flamboyance caricaturists and philistine patrons of the arts adore.

If I approach reverence to any conductor who ever lived, that conductor can only be Arturo Toscanini. He fulfilled the first duty of a head of orchestra by converting a heterogeneous body of men and women into a single instrument. He trained the NBC Symphony Orchestra, he knew by heart the scores he interpreted, and his interpretations were little more than the end products of endless lucubrations on the meanings of the composer's notes, tempi and expression marks. When you hear Toscanini's Wagner or Beethoven, you are, you believe, as close to what the composer intended as it is possible to conceive. Follow Toscanini with the score, and you will be impressed by his total fidelity to what is printed there. When Toscanini took his bow, you were expected to applaud the music, not the man. The cult of personality could never be applied to him: he left both Italy and Germany when those countries' regimes were based on such a cult. Thank God we have him preserved on record.

In a sense, he represented the fulfillment of a directorial tradition which had, of necessity, been started at Bayreuth (and which Toscanini would have continued had he not violently disagreed with the Nazi racial policy which excluded Jews from the theater there). No conductor could assume responsibility for a Wagner score unless he knew it technically: this meant a knowledge of every individual orchestral line and a capacity to teach the sometimes baffled players how to approach their parts. My father never tired of telling his own father's story about Hans Richter conducting the Hallé in a rehearsal of 'Siegfried's Rhine Journey'. The first horn player said his part was unplayable. Richter, who knew no English, asked for a translation, then for the cornist's instrument. He took a mouthpiece from his pocket and then played the passage with ease and panache. He handed the horn back and the rehearsal continued.[4] There was never again talk about Wagner's unplayability. This was great conducting.

Of the instrumental soloists I know, I admire most Yehudi Menuhin – chiefly for his humility not only toward the mysteries of the violin, but toward the music he plays. I was a little younger than he when, as a boy wonder, he first played Sir Edward Elgar's concerto under the composer himself (who at that time was, in response to British philistinism, professing more interest in horse racing than in music). The boy was an evident prodigy: he not only knew the notes, he seemed to know what the work was about, but the fact that a mere bare-kneed urchin could understand the curlicues of the mind of a complex and neurotic composer probably proves that music has no real content other than mere notes, and that learning to play a musical instrument well in extreme youth is a sign that there is not much in it. Yehudi had to outgrow the prodigy phase and, as a mature man, be accepted not with wonder but with affection. He turned himself into a conductor and was right to do so – he, if anyone, knows the problems of string players and precisely what a string section can do. Well, not exactly precisely: he has spoken to me of the unknown territory up there on the E string, he has disclaimed mastery, he retains his own sense of wonder in the presence of the music he performs. He is the perfect instrument for a composer.[5]

It is, alas, singers who, like actors, exhibit the least humility of all performers and, like actors, earn the most adulation.

The disease goes back a long way and was endemic among eighteenth-century castrati; hence, it may be taken to indicate some lack. Perhaps the disease is less prevalent than it was. There was a time when Enrico Caruso and Tetrazzini, grown gross physically, were above seeing the disparity between what they looked like in opera and what the public was expected to believe they looked like. They became bigger than the works they performed in; the composers shrank to mere providers of fodder; the exhibition of high C's was more important than characterization or expression. If their day is past, nevertheless there are still opera subscribers around who cling to their old philosophy: 'Let us go and see Stronzo or Cazzi in *Falstaff*', not 'Let us go and see *Falstaff*', and trust that the singers, whoever they are, are adequate.

There remains a humbler musical sphere where it is not really possible to separate the singer from the song – that of jazz, where the performer is also the creator. There is also the world of the popular song, where everything seems to depend on the performer's charisma and the rewards are higher than even those of a Karajan or Bernstein. It is more reasonable to line up for a Sinatra or Streisand recital than for a Fischer-Dieskau one, since the music they sing is actually given, through their interpretations, the substance it fundamentally lacks. They are scrupulous about putting across such verbal meaning as the lyrics have; they will not, in 'September Song', substitute 'I'll spend with you' for 'I'd... .'[6] They will convey the nuance of the comma in 'Lady, be good'. But some of them have inherited from the old opera gods and goddesses a damnable condition of swelled head. Who said, peeling an unripe banana, 'I'll give ya three minutes'? (I was proud, getting my hat, of saying, 'Two minutes too much.') Who turned up at Nice Airport and, finding Prince Rainier not there to meet him, cancelled his Monaco engagement? Who else was three hours late for rehearsal?

But, back on the subject of real music, let us learn a sense of proportion vis-à-vis the masterpiece and the maestro, reflecting on the possibility that, when a performance is merely adequate, the greatness of the work performed may shine through all the more clearly. When we talk of Karajan's Mahler or Bernstein's Stravinsky, we're rejoicing in a superaddition, as though the composer himself were not enough. I never enjoy Shakespeare more than when schoolchildren perform him: bring in your Olivier or James Earl Jones and you've interposed an animated curtain between yourself and the Bard. In Italy, the least musical country in the world (ask the shade of Toscanini), you can see most clearly, in a kind of caricature, where the adoration of the performer can lead. At La Scala, Milan, during a performance of *Madama Butterfly*, there was respectful silence while the soprano sang; when the orchestra played alone, the conversation happily buzzed. Aghast, I cried, 'Shut up!' and was asked to leave. No music lovers, these English. I met the soprano afterward and she sympathized.[7] I don't think otherwise I would have remembered her name. She would have sympathized with that too. Like myself, she cared about Puccini.[8]

My readers will, I know, now be saying, 'Nonsense: without the interpreter there is only silence; anyone who can convert silence into meaningful sound has wrought a miracle and deserves homage.' This view can only come from music lovers who can't read music. Do they feel the same about interpretations of Shakespeare or Ibsen, whom, presumably, they know how to read? Apparently, yes. The maestro heresy has, in our age, attached itself to the drama, and names like Peter Brook, Jonathan Miller and Joe Papp are granted bigger billing than the dramatists they interpret. Their status would be unintelligible to the great actor-managers like Irving, to whom the notion of interpretation and, more particularly, interpretation by a non-participant in the drama would contradict all tradition. In Shakespeare's company, the Lord

Chamberlain's (later the King's) Men, Richard Burbage presumably decreed cuts and moves, but he was primarily an actor, which Papp and Brook and Miller are not. Once the director cuts himself off from personal participation, he dreams dreams and has visions. He reads Freud and Jan Kott, he remakes his play from the outside.[9] The playwright becomes raw material for the expression of a philosophy or a sociology. Or else he is pitied for not having lived in the present and so must be brought up to date. I recently saw the Papp production of *The Pirates of Penzance* and mourned over the death of Sullivan's orchestra and the inaudibility of Gilbert's words.[10] But it is Papp who is filmed and G. and S. merely truckle to his image of Victorian England. The historical perspective, indispensable when we see Aeschylus or Sophocles, dissolves into a Freudian or Marxist overview. Stage directors no longer defer; deference is left to the ignorant dead.

Come, sir, be reasonable: without direction there is no play. Similarly, without translation there is no Dostoevsky or Proust. Alas, all too true, but translators preserve for the most part a decent subservience to the master whom they render (except for Sir Thomas Urquhart, who virtually remade Rabelais): there are no maestro translators. Instead, some will say, there are mere hacks, cursed alike by penury, ignorance and a lack of style. As one of the lesser translated, I know this to be true. But it is better perhaps to have one's meaning and style traduced than to be the raw stuff of somebody else's virtuosity. I once wrote a novel in which a character yawned. Instead of merely saying that he yawned, I made him utter the vocables 'War awe warthog Warsaw', which sound like yawning.[11] My German translator promptly turned the noises into *'Krieg Ehrfurcht Warzenschwein Warschau'*, where there is no yawning. There is incompetence, but it is more acceptable than creative virtuoso performances, in which the translator becomes bigger than his author.

We cannot read every book in the original, we are not all competent to turn our inner imagination into a well-lighted stage with brilliant actors walking across it, few of us can read music. But we can still deplore the contemporary glorification of the interpretative maestro. The singer is not greater than the song, nor is the conductor above the symphony. Somerset Maugham's Alroy Kear says: 'The Americans prefer a live dog to a dead lion. That's one of the things I like about the Americans.'[12] It is probably America, so much concerned with the present and palpable, that has done most to deify the interpreter: it may have something to do with the Hollywood star system, in which actors became gods and writers were merely schmucks with Remingtons. But the rest of the world has not been slow to regard Shakespeare and Beethoven as ghosts and Bernhardt and Bernstein as the living artistic reality. It's time to view the maestri as what they really are – schmucks with batons and voices.

The New York Times, 1982

1   Cecil William Turpie Gray was a Scottish music journalist, critic and author who also composed but preferred to promote the music of his friends Philip Heseltine (Peter Warlock), Constant Lambert and Bernard van Dieren over his own. Gray's opera *The Temptation of St Anthony* dates from 1937. He was also a passionate advocate of Sibelius's music and, beginning in 1917, lived next door to D.H. Lawrence, who based characters in *Aaron's Rod* (Cyril Scott) and *Kangaroo* (James Sharpe) on Gray.
2   Bernard van Dieren, a Dutch composer, critic, author, and writer on music who spent much of his career in England, having taken British citizenship in 1910. See *Byrne*, p. 19, for the strophe on 'English-born composers', which includes van Dieren, erroneously, since he was born in Rotterdam.

3 Fischer-Dieskau was renowned for his singing of art songs, especially those of Franz Schubert.

4 See ACC, p. 365.

5 Burgess composed a violin concerto for Menuhin in 1979. See Chapter 62 *The Vocation of a Virtuoso* and ACC, pp. 256-8.

6 See Chapter 43 *A Berliner on Broadway*.

7 The soprano, unnamed in 'Performers: A Necessary Evil', is identified as Renata Scotto (misspelled as Scotti) in HQY.

8 As published in *The New York Times*, the essay ends here. The three paragraphs below were added to the version published as 'The Maestro Heresy' in HQY.

9 Jan Kott was an noted critic and essayist on the theatre, and author of *Shakespeare, Our Contemporary* (1964), which drew parallels between Shakespeare and Beckett that influenced directors like Peter Brook. Born in Warsaw, Kott defected from Poland to the United States in 1965, becoming a professor at SUNY Stony Brook and contributor to *The New Republic, The New York Review of Books*, and other publications.

10 See Chapter 31 *His Objects Were Sublime.*

11 *The Doctor is Sick,* p. 167 in Chapter 21 (W.W. Norton, 1997). Burgess recounted the same anecdote in 'Novels are Made of Words', an essay on language and fiction first published in the *Times Literary Supplement* in 1965.

12 A quote from *Cakes and Ales* (1930), a satirical novel about London literary society, class snobbery, and hypocrisy. When Alroy Kear, official biographer of the successful novelist Edward Driffield, learns about his first wife Rosie, Driffield's voluptuous muse, and realizes that telling her story would cast an embarrassing light on his subject's respectable image, Kear faces difficult choices. See *The Real Life of Anthony Burgess* by Andrew Biswell, p. 8, for insight into Burgess's view of Rosie as his 'mythical mother'.

66. ANYBODY CAN CONDUCT

True. It requires no very special skill to get up on a podium and lash an orchestra to life. It is much more difficult to be a bus or train conductor. After all, you don't really need a stick-wagger up there. The early days of the Soviet Union were inflamed by such a spirit of equality that they got rid of the one man with the baton who enslaved one hundred blowing, scraping and banging to his will. Russian orchestras didn't noticeably play worse, though the percipient observed how the principal first violin or concertmaster (as Germans and Americans call him) became more self-assertive and wagged his bow about instead of setting it to his strings. There was, in fact, a reversion to the state that existed before conductors came along. *Somebody* had to keep the orchestra together, but not somebody *up there*, stick-wagging.

Naive music lovers love conductors for various reasons, few of which have much to do with music. A conductor provides visual relief from too much listening: he is a kind of one-man ballet. He is known to be richer than mere fiddlers and flautists, and this gives him star status even if he has little talent. Karajan, who conducts the Berlin Philharmonic, travels about in a private jet and, old as he is, looks glamorous, as Beethoven might have looked had he been successful. The admirers of conductors believe they could do the job themselves moderately well (compare the attitude rock lovers have to rock singers: success is a matter of luck, not genius: this is very comforting), and to some extent this is true. The orchestra has been playing the *Mastersingers* Prelude for years. The conductor drops dead of a heart attack. You, a member of the audience, are ordered to mount the podium. Give the downbeat. The orchestra starts to play. It plays well. But it plays well in spite of you. It knows the damned thing backwards. If it were a matter of a first performance of a new work by Berio or Boulez or Messiaen, the situation would be altogether different.

Watch Pierre Boulez conducting Stravinsky's *Le Sacre du Printemps*. He seems to do nothing except make unemphatic gestures. No flamboyance, no leaping in the air, no hair-tearing, no brow-mopping with a snowy handkerchief. What he is doing is *reminding* the orchestra of what he has taught them in rehearsal. There's nothing much for him to do now. The work has already been done, and now it's up to the players to discourse the notes in the manner he has, in rehearsal after rehearsal, imposed. But before the rehearsals there were months of work quite as important, in which the conductor was alone with the score – reading it, learning it, pencilling in expression marks. He had to decide on tempo – how fast, how slow. On deciding just how loud *fff* is, and how soft *ppp*. The composer's expression marks are never very exact. What does *allegro con fuoco* mean? Fast and fiery. But how fast? And what has fire to do with blown wood and scraped catgut?

When an amateur conductor is given charge of an orchestra, the work performed will always be something the players already know well. A symphony by Beethoven – preferably the Fifth. *The Flight of the Bumble Bee*. Give the downbeat to start the thing off, and, like the man who first conducted Berlioz's *Benvenuto Cellini*, you can get your snuffbox out.[1] If the work is Debussy's *L'Après-Midi d'un Faune,* you don't even need the downbeat: just nod at the first flute, saying: 'Start when you feel like it.' What the amateur conductor can't do, even with a work excruciatingly well known and a great bore to the orchestra, is organize balance, make sure the wind are not swamped by the strings and the brass by both. Composers like Beethoven gave the trumpets *f* and the flutes *f* in a *tutti*, thus ensuring that the flutes wouldn't be heard. The good conductor puts that right. He puts it right in rehearsal. At the performance the trumpet remembers that he must play *mf* and the flautist that he must play *ff* or even *fff*.

Many people think that the conductor's main job is to beat time. There is something in this. Downbeat, leftbeat, rightbeat, upbeat. But many conductors are very erratic about time. I was at a rehearsal once in which the conductor (very famous, but I had better not mention his name) lambasted the players unmercifully. 'Strings unforgivably ragged,' he yelled, 'and woodwind as pallid as lard. Brass brutal. A disgrace. But I'd better not say any more, or you'll have your revenge at the concert.' A little man in the back row of the second violins spoke up. 'Yes,' he said, 'we'll follow your beat.' What, then, was the orchestra getting out of this celebrated maestro? Chiefly his feeling for the music, expressed in his eyes and grimaces, his body language, the curious illusion that he himself was playing the music on a human keyboard called the orchestra. He *cared* – that was the important thing. A lot of orchestral players *don't* care. They do the job, get paid, are more concerned about union restrictions than about an agonized Beethoven or Schubert. My old violin teacher played in the Hallé Orchestra in Manchester.[2] He *hated* music, so he told me, but fiddling was the only job he could do. He needed a conductor to infuse him with a temporary love of music. All the rest was technique.

Orchestras need conductors, then (whether they wag a stick on the rostrum, nod from a solo pianoforte, or move their head and shoulders from a violin desk). They need them at rehearsal; they don't necessarily need them on the night. But it is wrong for music lovers to rush to buy tickets because Maestro Stronzo or Pferdescheisse is up there.[3] The music comes first, and badly conducted Beethoven is better worth hearing than well-conducted Victor Herbert. Beethoven can more or less look after himself; kitsch has to have glamour spread all over it, like peanut butter. You yourself can, with confidence, get up there, take the stick, give the downbeat and launch the players into 'The Star-Spangled Banner'. But you can't do it with Stravinsky or Schoenberg. You just can't spare the months of preparatory solitude and the hours of arduous rehearsal. Conducting is, finally, an art which goes on behind locked doors. What you see in the concert hall is hardly worth seeing.

Homage to QWERT YUIOP

1   Reference to an incident that Hector Berlioz relates in his memoirs except that Burgess has confused Berlioz's *Benvenuto Cellini* with his Requiem Mass. After receiving the good news that his Requiem would be premiered in Paris in December 1837 less than six months after he had completed the score, Berlioz was distressed to learn that François Habeneck, *premier chef* at the Paris Opéra, would conduct it instead of himself. Berlioz's concern proved to be well founded when, during the premiere, Habeneck neglected his conducting duties at a critical moment to take a pinch of snuff. In his annotated edition of Berlioz's autobiography, Ernest Newman casts doubt upon the veracity of this story. See *Memoirs of Hector Berlioz*, p. 210.

2   Nowhere else does Burgess mention studying violin with a member of the Hallé Orchestra. In *This Man and Music*, he claims to have taken violin lessons at Mr Bradshaw's School of Music in Manchester but was a 'hopeless' student who eventually stopped showing up for lessons. Nonetheless, his father was still charged for the supposed instruction. 'My truancy was discovered by a shop-customer. There was a terrible row.' See TMM, pp. 14/34-5.

3   Stronzo (It.) means 'piece of shit'; Pferdescheisse (Ger.) means 'horse-shit'

67. HAND TO MOUTH

It Ain't Necessarily So: The Autobiography of Larry Adler
London: Collins, 1984

There have been three great players of the harmonica – John Sebastian, Tommy Reilly and Larry Adler.[1] The achievement of all of them has been to show the artistic possibilities of a mere toy, though, if you look closely at the toy, you will see that it is rather remarkable. The mouth organ manufactured by Hohner in Germany has a stretch of four octaves and a lever which enables you to play a chromatic scale.

Give it to a naive player and he will blow-suck a major triad and a dominant ninth – a pair of folk-sounds which Vaughan Williams parodied in his 'London Symphony'. The skill of men like Adler lies in being able to cut off, by shoving the tongue-tip into the square holes, the built-in chords and to discourse a single melodic line. Sophisticated chords are possible too, but once hint at a dominant ninth and you've taken the mouth-organ back into the streets or the trenches or the sardonic scherzo of Vaughan Williams.

Vaughan Williams wrote a 'Romance' for Larry Adler. I remember Adler speaking on the radio in 1951 and begging composers to take the instrument seriously. Villa-Lobos wrote a concerto for Adler and then handed it over to the late John Sebastian. I myself wrote two works for John Sebastian, both for harmonica and guitar (a marvellously portable combination). I also wrote a piece for Tommy Reilly, and he and I played it together on BBC television.

I have also written a suite for Larry Adler, but he seems not to have played it yet. This being drawn into the world of the harmonica is one of the more bizarre aspects of my non-literary life. I know how the instrument works, but I cannot play it. I admire anyone who can play it. I admire Adler.

As a nice Jewish boy in Baltimore, he heard that the family was of Russian extraction and named Zelakovitch, but that his grandfather, tired of always being at the end of the queue, leapt over the alphabet and became a German eagle. This daring was transmitted to Lawrence Cecil, who was glad to be called Larry, and he got on because he took to an instrument which few could play properly. Rejected by Borrah Minevitch and His Harmonica Rascals ('Kid, you stink'), Larry determined to be a soloist and began a hard struggle to be accepted in the world of show business (a struggle to be duplicated when he tried to board the concert platform).

The world was not yet ready for Bach or Vivaldi on a mouth-organ, and it was hard enough to get audiences to accept 'I Wanna be Loved by You'. The turning-point came with Ravel's *Boléro*, which brought the house down because Larry didn't know it well and made desperate signals to the orchestra which were assumed to be cleverly balletic. When he played it properly the audience was less interested. That, as they say, is showbiz.

Larry needed *chutzpah* to get on, but he always had a plentiful supply of it. He boasts about being a coward, but he seems to have had courage enough. As a Jewish boy in Baltimore he met plenty of racial and sectarian prejudice and he was not willing, at the time of the McCarthy witch-hunts, to make a theological issue of Communism. He had toured the theatres of war with Jack Benny and brought tears to the eyes of Russian troops by playing 'Ochi cherniya' to them.[2] The Russians weren't all bad, and American communists had certain constitutional rights. He was blacklisted.

One of his reasons for living in England is the purely negative one of his American persecution. He wrote the music for the British film *Genevieve*, only to find his name removed from the credits for its American showing.[3] Things have changed now but he still lives in England. After all, it was under the aegis of Charles B. Cochran that he was first taken seriously as a musician.[4] It was a struggle to get to Carnegie Hall.

Larry speaks out. He spoke out against the Beatles because he considered their lyrics inept. He speaks out in this book against misuse of the English language: 'I have seen language gradually being eroded, helped on its way by too many journalists and broadcasters ... I detest jargon and I make an effort to avoid the *in* phrase.' It is dangerous for any writer to make such a declaration, especially as Larry has here, when he has committed himself to a loose slanginess which is probably meant to be disarming. To write in the orotund style of Sir Thomas Beecham or with the plain seriousness of Yehudi Menuhin's admirable autobiography might not be in order for a harmonica-player.

The title itself is meant to be disarming. It is the refrain of Sportin' Life's song in *Porgy and Bess*, which counsels scepticism even about the things you're li'ble to read in the Bible. Larry knows how treacherous memory can be, meaning how dangerous it is to tackle an autobiography at the age of seventy, when the imagined, the reported, the dreamt and the enacted are swirled into the one broth. But the title also enfolds a message for the young: 'Daddy isn't always right. Daddy has no monopoly on wisdom.' The wrongs done to him by the American state still rankle. 'Test the validity of the most dogmatic of beliefs. To many, faith is enough. Not for me. I respect the truth, if the truth is there to find.'

What the musical reader probably has a right to demand is the truth about playing the harmonica the way Larry plays it. How is it done? Vaughan Williams asked a pertinent question: 'You blow to get C and you suck to get D. How do you get a legato?' Larry's answer is a little evasive. If most things aren't necessarily so, the mouth-organ is a verifiable solidity. For my money, it isn't sufficiently in the foreground.

There are some good illustrations. Lord Mountbatten plays a duet with Larry and hogs the mike. Sheik Suleiman listens to a solo with the attentive wonder proper to a reading of the Koran. Larry says to Sargent: 'No no, no, Malcolm, you're supposed to *in*hale.' R.V.W. as G.O.M. snarls like an old lion as Larry presumably muffs a passage. The book is full of bitterness as well as humour, but the humour prevails. And, seriously though, that suck-blow toy has come a long way.

The Observer, 1984

1   See ACC, Chapter 28 *The Sad Suck-and-Blow.*
2   'Dark Eyes' ('Очи чёрные'), a popular nineteenth-century Russian romance song, with lyrics by Yevgeny Grebyonka set to the melody of Florian Hermann's piano piece *Valse hommage,* Op. 21. *It Ain't Necessarily So,* p. 120.
3   The score was nominated in 1953 for the Academy Award for Best Music Score, with the Scottish conductor-composer Muir Mathieson, the musical director of *Genevieve,* given sole credit for the music. In 1986, the Academy's Board of Governors removed Mathieson's name from the nomination and replaced it with Adler's. *It Ain't Necessarily So,* pp. 183-4.
4   Sir Charles Blake Cochran, known as C.B. Cochran, was an English theatrical manager and impresario who produced performances by the Ballets Russes and Harry Houdini and musicals by Jerome Kern and Cole Porter, was closely associated with Noël Coward, and managed the Royal Albert Hall for twelve years. *It Ain't Necessarily So,* pp. 48-9.

68. JOHN SEBASTIAN – A PERSONAL REMINISCENCE

I got to know John Sebastian when we were both living in Rome in the 1970s.[1] I knew him as a lover of art and literature before I was aware of his skill and reputation as a musician. He was, in fact, an all-round Renaissance man – handsome, a great reader, a great traveller, learned in painting and sculpture, a fine cook, and exquisitely well-informed in all branches of classical, romantic and modern music. As for popular music, he left that to his son, who carried the same name as himself and had a greater reputation – though only among young American aficionados of rock.[2] When he discovered that I had started my artistic career as a composer, abandoning music in favour of literature because I had a living to earn, he commissioned from me a couple of compositions for harmonica and guitar – a sonatina and a work called *Faunal Noon*.[3]

Of all musical instruments, the harmonica and the guitar are the most difficult to write for: you have to know how they work before you can scribble notes for them. And so I learned something about the technique for both. The result of this was that I composed music for solo guitar and for guitar quartet, including a concerto grosso for the latter which is under rehearsal as I write.[4] As for the harmonica, I wrote works for the other two great virtuosi of our day – Larry Adler and Tommy Reilly. I remember celebrating my sixtieth birthday by accompanying Reilly in a brief rhapsody on BBC television.[5] I doubt if I would have returned to music at all if it had not been for John Sebastian's encouragement. This encouragement forced me much further afield than the comparatively narrow limits of harmonica and guitar. In 1975 I composed a symphony that was performed in Iowa City, and John's ear was sharp and his response highly informed when I played the tape to him in my lakeside house in Bracciano.[6]

He was without doubt the finest harmonica virtuoso of our day, and I was angry when the new *Grove Dictionary of Music* (1980) gave lengthy entries for both Adler and Reilly but did not mention John Sebastian at all. It was he, and not those two, who persuaded composers like Villa-Lobos to write at length for the instrument, though Villa-Lobos had to be taught its resources and see the cadenza of his concerto rejected as unplayable.[7] John produced a very useful guide to the harmonica, showing what chords were possible and what not, and I keep this carefully in my files. Unfortunately, since John's untimely death, I have felt no urge to compose for this difficult and wayward instrument – though the faint strains of John Murray Ferguson may be heard in the score of my *Blooms of Dublin* – a musical version of Joyce's *Ulysses* recorded in Dublin in early 1982.

Difficult and wayward? It required enormous courage to convert the harmonica from a melancholy suck-blow travesty of music into a highly refined wind instrument of large range and poignant tone. John showed that Bach and Mozart were playable on it with no loss of sweetness or dignity. The suck-blow element – parodied in the third movement of Vaughan Williams's 'London Symphony' and technically described as an alternation of tonic and dominant chords – had to be eliminated by a cunning insertion of the tongue-point into the apertures; then the sweetness and power of single notes could be made manifest. One thanks God, or the resources of modern technology, that we have so much of John Sebastian on record, but nothing can replace the personality of the man on the concert platform, the charm and wit of his commentaries on the music he played, to say nothing of the aura of world culture that shone round his powerful presence. To me he was a good friend, a supreme intermediary between the American and European cultures, and the man who taught me to appreciate Italy. Of his greatness as a musician this book is an eloquent and informative testimony.

The 'Classic Harmonica' Series, 1988

1 See YH, pp. 267-8. John Murray Ferguson solicited this essay for inclusion in The "Classic Harmonica" Series. See Commentary.

2 Singer-songwriter John B. Sebastian founded the Lovin' Spoonful, and played guitar and harmonica in the band.

3 The two pieces Burgess composed for John Sebastian were a sonatina and a work called *Panique*, not *Faunal Noon*. Burgess composed *Panique* first; it is inscribed 'Bracciano July 10, 1972' and signed, waggishly, 'Antoine Bourgeois 1866-1922'. He composed the three-movement Sonatina in C for Harmonica and Guitar later that summer while crossing from Italy to the United States aboard the *SS Raffaello*. The sonatina is inscribed 'Rafaello [sic] - New York Aug. Sept. 1972'. In YH (p. 267), Burgess misidentifies the ocean liner as the *Leonard da Vinci*, which was, along with the *Michelangelo*, a sister ship of the *Raffaello*. Burgess wrote out the scores by hand, with dedications to John Sebastian on both manuscripts. In *The 'Classic Harmonica' Series*, Ferguson changes the end of this line to 'a sonatina and a work called PANIQUE', the latter underlined and in all caps.

4 The premiere of the *Concerto Grosso pour Quatuor de Guitares et Orchestre en La mineur* took place on 26 February 1989 in Cannes. (See Chapters 52 *Concerto Grosso for Guitar Quartet and Orchestra* and 53 *The Aïghetta Quartet*.) If written in December 1988 (the copyright notice of this essay is '© Anthony Burgess 1988'), then rehearsals for the *Concerto Grosso* would have begun at least two months prior to the premiere.

5 They performed Burgess's *Romanza* for harmonica and piano on a broadcast of Oscar Peterson's BBC-TV show that aired on 8 March

1977. Burgess's sixtieth birthday was 25 February 1977, which could have been the date that the episode was recorded.

6   John Sebastian would have noticed that several themes from the Sonatina in C were reused by Burgess in his Symphony in C.

7   Ferguson replaced the comment that Sebastian 'persuaded composers like Villa-Lobos' with 'persuaded composers like Tcherepnin, Cowell, Dello Joio and Villa-Lobos' to write for the instrument.

69. A CONDUCTOR WITH A TALENT FOR RESURRECTION

LONDON

Shakespeare's Prince Hal asks Falstaff for his reasons, and Falstaff replies that 'reasons are as plentiful as blackberries.' This makes little sense until we're told that our Elizabethan ancestors pronounced 'reasons' and 'raisins' in the same way. At once the silly pun sparks into life. We recognize that Chaucer's English makes no true impact on us until we learn how to pronounce it. Should we give to Shakespeare the same homage of antiquarian research? Most people, who like to think that plays at the Globe were given in the refined tones of Sir John Gielgud, say no. Let's have our Shakespeare modern, complete with 'Fraaance' and 'daaance' and 'show' pronounced like 'sheu-oo.' Of course, there's some sense in this, since Shakespeare, though four centuries old, is undoubtedly 'modern'. Chaucer is medieval, and he needs the so-called historical approach. But in general we're becoming more and more concerned with questions of authenticity.

My subject here is music, not literature. The connection will make sense, though, to Roger Norrington, the chief British advocate of antiquarian research into how old music actually sounded in its own day, since Mr. Norrington took a degree in English literature at the University of Cambridge before pursuing a musical career. I'm aware that musico-literary parallels can never be just, for a very simple reason, or raisin. Restoration of ancient phonemes affects meaning; resuscitation of mere phones is cosmetic, not at all semantic. The concern with musical authenticity is greatly tied up with the very twentieth-century passion for restoring the roots of European (and hence American) music. Neither Mozart nor

Beethoven cared much for Monteverdi. Even with a Baroque masterpiece like Handel's *Messiah*, Mozart had to refashion the orchestration to bring it in line with late-eighteenth-century expectations. The Victorians, such as Ebenezer Prout, made *Messiah* a loud celebration of the Crystal Palace rather than a comparatively subdued meditation on redemption.[1] The Age of Reason and the Age of Industrial Expansion alike assumed that old music was acceptable only if it could be wrenched into the frame of modernity.

In contrast, let us examine what Roger Norrington has done and is doing. Mr. Norrington, who is now fifty-seven years old, studied violin and voice before taking his Cambridge degree; he then went on to the Royal College of Music in London to specialize in conducting, composition and music history. He founded the Schütz Choir in 1962, and this did much to unlock the treasury of seventeenth-century music that had for so long slept in the dust. Mr. Norrington became music director of Kent Opera, a new enterprise that began in 1969, and he was responsible for some incredible productions over the fifteen years of his tenancy. He has been the chief conductor of the Bournemouth Sinfonietta and chief guest conductor of the Jerusalem Symphony Orchestra.

The work of purveying known tonalities goes on, but Mr. Norrington's true achievements lie in the work he has done for the London Classical Players, to which may be coupled the impact made in New York with the St. Luke's Orchestra. He is concerned with presenting Bach and Handel, Haydn and Mozart in the orchestral guise of their own epochs. More controversially, he has elected to historicize composers close enough to our own age to seem part of contemporary culture – Berlioz, Mendelssohn, Schumann, Brahms. Beethoven, with whom the modern consciousness in music may be said first to emerge, has also been given the historic treatment. He sounds like the Beethoven we thought we already knew, with certain subtle differences.

I have taped the entire presentation of the Beethoven symphonies that Mr. Norrington and his orchestra made for BBC television, and I frequently play them back. I like his rapport with his players. His face, that of a genial Mephistopheles, talks as much as his baton. The sounds are ravishing. Nevertheless, I have a sensation of a certain perversity, as of a man who disdains electric light and prefers the smell of lamp oil. This is not Karajan and the smooth perfection of the Berlin ensemble. In my youth the horns were always expected to bubble, and there was a kind of pleasure in that, as though nature were not yet quite conquered by man. Mr. Norrington's horns make no errors, but one is always expecting a salutary miscalculation. We are, in a word, closer to nature than we used to be.

The major difference between Mr. Norrington's instruments and ours is to be found in the brass department. Trombones, which have hardly changed at all since they were biblical sackbuts, are not the regular noisemakers of a Beethoven symphony. They are used sparingly in Nos. 5, 6 and 9 and nowhere else. But trumpets and horns are always there in pairs, and they were nothing like ours. Like the army bugle they were limited to the notes of the harmonic series. In a symphony in C, the two trumpets, playing in octaves, hammer out tonic and dominant (C and G), usually in unison with two timpani. The horns have rather more to do, being contemplative instruments as well as the brayers of the forest hunt. Still, they're limited, too. Both trumpets and horns have to adjust to the 12 major and 12 minor keys available to the composer by fitting on crooks that raise or lower the tone. A horn player of the old days had to have 12 crooks at his feet, ready to respond to the signal in the score – Corno in C, in F, in E flat.

The Beethoven Mr. Norrington has resurrected is still stuck with the old refined bugles. Look at the London Classical

Players at work, and you will see long trumpets hammering away at a pair of notes, and horns totally lacking valves. But something happened when Beethoven was preparing his Ninth Symphony. The valved horn was coming in. Beethoven knew of a man living outside Vienna who had one of these new-fangled marvels, and he wrote his fourth horn part for him. The Ninth was the first symphony to employ two pairs of horns, and the custom was thereafter pretty firmly established.[2] The fourth horn part of the Ninth is a virtuoso piece of writing, appropriate to the new valved resources. Surprisingly, Mr. Norrington clings to the valveless variety. The player copes well enough.

The Beethovenian woodwinds are, by our standards, comparatively primitive, meaning that there is no great array of polished steel accouterments: flute, clarinet, oboe and bassoon are more concerned with fingers on the holes than with keys and bars. The effect of Beethoven's woodwinds, like that of his brasses, is essentially rustic. There is an interesting linguistic parallel here. If we were to restore Shakespeare's pronunciation in our theaters, we would be shocked by a highly provincial, even hayseed, quality in the vowels. The restored original sounds of the 'Pastoral' Symphony sound appropriately rural, and the Norrington version is probably the one we ought to hear. Of the other, more sophisticated symphonies, we may have reservations, but they can be glossed as untenable prejudice.

As for the strings, we have become habituated to vast masses of violins, violas, cellos and basses against which the woodwinds sometimes have to struggle to make themselves heard. Mr. Norrington's string force is comparatively small. In the Ninth Symphony his choral finale, though noisy enough at the end, does not evoke the triumphalism for which the work, at national celebrations, seems to have been created. The orchestra of Beethoven's time, and even more of Mozart's, is closer to the chamber combination than to the Napoleonic army necessary for a work like Strauss's *Heldenleben* or Holst's *Planets*.

To me the most revealing of Mr. Norrington's revelations is his recording of Berlioz's *Symphonie Fantastique*. We like to think that this is a work looking forward to our own day, and that Berlioz himself, in heaven or purgatory, hears the fulfillment of his design in the orchestra of Strauss or Elgar. Not so. To begin with, Berlioz's brasses are not ours. He has a pair of the old valveless trumpets playing alongside keyed and lively cornets. He has the old narrow-bore trombones backed by ophicleides, which rasp on their deeper notes, lacking the comfortable roundness of the modern bass tuba. To hear the original brass in the 'March to the Scaffold' is to be impressed by a sardonic sneering quality as the opium-eating poet is carried to his execution. The English horn used in the recording is one made by Henry Brod, who, says Mr. Norrington, almost certainly played in the first performance of the work. The four harps Berlioz called for are a delight. They are smaller than our modern monsters and are very clear on the high notes. Though his strings are the same as ours, the technique is the one developed in the Paris Conservatoire, with the minimum of bow-bounce and vibrato. Classical, in other words: closer to Mozart than to Wagner. The total effect of the work in its new, or original, dress is Romantic enough, but it is not Wagnerian Romanticism. Mr. Norrington remarks, rightly, on a 'younger, leaner' quality. It is the Romanticism of the Wordsworthian period, not that of the full-blown petal-shedding Tennyson. It is, despite the grim program with its Edgar Allan Poe overtones, a curiously innocent work.

Finally, of course, it is the notes that count. Those of us who are growing old and prefer our concerts to be internalized, reading our scores in an armchair with a highball, are trying to hear what deaf Beethoven heard. Music is ultimately a tissue of relationships written down on lined paper. Sheer sounds are vulgar. We can understand this thirst for authenticity, slaked by Roger Norrington's remarkable endeavors. We're living in an age of artificial sounds, in which electronics seems likely to snatch the instruments from the players' hands and consign them to the garbage dump. There's a need to get back to the primal, if not the primitive, and Baroque and early Romantic blowers and scrapers are, by our standards, primal enough. And to hear what Mozart heard, and what Beethoven would have liked to hear, exalts us, enables us to touch the hands of long dead masters. When we become used to hearing Hamlet tehking arrrms agehnst a say of troobles, we shall similarly feel closer to Shakespeare. To recover the past is a legitimate human aim. Mr. Norrington has done a remarkable job of resurrection.

The New York Times, 1991

1 The English composer and arranger Ebenezer Prout was a heavy-handed editor of *Messiah* who added instruments (flutes, clarinets, horns, trombones) to the original orchestration and replaced Handel's phrasing and expression marks with his own.

2 Long before Beethoven composed his Ninth Symphony in 1822–4, Haydn used two pairs of horns in his Symphony No. 31 in D major ('Hornsignal') in 1765. Mozart employed four horns in his Symphony No. 18 in F major, K. 130, in 1772, and in four later symphonies: No. 19 in E-flat major, K. 132; No. 25 in G minor, K. 183; No. 32 in G major, K. 318; and No. 40 in G minor, K. 550. Cherubini used two pairs of horns in numerous works, including his Requiem, and Schubert included four horns in his 'Tragic' Symphony, composed in 1816 at the age of nineteen.

PART V
OPERA

70. INTRODUCTION TO *DON GIOVANNI* AND *IDOMENEO*

Don Giovanni and *Idomeneo* by Wolfgang Amadeus Mozart
London: Cassell, 1971

People who gain their notions of the character of musical genius from romantic literature, seeing composers as wild-haired piano-smashers, volcanoes of temperament, monomaniacs who go their own way, must cleanse their minds of such images before confronting Wolfgang Amadeus Mozart. The composer as angelic brute is an attractive fictional property, and it made a best-seller of Margaret Kennedy's *The Constant Nymph*. But only in the nineteenth century did composers fulfil the twentieth-century popular novelists' view of the archetypal composer. There were a few men who were, like Byron, bigger than life – Berlioz, with his opium-dreams and his thousand-piece orchestra; Wagner, whose huge Aryan visions were indulged by a mad king; Liszt, the womanizing abbé with his warts and white mane and cigars and magic keyboard. Before them came Beethoven, the true source of the archetype, who was a deaf colossus with terrible manners and an artistic single-mindedness that had never been known before. With him, the creation of music as the emanation of one's own personality, and not as artefacts made primarily for the enjoyment of others, accorded with the new romantic doctrines of Feeling and the revolutionary slogans about Liberty.

In previous centuries it had been very different. The musical composer had usually been a kind of upper servant, tied to a cathedral or an aristocratic court, ordered to write motets or minuets as his patron, bishop or prince, dictated. There was neither room nor time for temperament.

Temperament, anyway, has always been primarily an attribute of executants, not creators. Singers especially are traditionally notorious for rages, sulks, and an intransigence before which mere composers must bow, unless they are called Beethoven or Lewis Dodd.[1] Generally, the smaller the vocal talent the bigger the head.

Mozart was very much a child of the eighteenth century, when, as Jean-Jacques Rousseau saw, everybody was in chains and ready for a new deal or social contract. In England, that period was notable for Grub-street writers looking desperately for patrons (Dr. Johnson, who anticipated Beethoven, abandoned vassalage and struck out on his own). In the Habsburg Empire, it was notable for mediocre musicians trying to be salaried Kapellmeisters. That Empire was full of small aristocratic and episcopal courts, and these had to have music as they had to have art galleries and livery stables. A resident choir, organist and orchestra must be available for religious routine and secular junketing. Mass in the morning, a ball at night, a wedding to be solemnized, a triumphant return from the Grand Tour loudly TeDeumed. There were also concerts, with symphonies and virtuoso fireworks on solo instruments, but these were always private affairs, the notion of the public concert being a free-enterprise and democratic one and the times not yet ripe for it. The Habsburg Empire cultivated music diligently, but only as an aspect of the full aristocratic life.

With so many musicians around, one would have expected – fulfilling the statistical law – a flowering of musical genius. But such genius, meaning powerful originality and a strong individual vision, cannot easily come to birth in an environment where the artist's status is low and his function prescribed and circumscribed. It is not easy to imagine Beethoven's Ninth Symphony getting as far even as a first rehearsal in the court of the Archbishop-Elector at Bonn. Let music be kept in its proper station, and symphonies be tuneful and short. Eighteenth-century genius had to be considerable in order to manifest itself through routine jobs and speedy commissions (a week for a concerto, a month for an opera). Mozart's genius was very great indeed, and its greatness is attested by its civilized submission to accepted forms, even clichés. To shrug, smile, and still be a genius is granted to few. Mozart wrote for society, not for himself, but every bar of his mature work is instinct with his own personality. Sometimes, especially in such late works as the final symphonies, his genius threatened to smash the accepted forms in a Beethovenian way. Occasionally this genius made his lordly listeners uneasy; there is always a subversive whiff in a work of genius, its recognition glossed as failure to understand. But, for the most part, Mozart made himself very clearly understood; he had a supreme talent as well as a towering genius, and this talent was in the service of giving pleasure.

Mozart was born into the world of musical servitude. His father, Leopold, was a violinist and small composer in the court of the Archbishop Sigismund von Schrattenbach at Salzburg.[2] He and his wife Maria Anna produced seven children, but only two survived – Wolfgang Amadeus, born in 1756, and Marianne, nicknamed Nannerl, born in 1751. Both children showed considerable talent at an early age, but Wolfgang was, as all the world knows, a prodigy. At the age of three he was picking out thirds on the keyboard, at four he was playing the clavier, at five he was composing. His sheer musicality is attested in various legends – his fainting when first hearing a trumpet, his ability to distinguish between microtones (or minute divisions of the semitone), a faculty for reproducing from memory – at the keyboard or on paper – a complex composition heard once only. He and his sister were, inevitably, exploited by their father, who took them on concert tours to Munich, Vienna, London, Brussels, Paris. They were kissed and cosseted wherever they went, and Leopold Mozart, whose archiepiscopal master was very indulgent, took them everywhere. Youth's a stuff will not endure, and youthful genius does not always turn into mature genius. So Leopold drove both his children hard, but his son especially hard.

At seven Wolfgang was playing the violin; at eleven he wrote part of an oratorio, his first two symphonies, and four piano concertos, which, in the free and easy manner of the time, he made out of the piano sonatas of other composers. At twelve he was commissioned by the Emperor Joseph II himself to write a comic opera – *La finta semplice*. And at the house of the father of mesmerism, Dr. Franz Mesmer, the still delightful operetta *Bastien und Bastienne* was performed. Back in Salzburg, the Archbishop, aware of what talent he had vicariously bred, set Mozart to composing masses and other church compositions. But Leopold's feet itched to be on the road again, and his palm itched too: young geniuses must be seen as much as heard.

Verona, Milan, Bologna, Rome, Naples, Venice – Italy took Wolfgang to its heart, and Wolfgang's German-Austrian blood became tempered by the spirit of musical Italy: Italian became one of his languages and, very important, libretti in Italian were to inspire his greatest vocal-dramatic flowering. He was starting to take the writing of opera seriously now, but works like *Lucio Silla*, presented in Milan, achieved no large success. *La finta giardiniera* did well in Munich, with the Electress and the Dowager Electress crying *Bravo* and the common sort shouting *Viva Maestro*, but it was only a prentice work. Mozart the opera-maker needed a real librettist. He also needed to grow up and learn about human passion and intrigue.

Growing up presented its own problems. Not only the problem of love (Mozart, like most heterosexual artists, was susceptible to women, and the ladies of the aristocratic courts were inflammatory charmers), but the problem of finding a niche in the adult world. The time is short for being an infant prodigy. There were plenty of boys of nineteen who could touch the clavier divinely, but there were few of nine who could play it even moderately. And a dashed-off opera, like the *Il re pastore* Mozart had to write for his Archbishop, would be regarded as no large achievement for a young man touching twenty, not to be compared with a lisping child's derivative minuets. The glamour was going; the hard work had to begin. The Archbishop at Salzburg, once flattered by the compliments of Munich and Vienna on having so brilliant a musician in, or rather out of, his court, seemed ill-disposed to the mature young Mozart. So Mozart began to look for openings elsewhere.

He tried for a post in Bologna but had no luck. Conditions at Salzburg deteriorated, and, when Mozart asked the Archbishop for new leave of absence, His Grace suggested that he and his father take permanent leave. At this Leopold Mozart exhibited the fright of an ageing-employee. But the capricious cleric later assured him that his services were still required and let Wolfgang, accompanied by his mother, again go off on his travels. The boy wrote home regularly, as he had always done, and revealed in his letters the sense of fun that was to give such a champagne sparkle to his mature operas. He had the eye of the dramatist; he observed. He sums up with something like literary skill the absurdity of Graf, who wrote only flute concertos: 'His words are all on stilts and he generally opens his mouth before he knows what he wants to say; and often it shuts again without having done anything'. He is not only sharp and funny; he is frequently obscene. The whole family had a teutonic obsession with farts and faeces, and Mozart revelled, after putting notes of airy delicacy on paper, in gross lavatory mirth, 'My hole itches,' he says. 'Perhaps some shit wants to come out.' And then back to the creation of more aethereal emanations.

Mozart sought a post at Mannheim, but his father told him that musicians were poorly paid there. Still, said the son, there were clarinets in the orchestra, which they didn't have at Salzburg. There was something more than clarinets; there was the beautiful young singer Aloysia Weber, who sang Mozart's music divinely. Mozart fell in love with her and had no wish to leave Mannheim. His father, scenting that his son was making little money and fooling about instead of paying paternal debts (for this leave of absence had required heavy capitalising), tried to send him to Paris, but the attractions of Mannheim prevailed and begot an uncharacteristic unfiliality. When, at last, mother and son went to seek their father's fortune in Paris, the young composer became acquainted with true grief, not the fictitious emotion of conventional opera. His mother died. Later his pain was compounded by the refusal of Aloysia Weber to take his love seriously: she became a singer at the Munich court opera, well paid, too good for a mere composer. All this was part of Mozart's growing up.

At the age of twenty-three he was back in Salzburg. There was a new Archbishop there – Hieronymus Colloredo – and Mozart settled to a life of musical service in the court.[3] A good deal of music he wrote fails to reflect the spirit of the patronising commission – such free and original works as the Sinfonia Concertante for violin, viola and orchestra, for instance, and the Concerto for two pianos. But he had still produced no great masterpiece. A year after his appointment – in 1780 – the chance to display his genius in an extended work came at last, and it came only indirectly from Salzburg. 1780 is the year of *Idomeneo*.

Opera was essentially an Italian art-form. England developed its own sturdy operatic tradition out of the masque, producing in Purcell's *Dido and Aeneas* (1689) a universal masterpiece, but the rest of the world was very un-English, meaning Italian. Composers like Alessandro Scarlatti,

Porpora, Pergolesi and Cimarosa particularized Italian to Neapolitan, and librettists like Zeno and Metastasio laid down the standard verbal requirements. Scarlatti was very ready to taxonomize Neapolitan opera into permanent rigidities, decreeing that opera seria should not merely be serious but marbly monumental, and that opera buffa should be light and funny and racy. Operatic song had to be in the form of the *da capo* aria, meaning a melody stated and, after some bars of contrast, repeated. The dialogue was, of course, sung, but in a stylised form intended to convey the freedom and rapidity of speech – in other words, recitative. The run-of-the-mill recitative was called *secco* (or dry) and had a minimal harpsichord accompaniment; the more dramatic recitative was *stromentato*, or orchestrated. Scarlatti was a considerable composer, and was able to animate the set forms with a strong dramatic thrust and a high lyricism; with lesser composers, it all became a matter of vocal showing-off – icing piped on to bread pudding. Singing prevailed over acting, and the *castrati*, men who had had, as boys, their testicles sacrificed on the altar of art, shrilled out the main male parts in *opera seria*, doing in vocal fireworks what they could not do in bed.

In England, Handel tried to breathe back life into the empty Italian forms, but he failed and turned to oratorio – *opera seria* or even *religiosa* without stage action. In France, Gluck stuck to the stage but rebelled powerfully against pyrotechnics and tyrannical *castrati*. *Orfeo* appeared in 1762 and introduced, in addition to firm dramatic action and emotion sincerely expressed, two properties which Scarlatti had regarded as unnecessary – the chorus and the ballet. Librettists and composers, especially in England, France and Germany, began to see that opera could be true drama as well as true song, and they developed a medium in which there was scope for convincing spoken dialogue – the ballad opera in England, the *opéra comique* in France, the *Singspiel* in Germany. It was from this speech-song hybrid (examples of which are *The Beggar's Opera* and *Die Zauberflöte*) that the romantic national opera of the nineteenth century was able to proceed. *Opera seria* and *opera buffa* were, in a sense, *castrati:* they filled the eighteenth-century stage but could not breed. Stravinsky's *The Rake's Progress* is, like most of his work, genius happy in pastiche, a deliberate return to the *opera buffa* as Mozart was to practise it in *Don Giovanni.* The rest of twentieth-century opera is derived from Wagner. The *Singspiel* survives as musical comedy.

Idomeneo is *opera seria,* very *seria,* which has taken advantage of the reforms of Gluck. The chorus has important work to do; there is a ballet; there are marches in the French style; there is even a subterranean voice with trombones in the manner of the Oracle in Gluck's *Alceste.* But the music is wholly Mozartian. The commission came from the Elector Carl Theodor, who had known Mozart's work when the electoral court was at Mannheim. Now it had moved to Munich, whose carnival in 1781 was to be marked not only by false noses but by an *opera seria.* Mozart seemed the Elector's best election for composer; as he was stationed in Salzburg, it was considered that he ought to have a Salzburg librettist to work with. And so the Abbé Giambattista Varesco, chaplain to the Archbishop himself, undertook to provide – out of a small but undeniable poetic talent and a rather large ignorance of the requirements of the operatic stage – a suitably weighty text.

The Imperial Poet Metastasio, a pretty enough versifier and a very skilled librettist, was the best model that any tyro could take when planning the book of an opera. What Metastasio taught whole generations of poets was that there was not room for very much poetry in a good libretto: the music was doing the poet's work, the poet must humble himself and regard his texts as a mere handmaid. Metastasio knew the virtues of conciseness and directness, but Varesco, who dutifully read Metastasio, could not believe that words should so abase themselves. After all, religion was based on the Word, not the song, and Varesco was primarily a man of God. He produced a libretto which was far too impracticable for the mechanics of the eighteenth-century stage, and he complained bitterly when Mozart proposed that his lines be drastically cut. Out of this quarrel, out of the need to decide for himself what words could and could not be used, Mozart became his own best man of the theatre. He could make the drama if others would feed him situations and a few, a very few, words.

To give the Abbé his due, the material he chose was far from bad. His *Idomeneo, Re di Creta* was based on a theme essentially biblical and hence well enough known – the story of Jephtha, who returned from the wars and made a vow to sacrifice to Jehovah the first creature he met. This was, as Hamlet reminds us, his own daughter (what a treasure had he, etc.).[4] Varesco turned Jephtha into Idomeneo, King of Crete. He comes home from the Trojan wars, from which he has sent on in advance Ilia, daughter of Priam, as one of his prisoners. Pursued by the wrath of Poseidon, the sea-god, he vows to sacrifice to him the first living being he meets if only he will abate the fury of the storm and let him land safely. And so he reaches shore, encountering not a daughter but a son, Idamante. He does not dare reveal his vow and is, very properly, in extreme anguish. His confidant Arbace recommends that he permit Idamante to escape the danger by escorting Electra, daughter of Agamemnon, to Argos. Electra, improbably, has taken refuge in Crete after the murder of her mother. But Poseidon, being a god, realizes what is afoot and unleashes a new and more terrible storm at the moment of the refugees' departure. He does more: he sends a ghastly sea-monster which, in good classical Sphingine fashion, ravages the kingdom. Idamante goes forth to slay the beast, but the Cretan people, sorely and, as they see it, unfairly tried, come seeking the man who has offended the god and brought all this trouble on themselves. Idomeneo has to reveal the terrible secret, disclosing the name of his son as the necessary sacrificial victim. The priests make ready for the oblation, but Idamante returns, having killed the monster. Nevertheless, hearing of his father's vow, he is prepared to be slain on the altar. The prisoner Ilia, who loves Idamante, offers to take his place. Poseidon is pleased by this literal self-sacrifice, or intention of it, and the voice of an oracle is heard, stating that Idomeneo had better abdicate and hand over the throne to Idamante and, as his consort, Ilia. There is great rejoicing, except from Electra, who ends as she began, raging, jealous, unwanted. Metastasio might have tied things up neatly by marrying her to Idomeneo, but Varesco liked that sour note in the final concord. It is, in fact, a rather palatable acerbity, like a dash of good vinegar.

The story, then, is good, but Varesco's original script is verbose. He seems to have been unable to imagine the effect on the stage of a musical setting of his words as they stood. Mozart was, as always, very reasonable in his objections, but Varesco proved haughty and difficult. He insisted that he be paid extra for alterations and that, to show he was a victim of a mutilating musician, his script be published, if not performed, exactly as he wrote it. Mozart and he would not communicate with each other directly but used Leopold as an intermediary. As was his usual plan when composing an opera, Mozart wrote the earlier portion and then left a gap before completing the work. It was better to take a mere part of a new opera to rehearsals, and then finish it while the rehearsals proceeded. In that way the composer could see exactly what the performers were capable of doing, and the opera gained from the composer's awareness of the exigencies of cast and orchestra. So, fortunately for us, Mozart was away in Munich during the writing of much of *Idomeneo*, which meant that he had to commit to paper, in letters to his father in Salzburg, his problems and triumphs. We have a revealing record of the making of the opera.

Mozart shows himself a very astute stage-man. He saw that the work could not begin, as it does in Varesco's libretto, with Idomeneo scrambling up rocks at the rear of the stage after his shipwreck. It was absurd of Varesco to write run-on lines and stick asides into arias. In the *da capo* aria there had to be strophic regularity, and the repetition of an aside – imposed by the need to repeat the main melody – could only sound ridiculous. Here, in extenso, is an example of Mozart's good sense:

> Tell me, don't you think that the speech of the subterranean voice is too long? Consider it carefully. Picture to yourself the theatre, and remember that the voice must be terrifying – must penetrate – that the audience must believe that it really exists. Well, how can this effect be produced if the speech is too long, for in this case the listeners will become more and more convinced that it means nothing. If the speech of the Ghost in Hamlet were not so long, it would be far more effective. It is quite easy to shorten the speech of the subterranean voice and it will gain thereby more than it will lose.

And again,

> After the mourning chorus the king and all his people go away; and in the following scene the directions are 'Idomeneo prostrates himself in the temple'. That is quite impossible. He must come in with his whole suite. A march must be introduced here, and I have

therefore composed a very simple one for two violins, viola, cello and two oboes, to be played *a mezza voce*. While it is going on, the king appears and the priests prepare the offerings for the sacrifice. The king then kneels down and begins the prayer.

Not only did Mozart have the pigheadedness of Varesco to deal with; the singers, at least the male ones, gave trouble. The tenor Raaff took the title-part, but he was getting on in years – sixty-five – and very set in his ways. He obstructed, with the best of intentions, all Mozart's attempts to follow new and original paths, and he did not fail to draw on his long, but dated, experience in the theatre in order to give the young composer time-wasting homilies. Moreover, though he was still a fine singer, he could not act. Panzacchi, the other tenor, knew something of acting, but he insisted on his having the part of the confidant Arbace loaded with irrelevant display. Like Raeff, he was a senior man who saw the young Mozart as a clever-clever young whippersnapper who needed the advice of his elders and betters. Dal Prato – 'my molto amato castrato Dal Prato', as Mozart called him, with loving exasperation – was, on the other hand, totally unburdened with experience, and he was not over-gifted with either talent or intelligence. Yet the big part of Idamante was his. The composer showed himself, not for the first time, as a kindly, skilled and patient teacher; he could take stupidity better than he could take conceit. As for the ladies, Dorothea and Elisabeth Wendling, they gave no trouble, God bless them, and they knew how to sing.

The first performance of *Idomeneo* took place on 29 January 1781, two days after Mozart's birthday. His father and sister were present, and so we have no epistolary account of how things went. In fact, we have very few records indeed of that premiere, and those that we have totally fail to mention the composer's name. Of the importance of the opera – despite inevitable faults, derived as much from Varesco's libretto as the composer's own comparative immaturity – posterity has no doubt.

Idomeneo is *seria*, lofty, statuesque, and yet human and warm. This is no place for a detailed musical analysis, and perhaps it is enough to affirm that the mere reading of the orchestral and vocal score is a hugely educative experience. The deployment of orchestral colour, the boldness and poignancy of the harmonies, the elevation of conventional 'tags' (like the cadence of Ilia's first recitative) into highly dramatic devices – these, and many more, aspects of the composition are a great wonder. But the totality – the balance of chorus and aria and ensemble, the sense of movement, the economy – reveals an architectonic genius which a mere symphony or concerto cannot always adequately show. And yet the strength of the work is a symphonic one, in which purely musical devices of contrast – wind against strings, chromatic anguish against diatonic assertiveness – are a counterpart, not a mere accompaniment, to the human drama.

Mozart went back to purely instrumental writing after the Munich premiere of *Idomeneo*, producing, for instance, the masterly Oboe Quartet. But creation cannot flourish without the means of subsistence, and Mozart was suffering from the jealousy and tightfistedness of his Archbishop, who would not let his employee (whose genius he now certainly began to recognize) accept commissions or give performances outside the court, whether the court was in Salzburg or Vienna. Soon, after a blazing row with the proud prelate, Mozart left that servitude and tried to live as a free-lance teacher, composer and performer. Vienna became his centre, and it was here that he married Constanze Weber, the sister of Aloysia. He could be a fond husband and father but did not lose his artistic detachment: while his child was being born in one room he wrote his Quartet in D minor in the next. With a family to support, the need to raise money became a permanent obsession, and one means of raising it was the new device of the subscription concert. But debts always outgalloped income.

His output became, as we know, prodigious, and it raged over all the musical forms, not excluding opera – *Die Entführung aus dem Serail* (with a heroine named for his wife), which was produced at the Imperial Theatre, and the small but perfect *Der Schauspieldirektor* for the imperial palace at Schönbrunn, But the next great operatic masterpiece was a marvel of *opera buffa – Le Nozze di Figaro.* The librettist for this was Lorenzo Da Ponte, a half-Jew half-Gentile from Ceneda, north of Venice. His real name was Emanuele Conegliano, but, on his reception into the Catholic Church at the age of fourteen, he took the name of the officiating bishop. He was intended for the priesthood, 'though this', he said rightly, 'was utterly contrary to my vocation and my character.' But a seminary education made him skilful in Latin, including Latin versifying, and this proved no bad training for the managing of metre, as well as the compression of diction, in the Italian libretti which made his name. He became a somewhat dissolute priest, on the venerable Venetian model, and his profligacy, as well as his Rousseau-style rationalism, eventually led to his having to quit Venice.

Da Ponte was in Vienna in 1782, and in the following year he tried his hand at his first opera libretto, for the distinguished composer Salieri. A few years later, Mozart himself sought him out as a possible collaborator in a musical adaptation of Beaumarchais's *Le Mariage de Figaro.* The play itself had caused a scandal in Paris, because of its political implications (lost in the operatic version) – and it was banned in Vienna. Mozart foresaw no great difficulty in obtaining permission to produce a musical version, since music is supposed to draw the teeth of satire: the notoriety of the banned play would send the Viennese flocking to the unbanned opera.

There was some trouble with the libretto, both from the composer's point of view and the censor's, and it is hard to believe that, as Da Ponte was later to allege, the whole work was made ready for performance in six weeks. Indeed, of the background of the work we know little. We do know, however, that the first performance took place, at the command of the Emperor himself, on 1 May 1786, and that the general response to it was very enthusiastic. Yet the public is always fickle, and it soon let *Figaro* be eclipsed by the work of a very indifferent composer, Vicente Martín y Soler, whose opera *Una Cosa Rara* was immensely popular but is not now well remembered. *Le Nozze di Figaro* only managed to secure a revival in Vienna when *Don Giovanni* brought Mozart back into prominence.

Mozart did not repine at the short-lived popularity of the work in Vienna, for there was another city – deservedly famous for its musical taste – that loved his stage-work and could not have enough of it. This was Prague. Mozart visited the Bohemian capital in 1787, at the invitation of his admirers, and Prague and he got on very well together: his keyboard improvisations on themes from *Figaro* brought the house down. The manager of the local Italian Opera, Pasquale Bondini, was especially delighted with Mozart, for *Figaro* had played to full houses all the winter of 1786-7 and much strengthened the normally precarious finances of his organization. He was quick, then, to commission a new opera for production the following winter, and Mozart went back to Vienna to consult with Da Ponte about a suitable subject.

Da Ponte was busy. He was writing *L'Arbore di Diana* for Martín and *Axur, Re d'Ormuz* for Salieri. All he could think of for Mozart was the story of Don Giovanni or Don Juan, already well-known and much used on the stage, and all he had time to do was to draw heavily on an existing libretto by Giovanni Bertati. Mozart probably started work at once, producing enough material to commence rehearsals. Then he took lodgings in Prague and got down to the rest of the opera. On 29 October 1787, he conducted the first performance, having – according to a legend that may not be true, merely *ben trovato* – completed the composition of the overture while the audience was still coming in. That audience acclaimed the work, and so did the audiences that crammed the theatre night after night thereafter, recognising it as a great dual triumph. Da Ponte, however much he owes his immortality to Mozart, showed that a libretto – even a derivative one – could be important art. And the words of *Don Giovanni* are exquisite – tender, witty, precise. Mozart could hardly fail to make a wonderful duet out of these lines:

DON GIOVANNI	DON GIOVANNI
Là ci darem la mano,	There we'll take hands,
Là mi dirai di sì.	and you will whisper 'Yes'.
Vedi, non è lontano:	See, it's close by:
Partiam, ben mio, di qui.	let's leave this place, my dear.

ZERLINA	ZERLINA
Vorrei, e non vorrei...	I'd like to, but I dare not...
Mi trema un poco il cor...	My heart will not be still...
Felice, è ver, sarei;	I know I would be happy;
Ma può burlarmi ancor.	but he may yet deceive me.[5]

The story of Don Juan is an old one and appears to date back to a real, or mythical as opposed to literary, Spanish nobleman of Tenorio who was a noted profligate. Faust, Don Juan's cousin in sin, similarly derives from a personage real enough to be in the Acts of the Apostles – Simon Magus the Fortunate of Faustus. But, whereas the Faust story is one of the most terrible in Western culture, being the tale of a man who sells his soul for a few years of pleasure, the Don Juan legend has never seemed to be really tragic. Womanizers are admirable, pathetic, or comic, but – though they may deserve a thrashing on the bare buttocks in the Venetian manner – they are hardly hell-bait. And, if we look at the story closely, we will observe that Don Juan's being dragged to hell is only indirectly a punishment for his profligacy. His real crime is to insult the dead, which has traditionally been regarded as a terrible impiety with overtones of parricide about it. Thus, the Don Juan legend may be taken as a combination of two quite distinct stories, that of a man who lusts after women, and that of a man who wrongs the dead.

We need no particularized tale of philandering to produce a Don Juan image. Casanova – a real-life womanizer who actually, it is believed, helped with the preparation of *Don Giovanni* – will do for a great-lover myth, as will Frank Harris or Errol Flynn or even H.G. Wells.[6] Don Juan has his place in the mythology of the West because of the manner of his blasphemy and his subsequent end. He kills a high hidalgo, the Commendador or Commendatore, who happens to be the father of one of his amatory victims, the Lady Anna. A statue is erected in honour of the great man, and Don Juan sneers at it. The statue comes to life (a very ancient, indeed classical, fabular device) and there is a supper invitation. In the opera, it is Don Giovanni who invites the Commendatore; in the older versions of the story it is the Commendador who invites Don Juan. The latter version is the more terrible and the more characteristic, since Don Juan is foolhardy enough to go to a graveyard where adders and other inedibles are served, and, as a *bonne bouche*, is dragged down to the city of the dead which lies beneath the gravestones. Da Ponte and Mozart were not really in search of terror, except in a Pickwickian sense. To them the legend is material for a kind of black comedy which is a new, and original, variant of *opera buffa*.

Da Ponte's predecessors in the field of dramatizing the legend are many and distinguished. We begin with Gabriel Tellez – or Tirso de Molina – in the early seventeenth century, whose *El Burlador de Sevilla* is not particularly distinguished (too much moralizing), though it contains many of the prototypes of Da Ponte's own characters. There are a Doña Anna and a Don Octavio – a decent dull respectable lover – as well as a comic servant. In a mid-seventeenth-century Italian version of the story, put on at Naples, Harlequin took time off from the *Commedia dell'Arte* to act as Don Juan's servant, but the lineaments of Leporello can best be traced in Molière's *Le Festin de Pierre*, in 1665, where the servant is a well-rounded creation called Sganarelle. Moreover, Molière stresses the comic aspects of the story, dispensing with the hell-torments that were necessary to both Tirso de Molina and the Naples version. Here too are Donna Elvira, Masetto and Zerlina. Da Ponte obviously studied the play

England took over the Don Juan theme a decade after Molière, with Shadwell's *The Libertine,* to which the divine Purcell contributed incidental music.[7] In 1736, in Da Ponte's own Venice, Goldoni wrote a verse-play called *Don Giovanni Tenorio o sia il dissoluto,* less as an artistic venture than as an act of revenge on an actress – Signora Passalacqua – who had made a fool of him at the end of a protracted liaison. Don Giovanni would be recognized as his rival, Carino, the shepherd as himself, and the shepherdess Elsa as his former mistress. Here again, to judge from the similarity between Goldoni's last act and Da Ponte's finale, we seem to have another conscious source for the libretto. Finally, in 1775, came Bertati's version, the direct and immediate origin – not because of lack of inventive power on Da Ponte's part, solely because of lack of time – of the *Don Giovanni* that was the rage of Prague.

It is necessary for us to see the opera in relation to its time and to an existing stock of dramatic workings of the legend.

Neither Mozart nor Da Ponte was drawn by inner artistic necessity to the theme: there was none of the sense of creating great art, like Goethe brooding for a long time on the Faust story and then pouring his life's blood into it. There was a theatrical commission to be fulfilled, and the Don Juan theme was the only one quickly available. Bondini in Prague wanted a new *Figaro*, so *Don Giovanni* had to be comic, not serious and moralistic. Fortunately, the Don Juan stage tradition had become a *buffo* one – from Molière on – so there would be no sense of wrenching an essentially grave theme into an unsuitable comic mould.

The singers available for *Don Giovanni* were those already engaged on *Figaro* when the new opera went into rehearsal. This limited Da Ponte as to characters (early versions of the story had a large number of personages – especially women, since Don Juan's profligacy had to be given arithmetical authenticity). Figaro steps easily into the role of Leporello. The tenor part in *Figaro* is not of great importance, so the tenor – Don Ottavio – of *Don Giovanni* has to be a minor role similarly suitable for a minor artist. Luigi Bassi, who sang the baritone part of the Count in *Figaro*, was a godsend of a villain-hero for the eponym of the new work – a fine actor, good-looking, only twenty-two. The three female parts of *Figaro* – all of roughly equal importance – are exactly matched in *Don Giovanni*. Mozart, considerate of his singers, always ready to cut his musical cloth to their vocal measure, reveals himself always as a pre-Beethoven artist – willing to change, omit, throw away whole sheets of glorious music in the service of expediency.

If the music had to be changed, the libretto too had to undergo modifications during rehearsal, and, in the absence of Da Ponte, recalled to Vienna for the first night of his and Martín's *L'Arbore*, it seems that Giacomo Casanova, whose qualifications were not just amatory, was called in to make delicate emendations. The libretto we have is surely perfect of its kind, strong in character interest, lucid and concise in language, and eminently singable. Based on myth, *Don Giovanni* has itself become a source of myth. The figures of the *Don Juan in Hell* in *Man and Superman* are essentially Shaw's but primarily Mozart's and Da Ponte's. When we think of Don Juan, it is not the *Burlador* or the self-projection of Byron that comes to mind but a comic villain with a fine baritone voice singing pithy Italian.

Of the felicities of the music it is needless, indeed impossible, to speak; music must always speak for itself. There is a trombone triumph for the Commendatore, greater than that in *Idomeneo*, whose first intonations, says Shaw, represent a moment of dreadful joy for all musicians. The three orchestras in the ballroom, playing simultaneously in three different tempi, may have been primarily a tribute to the excellence of the Prague instrumentalists, who could cope with any ingenuity, but it is good drama in itself. And the final ensemble – too often omitted in performance, for it proclaims the essentially *buffo* character of a work that some, incredibly, would like to take for a serious morality – is a wonder of pseudo-profundity, a civilized grotesquerie to match the words:

Resti dunque quel birbon,	Let the scoundrel remain below
tra Proserpina e Pluton.[8]	with Proserpine and Pluto.

The rogue must dwell between Pluto and his queen for ever. Not the Christian inferno after all, but the stock classical Hades: three in a bed, Don Giovanni in the middle, but Pluto probably awake all the time. It is a pleasant conceit and a fitting punishment.

One of the results of the success of *Don Giovanni* was Mozart's elevation to Chamber Composer to the Emperor himself, but it was purely a nominal appointment and did nothing to ease circumstances that – however much music he wrote – were destined to remain wretched till the end of his life. He had no money sense, nor did his wife, and it is painful to think of the poverty, partly self-induced, that is the background to the last three great symphonies, written in a single summer, that came after *Don Giovanni*. But, besides Mozart's own improvidence, we have to remember that the system of royalties, which keeps today's composers alive, did not then exist, and that the outright fee paid for a commission was never exactly princely, even though a prince sometimes paid it. Many of Mozart's final letters are begging letters, requests for loans that, he assures his correspondents, will be repaid when the present 'temporary embarrassment' is over. But the embarrassments grew into one permanent embarrassment, and led to a pauper's grave. Mozart died in 1791. He was only thirty-five.

Perhaps it is worth dying young and in poverty if one can produce – among other masterpieces – an *Idomeneo* and a *Don Giovanni*. But we listeners to these works, entranced and elevated, ought occasionally to allow ourselves the luxury of anger. In Mozart's own works there is neither anger nor self-pity, only humour, elegance and a nobility sometimes – though always impersonally – tragic. His music contains the image of a perfectly ordered civilization which is itself an image of divine order.

Cassell Opera Guides, 1971

1 Dodd is the protagonist of *The Constant Nymph*. See Chapter 1 *The Writer and Music*.

2 As a youth, Wolfgang joined his father Leopold as a member of the episcopal court orchestra during the tenure of Sigismund Graf von Schrattenbach, Prince-Archbishop of Salzburg from 1753 to 1771; Michael Haydn, Franz Joseph's younger brother, was the court composer in Salzburg for 44 years starting in 1762.

3   Count Hieronymus von Colloredo was Prince-Archbishop of Salzburg from 1762 until 1803, when the post was secularized and the position of Prince-Archbishop discontinued.

4   Through reference to Jephthah, Hamlet insinuates that Polonius is willing to sacrifice his own daughter, Ophelia, for personal gain.
    Hamlet (to Polonius): O Jephthah, judge of Israel, what a treasure hadst thou!
    Polonius: What treasure had he, my lord? (II, ii, 393-5).

5   The English translation by Lionel Salter has been added to Burgess's introduction, which provides only the Italian text.

6   The Irish-American editor and writer Frank Harris is chiefly remembered for his four-volume memoir *My Life and Loves*, a sexually explicit autobiography recounting Harris's amatory adventures around the world, illustrated with his own drawings and photographs of naked women.

7   Purcell's incidental music to *The Libertine* (1691) includes the song 'Nymphs and Shepherds', with text by Thomas Shadwell. In 1929, the Manchester School Children's Choir sang a choral arrangement of 'Nymphs and Shepherds' with the Hallé Orchestra under the direction of Sir Hamilton Harty, and twelve-year-old John Burgess Wilson may have heard it, or even sung in the chorus, on that occasion. 'Nymphs and Satyrs', a parody of 'Nymphs and Shepherds', is the fourth movement of *The Brides of Enderby*, a setting of six Burgess poems attributed to his fictional poet F. X. Enderby, composed in 1977 as a song cycle for soprano and chamber ensemble of flute, oboe, violoncello, and keyboard. See ACC, pp. 214-22.

8   Burgess replaces 'con' (with) in the original text – *Resti dunque quel birbon / con Proserpina e Pluton* – with 'tra' (between) to support his conception of Don Giovanni spending eternity frustratingly sandwiched between Proserpine and Pluto. (Though wouldn't it be a harsher punishment for Don Giovanni to have Pluto lie between him and Proserpine?) Lionel Salter's unaltered translation (with 'with' and not 'between') has been added.

Romantic Opera and Literary Form by Peter Conrad
Berkeley, CA: University of California Press, 1977

Literature as Opera by Gary Schmidgall
Oxford, New York: Oxford University Press, 1977

Richard Wagner coined for his own works the term 'music-drama,' and Peter Conrad considers it to be an oxymoron. 'My argument is that music and drama are dubious, even antagonistic, partners and that opera's actual literary analogue is the novel.' There is sense in this. In opera, and most especially in Wagnerian opera, there is little room for dramatic action. The actors have to sing, not fight, make love, or indulge in aggressive stichomythia. Arias are single soliloquies, duets, trios and sextets multiple ones. To sing a thing takes longer than to say it, implying a kind of novelistic space for introspection. The orchestra, especially the Wagnerian one, stands for a huge complex of unspoken thought and feeling, often in contradiction to what is being phonated up there on the stage. Freud, though a Viennese, was uneasy about music, since music was close to the id. The novel is the place for the id; the stage is all prancing egos.

Shakespeare was a key figure in that process which turned rococo opera into nineteenth-century music-drama. The romantic composers, from Berlioz to Verdi, saw Shakespeare as a novelist forced, by the cultural and economic circumstances of his time, to work in the theatre. They couldn't rewrite his plays as novels, but they could at least orchestrate them. Boito and Verdi made of *The Merry Wives of Windsor* the enacted novel on Falstaff that Shakespeare wasn't allowed to write. None of us doubt that the opera is superior to the play (as, in a smaller figure, *The Boys from Syracuse* is better than *The Comedy of Errors*).[1] The Boito-Verdi *Falstaff* is no mere rutting buffoon. He is a knight and a soldier. The throbbing complexities of his mental life are all there in the orchestra. A hack job has been turned into a masterpiece.

Mr Conrad believes the culmination of the novelistic introversion of nineteenth-century opera was the symphonic poem. Human voices get in the way of introspection, which must be left wholly to the orchestra. Berlioz, in his *Roméo et Juliette*, indeed uses voices but not for the protagonists. The lovers become orchestral instruments. Eventually Richard Strauss was to claim an unlimited capacity for novelistic mimesis without uttering a word. The whole of Cervantes's novel is in that fifty-minute set of orchestral variations, cello as the Don, viola as Sancho Panza, sheep, windmills, monks, madness all present. It takes a page or so for a novelist to show a character dying. Strauss does it with a single cello glissando.

Literature becomes music. Can music become literature? Mr Conrad shows how both Goethe's and Auden's dissatisfaction with Schikaneder's confused libretto for *The Magic Flute* drove them to the writing of sequels whose intellectual dignity, wit and allegorical consistency should match the genius of Mozart. In other words, the music *suggests* a literature that isn't there. Auden wrote libretti because he saw opera as the last refuge of the high style. It is outside Mr Conrad's thesis to consider how far the reduction of the music-drama to the symphonic poem can be logically followed by the expansion of the symphonic poem into the novel. My own feeling is that the future of the novel may well lie in its willingness to absorb the lessons of symphonic form.

But, as Mr Schmidgall reminds us, 'the study of literature and music is a sadly neglected field.' Professors of literature either hate music or despise it. Their opposite numbers in the music department can at least *read* literature, while they themselves regard a score as so much technical gibberish. As both literature and music use sounds set in forms characterized by such properties as exposition, development, climax, dénouement, it would seem logical to study them together. Few students of *The Waste Land*, to my knowledge, are made to listen to Wagner. Shakespeare scholars are unexcited by the presence of an original six-note theme in a speech by Holofernes in *Love's Labour's Lost*.[2] The ground where the two disciplines meet most amicably (or at least with the appearance of amity) is opera. Mr Schmidgall's book takes operas from Handel to Benjamin Britten and examines the nature of the marriage, or forced yoking, between the two kinds of sound.

There have been a great number of operas based on libretti which had nothing literary about them. When an opera fails to survive it is usually because of a literary, rather than musical, insufficiency. It is not enlightening to examine the texts of *Oberon*, *Semiramide* and *Louise*.[3] Most great operas have a great literary provenance.[4] The question Mr Schmidgall sets himself is: how far can the adaptation to musical form enhance an existing work of literature?

Many will say that there is usually a diminution, rather than an enhancement, of aesthetic effects. We have Thomas Mann's novella, *Death in Venice*, and that's that. Let Visconti put it on the screen, and we have only the picturesque externals. Let Britten set it to music, and the notes get in the way of the words, there is a mere stylisation of the *mise en scene,* at best the lily has gilt on it. The answer might be that words try to do what music alone can – that the non-Aschenbach world of sensuality that Tadzio evokes is pre-verbal; that the cholera that hits Venice is only expressible through the irrationality of organic noise; that Aschenbach's conflicts can be conveyed synchronically in music, but only diachronically in words. What music has and literature does not have is counterpoint. To get it into literature entails the disruptive punning of

Finnegans Wake. Literature can only try to be music; music can enclose literature. This brings us back to the symphonic poem.

Mr Schmidgall regrets that contemporary music is tearing itself away from the word. The avant-gardistes of Beaubourg in Paris want to explore the possibilities of music as sheer sound, to perform a brutal surgical operation on the sphere-born harmonious Siamese twins.[5] And, he says, even with composers who don't despise words, there is no urge to accommodate operatic form to contemporary literature. This tends to confirm the lowbrow's view of opera as a dead scene, full of unreal romantic posturing. But Mr Schmidgall forgets Michael Tippett, as he forgets Hindemith's *News of the Day* and, for that matter, Menotti's *The Consul.* I myself, who have suffered both sonic disciplines, have produced an operatic version of *Ulysses* called *The Blooms of Dublin.* Joyce's novel is unique in having a professional soprano and a near-professional tenor, as well as a host of good amateurs, in its dramatis personae. But nobody wants my *Singspiel.* Opera houses are not yet ready, despite Peter Hall's production of *Moses and Aaron,* for the on-stage blatant prancings of the id.

The Observer, 1978

1   *The Boys from Syracuse,* which premiered on Broadway in 1938, is considered the first musical based on a Shakespeare play. Adapted by librettist George Abbott from *The Comedy of Errors* (based in turn on *The Menaechmi, or the Twin Brothers,* a Roman play by Plautus), it featured music by Richard Rodgers and lyrics by Lorenz Hart, including the hit song 'Falling in Love with Love'.

2   Burgess quotes Wagner in his musical setting of *The Waste Land* and uses Holofernes's six-note solfège theme as the main theme

of the finale of his Third Symphony. See Chapters 44 *Symphony in C* and 45 *How I Wrote My Third Symphony*, and ACC, pp. 185-97, 222-6.

3   Burgess created a radical new adaptation of the libretto of Weber's *Oberon* in 1985 for Scottish Opera. In his version, written in the aftermath of the Iranian Revolution that brought the Ayatollah Khomeini to power in 1979, Burgess replaced Planché's Baghdad with the fictional state of Naraka (representing Iran), with Caliph Harouin Alraschid represented as Harun, the ruler of Naraka. The realm of Charlemagne became the United States with the Franks converted into Americans and Charlemagne, the US President. See *Oberon Old and New* and ACC, pp. 294-7.

4   In 'Operatics', the revised version of this essay published in HQY, the word 'Most' is omitted from the start of this sentence and *Otello, Don Giovanni*, and *Death in Venice* are cited as examples.

5   a reference to the then new Pompidou Centre and IRCAM (Institut de Recherche et Coordination Acoustique/Musique) at Beaubourg, the subject of Burgess's 1977 *New York Times* article 'A $200 million Erector Set'. The 'sphere-born harmonious Siamese twins' are music and literature; see Chapter 15 *Blest Pair of Sirens?*

The Opera Libretto Library
New York: Avenel Books, 1980

I entered literature out of music, and quite by accident. I
wished to write an opera on a fantastic tale I had discovered in
Burton's *Anatomy of Melancholy* (Pt 3, Sec. 2, Mem. I, Subsec.
I – the one about the young man who puts a ring on the finger
of a statue of Venus and finds himself married to the goddess)
and, encouraged by the examples of Wagner, Berlioz and
Tippett, attempted my own libretto. It was far too long, so I
converted it into a play. The play was too long, so I ended up
with a novella.[1] I found that I was no longer a musician but a
writer of fiction.

I have never since tried again to rival Da Ponte or
Hofmannsthal, though Luciano Berio asked me to make
an eight-page libretto which should combine *Il Trovatore,*
Rigoletto and *La Forza del Destino* and yet confine characters
and action to a kind of shelfwork of boxes.[2] The brevity
desired seemed excessive, but Berio was right in implying that
no libretto can be too brief. Mozart suffered agonies from
Metastasio's *Idomeneo,* which was terribly wordy and yet could
not be cut without danger, since Metastasio was the Imperial
Poet.[3]

It is no use, in our own day or just earlier, pointing to
Wagner as a composer who approved long libretti and justified
them in the musical execution. Wagner thought of himself
as a poet (he is, incidentally, the poet most cited in *The Waste*
Land) and wanted his audiences to admire the words as much
as their setting, but there is not one of his operas which would
not benefit by the lopping of about half the text. Here is the
Landgrave in *Tannhäuser*:

Minstrels assembled here, I give you greeting.
Full oft within these walls your lays have sounded;
In veiled wisdom, or in mirthful measures,
They ever gladdened every listening heart.
And though the sword of strife was loosed in battle,
Drawn to maintain our German land secure,
When 'gainst the southern foe we fought and conquered,
And for our country braved the death of heroes,
Unto the harp be equal praise and glory!

And so on, for another twenty lines. All that was needed was something like: 'Welcome, minstrels. You've sung of war. Now sing of love.'

The realization that, in opera, music is doing the real talking, while the words, like the titles of anecdotal paintings, merely specify the subject of the sonic discourse, has come late to librettists, though even non-literary composers have always had a vague idea of what they wanted. Montagu Slater's libretto for *Peter Grimes* is a model of brevity. 'Young prentice come,' sings Grimes. 'Young prentice home.' Wagner would have written something like 'Now that thou, who wouldst learn the skills and agonies of my ancient hard-won craft, art arrived here in this populous town after enduring the rigours of a lengthy journey... .' When Britten's orchestra starts its rumbling, the chorus merely sings 'Storm?'

But Da Ponte knew all the tricks, and too few of his successors saw his greatness. From *Don Giovanni* you can learn two things – good colloquial Italian thoroughly viable today, and the capacity of that naturally prolix language to combine, in the hands of a master, the witty and the eloquent with the laconic. *Don Giovanni* is perhaps, with Verdi's *Falstaff*, the greatest opera we have and it is not just because of the beauty of the music. *Der Rosenkavalier* comes close, but even Hofmannsthal could be self-indulgently expansive. I have just been commissioned by the New York Met to convert *Der Rosenkavalier* into a novella (in my end is my beginning).[4] I thought I would have to expand. I find that mostly I have to contract.

In this curious volume you will find no Hofmannsthal and only the one masterpiece of Da Ponte. It is curious because it is not really a planned unity with a named editor but a mere stitching together of various libretti, in the original with translations, from various printed sources with a large and disconcerting typographical variety. All Wagner is here except *Rienzi*. There are *Faust*, *Fidelio* and *The Magic Flute* but also *Mignon* and *Lakmé*. *Cav* and *Pag* rub shoulders with *La Gioconda* (there's a bad libretto for you) and *Aida*. *Hansel and Gretel*, which has a very reasonable libretto, is here to remind us that Engelbert Humperdinck was no mean pop musician.[5] In practically all instances the English translations are damnable.

Of course, the damnability is partly the result of the translator's having to follow the stresses and durations of the music. I had the task about fifteen years ago of translating Berlioz's *Enfance du Christ* for a Christmas television transmission.[6] This is an oratorio not an opera, but the problems are no different, especially when rendering recitative. The French has *Jésus* with an accent on the second syllable; the English equivalent reverses the stress. What does one do? One changes the notes. This has evidently been done in the English translation of *Pelléas et Mélisande* which has recently earned such praise, and it is thoroughly legitimate.

In practically all of the translations in this volume – all of them hackwork, pre- and sub-sub-sub-Audenian – there is a slavish adherence to the beat of the music though very rarely an understanding of the primary and secondary stress elements in English. Moreover, there is a Wardour Street jargon which rarely fails to be dismally comic.[7] Here is Germont in *La Traviata*:

Some day, when love hath colder grown,
And time's broad gulf yawns wider;
When all the joys of life have flown,
What then will be? Consider!

Fidelio begins with Jacquino singing:

At last, my idol, we are alone,
And can have a pleasant chat together.

Hans Sachs sings after Walther's Trial Song:

Ha! What a flow
Of genius's glow!
My Masters, pray now give o'er!
Listen, when Sachs doth implore!

The way out is not to cling to the original. If the mass has been (mostly atrociously) vernacularized, opera should not, because of the ineptitude of libretto-translators, claim a superior right of exemption. If we go to the opera we have a right to know what is being sung on the stage, and there was never any substance to the argument that English is not a singable language. Not singable, when we have *Dido and Aeneas* and *At the Boar's Head* and *The Rake's Progress?*[8] Auden showed that Mozart's libretti could be translated superbly. The Arts Council or the various British opera trusts could do worse than organise contests for translations of the old warhorses of the repertory. Larkin and Amis would do well (Amis, incidentally, still owes me an opera libretto).[9] Then the curtain would no longer have to go up on either

Blaue Streifen
stiegen im Westen auf

or

Bluish stripes
are stretching along the west.[10]

The Observer, 1981

1   *The Eve of Saint Venus.* See Chapter 43 *A Berliner on Broadway.*

2   See Chapter 3 *Music at the Millennium.*

3   Did Burgess forget that Giambattista Varesco and not Metastasio wrote the libretto for *Idomeneo,* as he had explained ten years earlier in the Cassell Opera Guide? See Chapter 70 *Introduction to* Don Giovanni *and* Idomeneo.

4   Burgess's story adaptation of Hugo von Hofmannsthal's libretto was published in 1982 in *Der Rosenkavalier,* a volume in *The Metropolitan Opera Classics Library* series.

5   Engelbert Humperdinck was a German composer best known for his opera *Hansel and Gretel* (1893). The real name of the pop singer known as Engelbert Humperdinck is Arnold George Dorsey. After a relatively unsuccessful decade in the music industry as Gerry Dorsey, the singer adopted the pseudonym at the prompting of his manager in the mid-1960s, had a #1 hit with 'Release Me' in early 1967 recorded as Engelbert Humperdinck, and performed under that name from then on.

6   See Chapter 46 *A Writer and Music.*

7   Wardour Street English is a term for pseudo-archaic jargon used particularly by writers of historical fiction. Wardour Street in the Soho district of London, now occupied mainly by the

film industry, was once a center for antiquities and reproduction furniture, where unscrupulous dealers attempted to pass off modern imitations as authentic original items. In 1888, the term 'Wardour Street English' was coined by the historian Archibald Ballantyne in an article of that title; in it, he described William Morris's translation of the *Odyssey* as 'not literary English of any date; this is Wardour-Street Early English—a perfectly modern article with a sham appearance of the real antique about it.' H.W. Fowler included a definition of 'Wardour Street' in *A Dictionary of Modern English Usage*, which discourages the use of words such as *anent, aught, ere, howbeit, perchance,* and *thither*, among many others.

8   *At the Boar's Head*, based on Shakespeare's *Henry IV, Part 1* and *Henry IV, Part 2*, incorporates many folk melodies and dance tunes. Gustav Holst wrote the libretto himself and composed the music in 1924, describing the opera as 'A Musical Interlude in One Act'.

9   Philip Larkin and Kingsley Amis, who met as students at Oxford around 1941, became lifelong friends. In his autobiography, Burgess praised Amis as one of the few literary people who cared about sound. YH, p. 82.

10   *Tristan und Isolde*. Act 1, Scene 1.

Prime alla Scala by Eugenio Montale
Milan: Mondadori, 1981

It is not necessary for a poet to know about music, but it helps. If Swinburne had not been tone-deaf, he might have realized that it was not within his province to contrive pure patterns of euphony: there was another art that could quite satisfactorily exploit the allure of sound. Dr Johnson, who got on well enough without a liking for music, encouraged his literary successors to regard it as either noise or angels, but certainly incapable of discoursing sense. The tide turned with Browning. The two great literary productions of 1922, the seminal works of our century (both of which, it may be argued, owe something to Browning) rely heavily on music. There is as much Wagner as Shakespeare in *The Waste Land*, and *Ulysses* showed that the sentence could be an analogue of the musical phrase, the fugue could be imitated, and that the total structure of a novel could learn from sonata form.

James Joyce was a tenor and, had he not been diverted by literature, he might have been a great one. Montale was gifted with a fine baritone voice, and he might have attained professional status with it if his singing master, Ernesto Sivori, had not died untimely. He remained a musician and, between 1954 and 1967, contributed regular very well-informed articles on opera to the *Corriere d'Informazione*. There are certain ignoramuses who assume that to be Italian is to be musical anyway. To these it must be said that there is no such a thing as an Italian. There are, for instance, Neapolitans, who assume, as black drummers with rhythm, that they are naturally endowed with the singing gift, and there are Romans, who make no such claim. Italy is probably less musical than England, and audiences at La Scala, Milan, are regrettably limited in their operatic tastes. If opera, which does not include Wagnerian music drama, is the national art, it is because southern Italian life is operatic. That Montale, in this collected volume of his musical writings, is nearly always at the opera, and not listening to symphonies or quartets, must not, however, be ascribed to the limitations of Italian musicality: as a singer and poet, he was naturally interested in a form which uses words to a musical end.

It is the regular Scala repertoire that Montale usually witnesses, along with such comparative novelties as the *Abu Hassan* of Weber, *Il Convitato di Pietra* of Dargomyzhsky and Bellini's *Il Pirata*. When an opera is so neglected that a performance becomes a novelty, the fault usually lies in the words.[1] Of the Bellini work he says: 'Romani's execrable libretto... seems to have touched the imagination of the composer only in respect of the part of Imogene... the other characters are respectively a baritone and a bass, not a couple of living personages.'[2] Montale admits that the libretto of Verdi's *Nabucco* is incomprehensible, but he finds a primordial power in the music.[3] In an article called *'Parole in musica'* he faces up to the problem of the composer's poetic taste, often severely lacking, admitting the mystery of expressive excellence surviving critical rejection of the words set. 'The truth of the matter is that genuine poetry already contains its own music and will not tolerate any other;' it is poetic intention, realized through the musical setting, that comes through despite the banality of the words.[4] Verdi is one of those who *'si contentano della situazione espressa in parole'* – not the *parole* themselves.[5]

As befits a potential Nobel prize-winner already internationally acclaimed, Montale discloses an international musical, and literary, appetite.[6] He praises George Gershwin, suggesting that if ever the United States should produce a genuine national operatic tradition, that same Jacob Gershovitz must be seen as *'il Glinka, l'iniziatore'.*[7] The libretto of *The Rake's Progress* fascinates him, but, before the triumphant première at the Fenice in Venice, he doubts whether its diversity of styles – ranging from *Il Mikado* of Sullivan to *La Terra Desolata* of Eliot – can be matched musically even by Igor Stravinsky.[8] At the performance – at which the composer-conductor bounces like a *'burattino di gomma'* and has a look of Benedetto Croce doubled over an ancient codex – the libretto seems to lose much of its modernist savour but gains in stylistic coherence.[9] Then he wonders if it is less a matter of style than of technique – entities which Stravinsky likes to confound.

Montale is sympathetic to Walton's *Troilo e Cressida,* but finds the music basically insular, Latin only in its aspirations.[10] He sees Britten's *Giro di Vite* or *Turn of the Screw* at Venice and finds its *'atmosfera viziata'* not far distant from that of Graham Greene (he is always ready with a surprising analogue: Gershwin's *An American in Paris* suggests Hemingway's *Fiesta* to him), though he surmises Britten to be not a Catholic but a *'cristiano-pagano* trouble', an artist who needs to fish in dirty waters.[11]

Montale writes a graceful journalistic prose unsullied by musical technicalities. He is not comparable with 'Corno di Bassetto' in that he lacks the daring to anathematize the mediocre and is a little too ready to be pleased.[12] He dutifully, against the grain one would think, accepts Wagner but finds few Italian voices able to cope with him. He is urbane, catholic, a delight to read, and it is to be hoped that this exhaustive collective of his *ritratti* will soon find an English translator.[13] Apart from the distinction of its author, the book is an admirable guide to the whole operatic repertory.

Times Literary Supplement, 1982

1   Cf. Chapter 71 *The Music is the Message.*

2   *'Del cattivo libretto del Romani solo il canto bianco di Imogene sembra aver toccato il cuore del musicista; gli altri personaggi [– il duca Ernesto, partigiano delgi Angiò, e Gualtiero, partigiano del re Manfredi e ora capo di pirati aragonesi –] sono rispettivamente un baritono e un basso, non due figure vive.'* p. 259.

3   p. 261.

4   *'la verità è che la parola veramente poetica contiene già la propria musica e non ne tollera un'altra.'* p. 24.

5   'are satisfied with the situation expressed in words'. p. 24.

6   Potential? The Nobel Prize for Literature was awarded to Eugenio Montale in 1975, six years before this book was published.

7   'The Glinka, the founder', p. 439. Mikhail Glinka, the composer of *A Life for the Tsar* and *Ruslan and Lyudmila*, is considered the father of Russian classical music and opera.

8   *'Quale musica potrà sottolineare versi che saltano dallo stile del* Mikado *di Sullivan al monologo di Baba la Turca arieggiante certi pezzi della* Terra desolata *di Eliot?'* p. 32. 'What music could possibly suit verses that jump from the style of Sullivan's *Mikado* to Baba the Turk's monologue expressing certain aspects of *The Waste Land* of Eliot?'

9   *burattino di gomma* means 'rubber puppet'; Benedetto Croce was an Italian philosopher, historian, and politician who opposed Mussolini and Italian fascism and, after World War II, helped restore democracy in Italy. *'Stravinskij è stato tirato alla ribalta dove rimbalzava come un burattino di gomma. Quando dirige, indaffarato e assente, con largo gesto impreciso, sembra Benedetto Croce curvo su un vecchio codice…Il libretto di Auden attraverso il suo filtro ha perduto molti dei suoi sapori moderni ma ha acquistato in compattezza di stile. Stile o tecnica? Un uomo come Stravinskij che fa una non lieve confusione tra forma e tecnica e distingue assurdamente tra opera in musica e dramma musicale (venerando l'una e scorbacchiando l'altro) non poteva approdare a un diverso risultato.'* p.

35. 'Stravinsky was drawn into the limelight where he bounced like a rubber puppet. When he conducts, busy and absent, with large imprecise gestures, he looks like Benedetto Croce bent over an old codex...Through his filter, Auden's libretto seems to lose much of its modern flavor but gains in stylistic coherence. Style or technique? A man like Stravinsky, who confounds form and technique, and distinguishes absurdly between opera in music and musical drama (venerating one and dismissing the other), could not arrive at a different result.'

10 pp. 176-9.

11 *atmosfera viziata* means 'spoiled atmosphere' (60); *'ecco* Un americano a Parigi *che è un poco la* Fiesta *(Hemingway) di Gershwin'*, p. 441; *'Ma Britten, per quel che ne sappiamo, non è un cattolico: è semplicemente un cristiano-pagano* trouble, *un artista che ha bisogno di pescare nel torbido: e stavolta l'argomento lo ha magnificamente servito.'* p. 61. 'But Britten, as far as we know, is not a Catholic: he is simply a troubled Christian-pagan, an artist who needs to fish in turbid waters: and this time the subject has served him magnificently.'

12 'Corno di Bassetto' was George Bernard Shaw's pseudonym as a music critic. See Chapter 10 *Tuned to the Future.*

13 *ritratti* means 'reviews'. The book has never been translated into English.

74. A LIBRETTIST'S LAMENT

I have deliberately kept away from the English National Opera's new version of *Carmen*.[1] This is not because of forewarnings about its locale having been changed from nineteenth-century Seville to contemporary Acapulco, or wherever it is, and Micaela being converted into Don José's mother. It is because of fears about what has probably been done to my translation of the libretto.

One newspaper notice has praised me for lines I never wrote; others have imputed to my version duff rhymes and impossible accentuations. I cunningly published the script as written to coincide with the premiere, so that opera critics and even ordinary operagoers might have a chance to compare – or, it seems, contrast – what they actually hear with what I wanted them to hear.[2] I guessed beforehand that both the director and the singers would howl about unsingability, unactability and over-literariness. This sort of thing always happens. The question arises, and not for the first time – has the author any right to protect what he writes, or has he to regard his script as the mere raw material for directorial processing?

My primary trade is that of novelist, and what gets to the reader has always been, with absolutely no exceptions, precisely what I wanted to get to him. Publisher's editors may have desired to display their own creative talent – thwarted in the sphere of total artistic creation – by introducing change for the sheer sake of change, but one is always able to resist this. Stage and film are a different thing altogether.

Earlier this year my name was attached as chief scenarist to a television biblical epic called *A.D.*[3] The *Observer's* anonymous TV prospectist dismissed the dialogue as vapid, and an *Observer* reader gleefully picked on this to demolish my pretensions to literary competence. But the text so disparaged was not mine: it was what had been made out of mine by producer, director, actors and, for all I know, somebody in the cutting room with a gift for mimicry.

I worked myself in the cutting room throughout a sweltering Roman summer on the editorial stages of another biblical epic called *Moses the Lawgiver*.[4] It was only my own talent for mimicry that prevented Anthony Quayle, who played Aaron, from declaiming to the Israelites: 'God has chosen people like you and I.' It also stopped Burt Lancaster as Moses from substituting deplorable Americanisms for the staid patriarchal idioms I gave to him. Between the creative spasm and the cinematic act falls the shadow. Critics ought to know this.

What should the scenarist do when he discovers, as in the *Jesus of Nazareth* I also wrote with the dangerous assistance of Zeffirelli, that a minor character is talking of 'fake messiahs' or muttering 'That figures, I guess'?[5] It is too late to withdraw his material. The prospect of such withdrawal hovered when the premiere of the new *Carmen* drew near and my eyes misted over the inept changes that had been made in a laboriously worked over text. One weakens; one lets things go through because of the cognate claims of time and money. One looks for the possibility of a major general row in the whole field of directorial accountability which will possibly restore to the author the rights he believes he once traditionally had.

I do not think he ever really had them. I am fairly sure that that endless First Player's speech about the fall of Troy got into *Hamlet* because Richard Burbage cut it out of *Troilus and Cressida* (which never seems to have been produced, anyway). I have a feeling that the 'bad' quarto of *Hamlet* was what the Globe audiences actually heard, forcing Shakespeare to publish what he actually wrote. The pigheadedness of directors probably goes back a long way. There was a brief period in the history of Hollywood when they were subordinated to the writer and the producer ('First five pages in the can by noon or you're fired'). But now they are all *auteurs*, meaning lordly editors of their betters.

I don't think that this situation applies in the field of performed music. Conductors may be composers *manqués*, and they can and often do ride roughshod over the work of dead composers, especially when confronted with different versions of the same work. But in dealing with living composers they do little more than demand adjustments of tempo or dynamics. The rewriting of a page or so of full orchestral score is not really enforceable on the composer (too much work), and it is usually beyond the powers of the conductor. But with words it is different. Anybody can write, and everybody thinks he can write better than anybody else. *Hinc*, as one writer put it, *illae lachrimae*.[6] Perhaps everything should be put on in Latin, which few stage directors and, among film directors, only Joseph L. Mankiewicz and George Roy Hill seem to know.[7]

The New York Times, 1986

1   The English National Opera production opened on 27 November 1986 following the Scottish Opera premiere in Glasgow that September.

2   *Carmen: An Opera in Four Acts* – Translated into English by Anthony Burgess (London: Hutchinson, 1986).

3   *A.D. (Anno Domini)* was a nine-hour, five-part television miniseries about the birth of Christianity following Jesus's crucifixion. It aired in 1986 and was the last of Burgess's Biblical collaborations with producer Vincenzo Labella, preceded by *Moses the Lawgiver* and *Jesus of Nazareth*. Burgess composed approximately 40 minutes of music for *A.D.*, which, although not used in the series, provided themes for two later compositions:

Mr Burgess's Almanack, completed on 24 February 1987 (the eve of his seventieth birthday) and Sonata No. 2 for G.B.R. (great bass recorder), composed in 1992.

4   In 1972, Burgess wrote the verse novel *Moses: A Narrative* from which he crafted scripts for the television miniseries *Moses the Lawgiver*, which was filmed in Italy and Israel during the 'sweltering Roman summer' of 1973. The six-hour-long series aired in 1975.

5   Burgess completed the script for *Jesus of Nazareth* in 1974. The series, which was six and a half hours long, premiered in Europe on 3 April 1977 and was broadcast in the US the following year.

6   Hence those tears. From Terence, *Andria*, line 125. Originally literal, referring to the tears shed by Pamphilus at the funeral of Chrysis, it came to be used proverbially in the works of later authors, such as Horace (Epistula XIX, 41).

7   Joseph L. Mankiewicz was an American film director, screenwriter, and producer who won Academy Awards for both Best Director and Best Adapted Screenplay for two films in successive years: *A Letter to Three Wives* (1949) and *All About Eve* (1950). He was going to direct the Shakespeare film *Will!* for which Burgess wrote the script and composed the score in 1968, but Warner Brothers-Seven Arts studio canceled the project the following year. Burgess met the American film director George Roy Hill, best known for *Butch Cassidy and the Sundance Kid* (1969) and *The Sting* (1973), when they served together on the jury of the 1975 Cannes Film Festival.

Essays on Opera by Winton Dean
Oxford: Clarendon Press, 1990

As we have to start somewhere, let it be with the influence of
the British Isles on European opera. Naturally, this influence
has never been musical; except during the Middle Ages,
British music has not even minimally agitated the cilia of
the Continental ear, unless Handel be considered British. He
was, of course, though those damned foreigners continue to
deny this by spelling his name as Händel or Haendel or (in
Russia) Gendel. No, the influence has been wholly literary.
'One cause of this,' says Winton Dean, 'was the popularity of
Scott's novels; another was the discovery of Queen Elizabeth
I as a born coloratura soprano.'

Dean gives us an absorbing essay on Donizetti's devotion
to our great monarch, though unexpressed titularly as with
Rossini's *Elisabetta, regina d'Inghilterra* or Michele Enrico
Francesco Vincenzo Aloisio Paolo Carafa di Colbrano's
Elisabetta in Derbyshire. The fifty-first Donizetti opera was
Roberto Devereux in which the eponym (known here as the
Earl of Essex) is condemned to death but reprieved too late by
the queen who, in anger and frustration, abdicates in favour of
James VI of Scotland.

In 1964, to celebrate Shakespeare's quatercentenary, Dean
considers at length the operatisation of Elizabeth's greatest
subject. Who now knows, except for Mr Dean, of Caruso's
or Andreozzi's or Mercadante's or Buzzolla's or Zanardini's
or Moroni's or Faccio's *Amleto*, of Cagnoni's or Ghislanzoni's
or Frazzi's *Re Lear?* His particular conclusion is not just that
Shakespeare is inoperable – the exceptions are to be taken for
granted, and we are given a superb essay on Verdi's *Otello*, of

which the librettist Boito is the true hero – but that the history of opera is a morass of ghastly adaptations of promising plots and of even more unpromising ones.

Take Weber's *Euryanthe,* whose librettist was Helmine von Chézy, 'a middle-aged lady of letters; her only other contribution to history was the play for which Schubert wrote his *Rosamunde* music and whose loss it is difficult to deplore'. Her ineptitude has rendered some ravishing music dumb, as has Planché's equally abysmal *Oberon.* My own attempt to save this masterly score through the devising of a fresh libretto seems, after performances in Glasgow, Oxford and Venice, to have forfeited its chance to demonstrate Weber's vocal and dramatic genius.[1] The audience at the Fenice objected to an aeroplane's crashing onto the stage in the first act. Opera retains its conservative aspects. Italy, mother of opera, said no to Burgess-Weber.

Dean's raising of dust in the archives, his reading of scores unlikely to be realised in external sound, makes us realise how many operas have been written and how comparatively small the surviving repertory is. And how important such rarities as Da Ponte and Boito are. He is an expert on Handel and Bizet, and his long and brilliant essay on the latter's *Ivan IV* shows us how even Bizet's exceptional dramatic talent could not overcome the deficiencies of a mediocre libretto. As for *Carmen,* whose book is perfect, another essay asks the perennial question: what and where is the authentic version? This question drove me mad when I attempted a new translation for the ENO. Operas are not solid like symphonies; they are overfluid, subject to daily addition, excision, key-change. They have to be tinkered with, and this is like repairing an aircraft already on its journey.

Dean's collection, which covers nearly forty years, is musicology at its finest. Musicology is not music criticism: it addresses aesthetic questions only as aspects of factual research. It goes further than musical history in stopping clocks and examining spatial minutiae. It also consults the larger history in which the smaller is enclosed. Haydn wrote an opera, *Orfeo*, in 1791 for London presentation (the libretto, not exceptionally, was an 'amateurish muddle'). George III and the Prince of Wales were at loggerheads even in matters of artistic patronage; the Prince sponsored Haydn but the King withdrew the performing licence. We seem, as so often, to have been denied some glorious music because of a failure of enstaging which might have put the libretto right.

Musicology puts history right in the sense that it peers into gutters unilluminated by lamp posts. Beethoven's *Fidelio* is a shining light, but what do we know of Méhul or whole school of Cherubini which fuelled it? What, for that matter, do we know of the operatic ambitions of Beethoven, who did not wish solely to be the father of *Fidelio* but was ready to tackle any decent libretto. He played the viola in his youth in opera house orchestras; he saw *The Magic Flute* from the pit. Beethoven as operatic composer *manqué*. Discuss.

The book ranges from an excruciatingly specialist study of Handel's early copyists in London, complete with copious music-type illustrations and the magnifying glass poised above clef calligraphy, to a very human celebration of what musicology is about in a centennial tribute to Edward J. Dent. Dent was the first musicologist to transcend British notice and achieve international standing. He was a monument of prejudice, but prejudice is often the road to specialisation. He execrated Elgar as a heterosexual Catholic who aped the country squire. 'He detected the meretricious element in Puccini, but failed to detect anything else!' He wrote the first and perhaps still the best book on Scarlatti, and he killed the myth of Mozart as the periwigged sugar-sucker. In him we see the essential musicologist – too prejudiced and specialised to pen objective histories, too honest for the wine-tasting metaphors of the concert reviewer, above all concerned with good writing. Dean inherits the stylistic excellence which Dent initiated. We can only guess at his prejudices, but we are grateful for his specialisations.

The Observer, 1991

1   The Scottish Opera production opened in Glasgow on 23 October 1985 to mainly negative reviews. Hutchinson published *Oberon Old and New*, Burgess's contemporary adaptation paired with Planché's original libretto, the following day. See Chapter 71 *The Music is the Message*.

1. The Writer and Music

This early piece provides one of the first examples of Burgess's credo that novelists would benefit from knowledge of musical structure, such as sonata form, rondo, and fugue. He continued to advocate this belief in books that include *The Novel Now, The End of the World News* and *This Man and Music*, and put theory into practice in *A Clockwork Orange, Tremor of Intent, Nothing Like the Sun, Napoleon Symphony* and *Mozart and the Wolf Gang*.

2. Shakespeare in Music

The year 1964 marked the 400th anniversary of William Shakespeare's birth, which Burgess celebrated with the publication of a fictional biography written in faux Elizabethan style. Deriving its title from Sonnet 130, *Nothing Like the Sun: A Story of Shakespeare's Love-life* is structured in two parts, each consisting of ten chapters, with those in the second part exactly twice as long as the analogous chapters in the first part, like a set of musical variations with repeats. That quatercentennial year also produced this review, in which Burgess mourns the dissolution of the Elizabethan Age, when all of the arts were connected as a kind of 'continent', into separate artistic 'islands' of music, literature, and painting. Years later, Burgess would renew his praise of Winton Dean's writing on Shakespeare and Opera in his 1991 review of Dean's *Essays on Opera* (see Chapter 75 *Coloratura Work Amid the Archive*).

3. Music at the Millennium

For *High Fidelity*'s May 1976 'Twenty-Fifth Anniversary Issue, Part II: 25 Years Hence', titled '2001: Music and Audio of the Future', the magazine commissioned essays by eight writers, Burgess among them. Other contributors included Isaac Asimov, whose short story 'Marchin' In' shows how laser technology might be combined one day with musical inspiration in the service of medicine, and Mark F. Davis, an electrical engineer at MIT working in psychoacoustics, who, in 'Mahler in a Hangar', hypothesized about developments in directional recording and playback systems. In 'A Console for Would-Be Conductors', Ivan Berger presciently described a high-fidelity audio system that would follow the gestures of a 'phonograph conductor'; virtual reality conducting applications as envisioned by Berger first became available to the public around 2014. This essay, sans musical examples, was reprinted by *The Washington Post* on 16 May 1976.

4. Punk

On 30 June 1977, an op-ed by columnist William Safire in *The New York Times* attributed the origins of punk to a famous book by a certain British novelist:

> The godfather of punk is England's Anthony Burgess, author of *A Clockwork Orange*, a novel and movie of a few years ago that satirized our love of violence by portraying a future society run by goons. Their violent-looking clothes and makeup are the guiding spirit of punk.
>
> 'Horror show' was the goons' favorite adjective, meaning terrific. Most of us thought the irony lay in equating horror with good, but author Burgess, who is also an eminent linguist, had something deeper in mind: 'horror show' was a play on 'horosho', the expression for 'good' in the Soviet Union.
>
> Only a word play? Perhaps, but the brief and meteoric emergence of punk is rooted in a satiric reminder of the potential for brutality that lurks in every one of us.

Titled 'Punk's "Horror Show"', the column prompted Burgess to refute Safire's accusation in several writings disparaging punk and its practitioners. This essay was published in December 1977 as 'Punk Paradox' in *The Daily Mail* and 'Punk: The snarl of the underdog' in *The Sydney Morning Herald*.

5. Why Punk *Had* to End in Evil

This piece is remarkably prescient in its predictions that the self-destructive phenomenon of punk would lead to death and that a new pope would speak out forcefully against political oppression. Less than four months later, Sid Vicious, who had just been arrested for the murder of his girlfriend, died of a drug overdose. Karol Józef Wojtyła, who became Pope John Paul II one week prior to publication of this article, played a significant role in the fall of Communism in his native Poland and other Eastern European nations. As for Burgess's assertion that Jane Austen's novels remind us that pastoral life can be happy and productive, who could argue with that? A later article on the perils of punk and new wave, 'The Killing of Boy George' (*The Daily Mail*, 4 July 1986), so incensed its subject that Boy George scornfully quoted this 'scathing piece' in his 1995 autobiography *Take It Like a Man*.

6. Musical Autodidact

Burgess himself did not set out to be an autodidact. As he recounts in *Little Wilson and Big God*, he applied to the Royal College of Music to study composition but failed the entrance examination administered by Herbert Howells. Thenceforth Burgess took pride in being self-taught in music – 'Find middle C and you have found everything' – and was drawn to others who were. Occasionally, this fervor led Burgess astray, as when he claimed that Richard Wagner and Charles Ives were also musical autodidacts – they weren't – but in the case of Sir George Grove, the label was warranted.

7. A Mystery and its Monument

The daunting task of reviewing a twenty-volume dictionary of music containing over twenty-two million words is here dispatched with the utmost professionalism. Burgess examines the articles on major composers – Mozart, Beethoven, Rossini, Verdi, Wagner – along with the entries on Opera, Atonality, Twelve-note composition, Film music, and more. Minor British composers are well represented as are such literary music critics as Samuel Butler, George Bernard Shaw, and Ezra Pound. Burgess's interest in the Harmonica leads him to search for Tommy Reilly and Larry Adler, who have entries in *The New Grove*, and John Sebastian, who, to Burgess's dismay, does not. (See Chapters 67 *Hand to Mouth* and 68 *John Sebastian – A Personal Reminiscence*.)

A similar but shorter unpublished review by Burgess, titled 'The New Grove' and not included in this volume, covers much the same ground at just over one-third the length of this essay. Judging by a handwritten note on the typescript, it seems to have been intended for publication in France.

8. Turning the Handle

On 23 November 1980, the lead item in the 'Bookworld' section of the *Chicago Tribune* was a lengthy review of *Earthly Powers*. Accompanying the review was a profile of Burgess by Helen Dudar titled 'A novelist at home with papal politics and hurdy-gurdy', which ended with a description of Burgess's 'compulsive…need to keep working – serious writing in the morning, journalism in the afternoon', which was 'so intense… that in the old days he used to agree to take assignments without pay.'

> 'I'll do anything, anything,' he says. 'It's a great pride of mine never to reject any book for review. It keeps your brain alert.' Just the other day, he reported, a British

newspaper had sent him a history of the hurdy-gurdy, an instrument about which he was entirely ignorant but which he was more than happy to discuss in print.

This is that review, originally published in the *Times Literary Supplement* on 20 February 1981.

9. The Well-Tempered Revolution

The Lives of the Piano is an abundantly illustrated, 215-page coffee table book comprising writings by a varied array of British and American writers. 'The Well-Tempered Revolution', the first and longest of the book's eight chapters, traces the piano's development from the harpsichord to electronic keyboards equipped with 'ready-made chords and bongo drums activable at the touch of a switch.' Other chapters in *The Lives of the Piano* include Ned Rorem's 'Beyond Playing: A Composer's Life with the Piano', William Bolcom's 'Song and Dance: The American Way of Pianism', and Samuel Lipman's 'The Ordeal of Growth: Confessions of a Former Prodigy'.

10. Tuned to the Future

Burgess finds much to admire in Shaw's writings about music – his 'faultless' taste, embrace of Impressionism, enthusiasm for contemporary music and music of the future, and disinterest in dull Victorian cantatas and oratorios in favor of Wagner. Following Shaw's use of *The Ring* as a model for *Back to Methuselah*, Burgess based his novel *The Worm and the Ring* on Wagner's tetralogy. Shaw's enthusiasm for Wagner is the main focus of Burgess's other review of *Shaw's Music* (not included in this volume), one that was published in *Corriere della Sera* on 18 July 1981 as *'L'amore di Shaw per Wagner'* ('Shaw's love for Wagner') and reprinted in *One Man's Chorus* as 'Shaw as Musician'.

11. The Ruination of Music

As Burgess mourned the dissolution of the Elizabethan Age in his review of *Shakespeare in Music*, in this essay he bemoans the demise of Mozartian Classical music and what it represented in eighteenth-century society. Titled 'The Ruination of Music' in the typescript, it was published in *The Times* as 'The day the music died', a reference to Don McLean's 1971 hit song 'American Pie' about the plane crash on 3 February 1959 that killed Buddy Holly, effectively ending the early rock and roll era. Given Burgess's derision of popular music as 'a moronic sub-art', one can imagine his displeasure at the title chosen by *The Times*, which illustrated the article with four photos, arranged in a square, captioned: 'from top left: Wagner, impure; Mozart, glorious; Mahler, banal; Schoenberg, neurotic'. The article outraged Hans Keller, the Austrian-born British music journalist and musicologist, who accused Burgess of 'musical incompetence and incomprehension as well as sheer ignorance' in a Letter to the Editor written the day after this essay was published, intensifying a feud that would soon escalate when Burgess's *Blooms of Dublin* premiered on BBC Radio 3 five weeks later.

12. Food and Music

Following the same intrepid impulse that had led him to review a book on the hurdy-gurdy, Burgess accepted the challenge of writing an essay on food and music for *Cuisine Magazine*. Musical works associated with food are actually rather plentiful and one wonders why Burgess left out *Der Wein*, *The Love for Three Oranges*, *La Bonne Cuisine*, and *Belshazzar's Feast*, to name a few. This whimsical topic prompted Burgess, inspired by Richard Strauss's banquet scene in *Le Bourgeois Gentilhomme*, to conjure an ingenious blend of music, food, and evolution presenting 'a recapitulation of the world's history.'

13. The Mystery of Melody

This rumination on melody was written for *The Courier*, a periodical founded in 1948 by UNESCO (The United Nations Educational, Scientific and Cultural Organization) that, by 1986, was distributed internationally in 32 different languages. The April 1986 issue, 'Music on the Move', also included articles by Miguel Angel Estrella ('Music for all'), Lamine Konte ('The Griot: singer and chronicler of African life'), Daniel Viglietti ('Nueva canción: Latin America's song without frontiers'), and Iannis Xenakis ('Science and music, an interview with Iannis Xenakis').

14. Introduction to *Pianoforte: A Social History of the Piano*

This essay's emphasis on the Germanic aspect of the piano's history, especially as related to Romanticism, reflects the nationality of the book's author, Dieter Hildebrandt, and the language of the original edition, published by Hanser Verlag in 1985 as *Pianoforte: Der Roman des Klaviers*. The German edition did not include this introduction, which Burgess wrote in 1988 for the English version, translated by Harriet Goodman and published that year in the UK by Hutchinson and in the US by George Braziller. Hildebrandt, born in Berlin in 1932, is also the author of a biography of Graham Greene and books on Schiller and Beethoven.

15. Blest Pair of Sirens?

In this article for *The Listener*, also published in *Corriere della Sera* as *'Parole e note sono come sirene'* (Words and notes are like sirens), Burgess offers commentary on the compositions programmed at the 1988 Proms, emphasizing those works inspired by literary models. 'Blest Pair of Sirens', a phrase borrowed from Milton, had long been a term favoured by Burgess for comparisons of music and literature. He used it for the series of four T.S. Eliot Memorial Lectures that he delivered at the University of Kent from 28 April to 1 May 1980, in which he discussed the bonds between these complementary arts. For a second series of lectures – the John Crowe Ransom Memorial Lectures at Kenyon College from 13 to 17 October 1980 – Burgess converted the title of the Eliot Lectures, 'Blest Pair of Sirens: Thoughts on Music and Literature', into 'Disharmonious Sisters: Observations on Literature and Music' to emphasize points of dissimilarity between the sororal subjects. Burgess and his literary agent Gabriele Pantucci planned to publish revised versions of these lectures, along with other writings, in a book to have been titled *Blest Pair of Sirens,* but prudently decided instead on *This Man and Music* to avoid possible legal action by Faber and Faber, which maintained that it held the right to publish the original T.S. Eliot Memorial Lectures as *Blest Pair of Sirens* under its agreement. Having endowed the lectures, Faber had a strong case, but once *This Man and Music* was published in 1982, Faber let the matter rest, neither disputing the right of Burgess to publish revised versions of the Eliot Lectures nor publishing the original ones.

16. The Devil Prefers Mozart

When the Archbishop of New York denounced heavy metal as the Devil's means of invading its listeners' souls, Burgess weighed in with his own reasons to abhor this music – its infantile substance, its 'watery neutrality', and, above all, its brutally loud volume. He equates the danger of rock with that of chauvinistic music by composers such as Wagner and Elgar able to motivate ominous nationalistic tendencies. Alluding to *A Clockwork Orange* and its violent protagonist Alex, Burgess wrote, 'Play the scherzo of Beethoven's Ninth at an excessive volume and you will equally promote mindless aggression', ultimately avowing that Satan is too sophisticated for music as 'puerile' as heavy metal. Alex loves Beethoven, but the Devil prefers Mozart.

17. Beatlemania
This essay was commissioned for a special feature in the cultural pages of *Corriere della Sera* titled *'Beatles: trent'anni, ma sembra yesterday'* (Beatles: thirty years, but it seems like yesterday). The spread in *'Corriere Cultura'* included Burgess's contribution, translated into Italian by Laura Ferrari as *'Quattro ragazzi in band e una leggenda'* (Four guys in a band and one legend), along with three articles by Italian writers. From his Mancunian perspective, Burgess considers that the 'true significance' of the 'young men from Liverpool' might be their 'provincial assertiveness'; through their overwhelming success, they 'disputed London's claim to be the arbiter of thought, manners and morals.' His assessment of their musical importance is more equivocal. While acknowledging the group's 'considerable though untrained' musical talent and regarding 'sincere' songs like 'Eleanor Rigby' and 'She's Leaving Home', which are 'about suffering and bewildered members of the Liverpool working class', as their best, he denigrates the contributions of Ringo Starr, faults the Beatles for 'pretentiousness' while claiming that America exaggerated their significance, and, in his most derisible comment, asserts that 'The Beatles were not enough of musicians to sustain a genuine career in the art'. This would come as news to Paul and Ringo, who continue to sell out stadiums more than thirty years after this essay was published.

18. Pearls Before Swine
Music thrived in Elizabethan England thanks to the talent of such great composers as Thomas Tallis, William Byrd, John Dowland and Orlando Gibbons. But while their music was 'remarkable', the new style of music that Claudio Monteverdi

was composing in Mantua, Parma, and Venice, where he served as Director of Music at St Mark's Basilica, was 'revolutionary'. Yet, as these letters show, Monteverdi's stature as one of the most innovative composers in the history of Western music did not shield him from the indignity of having to beg clergy and noblemen for backing and benevolence, especially concerning his son Massimiliano, who was imprisoned for reading banned books.

19. Handel, not Händel – A Tricentennial Tribute
Music lovers revere 1685 as the birthyear of three towering composers: Johann Sebastian Bach, George Frideric Handel, and Domenico Scarlatti – two German giants and the Italian maestro of the keyboard sonata. Burgess commemorated Bach's *Well-Tempered Clavier* by composing his own set of twenty-four preludes and fugues in all of the major and minor keys, written at breakneck speed in November-December 1985 and flippantly titled *The Bad-Tempered Electronic Keyboard*. While he did not pen any known encomia to Scarlatti, Burgess celebrated Handel's tercentenary with this essay for *Corriere della Sera*, which published it as *'Seduceva le platee con gli effetti speciali'* (He seduced his audience with special effects) on 22 February 1985, the eve of Handel's birthday.

20. Handel Homage
This review of three recent books on Handel, also timed to celebrate the tercentennial, blends rather pithy comments about the books with more copious general remarks about the composer. Apart from noting its 'admirable illustrations', Burgess provides little information about *Handel and his world* by H. C. Robbins Landon, better known for his Haydn expertise than his Handel scholarship. He succinctly sums up Christopher Hogwood's monograph as 'the work of a man who has conducted Handel and been especially acclaimed for

his interpretations of *Messiah* and barely mentions Jonathan Keates, who went on to produce fourteen of his twenty-two books after this review appeared, including a book on *Messiah* published in 2016.

21. Good Gluck
This bicentennial commemoration highlights Christoph Willibald Gluck's importance to the history and development of music. By the mid-eighteenth century, opera seria and opera buffa, the principal Italian operatic genres of the time, had grown stale. Formulaic stage productions based on stilted libretti were predictable and tediously long, with obligatory ballet sequences that had become gratuitous. Glorification of the castrato and emphasis on florid solo singing above all else, especially in lengthy da capo arias, had stultified any sense of drama. As opera drifted further and further away from its origin as a dramatic art form focused on human passions and emotions, reform was desperately needed. The person who accomplished this was Gluck, whose 1862 opera *Orfeo ed Euridice*, based on a libretto by Calzabigi, demonstrated the path forward. With *Orfeo, Iphigénie en Aulide* and *Alceste*, Gluck forged a new style subsequently taken up by Haydn, Mozart, Beethoven, Weber, Schubert, Berlioz and Wagner, all of whom revered him and benefited from this new way of portraying real human drama through singing.

22. A Professional Music-Maker Beloved of God
Beginning in 1987, essays by Burgess appeared regularly in the pages of *The Independent*, with the elevated designation 'The Anthony Burgess Review' attached to the last sixty or so, published from February 1990 through May 1993. Of his nearly ninety writings for *The Independent*, seven are on musical subjects, including essays on Ivor Gurney, Alfred Brendel, Daniel Barenboim, Lerner and Loewe, and celebrated

conductors of the twentieth century. This Mozart essay from 1990 is representative of these writings, both in length (ca. 1300 words) and tone: Burgess's trademark combination of erudition, wit, and linguistic virtuosity often served up with an exaggerated certainty of expression. While the style is frequently entertaining, its provocative quality, deliberately distanced from scholarly prose, can be taken too far. While it may be true that Mozart often composed a kind of eighteenth-century *Gebrauchsmusik,* to disregard the sublime beauty of his many masterpieces feels churlish. And is it true that 'nothing was produced except on commission or for his own needs as a professional'? No entirely convincing reason has yet been presented to explain why Mozart, in the summer of 1788 during a bleak period of professional stagnation and financial despair, composed the miraculous trio of symphonies now known as No. 39 in E-flat, the great G Minor (No. 40), and the 'Jupiter' (No. 41) with neither a commission nor tangible prospects for performance as motivation.

In 1991, Burgess would go on to publish a 'bicentennial assessment' in *The Sunday Telegraph* titled 'The Magic of Mozart' and *Mozart and the Wolf Gang*, a highly original and idiosyncratic celebration in book form of the musical genius of Salzburg.

23. Notes from the Deep

The monographs by Maynard Solomon on Mozart, Beethoven, and Schubert are characterized by the application of Freudian and post-Freudian psychological interpretation to his biographical subjects, a relatively new approach in musicology at the time. Unlike most authors of scholarly works on classical composers, Solomon was neither an academic nor a professional musicologist when his Beethoven biography was published. With his older brother Seymour, he had co-founded Vanguard Records in

1950, a label known for folk, blues, and rock recordings as well as classical disks. Following the publication of *Beethoven*, Solomon held a series of teaching appointments at CUNY, SUNY-Stony Brook, Columbia, Harvard, and Yale before joining Juilliard's graduate faculty in 1998. Grouped with 'Music of the Spheres?' and 'Anthropomorphically analytical', this essay was reprinted as 'Ludwig Van' in *Homage to QWERT YUIOP* (pp. 541-8); it was also reprinted as 'Ludwig Van' in *A Clockwork Orange*: Restored Edition (Penguin, 2013, pp. 263-6), but without the other two essays.

24. Anthropomorphically Analytical

When a steady stream of books on Beethoven began to appear in 1977 during the sesquicentenary of his death and in the years to follow, Burgess was called upon to review them. As the author of *A Clockwork Orange*, with its aberrant characterization of Beethoven's music and its effect upon the novel's protagonist, this was inevitable. One of these books was this monograph on Beethoven's symphonies by Antony Hopkins, a composer, pianist, and conductor well known to BBC listeners for his *Talking About Music* radio programmes, which aired from 1954 to 1992. While Burgess is put off by Hopkins's 'slanginess' and incessant 'search for comedy', he generally approves of his 'anthropomorphic approach' to musical description. comparing Hopkins's book to *Beethoven and His Nine Symphonies*, Sir George Groves's seminal book on the subject, Burgess ranks it, surprisingly, above Grove, although not higher than the incomparable essays on the symphonies by Sir Donald Francis Tovey.

25. Music of the Spheres?

Wilfred Mellers was a composer of operas, chamber music, keyboard works, many songs, and much choral music, and incorporated aspects of folk, jazz, rock and indigenous music into his compositions. He was also the author of idiosyncratic writings much concerned with the spiritual side of music, which he discusses in combination with detailed harmonic analysis and multifarious correlations to literature.

26. The Ninth

Burgess wrote 'The Ninth' for BBC Radio 3 for a broadcast of the BBC Scottish Orchestra performing Beethoven's Ninth, which was recorded on 5 November and aired on 14 December 1990. In this essay, he asserts his belief in the myth – debunked by Basil Deane, Nicholas Cook, and others – that Friedrich von Schiller's 'Ode to Joy' had been originally an ode to freedom. Even Leonard Bernstein, who substituted *Freiheit* for *Freude* in his celebrated Berlin performance of the Ninth on Christmas Day 1989 shortly after the collapse of the Wall, acknowledged that *Freiheit* was not the original subject of Schiller's Ode, yet Burgess continued to maintain this belief, which he later repeated in *Mozart and the Wolf Gang*.

27. Strega in Do Maggiore

Symphonie Fantastique, which Harriet Smithson inspired, profoundly changed the musical landscape. Composers had written programmatic music long before Berlioz – *The Four Seasons*, for instance, and *Wellington's Victory* – but it was this work that led the way to the symphonic poems of Liszt, Romantic imaginings of Schumann, and tone poems of Richard Strauss.

Originally published in *The Observer* as 'Berlioz and the Bard', this essay was reprinted in HQY as 'Witch in C Major'. For republication in OMC as 'Strega in Do Maggiore' (Italian for 'Witch in C Major'), Burgess added an opening paragraph (included here) on Roger Norrington and his original instrument performances of nineteenth-century Romantic music while acknowledging recent advances in recording technology: the last line, which begins 'Turn on the cassette-player' in *The Observer* and HQY, becomes 'Turn on the compact disc player' in OMC.

28. Cosmos and Cosima
Wagner defined fundamental divisions of Burgess's musical world. As asserted in *This Man and Music*, music predating *Rienzi* held no allure for the young John Wilson (as Burgess was then known): 'Music before Wagner had little appeal: it was orchestrally naive, the trumpets and horns were mere bugles, the strings did not divide into a velvet shimmer, there was no bass clarinet or cor anglais or percussion section.' And not to understand the music that followed Wagner was a sure sign of musical ignorance. In his novel *A Vision of Battlements*, a fictionalization of Burgess's military service in Gibraltar, the autobiographical composer-protagonist Sergeant Richard Ennis disparages a fictional Professor of Harmony at the Royal College, scoffing, 'Coneybeare? That fool? Coneybeare doesn't know the first thing about any kind of music after 1883—', i.e., after Wagner's death.

29. Richard Wagner
A commemoration in *Corriere della Sera* of 'L'anno Wagner' – The Wagner Year – began with two articles written by Burgess in 1982: this brief overview of Wagner's life and achievements, titled *'L'anno di Wagner e i suoi eroi'* (The year of Wagner and his heroes) and the extensive summary of *The Ring* that follows. The text and titles of both essays are from the English typescripts that Burgess submitted to *Corriere della Sera*. Evidence suggests that they may have been intended for publication in *The Lamp*, Exxon's in-house magazine for publicizing its corporate achievements and and

philanthropic support of the arts. Burgess's essay 'Brideshead Revisited Revisited' had been published in the Winter 1981 issue of *The Lamp* to promote a new dramatization of the Evelyn Waugh novel for public television. In 1982, Exxon funded 'Wagner's *Ring*', a four-opera presentation on *Great Performances* of the centennial Bayreuth production of 1976, which was taped for television in 1980 and broadcast on *Great Performances* in early 1983, but instead of publishing another piece by Burgess, *The Lamp* printed an article about *The Ring* by John Ardoin, music critic of the *Dallas Morning News* and author of books on Maria Callas and Giancarlo Menotti, in its Winter 1982 issue.

30. Ring

In *Corriere della Sera*, this witty synopsis was called 'L'affascinante enigma della Tetralogia' (The fascinating enigma of the Tetralogy) instead of 'Ring', the terse title of the typescript. This essay relies heavily upon ideas articulated in 1898 by George Bernard Shaw in *The Perfect Wagnerite: A Commentary on the Niblung's Ring*, a Marxian interpretation of *The Ring* as an allegory for the demise of capitalism. A morbid comment about televisual broadcast of Wagner's tetralogy – 'Television, in the hundredth year after Wagner's death in Venice, has to be forced into accepting *The Ring*… and we ought to commit suicide rather than deny it to the small screen' – may explain why the editors of *The Lamp* decided not to print Burgess's article.

31. His Objects Were Sublime

When James Joyce competed in the *Feis Ceoil* (Festival of Music), a Dublin vocal competition for tenors, on 16 May 1904, it was his rendition of 'No Chastening' from Arthur Sullivan's oratorio *The Prodigal Son* that convinced Luigi Denza, the composer who judged the contest, to award Joyce the bronze medal. Although Burgess doesn't mention that oratorio or the connection to Joyce, he does refer to Jimmy Durante and his song 'I'm the guy who found the lost chord'. Once you've heard it, or (better) seen him perform it in the 1947 Esther Williams film *This Time for Keeps*, you'll never be able to hear 'The Lost Chord' again without breaking into a smile.

32. Native Wood-Notes

With the semicentennial on the horizon, Burgess began producing essays on Elgar in 1983 so as to gain a head start on what would be for him a highly meaningful commemoration. From his residence in Monte Carlo, Burgess wonders whether this 'music of a neurotic conservative Edwardian' is exportable to France, Germany and Russia. The revised and expanded version in HQY, entitled 'All Too English?', adds a final paragraph that quotes approvingly from a 1957 essay by Hans Keller, reprinted in *An Elgar Companion*, in which Keller asserts that Elgar's innovations will come to be understood through the music of Britten much as Wagner's musical advances become clearer once one has studied the twelve-tone music of Schoenberg.

The title of this essay in *The Observer* is drawn from the final line of this quatrain from John Milton's *L'Allegro*:

Then to the well-trod stage anon,
If Jonson's learned sock be on,
Or sweetest Shakespeare, Fancy's child,
Warble his native wood-notes wild.

33. Elgar non è volgare

First published in *Corriere della Sera* in July 1983 as '*Quel compositore fa 'Musica Inglese'*' (That composer makes 'English Music') in Luciano Conti's Italian translation, this essay appeared subsequently in *Harmonie-Panorama Musique* in September 1983 as 'Edward Elgar', with no French translation credit and this brief introduction (here translated into English):

> Composer (three symphonies, three concertos, various works of chamber music), writer *(Earthly Powers, A Clockwork Orange, Enderby)*, Anthony Burgess has agreed to collaborate regularly with *Harmonie-Panorama Musique*. It was natural that he devote his first 'paper' to a British composer – like him – and unknown – like him!

Its first publication in English appeared in OMC as 'Elgar non è volgare', the version reprinted here.

Burgess also wrote 'Elgarité = Vulgarité?' (not included in this volume), a review of three Elgar recordings on Chandos in which he repeats his contention that, apart from the first *Pomp and Circumstance* march, auditors outside the United Kingdom do not understand this composer's music, especially his Second Symphony: 'It baffled its first audience, and it still mystifies non-British listeners.' Evidently intended for a French readership, the review was submitted to *Harmonie-Panorama Musique* in October 1984 but was not published in that periodical.

34. Gentlemen v. Players
Elgar's socially humble background and Catholic religion did not fit in well with the South Kensington establishment, while the 'incessant pastoralism' of English music was unappealing to audiences abroad and to those Britons, like Burgess, who deplored the modal musical style of Ralph Vaughan Williams based on 'Tudor anthems and a folk-song tradition already near dead.' The battle over style determined who was in vogue and who wasn't: 'All English music subsided to the pastoral…

Walton was out, said RVW, as was Constant Lambert; both mocked pastoralism.' Written during his final year, Burgess's review sounds dispirited, concluding, 'We missed the boat somehow. We don't export well. Our music, as at the Proms, confirms an ironic chauvinism or encourages a cosy insularity.'

The era preceding the one examined in *The English Musical Renaissance 1860–1940* is the subject of another book, *Music and Tradition in Early Industrial Lancashire 1780–1840* (Ipswich: Boydell and Brewer, 1980), which Burgess discusses in an earlier review (not included here) titled 'Tunes and treadles' published in the *TLS* (27 June 1980, p. 735).

35. Mister Delius
Whereas Elgar and Holst resided in England throughout their lives, Delius spent much of his abroad, developing a unique style informed by residency in Paris, Leipzig, Florida, and Grez-sur-Loing. According to Burgess, this book places Frederick Delius 'firmly in that great artistic Europe which England has never learned properly to enter: it reminds us that Delius is international before he is British.' Originally published in *The Guardian* in December 1983, this essay was reprinted, in French translation, in *Harmonie–Panorama Musique* in February 1984.

36. Startalk
The powerful impact of *The Planets* on young John Wilson is described in *Little Wilson and Big God* and *This Man and Music*, where Burgess recalls having studied it in the 1930s and based the extensive instrumentation of his First Symphony upon it: 'from *The Planets* I stole a bass flute, six horns and four trumpets.' In later works he imitated the tritonal harmonic movement of 'Saturn' in his Sonatina in G Major for Anne Field (1952), mimicked a theme from 'Jupiter' in *A Glasgow Overture* (1980), and replicated a rhythmic figure from

'Mercury' in his music for *A.D.* (1983) before transcribing the entire movement for guitar quartet (1987). In this detailed review of a Channel One broadcast of *The Planets*, illustrated with musical examples that he wrote out by hand, Burgess celebrates the fact that the French are finally 'taking English music seriously' while fretting that *The Planets* not be deemed 'the beginning and end of Holst. He wrote better work, and the French deserve to hear it.' Burgess sent the typescript to France in May 1982 for publication in *Harmonie-Panorama Musique*, but it was not published in that journal and has remained unpublished until now.

37. In Tune with the Popular Soul

Like his contemporary countryman Gustav Holst, Samuel Coleridge-Taylor was a British composer whose fame rests principally on one work – *The Planets* in Holst's case, *Hiawatha's Wedding Feast* in Coleridge-Taylor's. Composed in 1898 when he was just 23 years old, Coleridge-Taylor's oratorio – a setting of *The Song of Hiawatha* by the American poet Henry Wadsworth Longfellow – propelled him to sudden international fame. *Hiawatha's Wedding Feast* was exceptionally popular for over fifty years, receiving thousands of performances throughout the English-speaking world. During the first half of the twentieth century, it rivaled Handel's *Messiah* and Mendelssohn's *Elijah* as the most popular oratorio in the UK, with over 200 performances in England alone by 1904. Coleridge-Taylor followed *Hiawatha's Wedding Feast* with two more oratorios based on Longfellow's epic poem: *The Death of Minnehaha* and *Hiawatha's Departure*, composed in 1899 and 1900, respectively. Collectively, the trilogy was published as *The Song of Hiawatha* and had its first complete performance in 1900 at the Royal Albert Hall.

The problem for Coleridge-Taylor is that, unlike *The Planets*, which remains a staple of the repertoire, *Hiawatha's*

Wedding Feast has virtually disappeared from the concert stage, sending its composer's reputation into eclipse. When the epic poem was first published in 1855, Longfellow was criticized for writing too sympathetically about Native Americans with his Romantic depiction of the 'noble Indian', but with increased awareness of cultural appropriation and rejection of insensitive portrayals of indigenous peoples, *The Song of Hiawatha* was rendered virtually unperformable except for rare revivals. Yet Samuel Coleridge-Taylor is too significant and talented a composer to be forgotten. Sir Edward Elgar considered him 'far and away the cleverest fellow going amongst the younger men' and recommended him to the Three Choirs Festival in 1896, which led to the *Hiawatha* commission. According to the musicologist Alasdair Jamieson, 'Although he had some quite serious struggles as a result of his skin colour, he was a popular young man who inspired the "guardian-angels" of his youth, and made friends easily. There is a typical and well-established story of his time at the Royal College, when Stanford, overhearing another student deliver a racial slur, rounded on the culprit and told him that Coleridge-Taylor had "more music in his little finger" than the other student had in "his whole body".'

38. Unravelling Ravel

In 1986, Burgess met Philippe Loli at Monaco's Académie de Musique and engaged him to give guitar lessons to his wife Liana. When Loli explained that he was a member of Aïghetta Quartet, an ensemble of four classical guitarists, Burgess offered to compose a work for the group. Loli gladly accepted and was shocked when Burgess presented him with the score of his *Quatuor (No 1) pour Guitares* just four days later. Burgess subtitled the work *Quatuor en hommage à Maurice Ravel* to commemorate the great French composer, whose semicentennial would be celebrated in 1987. This essay was published in *Corriere della Sera* as *'Quel sole rovente nelle note del Bolero'* ('That scorching sun in the notes of Bolero'), translated by Marina Meo Gentilucci, and later appeared, in English, in *One Man's Chorus*.

39. I Hear an Army

Burgess modestly neglects to mention in this review that he is one of the 141 composers listed by Myra Teicher Russel in her book as having written song settings of *Chamber Music* poems. When Russel, a Professor of English at Iona College, met Burgess at the International Joyce Symposium in 1982, he told her that in his youth he had set *Chamber Music* to music and would try to recall as many of those songs as he could. On 18 June, he wrote down his setting of 'Strings', the first poem in *Chamber Music*, in a music manuscript book that Russel had given him. Two days later, while riding a train from Dublin to Cork, he wrote out 'Ecce Puer', after which he returned the notebook to Russel. In 1998, while carrying out research for my book *A Clockwork Counterpoint* at the University of Texas, I learned about these songs and contacted Professor Russel about them. She promptly sent me copies and on 22 January 1999, soprano Kathryne Jennings, accompanied by me at the piano, performed the world premiere of both on a recital presented by the Longmeadow Chamber Music Society in Massachusetts.

In a Letter to the Editor published in the 29 October 1993 issue of *TLS* (p. 15), Russel mentions the pair of songs that Burgess wrote down for her in June 1982 before reproaching him for neglecting to mention the recording of Palmer's complete *Chamber Music* settings by tenor Robert White and pianist Samuel Sanders 'which *should* have been received with the book…(I can only assume that Mr Burgess did not receive the tape.)' She goes on to say: 'I do agree that Palmer's name should have been featured and hope this can be corrected for the second printing. But about George Antheil, Burgess is simply mistaken. His only setting of a Joyce poem was not from *Chamber Music* but from the much later *Pomes Penyeach*; entitled "Nightpiece", it appeared in *The Joyce Book* compiled by Herbert Hughes in 1932.'

What Myra Russel could not have known is that Burgess was suffering from late-stage cancer when he wrote this review, which was published less than eight weeks before his death on 22 November 1993. This essay is thus Burgess's last published writing on music or very close to it.

40. Engaging the Sensorium

Despite having come of age in the 1930s as an aspiring composer, Burgess wrote relatively little about Stravinsky in his autobiography. In *Little Wilson and Big God*, he recounts his frustration with Manchester's Hallé Orchestra, whose 'programmes were solid but unadventurous, like the cuisine of the city chophouses. We were always being promised *Le Sacre du Printemps*, but we never got it. Not even visiting Stravinsky could coax more than *L'Oiseau de Feu* out of that all-male hard-drinking body that regarded musical experiment as womanish frippery.' He came to know Stravinsky's music well and didn't hesitate to borrow from it: quoting the opening bassoon solo of *Le Sacre* in his musical setting of *The Waste Land*, parodying the scenario of *Mavra* – based on Pushkin's *The Little House at Colonna* – in *Honey for the Bears*, and so on. For someone like Burgess who wrote in a diversity of styles, Stravinsky was an important role model, one he celebrated in 1982 by writing the script for *Making It New – A Centennial Tribute to Joyce and Stravinsky*. In this review, written a few years prior to the centenary, Burgess awaits it with anticipation, hoping that by then 'the unity of Stravinsky's oeuvre may at last be understood'.

41. Stravinsky's Potent Spirit

In 1982, CBS Masterworks released *Stravinsky: The Recorded Legacy* – recordings of ninety-eight compositions, nearly all of them conducted or supervised by the composer, in a deluxe boxed set of fifteen albums. This limited edition, winner of the European 'Edison Award' for special issue recording of 'historical or documentary character', commemorated Stravinsky's centenary and his relationship with the late Goddard Lieberson, president of Columbia Records (CBS at the time, Sony Classical now), who produced most of these recordings, and Lieberson's widow Vera Zorina, former wife of George Balanchine, a Broadway and Hollywood star who danced in several Stravinsky-Balanchine ballets. Burgess's review focuses on these five albums:

1	In Rehearsal / In His Own Words
7	Le Baiser de la Fee • Jeu de Cartes • Scenes de Ballet
11	Persephone • The Flood • Monumentum Pro Gesualdo di Venosa • Dumbarton Oaks Concerto
13	Chamber Music / Short Pieces
14	Choral Works I & II

42. A Great Lady

Through the achievements of the eminent composers, conductors, instrumentalists and music producers whom she taught, the legacy of Nadia Boulanger extends to the present day. In addition to the individuals listed in Burgess's review, Grażyna Bacewicz, Burt Bacharach, Marc Blitzstein, Daniel Barenboim, İdil Biret, Elliott Carter, Jean Françaix, John Eliot Gardiner, Philip Glass, Roy Harris, Quincy Jones, Dinu Lipatti, Igor Markevitch, Astor Piazzolla, and George Walker all studied with her at Fountainebleau. In addition to being one of the most influential music pedagogues of the twentieth century, Nadia Boulanger was also a trailblazing keyboardist and conductor. She was the organ soloist in 1925 in the premiere performances of Aaron Copland's Symphony for Organ and Orchestra by the New York Symphony Orchestra conducted by Walter Damrosch and the Boston Symphony Orchestra led by Serge Koussevitzky, and conducted the first performance of Igor Stravinsky's 'Dumbarton Oaks' Concerto in 1938 in Washington, D.C. As the first woman to conduct an entire programme of the Royal Philharmonic in London (in 1937) and the first female conductor of the Boston Symphony, Philadelphia Orchestra, and New York Philharmonic (in 1938), she left a stamp on music history that will be long remembered.

43. A Berliner on Broadway

After a carefree young gentleman, about to wed his fiancée, passes by a sculpture of Venus and jokingly places the wedding band on one of its fingers, the statue curls her hand around the ring and demands that he marry her instead. In *The Anatomy of Melancholy*, Robert Burton attributes this fable to Florilegus, 'ad annum 1058, an honest Historian of our nation'. Subsequently it was adapted by F.J. Anstey into *The Tinted Venus*, a humorous novel that became the source of *One Touch of Venus*, the 1943 Broadway musical by Kurt Weill and Maxwell Anderson. Punning on the composer's name, this review of *The Days Grow Short*, Ronald Sanders's monograph on Weill, was reprinted in HQY as 'A Short Short While'.

44. Symphony in C

Burgess wrote this programme note for the premiere of his Symphony in C (Third Symphony), which took place in Iowa City on Wednesday, 22 October 1975 in Hancher Auditorium. James Dixon conducted the University Symphony Orchestra of The University of Iowa School of Music with tenor George

Tepping and baritone Norman Carlberg as the symphony's vocal soloists. The programme comprised four works, with pianist John Simms the featured soloist in the final two works:

JOHANNES BRAHMS	Tragic Overture, Op. 81 (1880)
ANTHONY BURGESS	Symphony in C (1974–5)
IGOR STRAVINSKY	Movements (for piano and orchestra; 1958-59)
MANUEL DE FALLA	Noches en los Jardines de España (1909-16)

45. How I Wrote My Third Symphony

This account of the genesis of his Third Symphony in *The New York Times* represented a major step in Burgess's effort to be regarded as a composer and musician as well as writer. Throughout the remaining eighteen years of his life, he composed prolifically, completing a ballet suite, an oratorio, a cantata, other choral works, two musicals, five concertos, two concertinos, two sinfoniettas, two overtures and several short orchestral works along with pieces for brass band and large chamber ensemble, eight recorder sonatas and sonatinas, three guitar quartets, one string quartet and other chamber works, two song cycles, numerous songs, a set of twenty-four preludes and fugues in all the major and minor keys, and other keyboard works. He also composed a setting of *The Waste Land* for narrator, soprano and chamber ensemble; wrote *A Clockwork Orange: A play with music*; composed incidental music for the television miniseries *A.D.* (Anno Domini) and a song for George Mikes's play *The Virgin and the Bull*; wrote multiple arrangements for guitar quartet; and began other compositions that he never finished. For anyone whose main occupation was composing this would have been a large output; for someone as busy as Burgess was writing books and journalism, it is almost incomprehensible.

46. A Writer and Music

With his outsize personality, trenchant wit and gift for the bon mot, Burgess was a popular interviewee from the late 1960s until the end of his life. Interviews and profiles appeared in *Life*, *The Observer*, *The Guardian*, *The Paris Review*, *The New York Times*, *Playboy*, *Penthouse* and *Modern Fiction Studies*, among other publications. Indeed, one could compile a sizable volume of the interviews alone, especially if transcriptions of his radio and television appearances were included. Titled '*Un écrivain et la musique: Anthony Burgess*', this interview stands apart from the rest owing to its emphasis on music. It appeared in the French monthly magazine *Harmonie hi-fi conseil* in its November 1981 issue, *La Musique au Moyen Age* (Music in the Middle Ages), and is presented here in English for the first time. The translation is by Veronika Schubert. As published in *Harmonie hi-fi conseil*, the interview is preceded by a brief introduction and followed by a list of twenty-six musical works composed by Burgess from 1934 through 1981, all of which were included in the longer catalogue published in *This Man and Music* in 1982.

47. The Making of a Writer

Elizabeth Burgess's career as a soubrette known as the Beautiful Belle Burgess was a cornerstone of Burgess's foundational story. In *This Man and Music*, *Little Wilson and Big God* and numerous interviews, he asserted that his mother was a music hall singer and dancer, adding the other key components of his musical development: his father's piano-playing activity in silent film theatres, music hall pit orchestras and pubs; teaching himself to play the piano and read music; and the epiphany of hearing Debussy's *Prelude to 'The Afternoon of a Faun'* on his handmade crystal radio set. These stories made their way into multiple writings about Burgess, including *The Real Life of Anthony Burgess* by Andrew Biswell, *Anthony*

511

Burgess by Roger Lewis, William Boyd's radio play *Homage to AB*, and my own *A Clockwork Counterpoint*.

On 3 July 2017, Simon Johnson, an English archivist based in Edinburgh, presented a meticulously researched paper at a conference of the International Anthony Burgess Foundation that contradicted the Beautiful Belle Burgess myth that Burgess had propagated for decades. Asserting that Burgess had created a fictionalized version of his mother based on a Lancashire-born prima donna with the same name, Johnson surmised that

> during his youth, Burgess encountered his mother's unrelated namesake in the local Manchester press during the 1920s and early 1930s, and was much taken by her musical career with the Carl Rosa Opera Company. This namesake was one Elizabeth Burgess (1869–1934), who hailed from the town of Ashton-under-Lyne, some six miles to the east of Manchester. As a touring member of London's Carl Rosa Opera Company, this 'Lizzie' Burgess became one of England's most prominent operatic singers around the turn of the century. The Carl Rosa regularly toured the provinces, and Lizzie Burgess often performed in Manchester. Burgess was certainly aware of its existence, stating in his autobiography that 'The [Holy Name] church itself has theatrical associations. The Carl Rosa Opera Company would sing a flamboyant high mass with orchestral accompaniment.' By the time Burgess reached his teens, the soprano Lizzie Burgess had retired from her career as a performer, but remained well-regarded locally as a teacher of singing and voice production on behalf of the Carl Rosa.

> (quoted with Mr. Johnson's permission from his unpublished research paper, *'The Beautiful Belle Burgess': A Biography of*

Elizabeth Burgess – The Mother Anthony Burgess Never Knew, 2015)

Autobiographical clues in Burgess's fiction, especially his final novel *Byrne*, lend additional support to this theory.

No evidence has surfaced to suggest that Elizabeth Burgess, who was born in Manchester in 1888, was ever a music hall performer. She married Joseph Wilson on 26 December 1908 and gave birth to two children: a daughter, Muriel Burgess Wilson, on 2 December 1909, and son John on 25 February 1917. Sadly, Elizabeth and Muriel were both victims of the Spanish influenza that spread worldwide in 1918. Muriel succumbed first, dying on 15 November 1918; Elizabeth died of the virus four days later on 19 November.

Despite references to America and New York (and the inked words '*NY Times Book Review*' in Burgess's handwriting above the typescript's title) indicating that this essay was intended for publication in the US, that did not occur. Instead, an abridged version was published as 'Words pay, but the melody lingers on' in *The Times* on 19 March 1983.

48. Musicalising *Ulysses*

Given his lifelong love of Joyce's writing, the deeply musical nature and literary style of both authors, and his passion for music composition, transforming *Ulysses* into a musical was a labour that Burgess seemed destined to fulfill. A remark in *ReJoyce* that *Ulysses* could 'be turned into an opera' indicates that by 1965, he was already considering how to do it. Once he got to work writing out the piano-vocal score, Burgess accomplished the task speedily even by his own remarkable standards, as reported in a letter to the novelist and literary scholar Geoffrey Aggeler, dated 21 August 1971, in which he states that he has just completed book, lyrics and music for a musical of ULYSSES I tentatively call BLOOMS OF DUBLIN. All done in three weeks, quite a record really, but one has to kill the Italian heat somehow.

The first page of 'Flower of the Mountain', dated '9 Aug '71', supports this chronology, as do his assertions that he 'started drafting a musical version of *Ulysses*' just after writing *Joysprick* (YH) and that a 'draft of both the libretto and the score had been available in 1971 when I was living in New York' (*Blooms of Dublin*, 'A Prefatory Word').

49. Blooms of Dublin

After the broadcast of *Blooms of Dublin*, a co-production for radio by the BBC and Radio Telefís Eireann on 1 February 1982, reviews appeared in *The Guardian* (W. L. Webb), *Sunday Times* (Susie Cornfield), *The Times* (David Wade), *The Observer* (Paul Ferris) and *The Listener* (Anne Karpf). All were generally positive except for one scathing critique: 'Phoneydom' by Hans Keller, published in *The Listener*. Upon reading Keller's blistering takedown, Burgess typed a letter to the editor of *The Listener* that he refrained from posting, as confirmed by the handwritten comment '*(not sent)*' in the top margin. Instead, he sent a brief 'Letter to the Editor', dated 16 February 1982, criticizing Keller's misconception and misuse of the phrase 'Scotch snap', the term mentioned at the end of the unsent letter.

50. The Guitar and I

Colin Cooper was a playwright, novelist, music critic, and champion of the classical guitar. Inspired by recordings of Segovia, Cooper took up the classical guitar at the age of thirty-six in 1962, co-founded *Guitar Magazine* ten years later, and co-founded *Classical Guitar* a decade after that. According to his son Ben,

Music had always been important, but when Colin first picked up a guitar in 1962 he developed an obsession which gradually took over his working life. From 1982 until his death, much of his writing was for one magazine, *Classical Guitar*. He edited, reviewed, and interviewed luminaries, including Andrés Segovia and Astor Piazzolla. He corresponded with Anthony Burgess who had composed for the instrument. 'The guitar,' wrote Burgess, in his one contribution to the magazine, 'has the difficult nobility of a great disease.' Burgess's only payment was a box of cigars Colin had brought back from Havana. (*The Guardian*, 5 November 2012)

Burgess actually contributed two articles to *Classical Guitar*, the other in 1988. When he wrote this essay in 1982, his guitar-related activities were limited to the few compositions described in the article and half-hearted attempts to play the instrument: 'I can fake flamenco, and I can strum, but I can't ever hope to be a guitarist.' Within the next few years, his interest in the guitar increased dramatically once he became acquainted with the members of the Aïghetta Quartet and began to compose for them.

51. A Few Words About a Guitar Concerto
Burgess completed the orchestral score of his *Concerto per Chitarra ed Orchestra en Mi minore* (Concerto for Guitar and Orchestra in E minor) on 21 January 1987 and the score of the solo guitar part with piano reduction a week later. The three-movement concerto is thirty-one minutes long, scored for full orchestra, and dedicated to guitarist Philippe Loli, a founding member of the Aïghetta Quartet. Loli made a promotional recording of the concerto with piano accompaniment, as Burgess explains in 'The Twenty-Four-String Guitar' (Chapter

55). The text of the typescript describes the concerto and was evidently written to accompany the promotional recording made to support Loli's attempts to secure an orchestral performance. These efforts proved unsuccessful and, to date, the work has not yet been performed with orchestra.

52. Concerto Grosso for Guitar Quartet and Orchestra
On 26 February 1989, the Aïghetta Quartet performed the world premiere of Burgess's *Concerto Grosso pour Quatuor de Guitares et Orchestre en La mineur* (Concerto Grosso for Guitar Quartet and Orchestra) in Cannes with the Orchestre Régional de Cannes Provence-Alpes-Côte d'Azur conducted by Philippe Bender. The work is in three movements, 23 minutes long, and scored for full orchestra. The complete programme was:

LUDWIG VAN BEETHOVEN	Symphony No. 1 in C Major, Op. 21
ANTHONY BURGESS	*Concerto Grosso pour Quatuor de Guitares et Orchestre en La mineur*
MARCEL LANDOWSKI	*La Sorcière du Placard aux Balais* (Mini-Opéra pour enfants)

The concert was titled *Hommage à Anthony Burgess et Marcel Landowski* and took place in the Théâtre Claude Debussy in the Palais des Festivals et des Congrès. Burgess's programme note, dated November 1988, was printed in French in the programme; here it appears in the editor's English translation.

53. The Aïghetta Quartet
In the 1987, the Aïghetta Quartet released an album titled *Oeuvres pour Quatuor de Guitares* (Works for Guitar Quartet), with this liner note by Burgess. Burgess's Guitar Quartet No. 1 is among the five compositions on the recording (REM No 11032):

JOHANN SEBASTIAN BACH	Concerto en La Mineur BWV 1065
FERDINAND CARULLI	Quatuor en Do Majeur, Op. 21
ANTHONY BURGESS	Quatuor en Hommage à Maurice Ravel
ANTONIO RUIZ-PIPÓ	Cuatro para Cuatro
ROBERT DELANOFF	Ein Türkisches Volkslied

54. Concert Introductions

The first introduction (here translated into English by the editor) was written in French by Burgess in Lugano on 12 November 1987 for a Celtic festival at which his Concerto Grosso for Guitar Quartet and Orchestra would be played. The second was written by Burgess in English for a concert performed on 18 January 1989 by the Aïghetta Quartet in the theatre at the Princess Grace Irish Library in Monaco. The introduction appeared in the printed concert programme; on Burgess's personal copy of the programme, he struck through the word 'appropriate' in the first sentence and replaced it with 'all too Irish'. Titled 'An Evening with Anthony Burgess and His Music', the concert consisted entirely of music for four guitars composed or arranged by Burgess:

ANTHONY BURGESS	Quatuor en Hommage à Maurice Ravel
CARL MARIA VON WEBER	Overture to Oberon (arr. by Burgess)
GUSTAV HOLST	'Mercury' from The Planets (arr. by Burgess)
ANTHONY BURGESS	Quatuor No. 2
TRADITIONAL	Two Irish Airs (arr. by Burgess)
	The Lark in the Clear Air
	The Irish Washerwoman

55. The Twenty-Four-String Guitar

This article on writing for guitar quarter was published in the May 1988 issue of *Classical Guitar* preceded by a short introduction by Colin Cooper, the journal's general editor. On 22 January 1988, Cooper sent Burgess a letter requesting that he write something new for the magazine, whose readership, he explained, had greatly expanded to ninety-two different countries. Cooper congratulates Burgess on the Aïghetta Quartet's recent recording of his *Quatuor en hommage à Maurice Ravel*, 'which after a first hearing sounds very interesting'. Without mentioning a fee, Cooper suggests that Burgess write about the problems of composing for guitar quartet, a topic that would interest 'a large number of our readers'. With his customary alacrity, Burgess sent Cooper the typescript on 2 February 1988 together with a note expressing his determination to get his Guitar Concerto performed:

> I wish you could hear the concerto I wrote for Loli, but I think you'll be seeing him in London. I have three or four copies of the full score and innumerable recordings of the reduction. We'll get that damned thing played before the year's out.

56. Petite Symphonie pour Strasbourg

Burgess composed his *Petite Symphonie pour Strasbourg* to commemorate the bimillennium of the city's founding in 12 B.C. Completed in June 1988, it is scored for a chamber orchestra of single winds, timpani, piano, and strings. At the premiere, which took place in Strasbourg on 25 November 1988 with Étienne Bardon conducting l'Orchestre de Chambre du Conservatoire National de Région de Strasbourg, Burgess delivered these remarks, which the editor has transcribed from an audio recording and translated from French into English.

57. Britten, Adler, Jazz

In this 1964 column for *The Listener*, Burgess touches upon musical subjects ranging from Britten's *War Requiem* and Ravel's *Boléro* to *Don Giovanni* and Larry Adler. Kurt Weill is mentioned in the context of a review of *Brecht on Music*. In a review of a new BBC jazz programme, Burgess displays surprising coolness and skepticism: 'Jazz is not expressive, nor is it concerned (unless it is played by Brubeck, who I am told is no jazzman) with extending its melodic, rhythmical, or harmonic scope.'

58. Beethoven Violin Concerto

In *A Clockwork Orange*, Beethoven's Violin Concerto impels Alex to knife his droogs Georgie and Dim to assert his authority, yet in this 1964 review of a performance by Yehudi Menuhin with the London Symphony Orchestra conducted by Colin Davis, written several years after ACO was published, Burgess confesses doubt about the concerto's power: 'Mr Menuhin played beautifully but failed to move me. Can it be that the work itself is not good enough for these great combined talents?... I declare it a bore.' Later that fall, Burgess met Menuhin for the first time when they appeared together on a BBC television programme, which led to his cordial friendship with the renowned violinist and his wife Diana. In a letter to Diana Menuhin, Burgess reiterates his doubts about the work, comparing it unfavourably to the violin concertos of Elgar and Brahms.

59. Britten *War Requiem*

While English composers of the early twentieth century such as Elgar, Holst, Delius and Walton exerted a powerful influence on Burgess's musical style, his attitude toward Benjamin Britten was more ambivalent. Britten, just four years older than Burgess, was the most acclaimed classical British composer of his generation, with the greatest international reputation, yet Burgess finds much to criticize: 'Britten seems hardly able to start a movement without a percussive exordium; when we hear his own voice it is in those arpeggios of the thirteenth which have become too much of a habit; the style is too eclectic; to set Owen is supererogatory.' Having spent six years in military service during the Second World War, could Burgess have resented Britten's conscientious objector status as a pacifist? Perhaps this helps explain why his 'judgment on the *War Requiem* has to remain very tentative.'

60. Reflections on a Golden Ring
This discussion of the relative merits of radio and television as means of transmitting music offers thoughtful suggestions on broadcasting opera and orchestral concerts on television along with mixed feelings about watching Leonard Bernstein's *Young People's Concerts*. Concern about television's tendency to distract the listener from music's essence generates the comment that a BBC programme on *Götterdämmerung* does 'nothing except grope after a nexus between eye and ear, trying to justify television's concern with music. But it was really all eye... Radio is the only substitute for the concert-hall experience.'

61. Enjoying Walton
Walton's influence on Burgess's musical style was profound. The robust, thickly scored sound of such orchestral works as *A Manchester Overture, Mr W.S.*, Third Symphony, and Concerto for Pianoforte and Orchestra in E flat owes much to Walton, which Burgess acknowledges in this review: 'This was a fine and greatly needed tribute to a composer who has meant more to some of us than anyone since Stravinsky.'

62. The Vocation of a Virtuoso
Burgess's acquaintance with Yehudi Menuhin began in 1964 when they appeared together as guests on a BBC television

programme. Later that year, Burgess exchanged letters with Yehudi's wife Diana, but the friendship appears to have lapsed until 1977, when Burgess's review of Menuhin's autobiography, and the latter's courteous correction of several errors in that review, led to further correspondence and a meeting the following year when Burgess attended Menuhin's performance of Max Bruch's Concerto in G minor with the National Opera Orchestra of Monte Carlo at the Palais de Monaco in July 1978. A year later, Burgess surprised Menuhin with the full score of his Concerto for Violin and Orchestra in E minor, which he dedicated to him. Burgess based this three-movement, thirty-five-minute-long work on his memory of the Sonata for Violoncello and Piano in G minor that he had composed as a British soldier in Gibraltar during the summer of 1945. Despite Menuhin's suggestion that he perform the concerto someday in Monte Carlo, he never did, and to this day Burgess's Violin Concerto has remained unperformed.

63. The Prince of Percussion

James Blades was no ordinary drummer. During his long association with Benjamin Britten, Blades advised him on distinctive uses of percussion in his operas. He played with many of the great British symphonic orchestras as well as the Melos Ensemble and English Chamber Orchestra, wrote six books (including *Drum Roll*), co-authored three more, and was Professor of Percussion at the Royal Academy of Music. His students included the rock drummer Carl Palmer and percussion soloist Evelyn Glennie.

64. Highly Vocal

In his discussion of the high male voice, Burgess cites *The Alteration*, Kingsley Amis's novel about a world in which the Protestant Reformation never took place and archaic religious practices continue to the present, such as gelding boys to produce castrati for ecclesiastical singing. In *You've Had Your Time*, Burgess compares Amis's counterfactual history to the bleak vision of *A Clockwork Orange* and the troubles it brought him, concluding that greater danger lies in imagining future dystopias than in writing books like *The Alteration*: 'Remake the past... and you are safe.'

65. Performers: A Necessary Evil

This essay, originally published in *The New York Times* and later reprinted as 'The Maestro Heresy' in HQY, is one of several on the theme of performers and interpretation. In 'Egos as Big as the Met', a 1985 *New York Times* review of Harold C. Schonberg's book *The Glorious Ones: Classical Music's Legendary Performers*, narcissistic conductors and opera singers ('schmucks with batons and voices') are, as here, the principal targets of Burgess's tirades. This view is counterbalanced by accolades to performers who earn Burgess's esteem for their musical artistry coupled with skill as a writer, such as the pianist Alfred Brendel (*Music Sounded Out*) and conductor-pianist Daniel Barenboim (*A Life in Music*), subjects of laudatory reviews in *The Independent* titled, respectively, 'Practical wisdom recited from the piano stool' (30 November 1990, p. 21) and 'Quixotic explorations into the sound of silence' (8 November 1991, p. 21).

66. Anybody Can Conduct

A counterpart to this essay, which first appeared in HQY, is one titled 'Timing, perfection and the power of the podium', a review of *Conductors in Conversation* published in the 4 May 1990 issue of *The Independent* that begins with this humblebrag: 'I am not an orchestral player but, as a composer, I have waved the occasional diffident stick.' Burgess proceeds to describe his conducting experience in detail: 'It was a matter of giving cues, bringing everybody in with a strong downbeat, stressing *sforzandi*, accelerating, cutting a held final chord neatly off. It struck me as something of a mechanical craft: it brought back my wartime days as a sergeant-major.' As in 'Anybody Can Conduct', Burgess displays a deep ambivalence toward the art of conducting and those who practice it: 'Grudgingly, I accept the conductor, but only as the slave of the score.'

67. Hand to Mouth

During a publicity tour for his novel *Earthly Powers*, Anthony Burgess met Larry Adler at a London cocktail party. Having already composed harmonica pieces for John Sebastian and Tommy Reilly, Burgess was eager to do the same for Adler. In November 1980, shortly after they met, he sent him a three-movement suite for harmonica and piano titled *Pieces for Harmonica*, which he had composed for Adler and dedicated to him. In 1986, Burgess composed another piece for him, *Sonatina for Harmonica and Guitar* in D major. Yet Adler, a self-described 'melody man', considered Burgess's music awkwardly written and insufficiently tuneful, and never played either one.

68. John Sebastian – A Personal Reminiscence

Born in Philadelphia in 1914 to an affluent Italian family, John Sebastian Pugliese exhibited extraordinary musical talent at a young age, appearing as harmonica soloist with John Philip Sousa's band in 1926 and defeating thousands of competitors to win Philadelphia's harmonica championship in 1930. Known professionally as John Sebastian, he greatly expanded the classical harmonica repertoire by commissioning new works that he performed worldwide. Upon meeting Burgess in Rome, he encouraged him to write works for harmonica and guitar that he take on tour, which led Burgess to compose *Panique* and *Sonatina in C for Harmonica and Guitar* for Sebastian in 1972 soon after they met.

When John Sebastian died on 18 August 1980 in Périgord, France, his substantial collection of music – which included the original manuscripts of the works Burgess had composed for him – passed to his friend John Murray Ferguson, who donated it to Haverford College, Sebastian's alma mater, in 1986. Subsequently, in tribute to Sebastian, Ferguson assembled, edited, and self-published *The 'Classic Harmonica' Series* in 1991. Burgess's essay retitled 'John Sebastian – A Personal Recollection', appears in the first volume of that six-part series, which is followed by a primer on harmonica technique and four volumes of arrangements for harmonica and piano of works by composers ranging from Bach, Mozart, and Gluck to Prokofiev, Gershwin, and Kleinsinger. The only extant copy of *The 'Classic Harmonica' Series* was donated by Sebastian's accompanist Glen Clugston to Clugston's alma mater, Pittsburg State University in Kansas.

69. A Conductor with a Talent for Resurrection

At the time this essay appeared in *The New York Times*, Roger Norrington had expanded his dominance of the Historically Informed Practice movement from London to New York in his new role as music director of the Orchestra of St. Luke's. Through Norrington's concerts and recordings with the London Classical Players, listeners were introduced to light, fleet, vibrato-less renderings of works by Beethoven, Schubert, Brahms, and eventually Wagner. In 1996, musicologist Richard Taruskin would launch a broadside at Norrington and the HIP movement in the pages of this same newspaper, declaring that 'it is high time Mr. Norrington and other "historical" performers dropped the historical pretense', for 'Norrington's prejudices are demonstrably those of a modernist.' Back in 1991, when Burgess wrote this article, he was especially taken with Norrington's recording of *Symphonie Fantastique* and the 'sardonic sneering quality' of the sound of ophicleides and valveless brass, yet even then expressed skepticism over HIP extremism in a Beethoven recording by the LCP: 'The fourth horn part of the Ninth is a virtuoso piece of writing, appropriate to the new valved resources. Surprisingly, Mr. Norrington clings to the valveless variety. The player copes well enough.'

70. Introduction to *Don Giovanni and Idomeneo*
Lionel Salter, a multi-talented musician and prolific writer at the BBC for most of the period from 1936 to 1974, translated 130 operas into English. Six of his translations of Mozart operas were published in 1971 in three volumes, each containing a pair of libretti in the original language side-by-side with the translation: *Le Nozze di Figaro* and *Così fan tutte* with an introduction by Dennis Arundell, *Die Zauberflöte* and *Die Enführung aus dem Serail* with an introduction by Brigid Brophy, and *Don Giovanni* and *Idomeneo* with an introduction by Burgess. In London, the volumes were published as *Cassell Opera Guides*; in New York, as *Universe Opera Guides*.

71. The Music is the Message
In this 1978 *Observer* review of books on opera by Peter Conrad and Gary Schmidgall, Burgess expresses favorite themes also articulated in *Shakespeare in Music* (Chapter 2), *A Mystery and its Monument* (Chapter 7), *Blest Pair of Sirens?* (Chapter 15), *Elgar non è volgare* (Chapter 33): the superiority of *Falstaff* to *The Merry Wives of Windsor* thanks to the mastery of Boito and Verdi, Richard Strauss's ability to miraculously transform Cervantes's *Don Quixote* into a symphonic poem, and his conviction that 'Most great operas have a great literary provenance.' In the revised version of this essay published in HQY as 'Operatics', Burgess takes this assertion a step further by omitting the word 'Most', leaving opera lovers to wonder if *Don Pasquale, Il Trovatore,* and *Tosca,* not to mention *Die*

Zauberflöte and *Der Freischütz,* are no longer to be regarded as great operas.

72. When Music Does the Talking

After mentioning his attempt at writing the libretto for *The Eve of Saint Venus*, Burgess claims that he has 'never since tried again to rival Da Ponte or Hofmannsthal' despite having written the words for the 1973 Broadway musical *Cyrano!*, which garnered a Tony Award for Christopher Plummer in the title role. During that decade, Burgess also wrote the words for two projects with composer Stanley Silverman – *The MND Show: A Madrigal Comedy Celebration in E major,* based on *A Midsummer Night's Dream,* for chamber singers, large choir, and instrumental ensemble (1971) and *King Oedipus,* for Speaker, Chorus and Orchestra (1973). He also wrote the words and music for *Blooms of Dublin,* adapted from Joyce's *Ulysses,* and *Trotsky's in New York!,* whose libretto he later incorporated into *The End of the World News.* In the 1980s, Burgess adapted the libretti of Weber's *Oberon* (1985) and Bizet's *Carmen* (1986) and wrote *1789: An Opera Libretto,* which was set to music by Lorenzo Ferrero and produced in 1989 as a marionette opera titled *Le Bleu-Blanc-Rouge et le Noir.*

73. Sounds and Settings

Burgess's critique of *Prime alla Scala* (Opening Nights at La Scala) by Eugenio Montale is the only review in this volume of a book not published in English. About two-thirds of Montale's writings in this volume are opera reviews, with the rest divided mainly between concert reviews and reports from The Festivals of Spoleto and Venice. Most were written between the early 1950s and middle 1960s, primarily for *Corriere della Sera* and *Corriere d'Informazione,* an afternoon daily newspaper published in Milan that ceased publication in 1981.

74. A Librettist's Lament

Fear of 'what has probably been done to my translation of the libretto' keeps Burgess from attending the English National Opera's new production of his adaptation of *Carmen*. As a novelist, he expects that 'what gets to the reader has always been, with absolutely no exceptions, precisely what I wanted to get to him.' But for the librettist and scenarist, there are no such guarantees. Actors, singers, and directors routinely substitute alternate language in librettos and scripts for which the poor writer is inevitably blamed. Burgess cites examples of mangled words and phrases in *A.D., Moses the Lawgiver,* and *Jesus of Nazareth* – three television scenarios on Biblical subjects that he wrote in the 1970s and '80s. The text published in *The New York Times* in December 1986 is reproduced here; ironically, several lines were cut from the version later published in *The Observer* as 'Changing one's tune'.

75. Coloratura Work Amid the Archive

Burgess finds much to praise in this collection of thirty essays starting with those about European opera based on British history and literature: 'Donizetti and Queen Elizabeth', 'Verdi's *Otello* – A Shakespearian masterpiece', and 'Shakespeare in the Opera House'. Covering subjects ranging from late Baroque Opera to Shostakovich's *Katya Kabanova*, Dean's writing style varies from lighter articles for *The Listener* intended for a general readership to meticulous original research, such as 'an excruciatingly specialist study of Handel's early copyists in London'. The final essay is a centennial tribute to Edward J. Dent, the first British musicologist to gain international recognition. In contrast to Dent, whose prejudices rendered him unable 'to pen objective histories', Winton Dean earns Burgess's highest praise: 'Dean's collection, which covers nearly 40 years, is musicology at its finest.'

TEXT SOURCES

For texts with more than one source, **bold type** indicates the
principal source of the version printed in this volume, with
the chapter title matching that of the source unless otherwise
indicated.

1. **The Writer and Music.** *The Listener,* **3 May 1962, Vol.
    67, Issue 1727, pp. 761-2** / *This Man and Music* (2020),
    pp. 242-4
2. **Shakespeare in Music.** *The Musical Times,* Vol. 105, No.
    1462, December 1964, pp. 901-2
3. **Music at the Millennium.** *High Fidelity,* **Vol. 26, No. 5,
    May 1976, pp. 47-9** / '2001, a Music Odyssey: What Can
    We Expect?', *The Washington Post,* 16 May 1976, pp. M1, M3
4. **Punk. Typescript** / 'Punk Paradox', *The Daily Mail,* 2
    December 1977, p. 7 / 'Punk: The snarl of the underdog',
    The Sydney Morning Herald, 10 December 1977, p. 12
    / 'Punk's "Horror Show"', *The New York Times,* 30 June
    1977 © 1977 The New York Times Company. All rights
    reserved. Used under license
5. **Why Punk** *had* **to end in evil.** *The Daily Mail,*
    23 October 1978, p. 6
6. **Musical autodidact.** *The Observer,* 4 May 1980, p. 38
7. **A mystery and its monument.** *TLS,* **20 February 1981,
    pp. 183-4** / 'Wandering Through the Grove', *Homage to
    QWERT YUIOP,* pp. 531-9,
8. **Turning the handle.** *TLS,* **20 February 1981, p. 205** /
    Homage to QWERT YUIOP, pp. 549-50
9. **The Well-Tempered Revolution: A Consideration of
    the Piano's Social and Intellectual History.** *The Lives of
    the Piano,* edited by James R. Gaines, Chapter I, pp. 3-39.
    New York: Holt, Rinehart and Winston, 1981

10. Tuned to the future. *The Observer*, 21 June 1981, p. 32 / 'Shaw's Music', *Homage to QWERT YUIOP*, pp. 539-41

11. The Ruination of Music. Typescript, 1981 / 'The day the music died', *The Times*, 29 December 1981, p. 8 / *'Forse con Mozart finisce la musica'* (trans. Luciano Conti), *Corriere della Sera*, 16 March 1982, p. 3

12. Food and Music. Typescript, 1983 / 'Food for Thought: Sweet & Savory Sounds', *Cuisine*, June 1984, Vol. 13, No. 6, pp. 13-14

13. The mystery of melody. *The Courier*, April 1986, Vol. XXXIX, No. 4, pp. 12-13

14. Introduction to *Pianoforte: A Social History of the Piano*. Written by Dieter Hildebrand, translated by Harriet Goodman, pp. v-ix. London: Hutchinson and New York: Braziller, 1988

15. Blest Pair of Sirens? Typescript, 1988 / 'Blest Pair of Sirens?', *The Listener*, 14 July 1988, Vol. 120, Issue 3071, pp. 4-5 / *'Parole e note sono come sirene'* (no translation credit), *Corriere della Sera*, 25 July 1988, p. 3 / *This Man and Music* (2020), pp. 245-7

16. The Devil prefers Mozart. *Evening Standard*, 7 March 1990, p. 7

17. Beatlemania. Typescript, 1992 / *'Quattro ragazzi in band E una leggenda'* (trans. Laura Ferrari), *Corriere della Sera*, 27 September 1992, pp. 23-4

18. Pearls before swine. *The Observer*, 12 October 1982, p. 32 / 'Artist and Beggar', *Homage to QWERT YUIOP*, pp. 553-6

19. Handel, not Händel – A Tricentennial Tribute. Typescript, 1984 / *'Seduceva le platee con gli effetti speciali'* (trans. Luciano Conti), *Corriere della Sera*, 22 February 1985, p. 3

20. Handel homage. *The Observer*, 24 February 1985, p. 26

21. Good Gluck. *One Man's Chorus*, 1987

22. **A professional music-maker beloved of God.** *The Independent,* 8 June 1990, p. 17

23. **Notes from the deep.** *The Observer,* 22 October 1978, p. 34 / 'Ludwig Van', *Homage to QWERT YUIOP,* pp. 541-3 / 'Ludwig Van', *A Clockwork Orange: Restored Edition,* Penguin, 2013, pp. 263-66

24. **Anthropomorphically analytical.** *TLS,* 1 May 1981, p. 480 / 'Ludwig Van', *Homage to QWERTYUIOP,* pp. 546-8

25. **Music of the spheres?** *The Observer,* 13 February 1983, p. 33 / 'Finding God in Beethoven', South China Morning Post, 13 March 1983, p. 18 / 'Ludwig Van', *Homage to QWERTYUIOP,* pp. 544-5

26. **The Ninth.** Typescript of BBC radio talk, 1990

27. **Strega in Do Maggiore.** 'Berlioz and the Bard', *The Observer,* 12 December 1982, p. 30 / 'Witch in C Major', *Homage to QWERT YUIOP,* pp. 587-9 / **One Man's Chorus, pp. 266-9**

28. **Cosmos and Cosima.** *The Observer,* 30 March 1980, p. 38 / 'Wagner in Brown', *Homage to QWERT YUIOP,* pp. 564-6

29. **Richard Wagner. Typescript, 1982** / *'L'anno di Wagner e i suoi eroi'* (trans. Luciano Conti), *Corriere della Sera,* 8 January 1983, p. 11

30. **Ring. Typescript, 1982** / *'L'affascinante enigma della Tetralogia'* (trans. Luciano Conti), *Corriere della Sera,* 8 January 1983, pp. 11-12 / 'Ring', *One Man's Chorus,* pp. 180-9

31. **His Objects Were Sublime.** *The New York Times Book Review,* 26 August 1984, Section 7, pp. 8-9 / 'S. Without G.', *Homage to QWERTYUIOP,* pp. 569-72

32. **Native wood-notes.** *The Observer,* 29 May 1983, p. 30 / 'All Too English?' *Homage to QWERTYUIOP,* pp. 567-9

33. **Elgar non è volgare.** *'Quel compositore fa "Musica Inglese"',* *Corriere della Sera,* 1 July 1983, p. 3 / 'Edward Elgar',

Harmonie Panorama Musique, No. 34, September 1983, pp. 28-30 / ***One Man's Chorus*, pp. 213-6**

34. **Gentlemen v. Players.** *The Observer*, 1 August 1993 – Books 1, p. 52

35. **Mister Delius.** 'Delius – A Life in Letters 1862-1908', Typescript, 1983 / ***The Guardian*, 15 December 1983, p. 12** / 'Delius', *Harmonie Panorama Musique*, No. 39, February 1984, pp. 16-17

36. **Startalk.** Typescript, 1982

37. **In tune with the popular soul.** *TLS*, 15 February 1980, p. 167

38. **Unravelling Ravel. Typescript, 1987** / *'Quel sole rovente nelle note del Bolero'*, *Corriere della Sera*, 21 December 1987, p. 3 / *One Man's Chorus*, pp. 312-5

39. **I hear an army.** *TLS*, 1 October 1993, p. 18

40. **Engaging the sensorium.** Typescript, 1980 / ***TLS*, 2 February 1980, p. 227**

41. **Stravinsky's potent spirit.** Typescript, 1982 / ***Spectator*, 24 July 1982, pp. 24-5**

42. **A great lady.** *The Observer*, 21 July 1985, p. 23

43. **A Berliner on Broadway. *TLS*, 5 September 1980, p. 968** / 'A Short Short While', *Homage to QWERT YUIOP*, pp. 573-5

44. **Symphony in C. Programme Note, University Symphony Orchestra of the University of Iowa, 22 October 1975** / *This Man and Music* (2020), pp. 253-62

45. **How I Wrote My Third Symphony. The New York Times – Arts and Leisure/Section 2, 28 December 1975, pp. 1, 19** / *This Man and Music* (2020), pp. 249-52

46. **A Writer and Music.** *Harmonie hi-fi conseil*, No. 14 November 1981, pp. 56-60

47. **The Making of a Writer. Typescript © 1982** / 'Words pay, but the melody lingers on', *The Times*, 19 March 1983, p. 8

48. **Musicalising *Ulysses*.** Typescript © 1982
49. **Blooms of Dublin. 'Phoneydom' by Hans Keller,** *The* **Listener, 11 February 1982, Vol. 107, Issue 2747, pp.** **26-7;** *This Man and Music* (2020), pp. 236-9 / **Unsent** **response by Anthony Burgess, typescript, February** **1982 / 'Letter to the Editor' by Anthony Burgess,** *The* **Listener, 25 February 1982, Vol. 107, Issue 2749, p. 18;** *This Man and Music* (2020), p. 240
50. **The Guitar and I.** *Classical Guitar*, Vol. 1, No. 3, Jan-Feb 1983, p. 23
51. **A Few Words About a Guitar Concerto.** Typescript, 1987
52. **Concerto Grosso for Guitar Quartet and Orchestra.** Programme note (November 1988), Orchestre Régional de Cannes, Provence, Alpes, Côte d'Azur, 26 February 1989
53. **The Aïghetta Quartet. Typescript** / liner note, *Oeuvres pour Quatuor de Guitares (Works for Guitar Quartet)*, Aïghetta Quartet, 1987
54. **Concert Introductions.** Typescript 1987, Concert programme 1989
55. **The Twenty-four-string Guitar. Typescript 1988** / 'The Twenty-Four String Guitar', *Classical Guitar*, Vol. 6, No. 9, May 1988, p. 48
56. **Petite Symphonie pour Strasbourg.** Spoken introduction, 25 November 1988
57. **Britten, Adler, Jazz.** 'The Arts' in *The Listener* – 20 August 1964, Vol. 72, Issue 1847, p. 283
58. **Beethoven Violin Concerto.** 'The Arts' in *The Listener* – 15 October 1964, Vol. 72, Issue 1855, p. 603
59. **Britten** *War Requiem*. 'The Arts' in *The Listener* – 12 November 1964, Vol. 72, Issue 1859, p. 775
60. **Reflections on a Golden Ring.** 'Television' in *The Listener* – 28 December 1967, Vol. 78, Issue 2022, pp. 858-9
61. **Enjoying Walton.** *The Listener* – 6 June 1968, Vol. 79, Issue 2045, p. 750

62. **The vocation of a virtuoso.** *TLS*, 8 April 1977, p. 419

63. **The prince of percussion.** *TLS*, **10 June 1977, p. 706** / *Homage to QWERT YUIOP*, pp. 575-7

64. **Highly vocal.** *TLS*, **2 April 1982, p. 378** / 'Highly Vocal', *Homage to QWERT YUIOP*, pp. 551-3

65. **Performers: A Necessary Evil.** *The New York Times* – **17 October 1982, Section 6, pp. 98-102** / 'The Maestro Heresy', *Homage to QWERT YUIOP*, pp. 578-84

66. **Anybody Can Conduct.** *Homage to QWERT YUIOP*, pp. 584-6

67. **Hand to mouth.** *The Observer*, 11 November 1984, p. 25

68. **John Sebastian – A Personal Reminiscence. Typescript 1988** / 'Foreword – A Personal Recollection', *The 'Classic Harmonica' Series*, Vol. 1, 1988

69. **A Conductor with a Talent for Resurrection.** *The New York Times*, 8 September 1991, Section 2, p. 33

70. **Introduction to *Don Giovanni* and *Idomeneo*.** Universe Opera Guides: *Don Giovanni* and *Idomeneo* by Wolfgang Amadeus Mozart, pp. 7-22. New York: Universe Books, 1971.

71. **The music is the message.** *The Observer*, **26 February 1978, p. 36** / 'Operatics', *Homage to QWERT YUIOP*, pp. 561-3

72. **When music does the talking.** *The Observer*, **20 December 1981, p. 20** / 'Words Without Music', *Homage to QWERT YUIOP*, pp. 558-61

73. **Sounds and settings.** *TLS*, **8 January 1982, p. 25** / 'A Poet at the Opera', *Homage to QWERT YUIOP*, pp. 556-8

74. **A Librettist's Lament.** 'Not Only Carmen', Typescript, 1986 / *The New York Times*, **21 December 1986, Section 2, p. 21** / 'Changing one's tune', *The Observer*, 28 December 1986, p. 20

75. **Coloratura work amid the archive.** *The Observer*, 13 January 1991, p. 55

Articles, Chapters, and Research Papers

Barnes, Clive. 'Langham Revitalizes the Guthrie Theatre', *The New York Times*, 20 September 1971, p. 31

Bowden, Sylvia. 'The Theming Magpie: The influence of Birdsong on Beethoven Motifs', *The Musical Times*, Summer 2008, Vol. 149, No. 1903, pp. 17-35

Burgess, Anthony. 'A $200 million Erector Set', *The New York Times*, 23 January 1977, pp. 181-2, 184-5

Collins, Glenn. 'Princeton's Small World of Big Writers', *The New York Times*, 20 May 1983, Section A, p. 14

Johnson, Simon. *'The Beautiful Belle Burgess': A Biography of Elizabeth Burgess – The Mother Anthony Burgess Never Knew.* Unpublished, 2015

Martin, Paul. 'Mr. Bloom and the Cyclops: Joyce and Antheil's Unfinished Opéra Mécanique', *Bronze by Gold: The Music of Joyce*, Sebastian D.G. Knowles, editor. New York: Routledge, 1999

Martin, Timothy. '"Cyclops" as Opera', *James Joyce Quarterly: Joyce and Opera' issue*, Fall 2000–Winter 2001, Vol. 38, No. 1/2, pp. 227-230

Phillips, Paul. 'Burgess and Music', Norton Critical Edition of *A Clockwork Orange* by Anthony Burgess, edited by Mark Rawlinson. New York: Norton, 2011, pp. 236-45

Rothstein, Edward. 'Creating a Stravinsky Monument', *The New York Times*, 15 August 1982, Section 2, pp. 1, 16

Taruskin, Richard. 'Dispelling the Contagious Wagnerian Mist', *The Danger of Music and Other Anti-Utopian Essays.* Berkeley: University of California Press, 2009, pp. 81-5

Books

Berlioz, Hector. *Memoirs*. New York: Dover, 1966 (reprint of 1932 Knopf edition)

Biswell, Andrew. *The Real Life of Anthony Burgess*. London: Picador, 2005

Burgess, Anthony. Works listed chronologically by original publication date

— *Beds in the East*. London: Heinemann, 1959

— *The Doctor is Sick*. London: Heinemann, 1960

— *A Clockwork Orange*. London: Heinemann, 1962

— *Inside Mr Enderby*. London: Heinemann, 1963

— *The Eve of Saint Venus*. London: Sidgwick and Jackson, 1964

— *The Eve of St Venus: A Fantasy about Love and Marriage*. London: Hesperus, 2006

— *Enderby Outside*. London: Heinemann, 1968

— *Joysprick*. London: André Deutsch, 1973

— *Napoleon Symphony*. London: Jonathan Cape, 1974

— *The Clockwork Testament, or Enderby's End*. London: Hart-Davis, MacGibbon, 1974

— *Moses: A Narrative*. London: Dempsey and Squires, 1976

— *Ernest Hemingway and his World*. London: Thames and Hudson, 1978

— *They Wrote in English*. Milan: Tramontana, 1979

— *The Pianoplayers*. London: Hutchinson, 1986

— 'The Cavalier of the Rose' (story adaptation, pp. 21-68) in *Der Rosenkavalier* by Richard Strauss and Hugo von Hofmannsthal. Boston: Little, Brown and Company, 1982

— *This Man and Music*. London: Hutchinson, 1982

— *This Man and Music* [Irwell Edition]. Manchester: Manchester University Press, 2020

— *Oberon Old & New*. London: Hutchinson, 1985

— *Blooms of Dublin*. London: Hutchinson, 1986
— *Carmen: An Opera in Four Acts*. London: Hutchinson, 1986
— *Homage to QWERT YUIOP: Selected Journalism 1978-1985*. London: Hutchinson, 1986
— *Little Wilson and Big God*. London: Heinemann, 1987
— *The Devil's Mode and Other Stories*. London: Hutchinson, 1989
— *1789: An Opera Libretto*. 1989 unpublished
— *You've Had Your Time*. London: Heinemann, 1990
— *Mozart and the Wolf Gang*. London: Hutchinson, 1991
— *Byrne: A Novel*. London: Hutchinson, 1995
— *One Man's Chorus: The Uncollected Writings*. New York: Carroll & Graf, 1998
— *Revolutionary Sonnets and other poems*, edited by Kevin Jackson. Manchester: Carcanet, 2002
— *Collected Poems*, edited by Jonathan Mann. Manchester: Carcanet, 2020
Daniel, Oliver. *Stokowski: A Counterpoint of View*. New York: Dodd Mead & Company, 1982
Drew, David. *Kurt Weill: A Handbook*. London: Faber & Faber, 1987
Eliot, T.S. *The Complete Poems and Plays 1909-1950*. New York: Harcourt, Brace & World, 1971
— *Selected Essays*. New York: Harcourt, Brace & World, 1960
Hayman, Ronald. *Nietzsche: A Critical Life*. New York: Oxford University Press, 1980.
Hinton, Stephen. *Weill's Musical Theater: Stages of Reform*. Berkeley: University of California Press, 2012
Keller, Hans. *Criticism*. Julian Hogg, editor. London: Faber & Faber, 1987.
Knowles, Sebastian D.G., editor. *Bronze by Gold: The Music of Joyce*. Taylor & Francis, 1999

Levant, Oscar. *The Unimportance of Being Oscar*. New York: G.P. Putnam's Sons, 1968

Mawer, Deborah. *French Music and Jazz in Conversation: From Debussy to Brubeck*. Cambridge: Cambridge University Press, 2015

Moore, Jerrold Northrop. *Edward Elgar: A Creative Life*. Oxford; New York: Oxford University Press, 1984

Phillips, Paul. *A Clockwork Counterpoint: The Music and Literature of Anthony Burgess*. Manchester: Manchester University Press, 2010

Smith, Dr. Rollin. *Stokowski and the Organ*. Hillsdale, New York: Pendragon Press, 2004

Whone, Herbert. *The Hidden Face of Music*. London: Gollancz, 1974

A

'Metalogue to *The Magic Flute*', 238, 240n

Austen, Jane, 47, 48, 49, 487

B

Bacewicz, Grażyna, 508

Bach, Carl Philipp Emanuel, 80

Bach, Johann Christian, 80

Bach, Johann Sebastian, 39n, 77, 78, 79, 80, 81, 82, 116, 117, 120-1, 124, 131, 153, 154, 155, 156, 157, 158, 159, 160, 163, 164, 167, 187, 188, 190n, 192, 229, 231, 233n, 280, 288, 292, 293, 294, 321n, 332, 347, 353, 355, 360, 370, 371, 408, 423, 427, 431, 494, 517, 524. Musical works: Air on the G String, 353; Cello Suite No. 3, 370; *Coffee Cantata*, 116; Choral Prelude *Sheep May Safely Graze*, 117; Choral Prelude *Wachet Auf*, 120-1; Concerto in A Minor, 517; Concerto in B Minor, 347; Fugues, 116; Minuet, 353; *A Musical Offering*, 80, 293, 294n; *Passions*, 164; Toccata and Fugue in D minor, 371; Violin Concerto in E major, 360; *The Well-Tempered Clavier*, 158, 293, 494

Bach, Wilhelm Friedemann, 80

Bacharach, Burt, 508

Bacon, Roger, 58

Badura-Skoda, Paul, 114n

Baines, Francis, 70

Baker, Josephine, 96, 391, 392

Baker, Richard, 365, 370, 373n

Bakunin, Mikhail Alexandrovich, 48, 50n, 216, 222

Balanchine, George, 508

Baldwin piano, 96

Balfe, Michael William, 63, 121; *The Bohemian Girl*, 121

Ballantyne, Archibald, 471n

Bantock, Granville, 254, 292, 294n

Barenboim, Daniel, 114n, 495, 508; *A Life in Music*, 522

Barnes, Clive, 400n

Bartók, Béla, 60, 95, 382n, 384, 388. Musical works: Sonata for Solo Violin, 389; Sonata for Two Pianos and Percussion, 395; Violin Concerto, 389

Bax, Arnold, 248, 251n

Bayreuth 208, 224, 248, 257, 411, 500

Beatles, 39n, 42, 43, 46n, 58, 122, 140-44, 187, 190n, 229, 233n, 324, 424, 493. Songs, recordings: 'Eleanor Rigby', 141; 'Lucy in the Sky with Diamonds', 141; 'She's Leaving Home', 141; 'A Day in the Life', 46n; 'Revolution 9', 46n; *Sgt Pepper's Lonely Hearts Club Band*, 46n, 140-1; 'Yellow Submarine', 141

Beatlemania, 140-44, 493, 529

Beaubourg, 464, 465n

Beaumarchais, Pierre: *Le Mariage de Figaro*, 452

Bechstein piano, 96

Beckett, Samuel, 39n, 42, 46n, 150, 417n

Beckford, Peter, 83, 101n

Beckford, William Thomas, 83, 101n

Bede, Venerable, 297, 299n

Beecham, Sir Thomas, 254, 424

Beethoven, Johann, 177

Beethoven, Ludwig van, 23, 36, 39n, 51, 52, 53, 56, 57, 58, 60, 61, 82, 84, 85, 86, 87, 88, 89, 91, 92, 93, 94, 99, 109, 110, 111, 112, 113, 114n, 115, 117, 120, 123n, 124, 125, 127, 128, 129, 129n, 131, 134, 136, 148, 152, 154, 155, 162, 166, 172, 173, 176-9, 181-5, 187-90, 190n, 192-201, 201n, 205, 215, 226, 229, 233n, 241, 257, 264, 273, 293, 313, 314, 320, 324, 330, 334, 335, 338, 342, 349, 352, 364, 365, 366, 367, 375, 386, 393n, 394n, 396, 399n, 407, 408, 411, 416, 418, 419, 420, 431, 432, 433, 434, 435, 435n, 439, 440, 441, 457, 483, 488, 491, 492, 493, 495, 496, 497, 498, 516, 519, 524, 525, 530, 532. Musical works:
Choral Fantasia, 185; 'Emperor' Concerto (Piano Concerto No. 5), 89, 407; *Fidelio*, 179, 201, 468, 469, 483; *Hammerklavier* Sonata, 124; *Leonora* Overture No. 3, 179; Missa Solemnis, 187; 'Moonlight' Sonata, 93; Piano Sonata, Op. 111, 188; *Prometheus* ballet music, 182, 193; String quartets (late), 61, 112, 120; symphonies, 52, 56, 94, 181-5, 194, 432, 497; Symphony No. 1, 109, 183, 194, 516; Symphony No. 2, 194; Symphony No. 3,

Bernstein, Leonard, 294, 374, 375, 413, 414, 416, 498, 520. Musical
    works: *The Age of Anxiety*, 99; *La Bonne Cuisine*, 490, *West Side
    Story*, 298n
Berthoux, André Michel (Aïghetta Quartet), 346
Bird, George, 208
Biret, İdil, 508
Biswell, Andrew: *The Real Life of Anthony Burgess*, 417n, 511
Bizet, Georges, 482, 526. Operas: *Carmen*, 526; *Ivan IV*, 482
Blades, James (Jimmy), 395-8, 399n, 521
Blake, Carice (daughter of Edward Elgar), 236
Blake, William, 187, 190n, 247, 365-6. Poems: 'And did those feet?',
    247; *Jerusalem*, 365-6, *Milton*, 247
Bliss, Arthur, 247; Musical works: *Lie Strewn the White Flocks*, 247;
    Morning Heroes, 247
Blitzstein, Marc, 508
Boito, Arrigo, 30, 31, 67, 134, 244-5, 461-2, 482, 525. Operas:
    Otello, 30, 482; *Falstaff*, 67, 134, 244-5, 461-2, 525; *La
    Gioconda*, 468
Bolcom, William, 489
Bonaparte, Joseph, 399
Bonaparte, Napoleon, 85, 86, 87, 88, 97, 98, 99, 109, 115, 124, 125,
    126, 177, 178, 179n, 193, 194, 200, 313, 349, 399, 434
Bondini, Pasquale, 453
Bösendorfer piano, 96
Boughton, Rutland, 247; *The Immortal Hour*, 248, 250n
Boulanger, Louie, 204, 207n
Boulanger, Nadia, 291-2, 508-9
Boulez, Pierre, 39n, 112, 126, 249, 293, 318, 322n, 331, 345, 380,
    389, 396, 411, 419; *Pli selon pli*, 114n
Boult, Adrian, 235, 239n
Bowie, David, 43
Bowman, James, 401, 403, 405n
Boy George (George O'Dowd), 487
Boys from Syracuse (Rodgers & Hart), 462, 464n
Boyd, William: *Homage to AB*, 512

Fonda, Jane, 327
Forkner, Ben, 18
Forman, Miloš: *Amadeus*, 171
Forsyth, Cecil: *Orchestration*, 60
Foss, Hubert, 266
Foulds, John: *World Requiem*, 249
Fowler, H.W., 471n
Françaix, Jean, 256, 508
Francis, Pope, 250n
Frazzi, Vito: *Re Lear*, 481
Frederick the Great (King Frederick II of Prussia), 79, 177, 293, 294n
Freud, Sigmund, 54, 57, 111, 132, 138, 176, 177, 225, 271, 409, 415, 461, 496
Fricker, Peter Racine, 382n
Friedrich Wilhelm II, 177
Fry, Christopher, 229, 233n
Fuller, Margaret, 332n, 333n
Furtwängler, Wilhelm, 387, 394n

G

Gable, Christopher, 255n
Gardiner, John Eliot, 508
Garfield (comic), 327
Garofalo, Raffaele, 374, 379n
Gay, John: *The Beggar's Opera*, 156, 164, 165n
George V, King, 237, 239n
Gershwin, George, 122, 139, 264, 296, 297, 299n, 335, 473, 524;
        Musical works: *An American in Paris*, 474, 476n;
        'Lady, be good', 413; *Rhapsody in Blue*, 64, 271
Gerstl, Richard, 63
Gesualdo, Carlo, 64, 65, 288, 289, 290n, 508
Ghislanzoni, Antonio: *Re Lear*, 481
Gibson, Alexander, 108n
Gide, André, 287
Gielen, Michael, 337

Horace, 480n
Horowitz, Vladimir, 407
Houdini, Harry, 425n
Housman, A. E.: *On Wenlock Edge*, 266
Howells, Herbert, 183, 186n, 246, 250n, 487
Hughes, Meirion, 246
Humperdinck, Engelbert (composer): *Hansel and Gretel*, 468, 470n
Humperdinck, Engelbert (singer; pseudonym of Arnold George
    Dorsey): 470n
Hunt, Holman, 378
hurdy-gurdy, 70-2, 176, 488-9, 490
Hurst, George, 336
Huxley, Aldous, 286, 289. Novels: *Antic Hay*, 24; *Crome Yellow*, 24;
    Island, 24; *Point Counter Point*, 24, 197
Hylton, Jack, 278, 279, 283n

I

Ibsen, Henrik, 364, 368n, 414
Independent, The, 174, 495, 522
Institut de Recherche et Coordination Acoustique/Musique
    (IRCAM), 465n
Ireland, John, 117, 251n; *These Things Shall Be*, 248
Irish Times, The, 333n, 335
Iron Maiden, 136
Irving, Henry, 414
Ives, Charles, 317, 322n, 487
Ives, George, 322n

J

Jaeger, August, 52, 237, 239n
Jagger, Mick, 43
James, Henry, 311, 326, 333n
James VI (King of Scotland), 481
Jamieson, Alasdair, 505

Jarvis, Charles, 85

Jasper Corporation of Indiana, 96

Jennings, Kathryne, 506

John Paul II, Pope, 47-9, 50n, 487

Johnson, Simon, 100n, 321n, 328n, 512

Johnson, Dr Samuel, 24, 27, 55, 162, 440, 472

Johnston, Johnnie, 233n

Jones, James Earl, 414

Jones, Quincy, 508

Joseph II, Emperor, 83, 173, 174, 442, 453, 458

Joyce, James, 193, 216, 341, 351, 472, 500. Writings: *Chamber Music*,
    274-6; *Finnegans Wake*, 277, 282n, 286, 331, 464; *A Portrait of
    the Artist as a Young Man*, 277, 282n; *Ulysses*, 24, 55, 283n, 326,
    329-32, 351

Jung, Carl, 225

K

Kant, Immanuel, 57, 176, 179, 188; *Critique of Pure Reason*, 196

Kantorei, 312n

Karajan, Herbert von, 375, 406, 413, 414, 418, 432

Karno, Fred, 325, 359, 363n

Karpf, Anne, 514

Keates, Jonathan, 162, 165, 495

Keats, John, 174, 325, 408

Keller, Hans, 34, 100n, 113, 139n, 188, 190n, 240n, 334-9, 339n,
    490, 501, 514

Kemble, Charles, 204, 207n

Kemble, Sarah, 207n; see Siddons, Sarah

Kemp, Will, 410

Kennedy, Margaret: *The Constant Nymph*, 23, 25n, 175n, 439

Kenyon College, 100n, 492

Kern, Jerome, 425n

Kesey, Ken, 326

Keynes, Milo, 405n

Love for Three Oranges, The (Prokofiev), 490

Lovin' Spoonful, 428n

Ludwig I, King of Bavaria, 102n

Ludwig II, 'Mad' King of Bavaria, 208, 210, 212n, 214, 223, 224, 375

M

Marx, Chico, 96

Marx, Karl, 216; Marxism, 415, 500

Massenet, Jules, 255n

Mathieson, Muir, 425n

Maugham, Somerset: *Cakes and Ales*, 416, 417n

Mazzetti, Jr., Remo, 192, 201n

McCarthy, Joseph, 297, 423

McCartney, Paul, 140, 493; *Liverpool Oratorio*, 144, 144n

McPherson, Aimee Semple, 381, 383n

Méhul, Étienne, 483

Mellers, Wilfred, 187-90, 190n, 497

Mendelssohn, Felix, 52, 88-9, 160, 228, 229, 241, 256, 318, 321n,
     431, 504, 553. Musical works: *Elijah*, 106, 504; *A Midsummer
     Night's Dream*, 29-30; 'Scots' Symphony, 117; *St Paul*, 106;
     Violin Concerto, 394n

Menotti, Giancarlo, 500; *The Consul*, 464

Menuhin, Diana, 366, 387, 390, 392, 519, 521

Menuhin, Yehudi, 293, 317, 322n, 365, 366, 384-8, 389, 392, 393-
     4n, 396, 412, 417n, 424, 519, 520, 521

Mercadante, Saverio: *Amleto*, 481

Messiaen, Olivier, 320, 419

Metastasio, 66, 167-8, 445-8, 466, 470n; *Artaserse*, 167

Meyerbeer, Giacomo, 211, 214, 226

Middleton, Stanley: *Harris's Requiem*, 24, 25n; *Holiday*, 25n

Mikes, George: *The Virgin and the Bull*, 510

Milhaud, Darius, 36, 259, 319, 349

Miller, Jonathan, 414, 415

Milton, John: *L'Allegro*, 158, 163, 164, 501; 'At a Solemn Music', 131,
     135n, 491; *Lycidas*, 80; *Il Penseroso*, 158; *Samson Agonistes*, 160

Minevitch, Borrah, 423

Molière, 204; *Le Festin de Pierre*, 456-7

Montale, Eugenio, 472-4, 475n, 526

Monteverdi, Claudio, 147-50, 151n, 293, 294, 431, 493, 494

Montez, Lola, 89, 102n

Moog, Robert, 35, 36, 39n

Moiseyev Dance Company, 372

Moke, Marie, 205, 207n

Morgann, Maurice, 134, 135n

Moroni, Luigi: *Amleto*, 481

Mossolov, Alexander Vasilyevich, 407; *Factory: the Music of Machines*, 117, 119n

Motörhead, 136

Mountbatten, Lord, 425

Mozart, Constanze, 172, 174, 451

Mozart, Franz Xaver Wolfgang, 172

Mozart, Karl Thomas, 172

Mozart, Leopold, 441-3, 448, 459n

Mozart, Marianne (Nannerl), 441

Mozart, Wolfgang Amadeus, 24, 35, 60, 66, 77, 83, 84, 88, 91, 92, 101n, 109-12, 114n, 115, 125, 136, 139, 147, 165, 166, 171-4, 187, 226, 228, 230, 231, 238, 240n, 257, 272, 287, 292, 293, 294, 321n, 334, 374, 375, 427, 430, 431, 433, 434, 435, 439-59, 459n, 462, 466, 469, 483, 485, 488, 490, 492, 493, 495, 496, 498, 524, 529. Musical works: *Bastien und Bastienne*, 442; Concerto for Flute and Harp, 370; 'Coronation' Concerto, K. 537, 171; *Così fan tutte*, 525; *Die Entführung aus dem Serail*, 452, 525; *Don Giovanni*, 107, 120, 169, 173, 361, 404, 409, 439, 446, 453-459, 460n, 465n, 467, 470n, 519, 525; *La finta giardiniera*, 442; *La finta semplice*, 442; *Idomeneo*, 446-451, 525; *Lucio Silla*, 442; *Le Nozze di Figaro*, 173, 409, 452, 453, 457, 525; Oboe Quartet, 451; Quartet in D minor, 452; *Il re pastore*, 443; Requiem, 173; *Der Schauspieldirektor*, 452; symphonies, 109, 193, 315, 435n, 496; *Die Zauberflöte*, 169, 173, 446, 525

Munch, Edvard, 254

Musgrave, Thea, 292

Musical Times, The, 31, 114n, 183

Musset, Alfred de, 204, 206, 207n

Mussolini, Benito, 475n

P

Q

R

Silverman, Stanley, 59, 526

Sinatra, Frank, 215, 282, 413

Slater, Montagu, 467

Smith, Rollin, 262n

Smithson, Harriet, 131, 203-6, 207n, 498

Smyth, Dame Ethel, 60

Solomon, Maynard, 176-9, 496-7, 560

Solomon, Seymour, 496

Solti, Georg, 375

Sophocles, 415

Sousa, John Philip, 523

Spectator, 289

Spanish Tragedy (Kyd), 133

Sparshott, F. E., 57

Spengler, Oswald, 212

Spohr, Luigi, 228-9, 233n

Spoleto Festival, 526

Staël, Madame de, 316

Stainer, John, 266

Stanford, Charles Villiers, 53, 246-7, 250-1n, 256, 265, 268n, 275, 505

Stanley, Arthur Penrhyn, 53

Staps, Friedrich, 179n

Starr, Ringo, 140-1, 144n, 493

Steibelt, Daniel, 86-7

Steiner, George, 57, 384-5, 388

Steinway pianos, 95, 96

Stendhal, 61, 179, 203

Stephenson, B. C., 233n

Sternfeld, Frederick, 284n

Stevens, Denis, 147, 148

Stevens, John, 27

Stockhausen, Karlheinz, 39n, 43, 46n, 126, 142, 380, 396

Stokowski, Leopold, 256, 262n, 371

Stradling, Robert, 246

Strauss, Johann, 243

Strauss, Richard, 27, 37, 103n, 107n, 126, 132, 170, 203, 226, 243, 250-1n, 253, 254, 266, 310, 344, 348, 396, 498. Musical works: *Also Sprach Zarathustra*, 133; *Le Bourgeois Gentilhomme*, 116, 490; *Capriccio*, 66, 170; *Don Quixote*, 111, 116, 132, 149-50, 375, 462, 525; *Ein Heldenleben*, 375, 434; *Metamorphosen*, 132; *Der Rosenkavalier*, 467-8, 470n; *Salome*, 111; *Till Eulenspiegel*, 133

Stravinsky, Igor, 36, 39n, 65, 94, 124, 161n, 244, 251n, 255n, 277-82, 278-85n, 286-89, 290n, 293, 318, 333n, 344, 355, 361, 381, 406, 414, 421, 509, 510, 520. Musical works: *Aldous Huxley In Memoriam*, 286; *Le Baiser de la Fee*, 508; 'Dumbarton Oaks' Concerto, 288, 508, 509; *Elegy for JFK*, 286, 290n; *Epitaphium*, 282n; *The Firebird*, 277-8, 280; *The Flood*, 286, 287, 508; Four Studies for Orchestra, 102n; *L'Histoire du Soldat*, 279, 396; *Jeu de Cartes*, 508; *Mass*, 279; *Mavra*, 278, 283n, 507; *Monumentum Pro Gesualdo di Venosa*, 64, 288, 290n, 508; *Movements* for piano and orchestra, 33, 510; *Les Noces*, 102n; *Oedipus Rex*, 287; *The Owl and the Pussy-Cat*, 277, 287, 290n; *Persephone*, 286, 287, 508; *Petrouchka*, 96, 102n, 128, 279, 284n; *The Rake's Progress*, 446, 474, 475-6n; *Requiem Canticles*, 277; *Le Sacre du Printemps*, 102n, 280, 281, 285n, 286, 287, 407, 419, 507; *Scenes de Ballet*, 508; 'The Star-Spangled Banner' (arrangement), 288; Study for pianola, 102n; *Symphony of Psalms*, 287; Violin Concerto in D, 280, 284n

Streicher, Nanette, 129n

Streisand, Barbra, 413

Striggio, Alessandro, 148, 151n

Strindberg, August, 254

Strozzi, Bernardo, 151n

Stuart-Wortley, Alice, 236

Suleiman, Sheik, 425

Sullivan, Sir Arthur, 228-32, 233-4n, 364, 548, 561. Musical works: *Cox and Box*, 232; *The Foresters*, 232, 234n; *The Golden Legend*, 228; *The Gondoliers*, 233n; *Hadden Hall*, 230, 234n; *H.M.S. Pinafore*, 230; *Iolanthe*, 364; *Ivanhoe*, 230; 'The Lost Chord', 228, 233n; *The Martyr of Antioch*, 228; *The Mikado*, 228, 231,

233n, 264, 474, 475n; 'Onward, Christian Soldiers', 228, 232;
    Overture di Ballo, 228; *The Pirates of Penzance*, 228, 415; *The*
    Prodigal Son, 500; *Trial by Jury*, 232
Sunday Times, The, 107n, 514
Svetlanov, Yevgeny, 235, 240n
Swinburne, Algernon, 25, 27, 472
Symonds, J. Addington, 248
Székely, Zoltán, 389
Szönyi, François (Aïghetta Quartet), 346, 347

T

Tallis, Thomas, 493
Tansman, Alexandre, 103n
Taruskin, Richard, 524
Tasso, Torquato, 242
Taylor, Thomas 190n
Tchaikovsky, Pyotr Ilich, 89, 288. Musical works: *Francesca da*
    Rimini, 132; *Hamlet*, 133; *Manfred Symphony*, 133;
    Piano Concerto No. 1, 90
Tcherepnin, Alexander, 429n
Tennyson, Alfred Lord, 55, 98, 434; *The Foresters*, 232, 234n
Tepping, George, 509-10
Terence, 480n
Tertullian, 191n
Tetrazzini, Luisa, 406, 413
Thackeray, William Makepeace: *Vanity Fair*, 378
Thayer, Alexander Wheelock, 176
Thomson, Virgil, 292
Thornton, Bonnel, 70
Times, The, 97, 112, 113, 114n, 190n, 327, 328n, 334, 336, 337, 490,
    513, 514
Times Literary Supplement (TLS), 59, 68, 68n, 72, 114n, 185, 186n,
    267, 268n, 276, 282, 284n, 298, 299n, 388, 389, 398, 404, 417n,
    474, 489, 503, 506,
Tippett, Michael, 371, 372n, 382n, 403, 464, 466